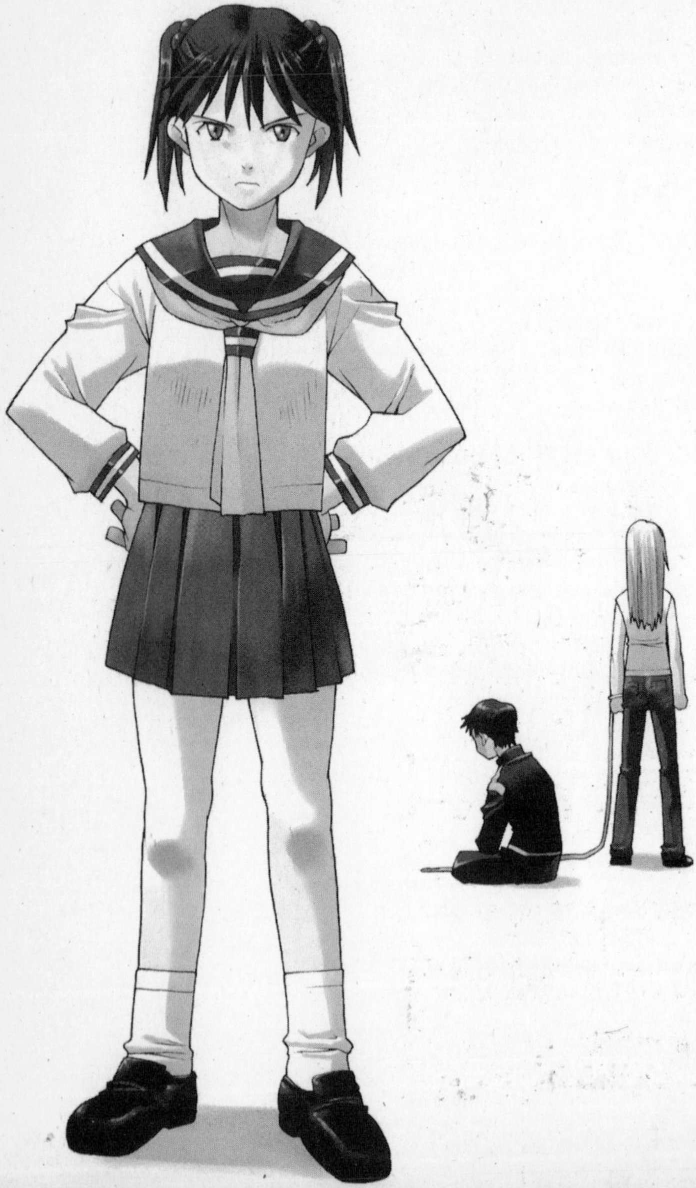

Translation and Adaptation – Christine Schilling
Production Assistant – Mallory Reaves
Lettering – TeamPokopen
Production Manager – James Dashiell
Editor – Brynne Chandler

A Go! Comi manga

Published by Go! Media Entertainment, LLC

Train + Train Volume 2
© HIDEYUKI KURATA - TOMOMASA TAKUMA 2000
First published in 2000 by Media Works Inc., Tokyo, Japan.
English translation rights arranged with Media Works Inc.

Visit us online at www.gocomi.com
e-mail: info@gocomi.com

ISBN 978-1-933617-19-0

First printed in April 2007

1 2 3 4 5 6 7 8 9

Manufactured in the United States of America

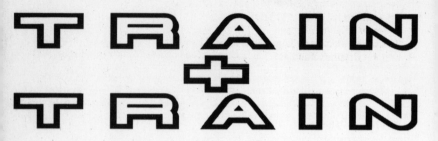

Volume 2

Original Story by

HIDEYUKI KURATA

Art by

TOMOMASA TAKUMA

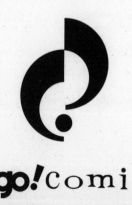

go!comi

Concerning Honorifics

At Go! Comi, we do our best to ensure that our translations read seamlessly in English while respecting the original Japanese language and culture. To this end, the original honorifics (the suffixes found at the end of characters' names) remain intact. In Japan, where politeness and formality are more integrated into every aspect of the language, honorifics give a better understanding of character relationships. They can be used to indicate both respect and affection. Whether a person addresses someone by first name or last name also indicates how close their relationship is.

Here are some of the honorifics you might encounter in reading this book:

-san: This is the most common and neutral of honorifics. The polite way to address someone you're not on close terms with is to use "-san." It's kind of like Mr. or Ms., except you can use "-san" with first names as easily as family names.

-chan: Used for friendly familiarity, mostly applied towards young girls. "-chan" also carries a connotation of cuteness with it, so it is frequently used with nicknames towards both boys and girls (such as "Na-chan" for "Natsu").

-kun: Like "-chan," it's an informal suffix for friends and classmates, only "-kun" is usually associated with boys. It can also be used in a professional environment by someone addressing a subordinate.

-sama: Indicates a great deal of respect or admiration.

Sempai: In school, "sempai" is used to refer to an upperclassman or club leader. It can also be used in the workplace by a new employee to address a mentor or staff member with seniority.

Sensei: Teachers, doctors, writers or any master of a trade are referred to as "sensei." When addressing a manga creator, the polite thing to do is attach "-sensei" to the manga-ka's name (as in Takuma-sensei).

Onii: This is the more casual term for an older brother. Usually you'll see it with an honorific attached, such as "onii-chan."

Onee: The casual term for older sister, it's used like "onii" with honorifics.

[blank]: Not using an honorific when addressing someone indicates that the speaker has permission to speak intimately with the other person. This relationship is usually reserved for close friends and family.

TRAIN

TRAIN + TRAIN
VOLUME 2

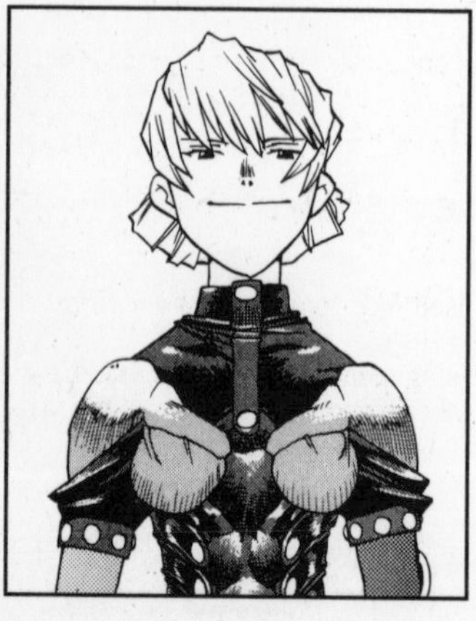

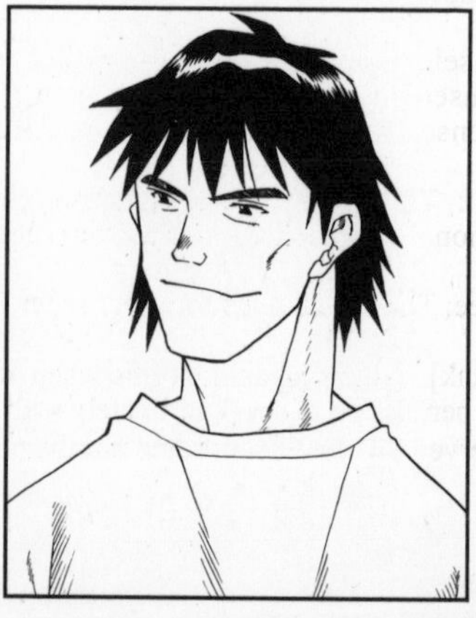

TRAIN

TRAIN
+
TRAIN

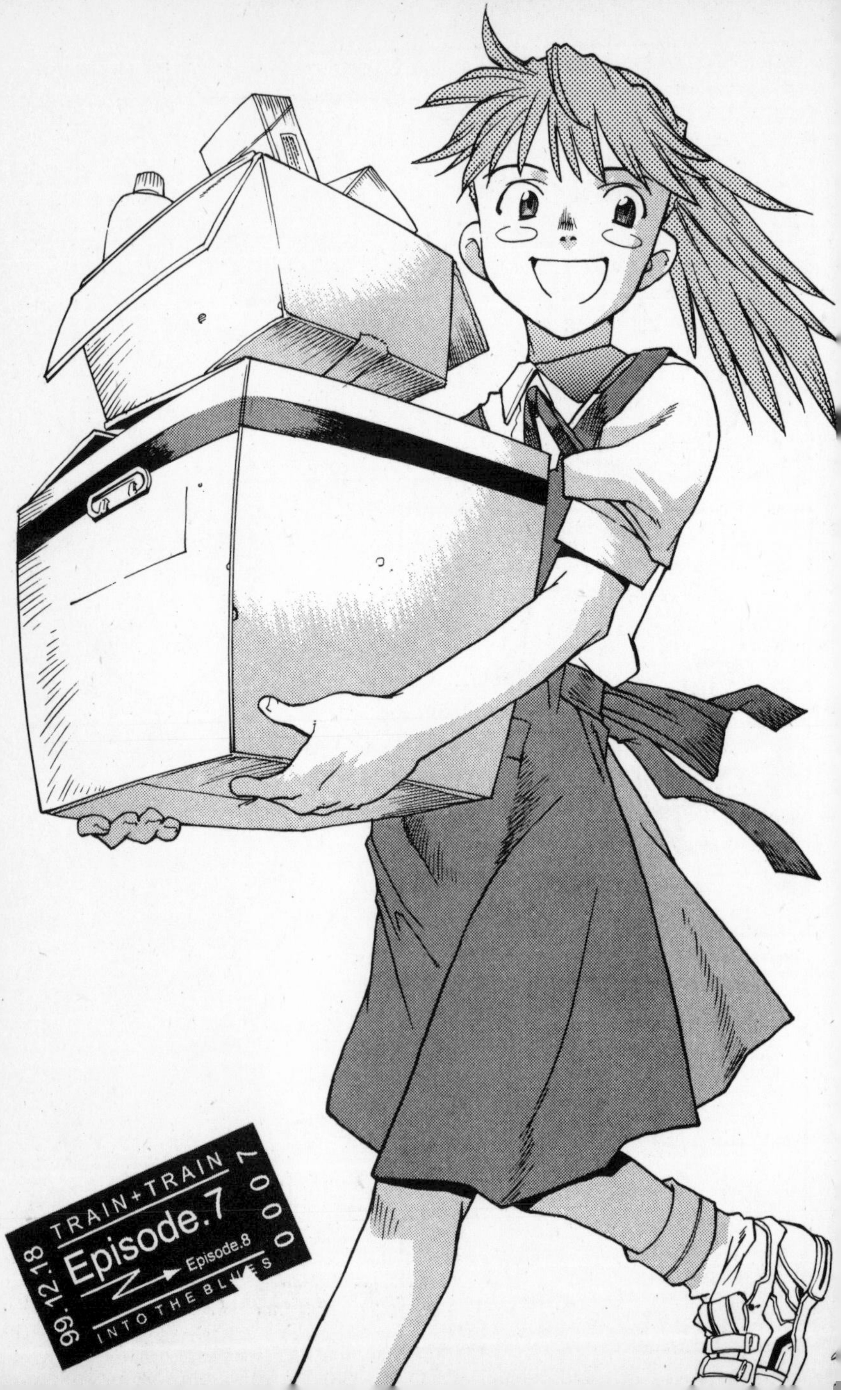
99.12.18
TRAIN+TRAIN
Episode.7
Episode.8
INTO THE BLUES
0007

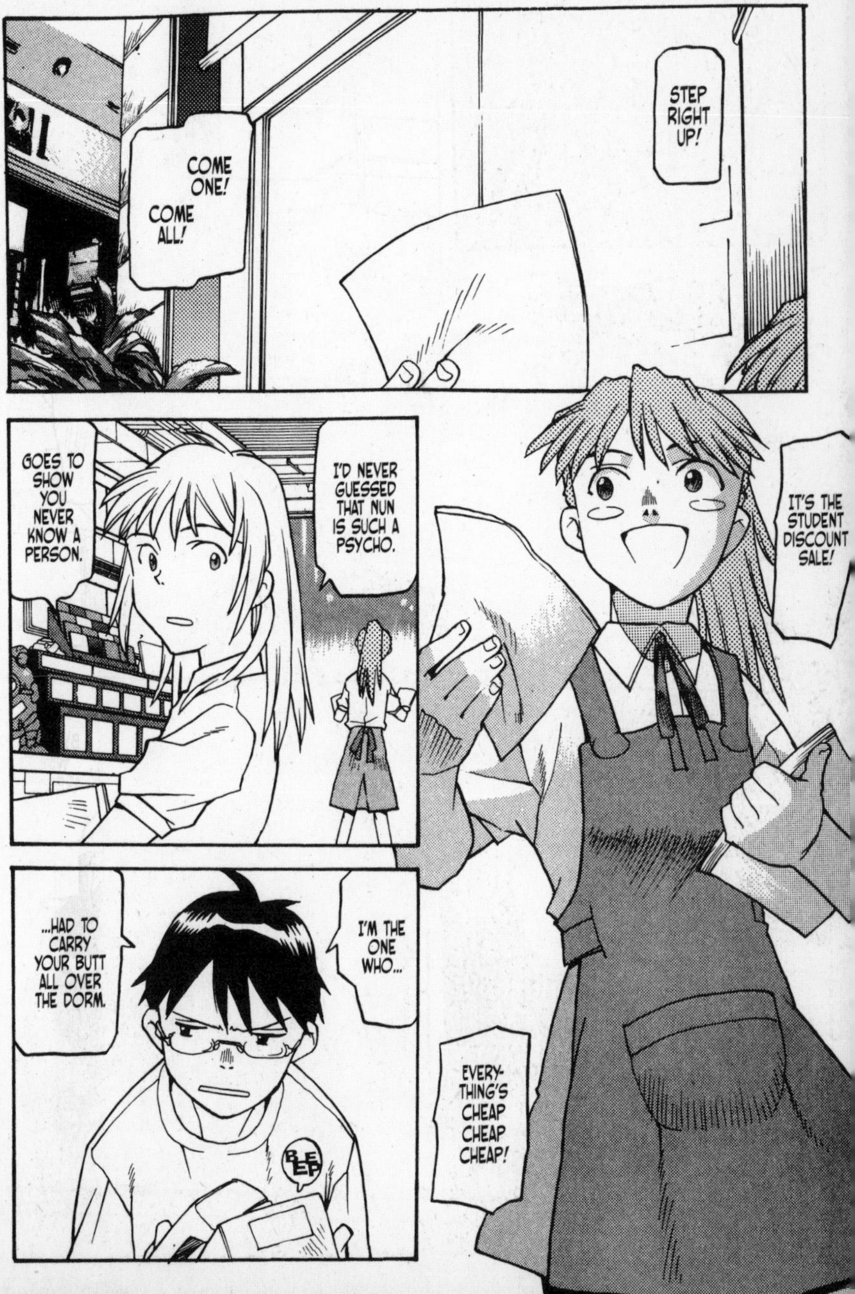
STEP RIGHT UP!
COME ONE!
COME ALL!
IT'S THE STUDENT DISCOUNT SALE!
EVERY-THING'S CHEAP CHEAP CHEAP!
I'D NEVER GUESSED THAT NUN IS SUCH A PSYCHO.
GOES TO SHOW YOU NEVER KNOW A PERSON.
I'M THE ONE WHO...
...HAD TO CARRY YOUR BUTT ALL OVER THE DORM.
BEEP

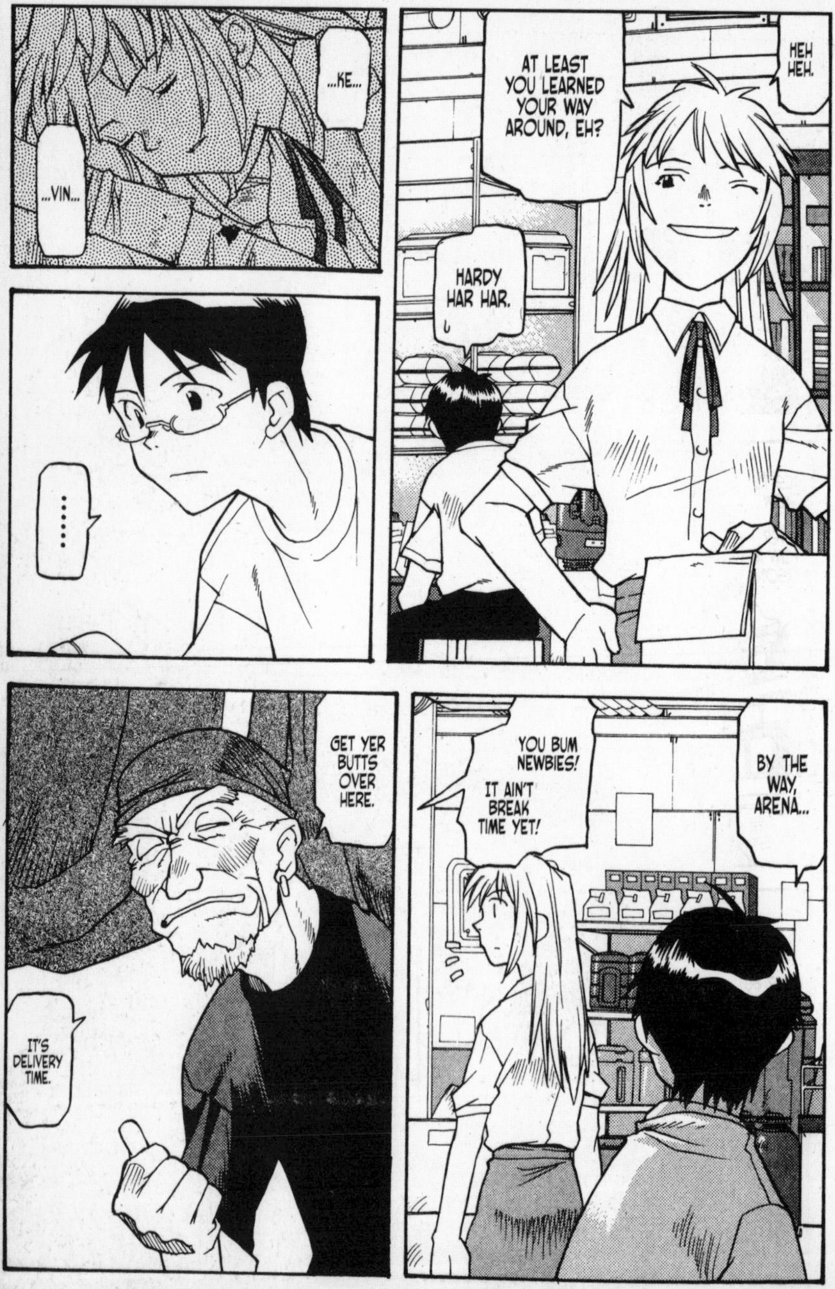
HEH HEH.
AT LEAST YOU LEARNED YOUR WAY AROUND, EH?
HARDY HAR HAR.
...KE...
...VIN...
......
BY THE WAY, ARENA...
YOU BUM NEWBIES!
IT AIN'T BREAK TIME YET!
GET YER BUTTS OVER HERE.
IT'S DELIVERY TIME.

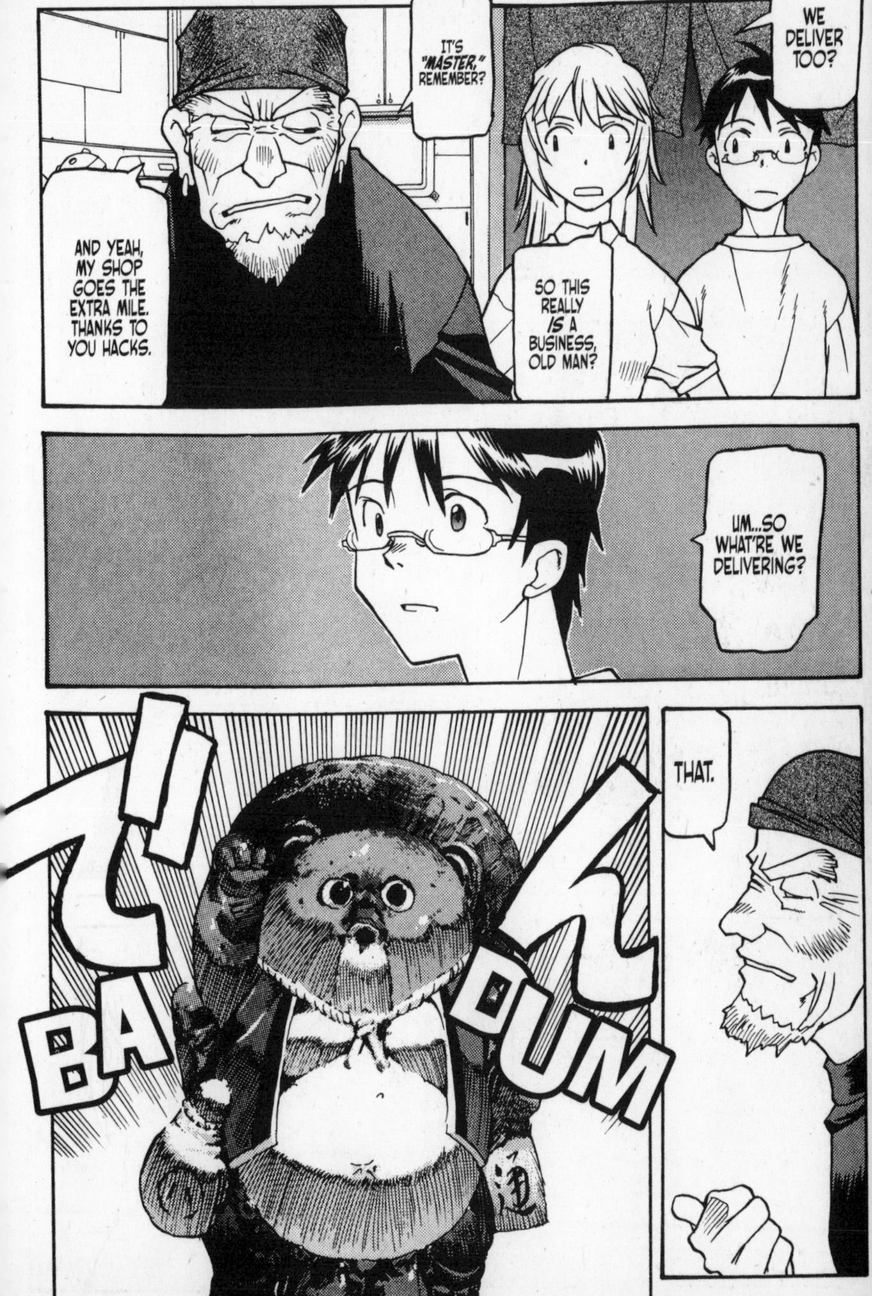
WE DELIVER TOO?
SO THIS REALLY *IS* A BUSINESS, OLD MAN?
IT'S "MASTER," REMEMBER?
AND YEAH, MY SHOP GOES THE EXTRA MILE. THANKS TO YOU HACKS.
UM...SO WHAT'RE WE DELIVERING?
THAT.
BA DUM

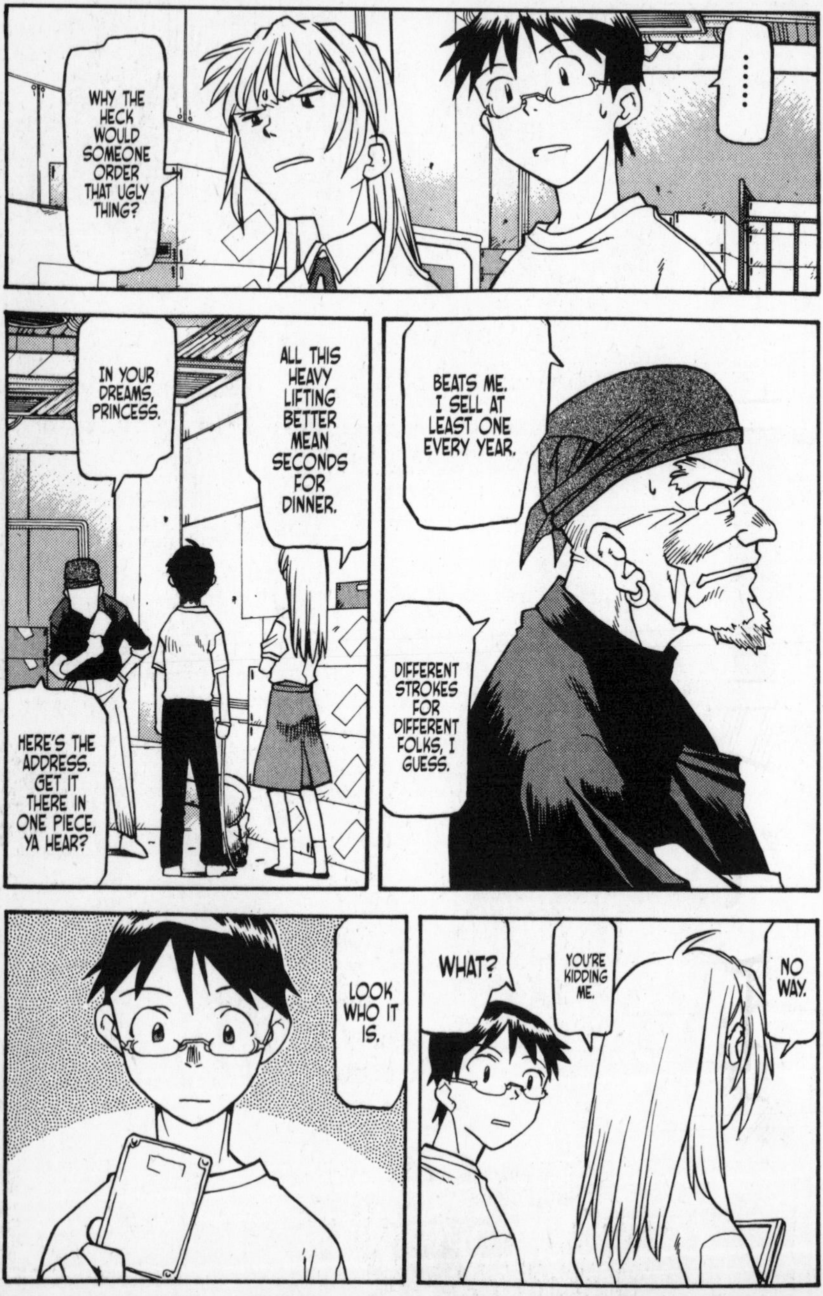
......
WHY THE HECK WOULD SOMEONE ORDER THAT UGLY THING?
BEATS ME. I SELL AT LEAST ONE EVERY YEAR.
DIFFERENT STROKES FOR DIFFERENT FOLKS, I GUESS.
ALL THIS HEAVY LIFTING BETTER MEAN SECONDS FOR DINNER.
IN YOUR DREAMS, PRINCESS.
HERE'S THE ADDRESS. GET IT THERE IN ONE PIECE, YA HEAR?
NO WAY.
YOU'RE KIDDING ME.
WHAT?
LOOK WHO IT IS.

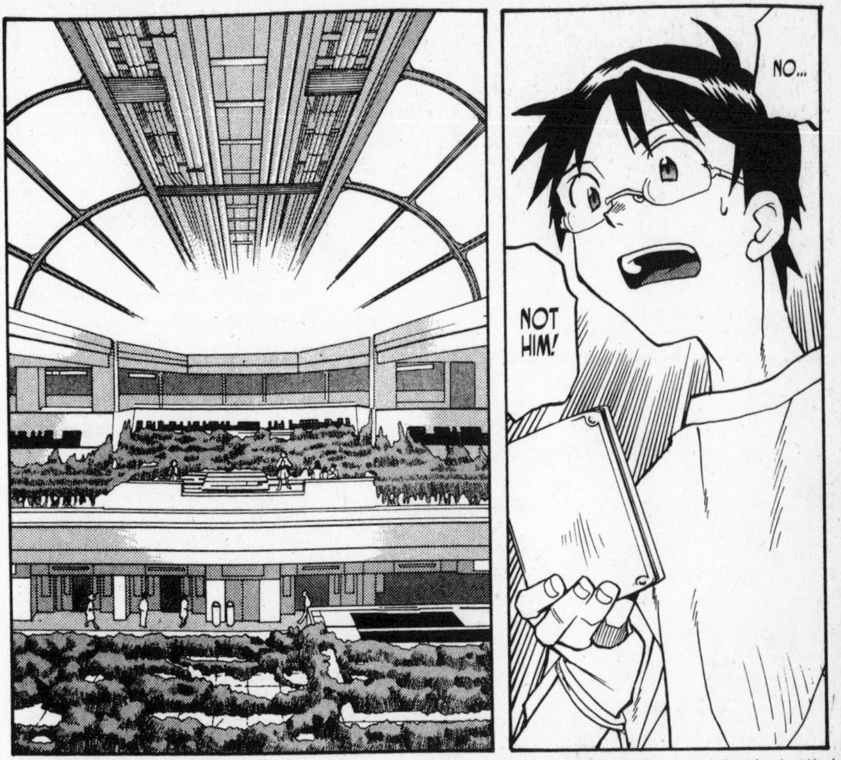
NO...
NOT HIM!

*Tanuki - This statue depicts the mythical raccoon dog or "tanuki" believed to be a mischievous but amiable creature. Statues like this are popular items found outside of Japanese temples and restaurants and always have the trademark wide-brimmed hat, big belly and large testicles. Their appearance represents plenty, fertility, and luck.

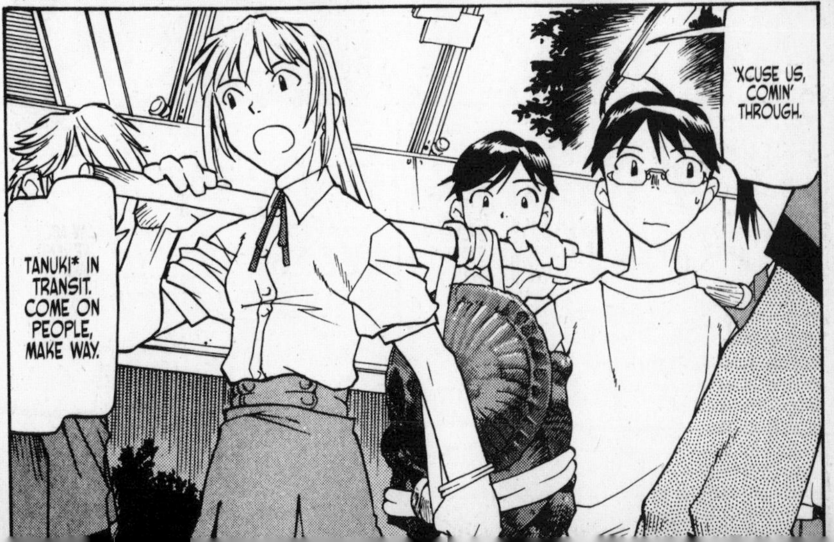
'XCUSE US, COMIN' THROUGH.
TANUKI* IN TRANSIT. COME ON PEOPLE, MAKE WAY.

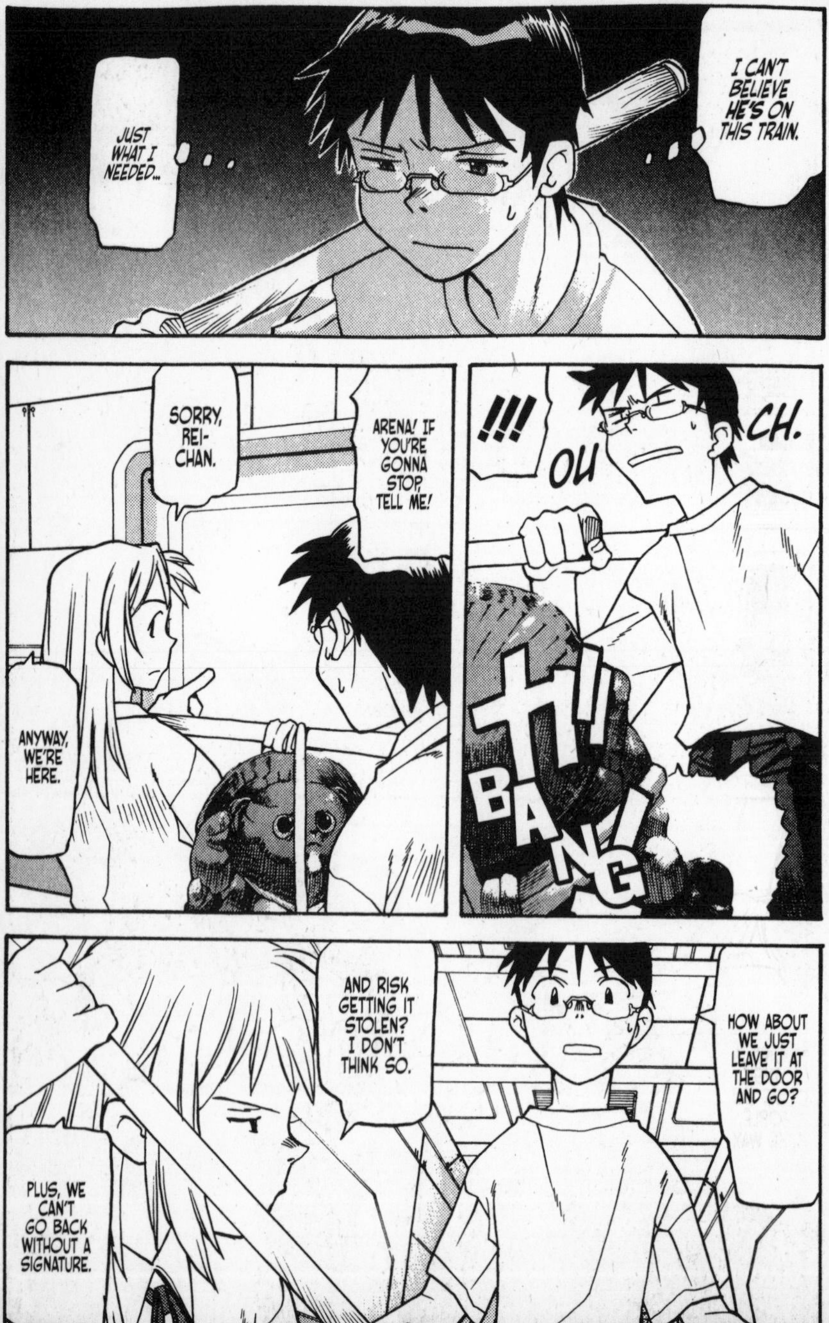
I CAN'T BELIEVE HE'S ON THIS TRAIN.
JUST WHAT I NEEDED...
!!!
OU CH.
HIT!
BANG!
ARENA! IF YOU'RE GONNA STOP, TELL ME!
SORRY, REI-CHAN.
ANYWAY, WE'RE HERE.
HOW ABOUT WE JUST LEAVE IT AT THE DOOR AND GO?
AND RISK GETTING IT STOLEN? I DON'T THINK SO.
PLUS, WE CAN'T GO BACK WITHOUT A SIGNATURE.

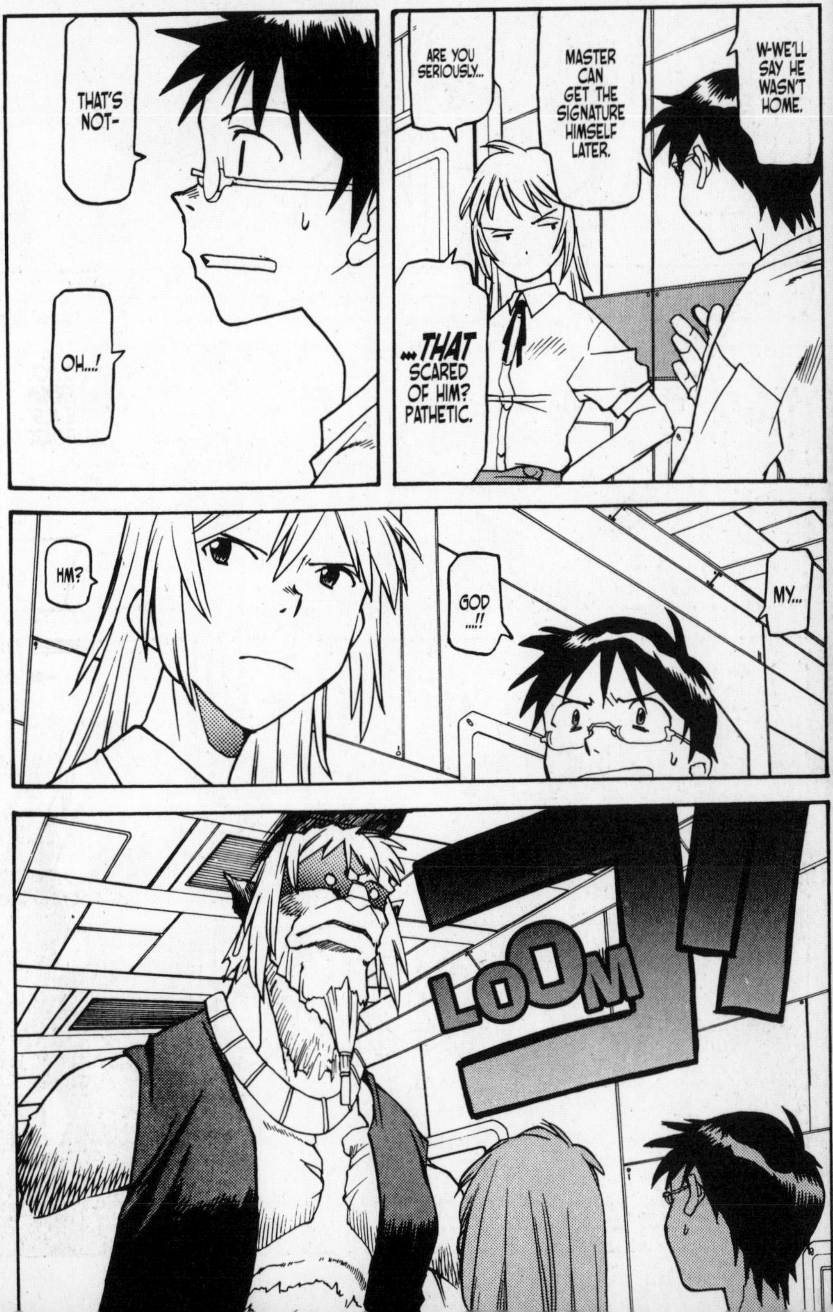
W-WE'LL SAY HE WASN'T HOME.
MASTER CAN GET THE SIGNATURE HIMSELF LATER.
ARE YOU SERIOUSLY...
...THAT SCARED OF HIM? PATHETIC.
THAT'S NOT-
OH...!
MY...
GOD ...!!
HM?
LOOM

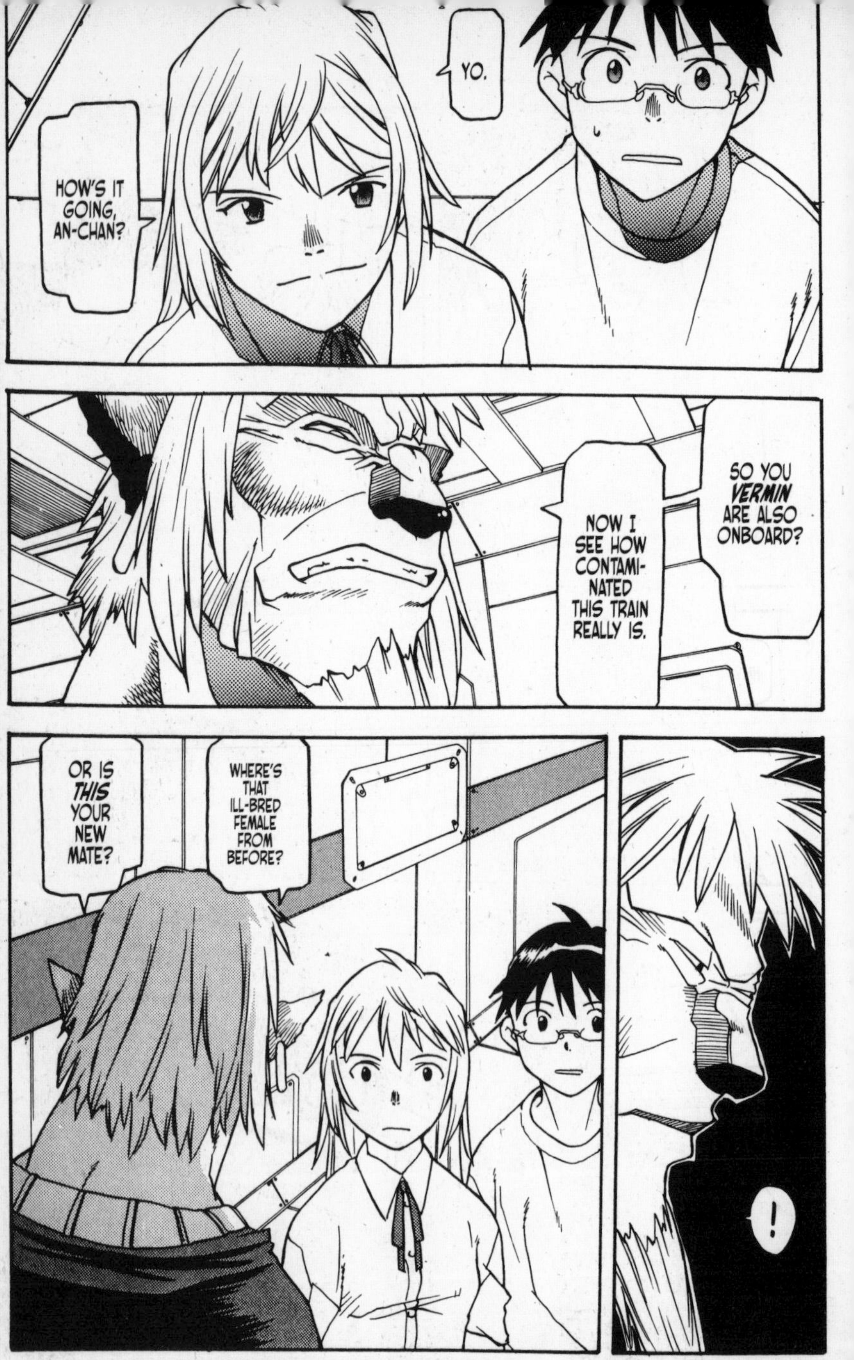
YO.
HOW'S IT GOING, AN-CHAN?
SO YOU *VERMIN* ARE ALSO ONBOARD?
NOW I SEE HOW CONTAMI-NATED THIS TRAIN REALLY IS.
!
WHERE'S THAT ILL-BRED FEMALE FROM BEFORE?
OR IS *THIS* YOUR NEW MATE?

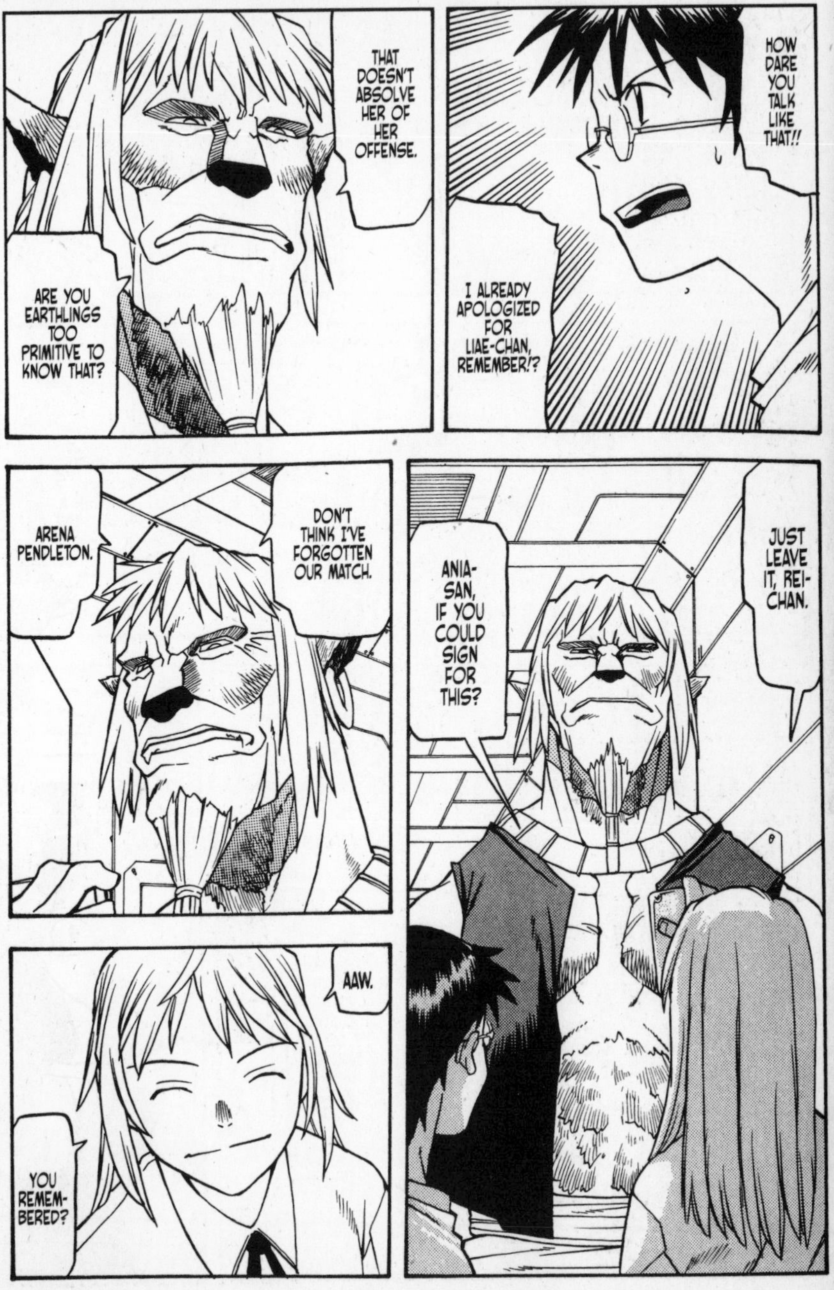
HOW DARE YOU TALK LIKE THAT!!
I ALREADY APOLOGIZED FOR LIAE-CHAN, REMEMBER!?
THAT DOESN'T ABSOLVE HER OF HER OFFENSE.
ARE YOU EARTHLINGS TOO PRIMITIVE TO KNOW THAT?
JUST LEAVE IT, REI-CHAN.
ANIA-SAN, IF YOU COULD SIGN FOR THIS?
DON'T THINK I'VE FORGOTTEN OUR MATCH.
ARENA PENDLETON.
AAW.
YOU REMEMBERED?

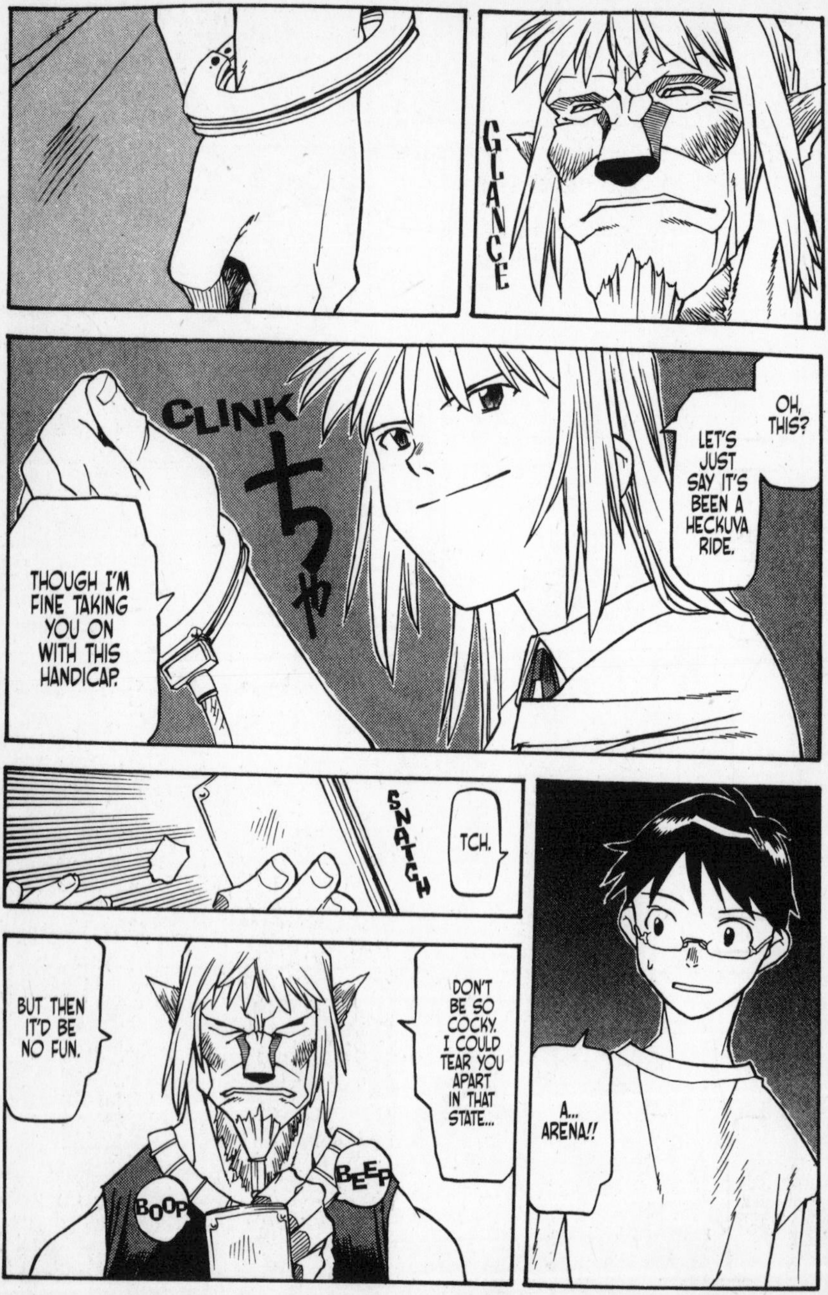
GLANCE
OH, THIS?
LET'S JUST SAY IT'S BEEN A HECKUVA RIDE.
CLINK
ちゃ
THOUGH I'M FINE TAKING YOU ON WITH THIS HANDICAP.
A... ARENA!!
TCH.
SNATCH
DON'T BE SO COCKY. I COULD TEAR YOU APART IN THAT STATE...
BUT THEN IT'D BE NO FUN.
BEEP
BOOP

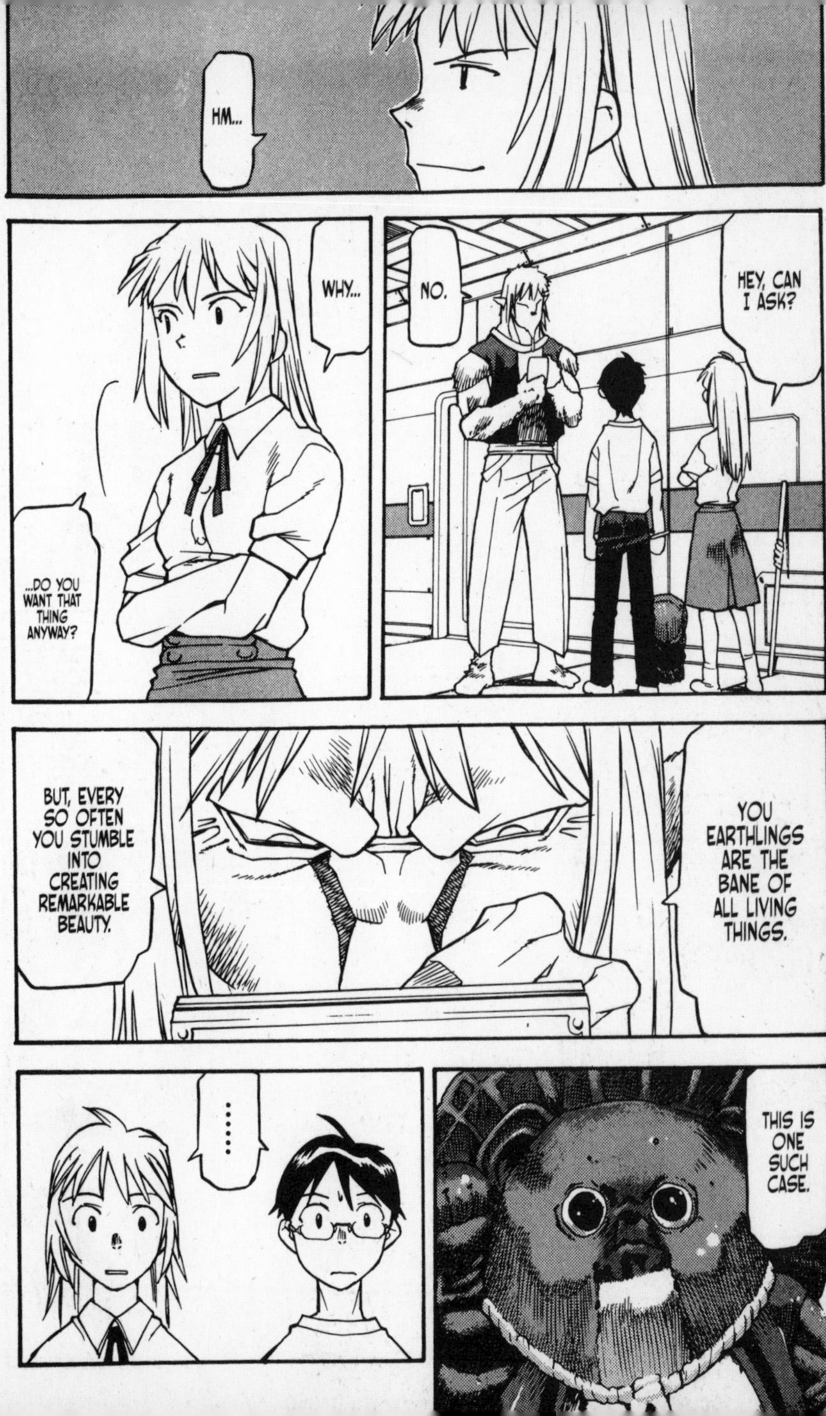
HM...
HEY, CAN I ASK?
NO.
WHY...
...DO YOU WANT THAT THING ANYWAY?
YOU EARTHLINGS ARE THE BANE OF ALL LIVING THINGS.
BUT, EVERY SO OFTEN YOU STUMBLE INTO CREATING REMARKABLE BEAUTY.
THIS IS ONE SUCH CASE.
......

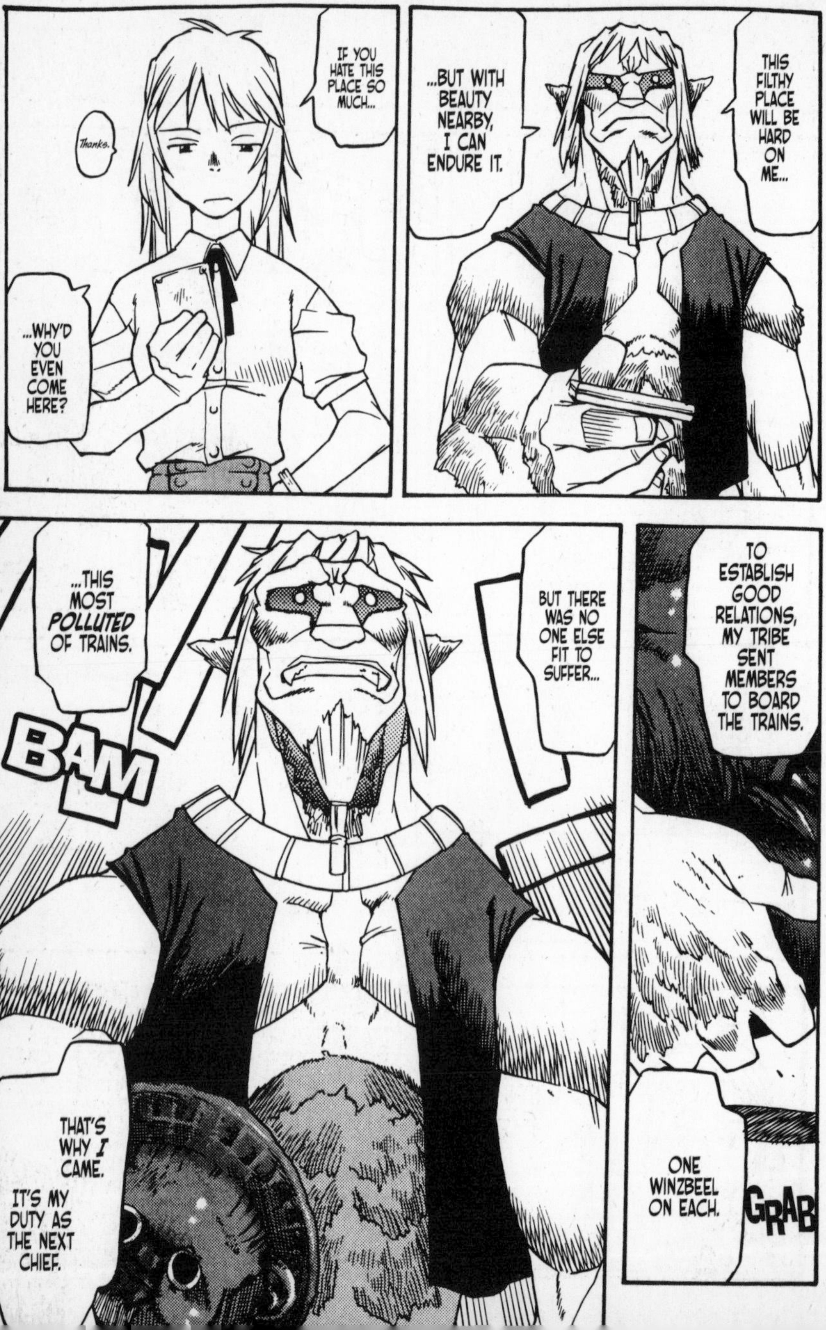
THIS FILTHY PLACE WILL BE HARD ON ME...
...BUT WITH BEAUTY NEARBY, I CAN ENDURE IT.
IF YOU HATE THIS PLACE SO MUCH...
Thanks.
...WHY'D YOU EVEN COME HERE?
TO ESTABLISH GOOD RELATIONS, MY TRIBE SENT MEMBERS TO BOARD THE TRAINS.
ONE WINZBEEL ON EACH.
GRAB
BUT THERE WAS NO ONE ELSE FIT TO SUFFER...
...THIS MOST *POLLUTED* OF TRAINS.
BAM
THAT'S WHY *I* CAME.
IT'S MY DUTY AS THE NEXT CHIEF.

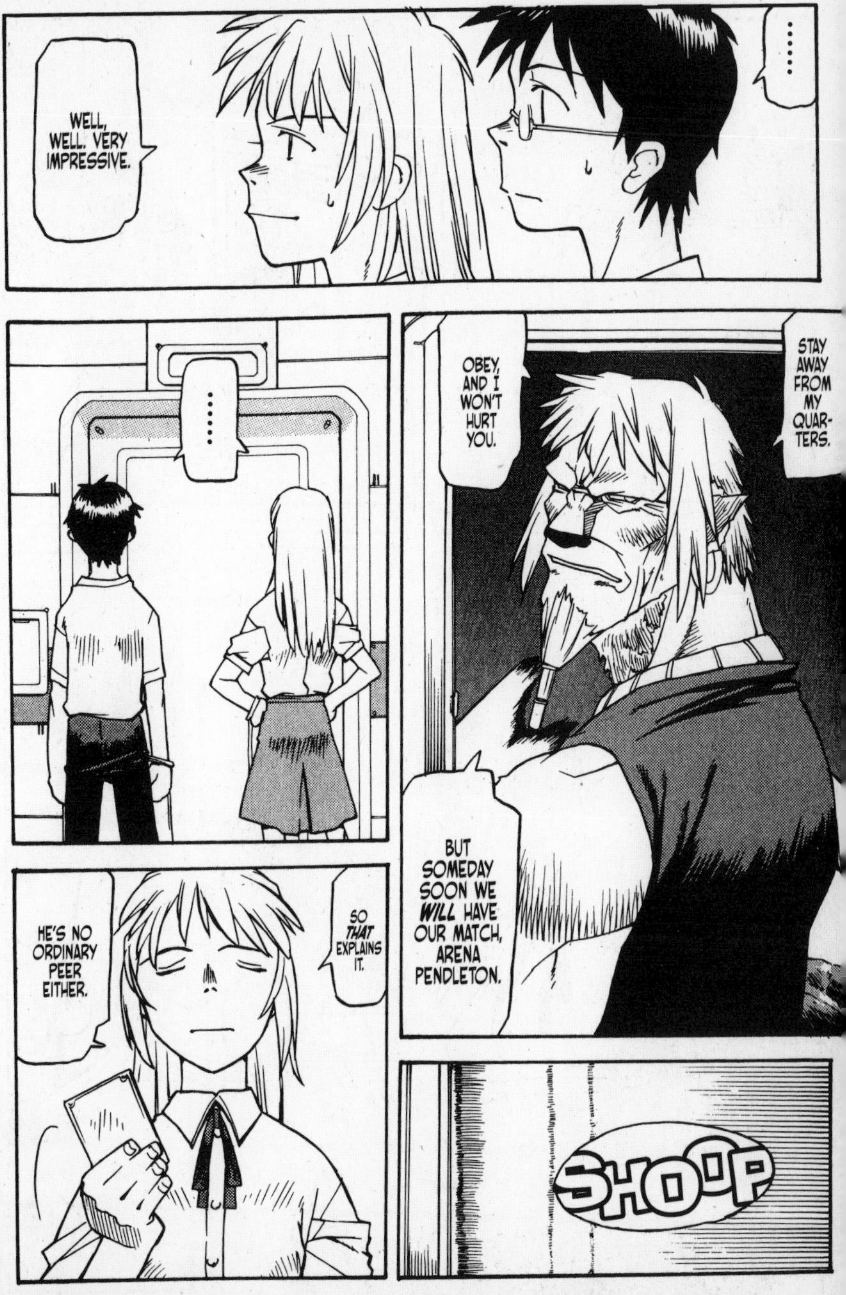
......
WELL, WELL. VERY IMPRESSIVE.
STAY AWAY FROM MY QUAR-TERS.
OBEY, AND I WON'T HURT YOU.
BUT SOMEDAY SOON WE *WILL* HAVE OUR MATCH, ARENA PENDLETON.
SHOOP
......
SO *THAT* EXPLAINS IT.
HE'S NO ORDINARY PEER EITHER.

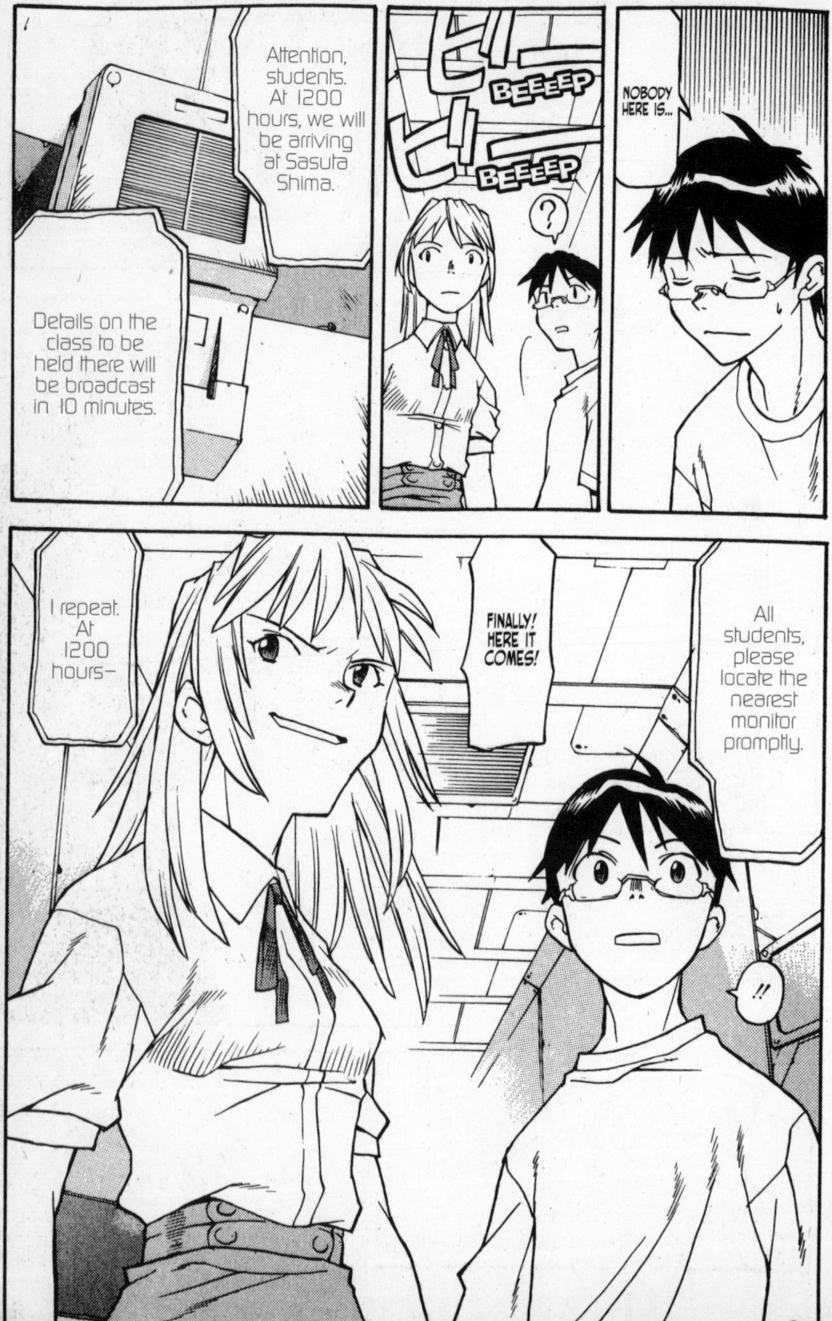
NOBODY HERE IS...
ビー
BEEEEP
ビー
BEEEEP
?
Attention, students. At 1200 hours, we will be arriving at Sasuta Shima.
Details on the class to be held there will be broadcast in 10 minutes.
All students, please locate the nearest monitor promptly.
FINALLY! HERE IT COMES!
I repeat. At 1200 hours–
!!

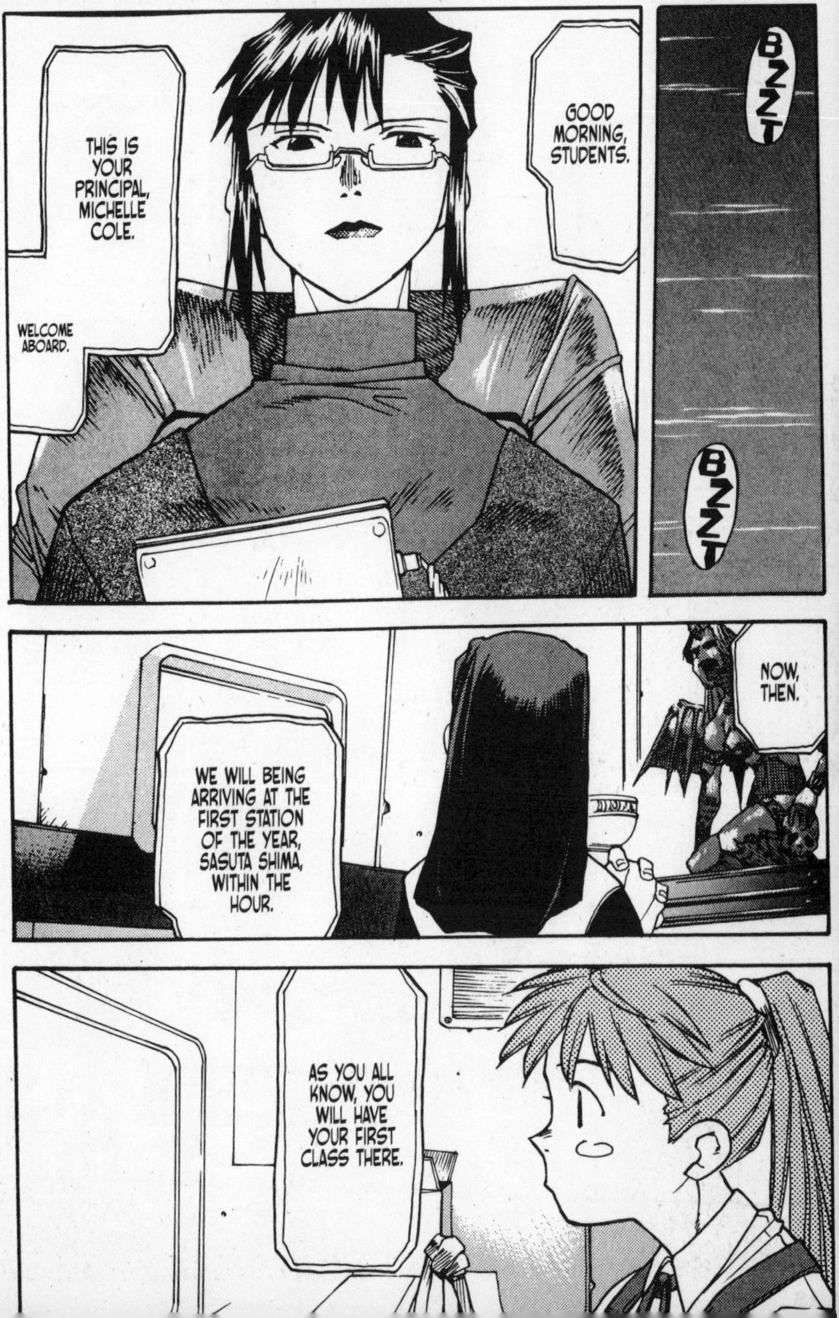
BZZT
BZZT
GOOD MORNING, STUDENTS.
THIS IS YOUR PRINCIPAL, MICHELLE COLE.
WELCOME ABOARD.
NOW, THEN.
WE WILL BEING ARRIVING AT THE FIRST STATION OF THE YEAR, SASUTA SHIMA, WITHIN THE HOUR.
AS YOU ALL KNOW, YOU WILL HAVE YOUR FIRST CLASS THERE.

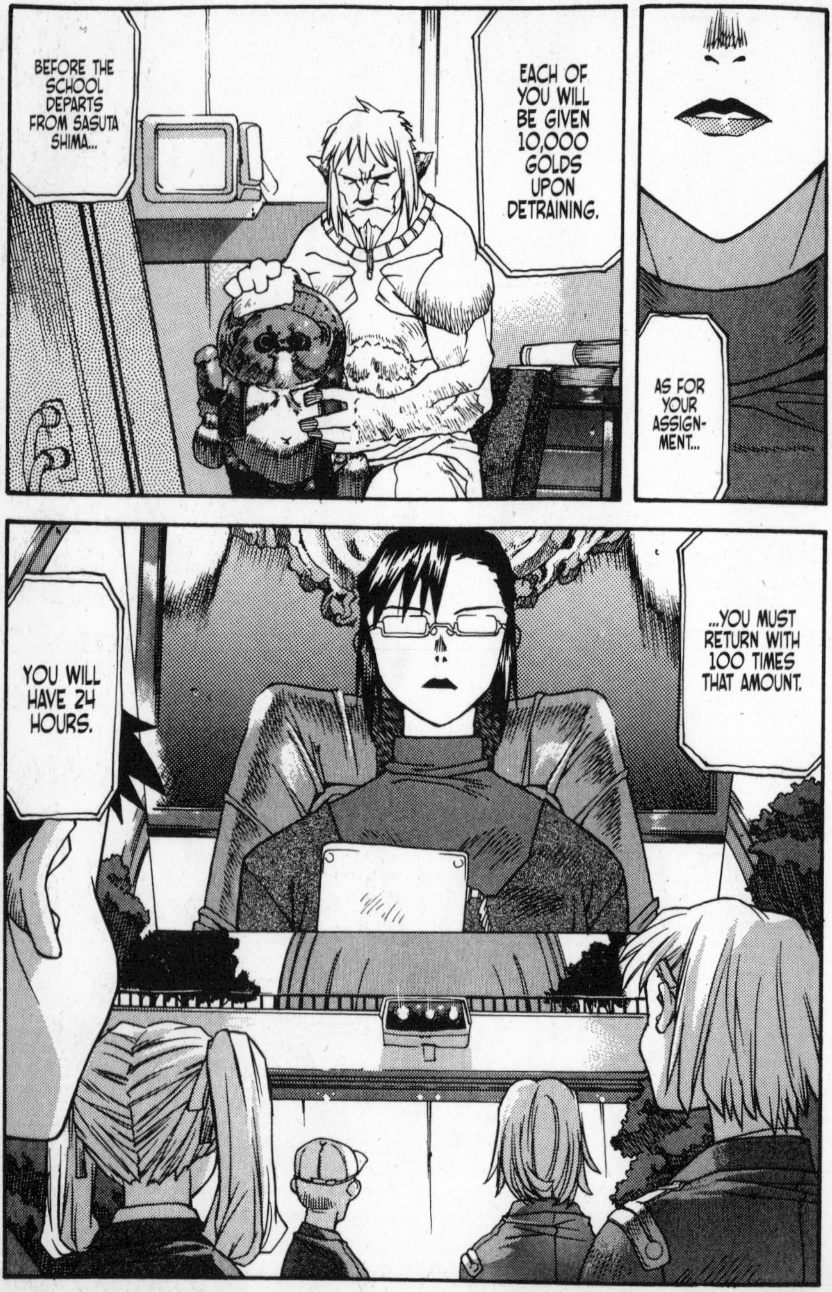
AS FOR YOUR ASSIGNMENT...
EACH OF YOU WILL BE GIVEN 10,000 GOLDS UPON DETRAINING.
BEFORE THE SCHOOL DEPARTS FROM SASUTA SHIMA...
...YOU MUST RETURN WITH 100 TIMES THAT AMOUNT.
YOU WILL HAVE 24 HOURS.

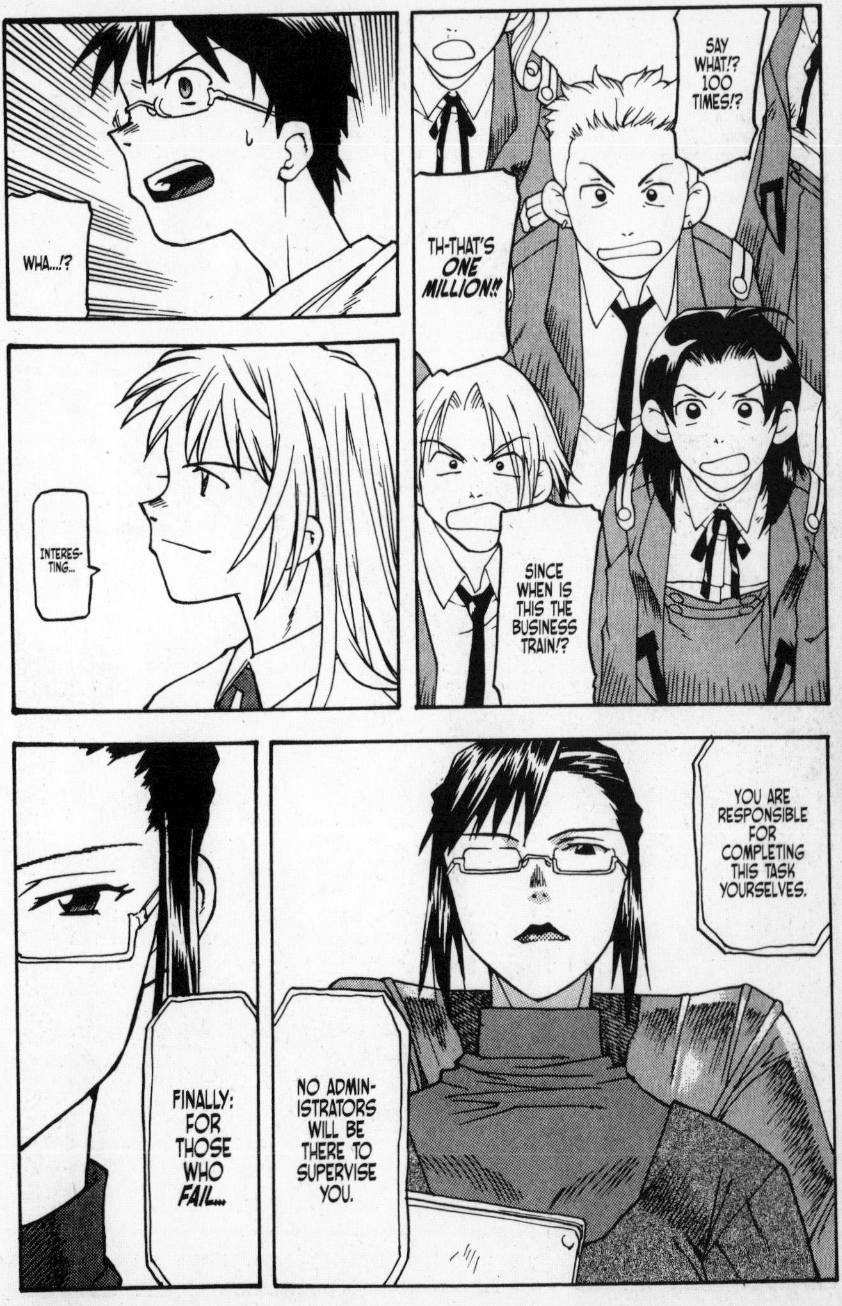
SAY WHAT!? 100 TIMES!?
TH-THAT'S ONE MILLION!!
SINCE WHEN IS THIS THE BUSINESS TRAIN!?
WHA...!?
INTERESTING...
YOU ARE RESPONSIBLE FOR COMPLETING THIS TASK YOURSELVES.
NO ADMINISTRATORS WILL BE THERE TO SUPERVISE YOU.
FINALLY: FOR THOSE WHO FAIL...

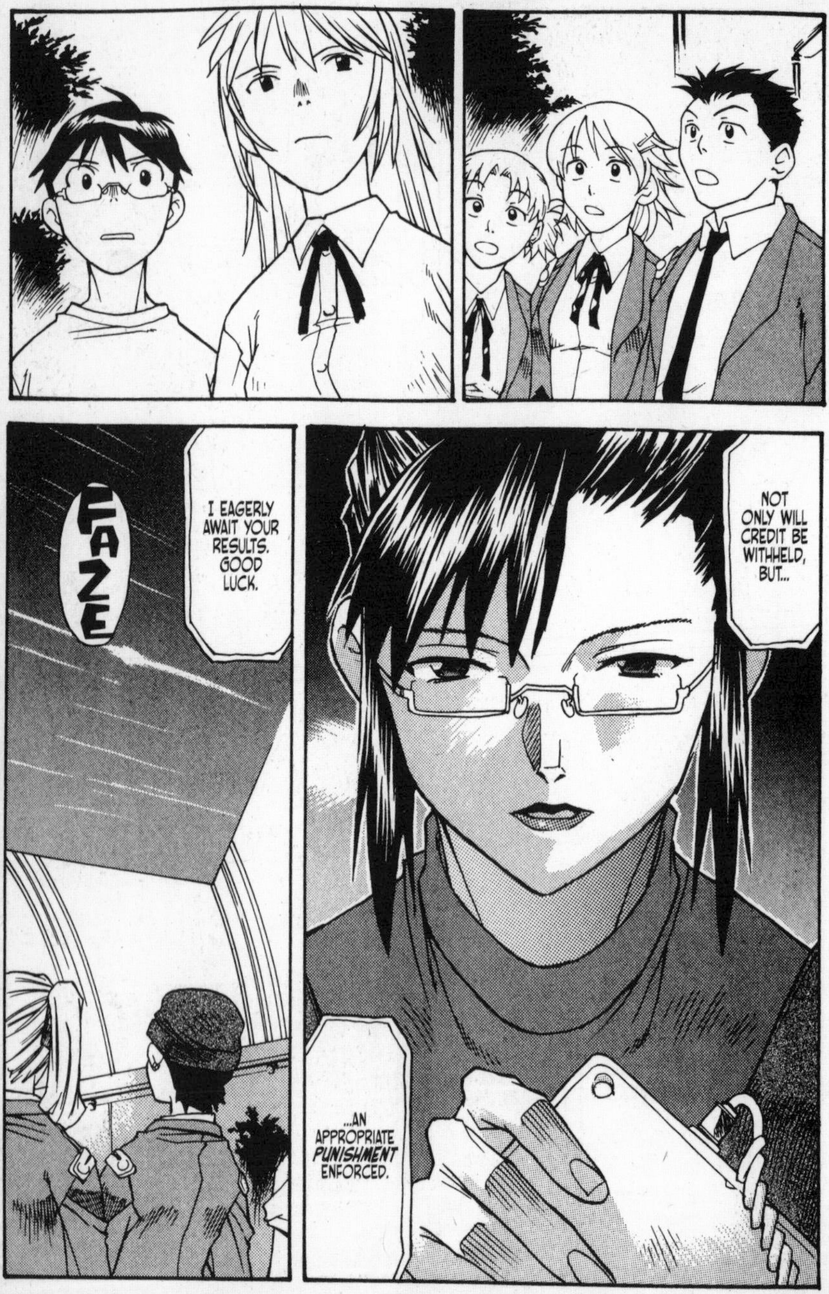
NOT ONLY WILL CREDIT BE WITHHELD, BUT...
...AN APPROPRIATE *PUNISHMENT* ENFORCED.
I EAGERLY AWAIT YOUR RESULTS. GOOD LUCK.
FAZE

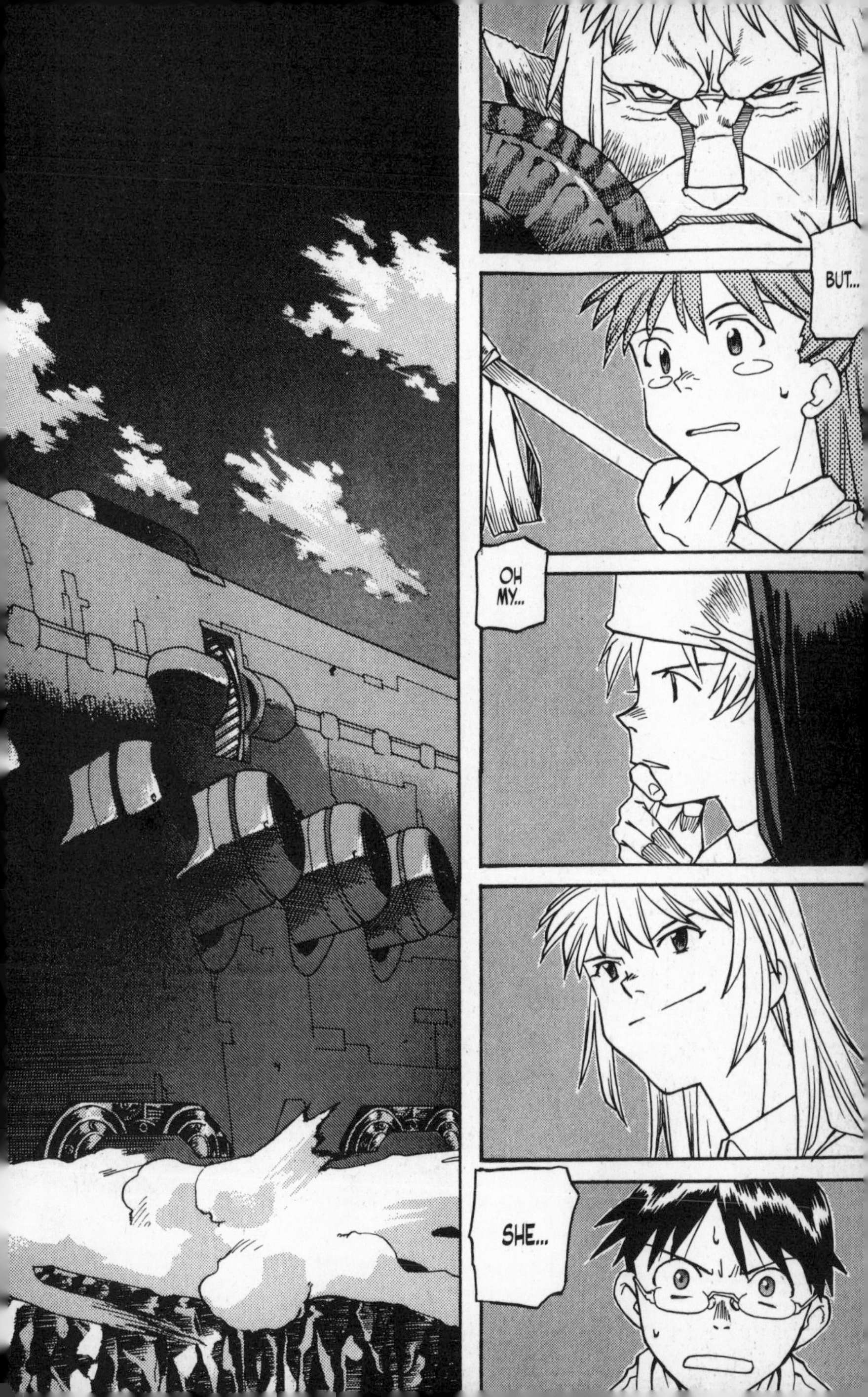
BUT...
OH MY...
SHE...

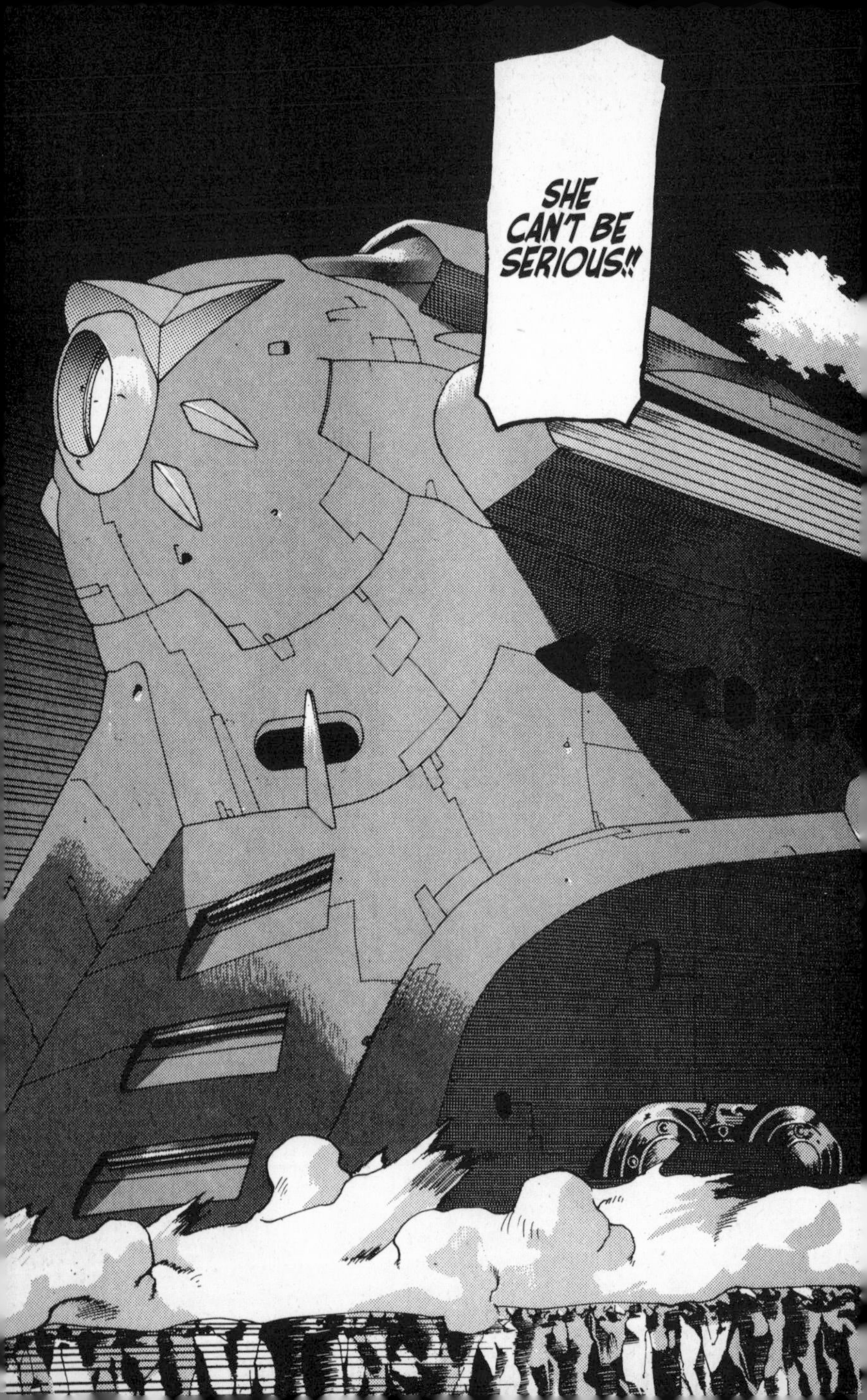
SHE CAN'T BE SERIOUS!!

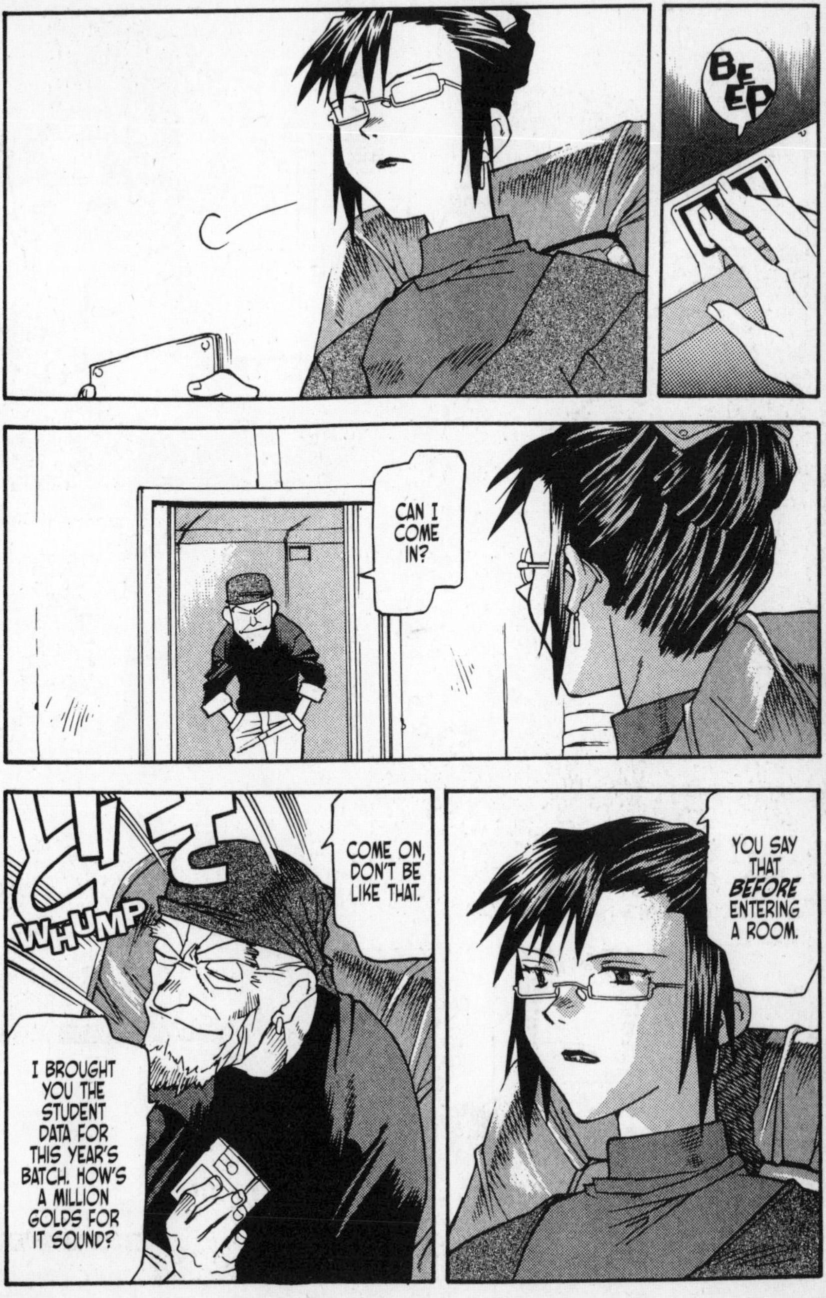
BEEP
CAN I COME IN?
YOU SAY THAT *BEFORE* ENTERING A ROOM.
COME ON, DON'T BE LIKE THAT.
WHUMP
I BROUGHT YOU THE STUDENT DATA FOR THIS YEAR'S BATCH. HOW'S A MILLION GOLDS FOR IT SOUND?

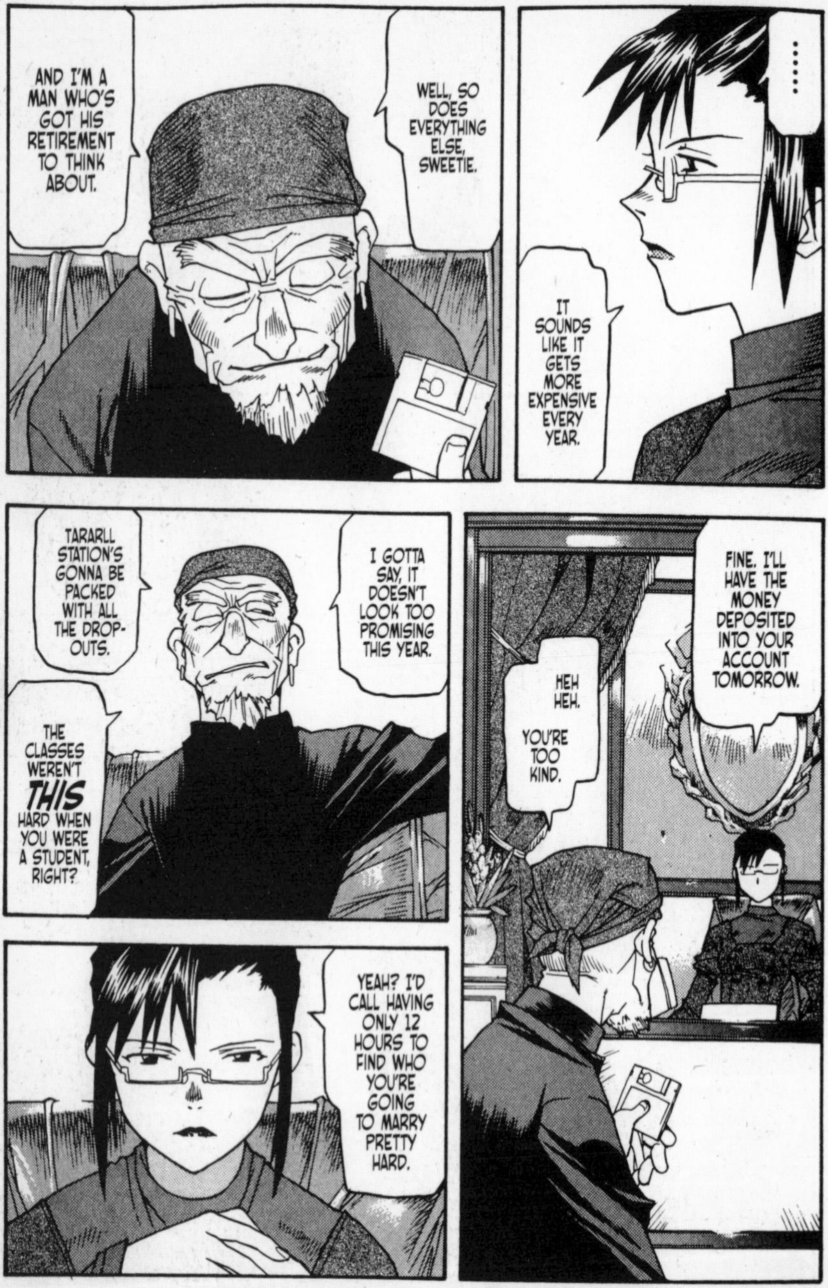
......
IT SOUNDS LIKE IT GETS MORE EXPENSIVE EVERY YEAR.
WELL, SO DOES EVERYTHING ELSE, SWEETIE.
AND I'M A MAN WHO'S GOT HIS RETIREMENT TO THINK ABOUT.
FINE. I'LL HAVE THE MONEY DEPOSITED INTO YOUR ACCOUNT TOMORROW.
HEH HEH.
YOU'RE TOO KIND.
I GOTTA SAY, IT DOESN'T LOOK TOO PROMISING THIS YEAR.
TARARLL STATION'S GONNA BE PACKED WITH ALL THE DROP-OUTS.
THE CLASSES WEREN'T THIS HARD WHEN YOU WERE A STUDENT, RIGHT?
YEAH? I'D CALL HAVING ONLY 12 HOURS TO FIND WHO YOU'RE GOING TO MARRY PRETTY HARD.

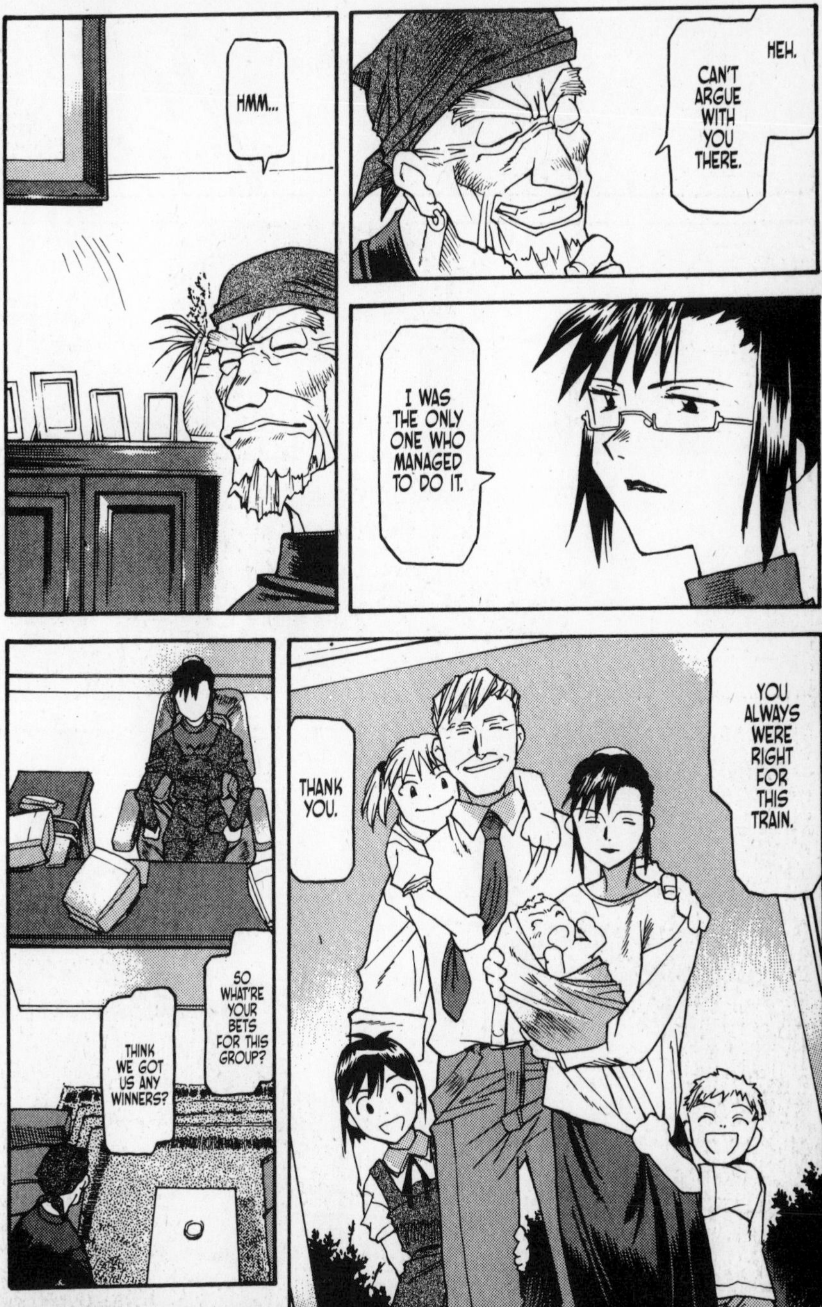
HEH.
CAN'T ARGUE WITH YOU THERE.
I WAS THE ONLY ONE WHO MANAGED TO DO IT.
HMM...
YOU ALWAYS WERE RIGHT FOR THIS TRAIN.
THANK YOU.
SO WHAT'RE YOUR BETS FOR THIS GROUP?
THINK WE GOT US ANY WINNERS?

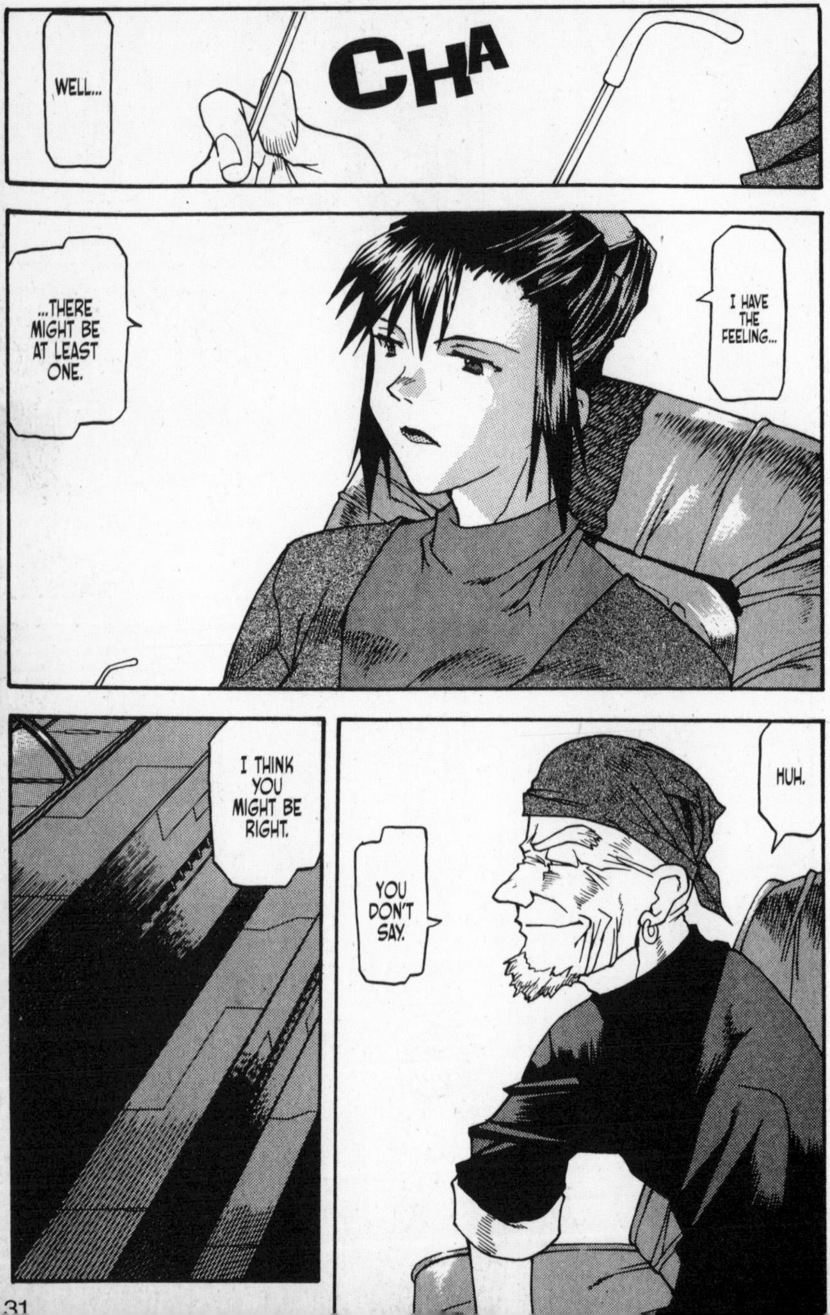
CHA
WELL...
I HAVE THE FEELING...
...THERE MIGHT BE AT LEAST ONE.
HUH.
YOU DON'T SAY.
I THINK YOU MIGHT BE RIGHT.

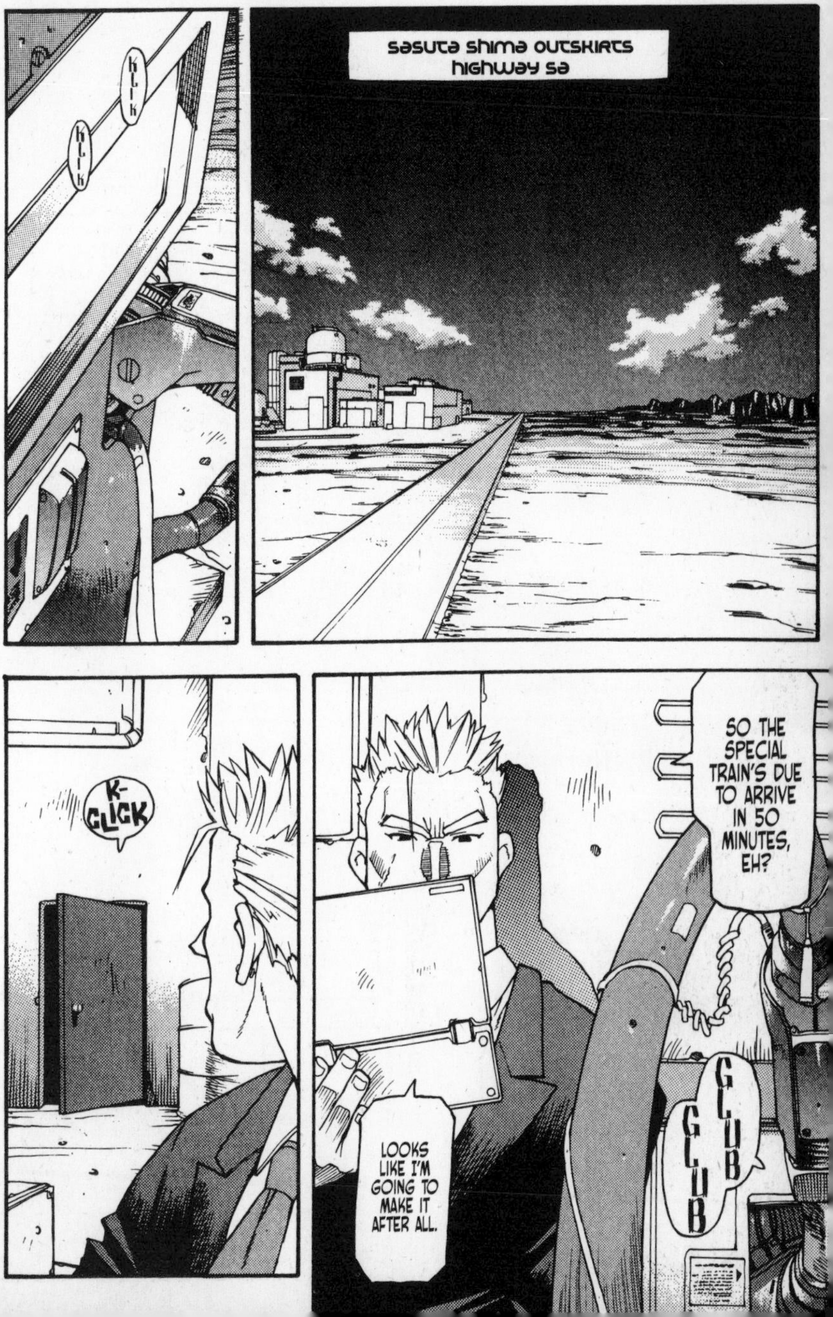
SASUTA SHIMA OUTSKIRTS
HIGHWAY SA
KLIK
KLIK
SO THE SPECIAL TRAIN'S DUE TO ARRIVE IN 50 MINUTES, EH?
GLUB
GLUB
LOOKS LIKE I'M GOING TO MAKE IT AFTER ALL.
K-CLICK

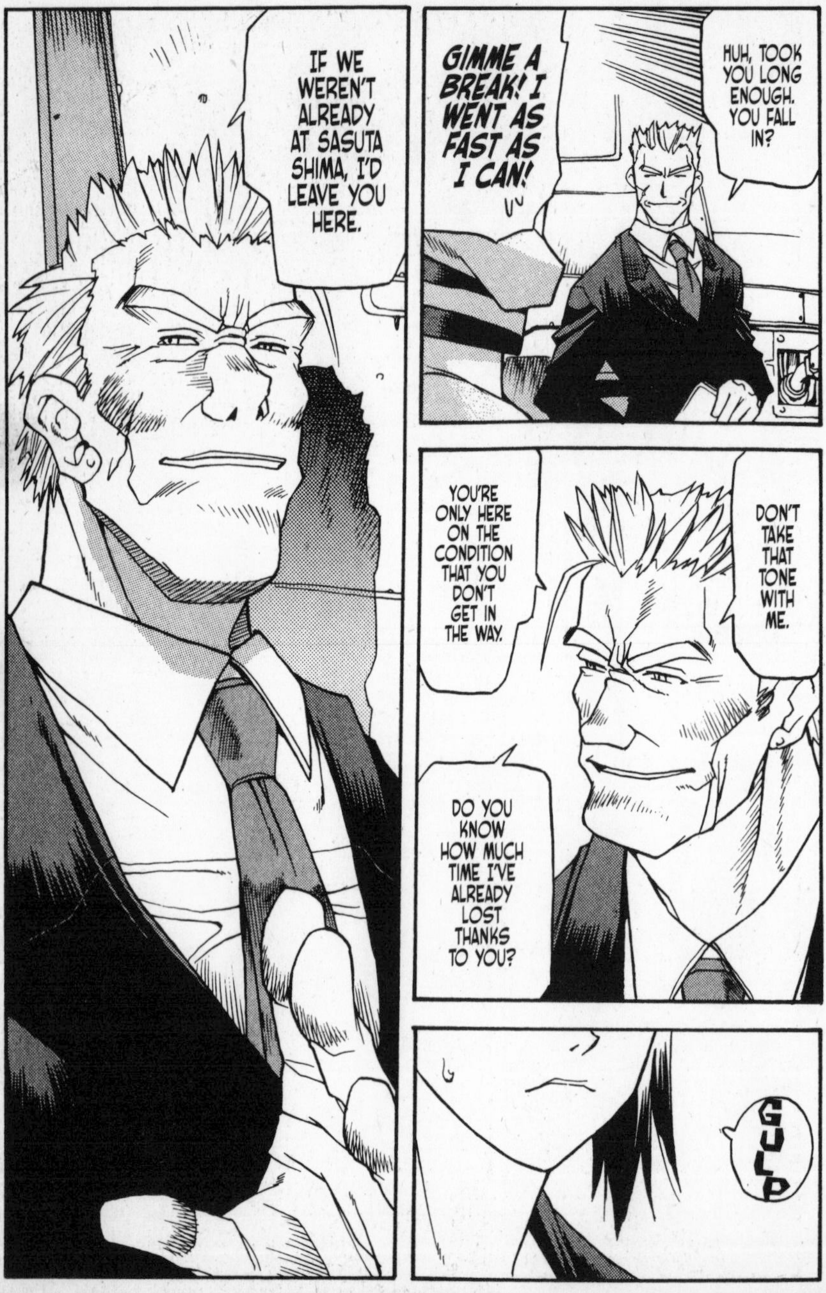
HUH, TOOK YOU LONG ENOUGH. YOU FALL IN?
GIMME A BREAK! I WENT AS FAST AS I CAN!
DON'T TAKE THAT TONE WITH ME.
YOU'RE ONLY HERE ON THE CONDITION THAT YOU DON'T GET IN THE WAY.
DO YOU KNOW HOW MUCH TIME I'VE ALREADY LOST THANKS TO YOU?
GULP
IF WE WEREN'T ALREADY AT SASUTA SHIMA, I'D LEAVE YOU HERE.

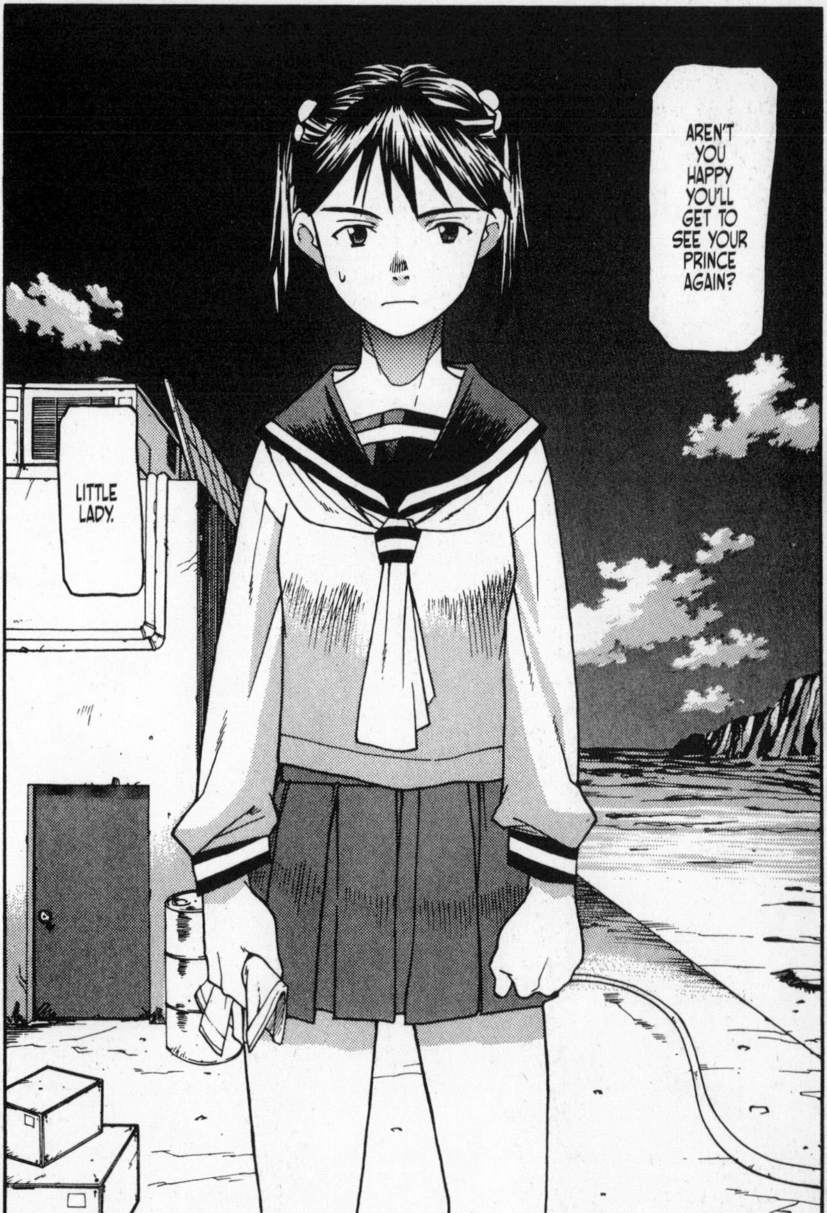

LITTLE LADY.
AREN'T YOU HAPPY YOU'LL GET TO SEE YOUR PRINCE AGAIN?

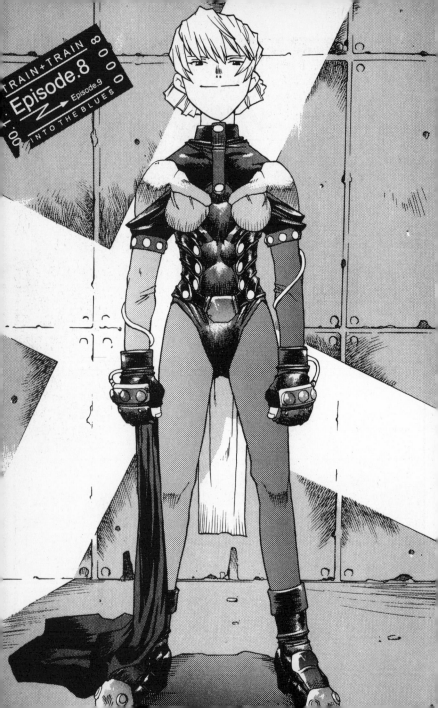

TRAIN+TRAIN
Episode.8
Episode.9
INTO THE BLUES

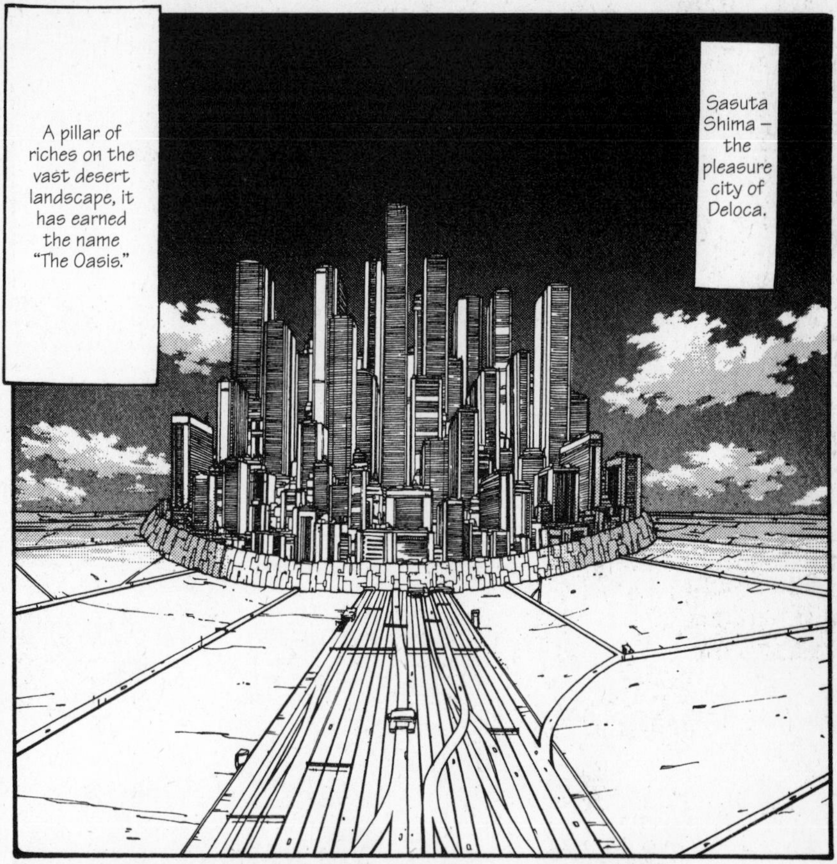
Sasuta Shima – the pleasure city of Deloca.
A pillar of riches on the vast desert landscape, it has earned the name "The Oasis."

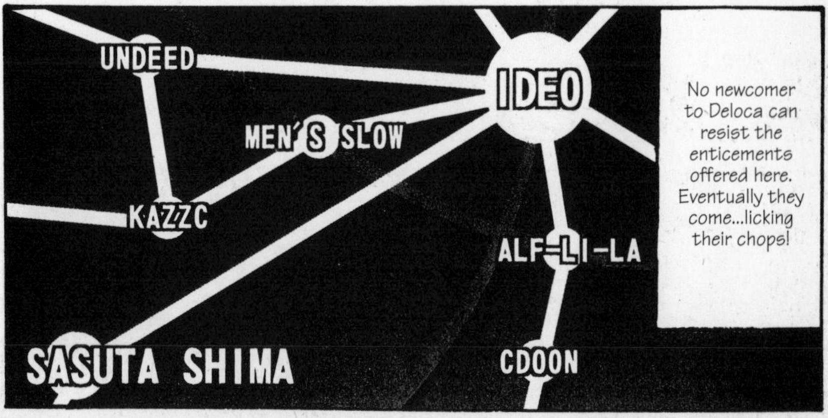
No newcomer to Deloca can resist the enticements offered here. Eventually they come...licking their chops!
IDEO
UNDEED
MEN'S SLOW
KAZZC
ALF-LI-LA
CDOON
SASUTA SHIMA

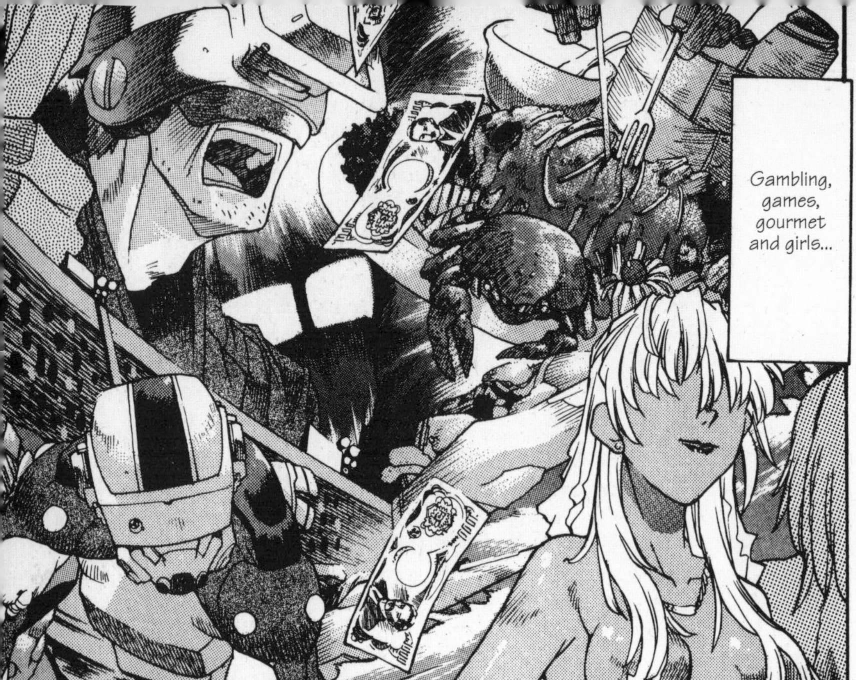
Gambling, games, gourmet and girls...
Every possible craving can be satisfied... with enough money. In Deloca, money is justice!
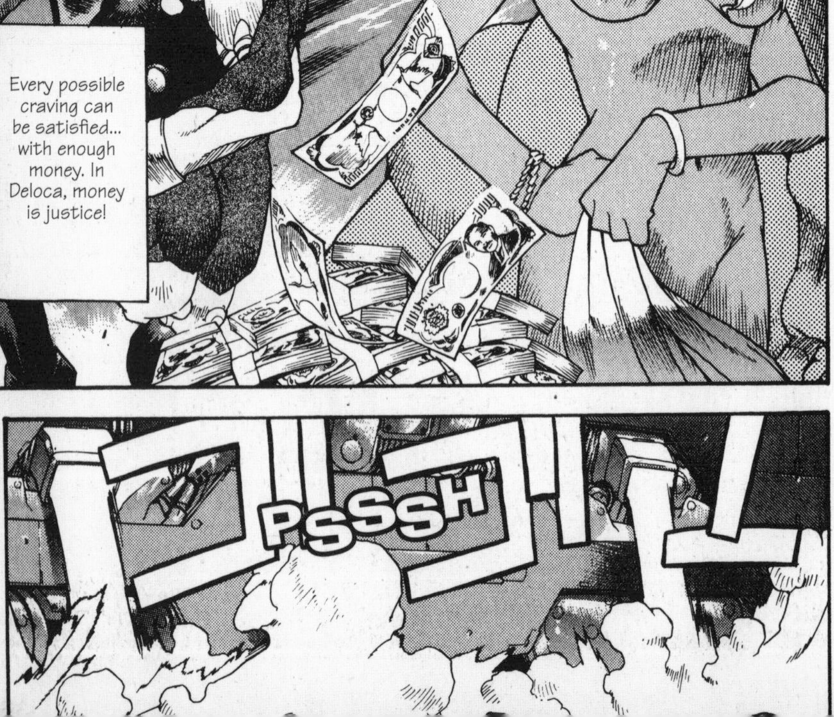
PSSSH

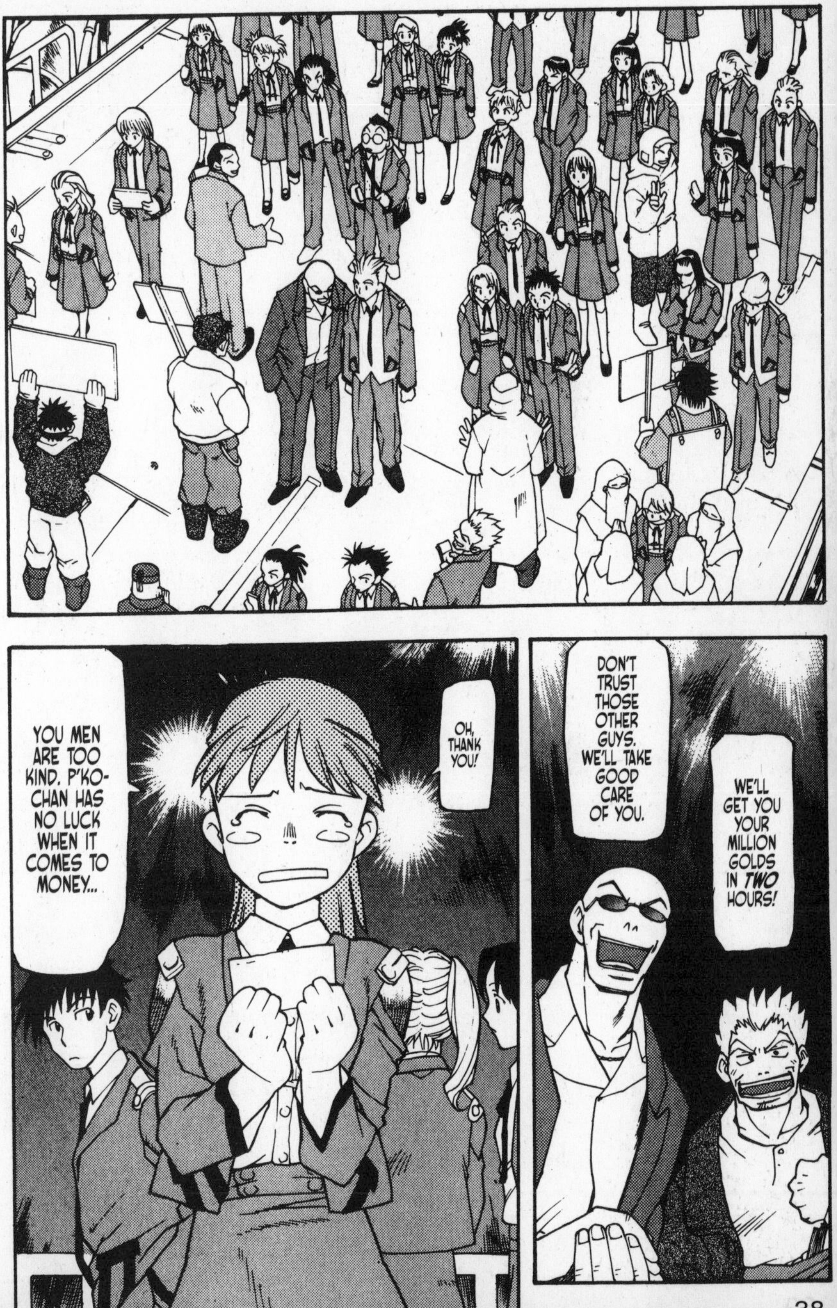
DON'T TRUST THOSE OTHER GUYS. WE'LL TAKE GOOD CARE OF YOU.
WE'LL GET YOU YOUR MILLION GOLDS IN TWO HOURS!
OH, THANK YOU!
YOU MEN ARE TOO KIND. P'KO-CHAN HAS NO LUCK WHEN IT COMES TO MONEY...

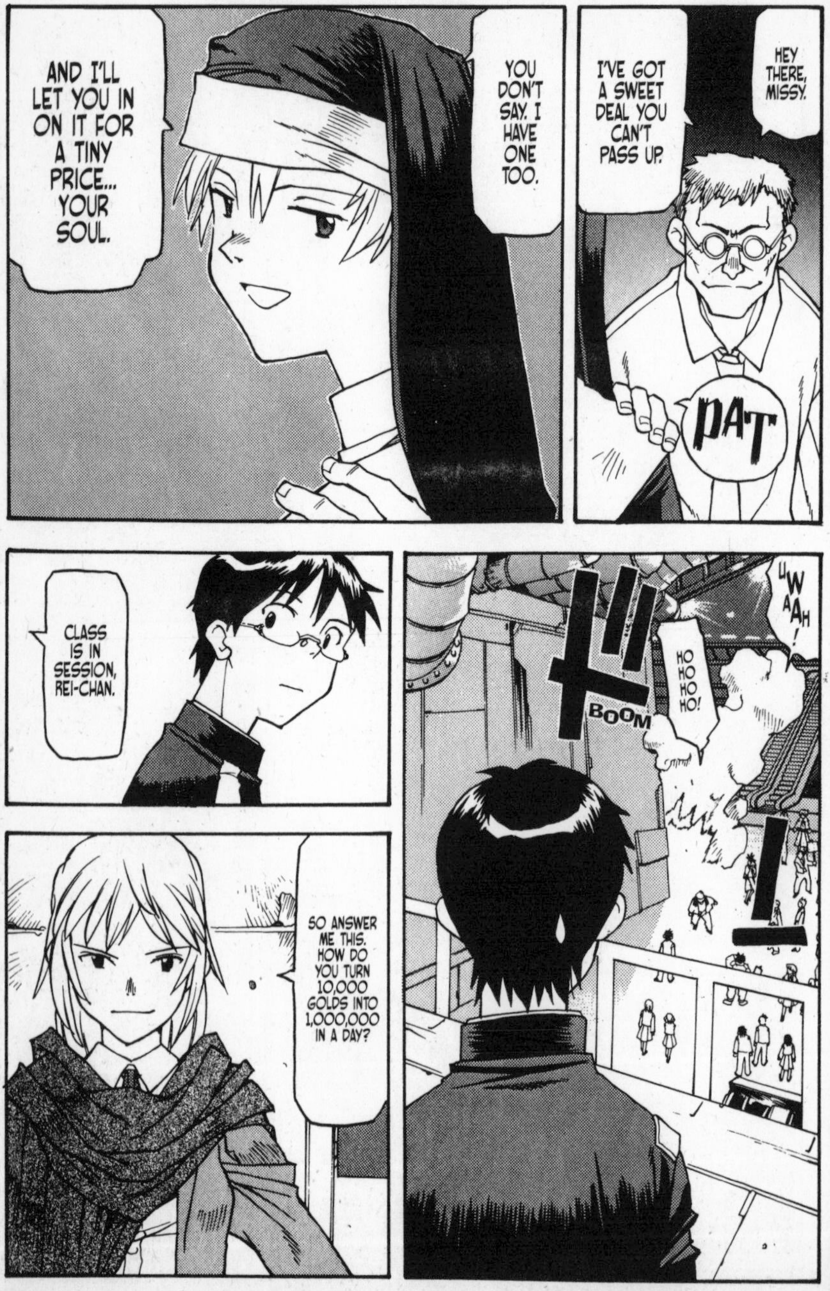
HEY THERE, MISSY.
I'VE GOT A SWEET DEAL YOU CAN'T PASS UP.
PAT
YOU DON'T SAY. I HAVE ONE TOO.
AND I'LL LET YOU IN ON IT FOR A TINY PRICE... YOUR SOUL.
UWAAH!
HO HO HO HO!
BOOM
CLASS IS IN SESSION, REI-CHAN.
SO ANSWER ME THIS. HOW DO YOU TURN 10,000 GOLDS INTO 1,000,000 IN A DAY?

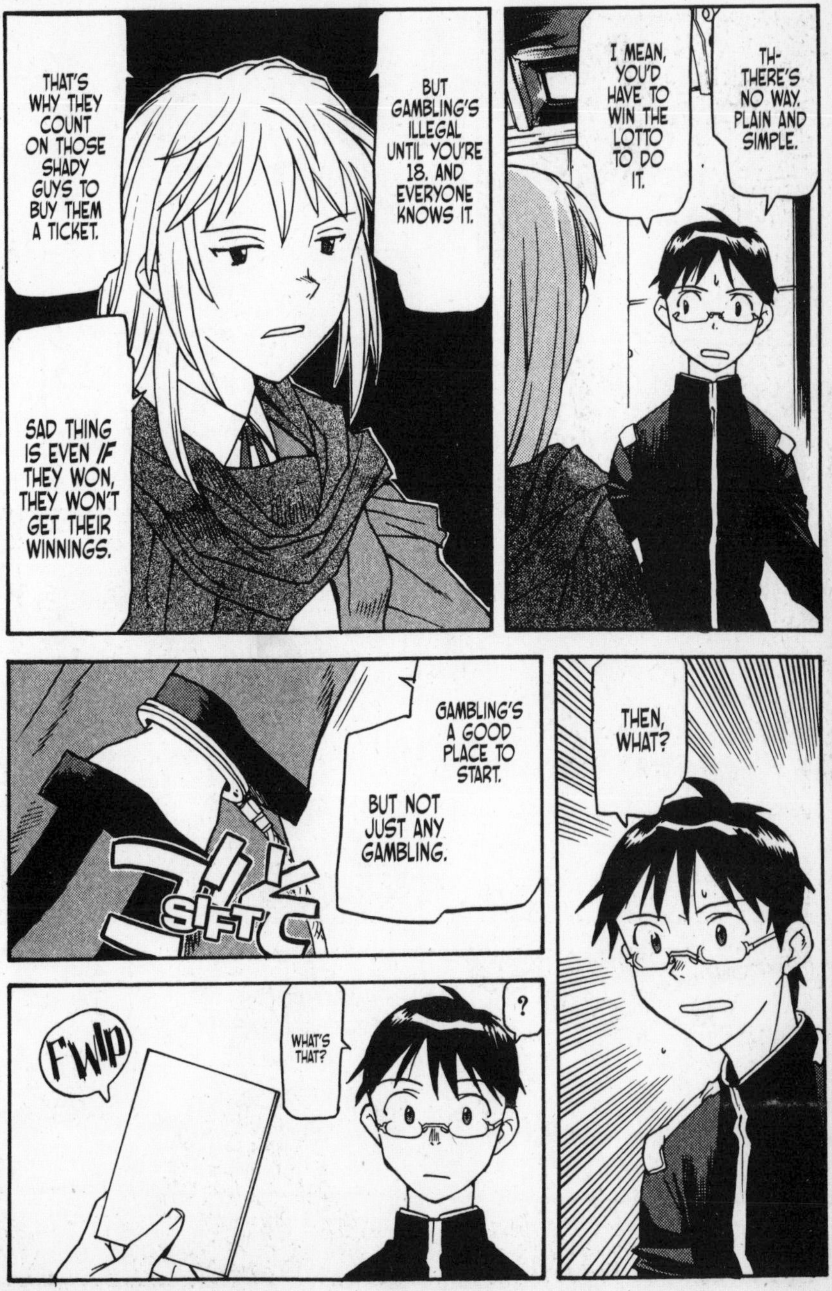
TH- THERE'S NO WAY. PLAIN AND SIMPLE.
I MEAN, YOU'D HAVE TO WIN THE LOTTO TO DO IT.
BUT GAMBLING'S ILLEGAL UNTIL YOU'RE 18. AND EVERYONE KNOWS IT.
THAT'S WHY THEY COUNT ON THOSE SHADY GUYS TO BUY THEM A TICKET.
SAD THING IS EVEN *IF* THEY WON, THEY WON'T GET THEIR WINNINGS.
THEN, WHAT?
GAMBLING'S A GOOD PLACE TO START.
BUT NOT JUST ANY GAMBLING.
SIFT
?
WHAT'S THAT?
FWIP

*WAREZ = an illegal internet database

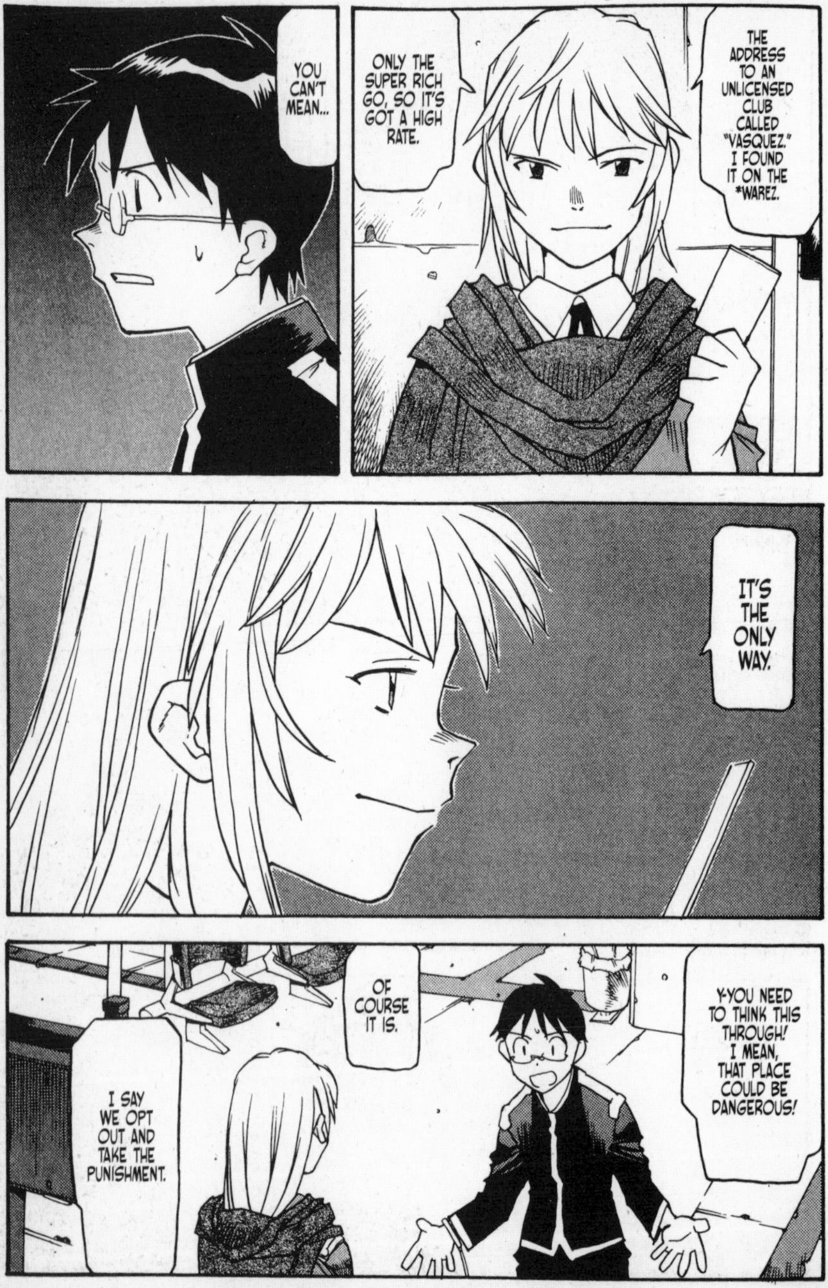

THE ADDRESS TO AN UNLICENSED CLUB CALLED "VASQUEZ." I FOUND IT ON THE *WAREZ.
ONLY THE SUPER RICH GO, SO IT'S GOT A HIGH RATE.
YOU CAN'T MEAN...
IT'S THE ONLY WAY.
Y-YOU NEED TO THINK THIS THROUGH! I MEAN, THAT PLACE COULD BE DANGEROUS!
OF COURSE IT IS.
I SAY WE OPT OUT AND TAKE THE PUNISHMENT.

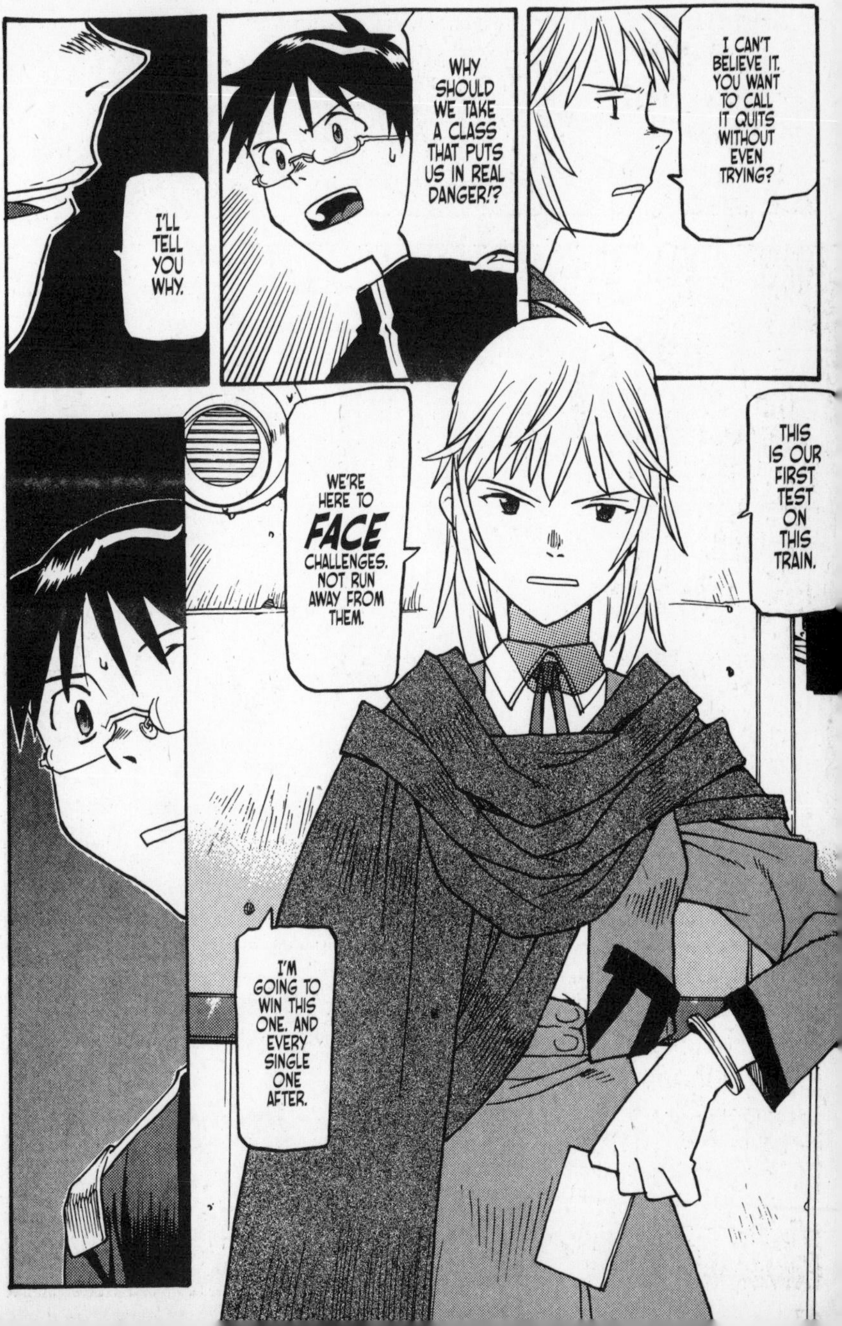
I CAN'T BELIEVE IT. YOU WANT TO CALL IT QUITS WITHOUT EVEN TRYING?
WHY SHOULD WE TAKE A CLASS THAT PUTS US IN REAL DANGER!?
I'LL TELL YOU WHY.
THIS IS OUR FIRST TEST ON THIS TRAIN.
WE'RE HERE TO FACE CHALLENGES. NOT RUN AWAY FROM THEM.
I'M GOING TO WIN THIS ONE. AND EVERY SINGLE ONE AFTER.

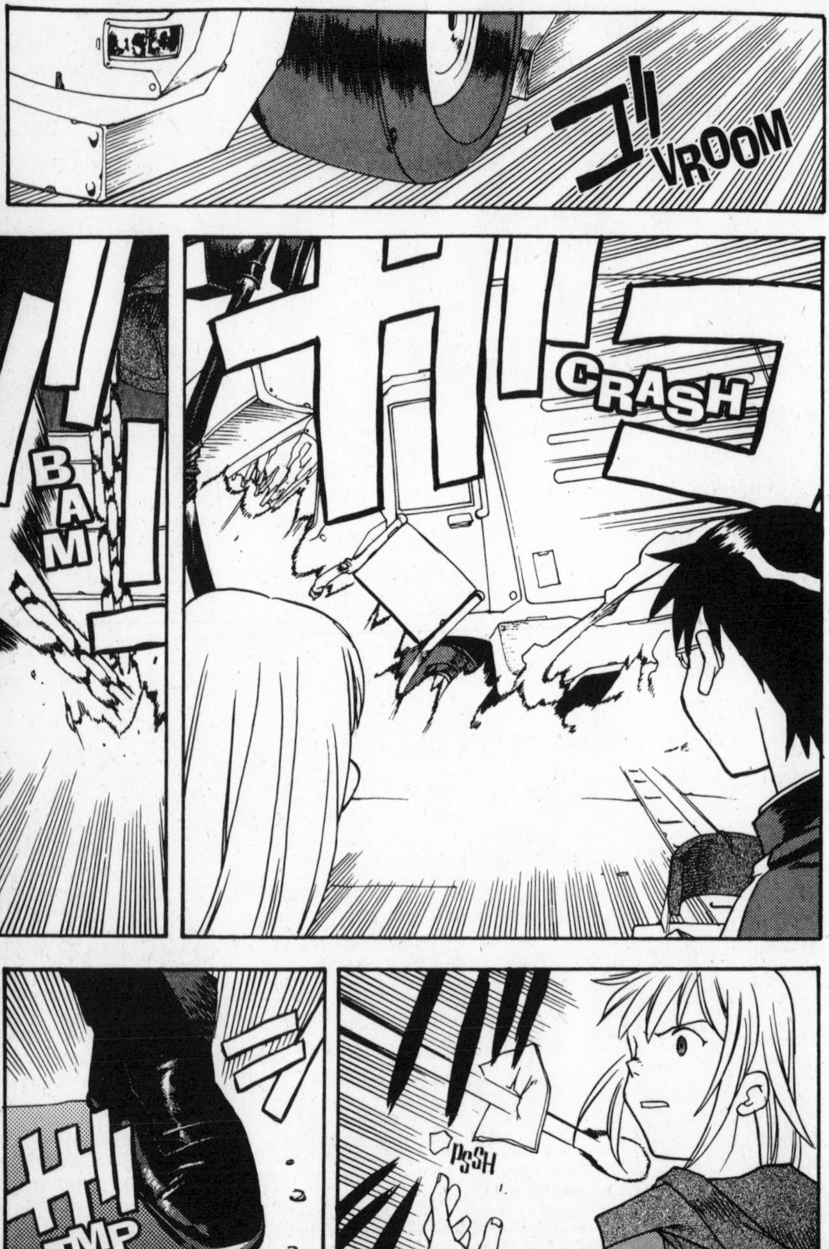
VROOM
CRASH
BAM
PSSH
TMP

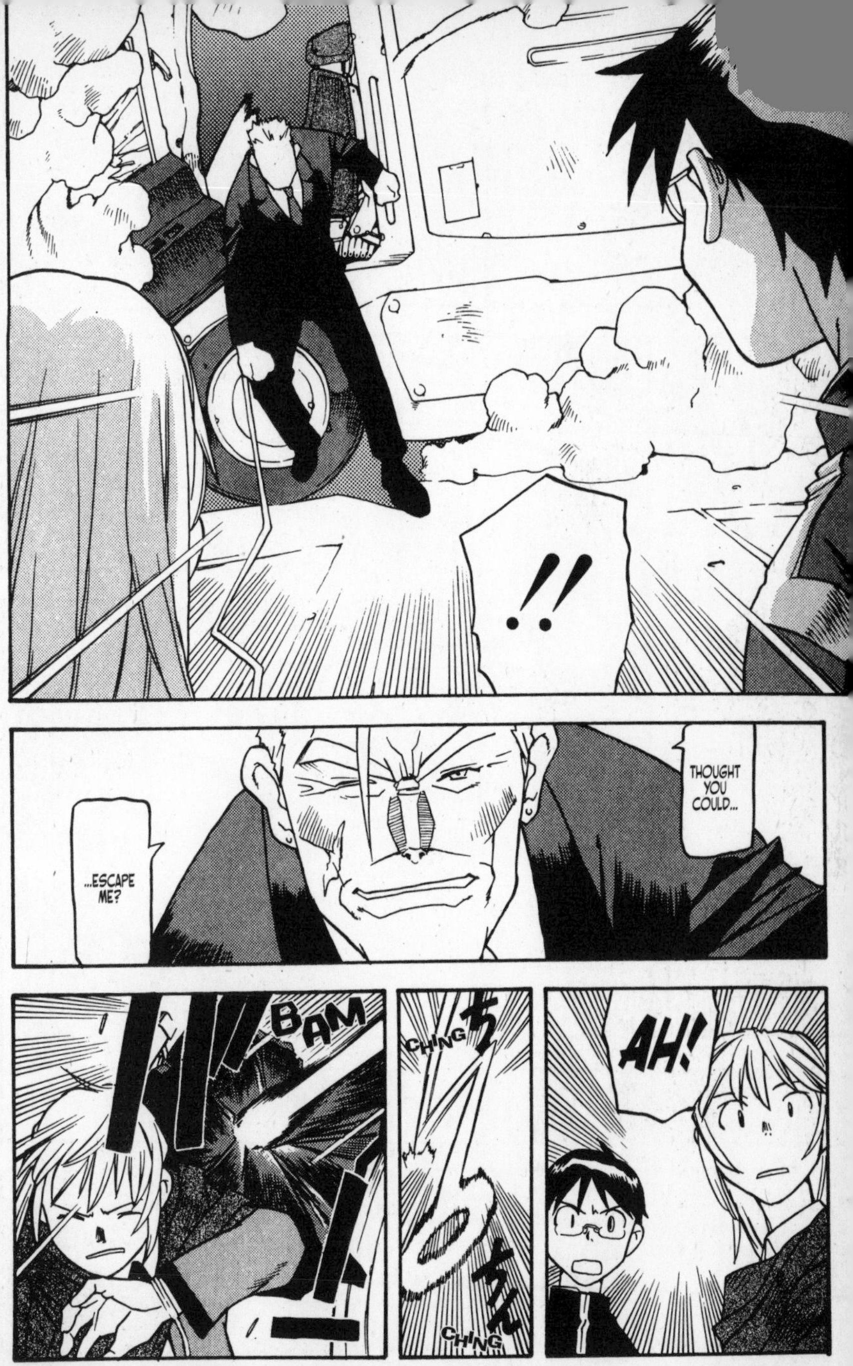
!!
THOUGHT YOU COULD...
...ESCAPE ME?
AH!
CHING
CHING
BAM

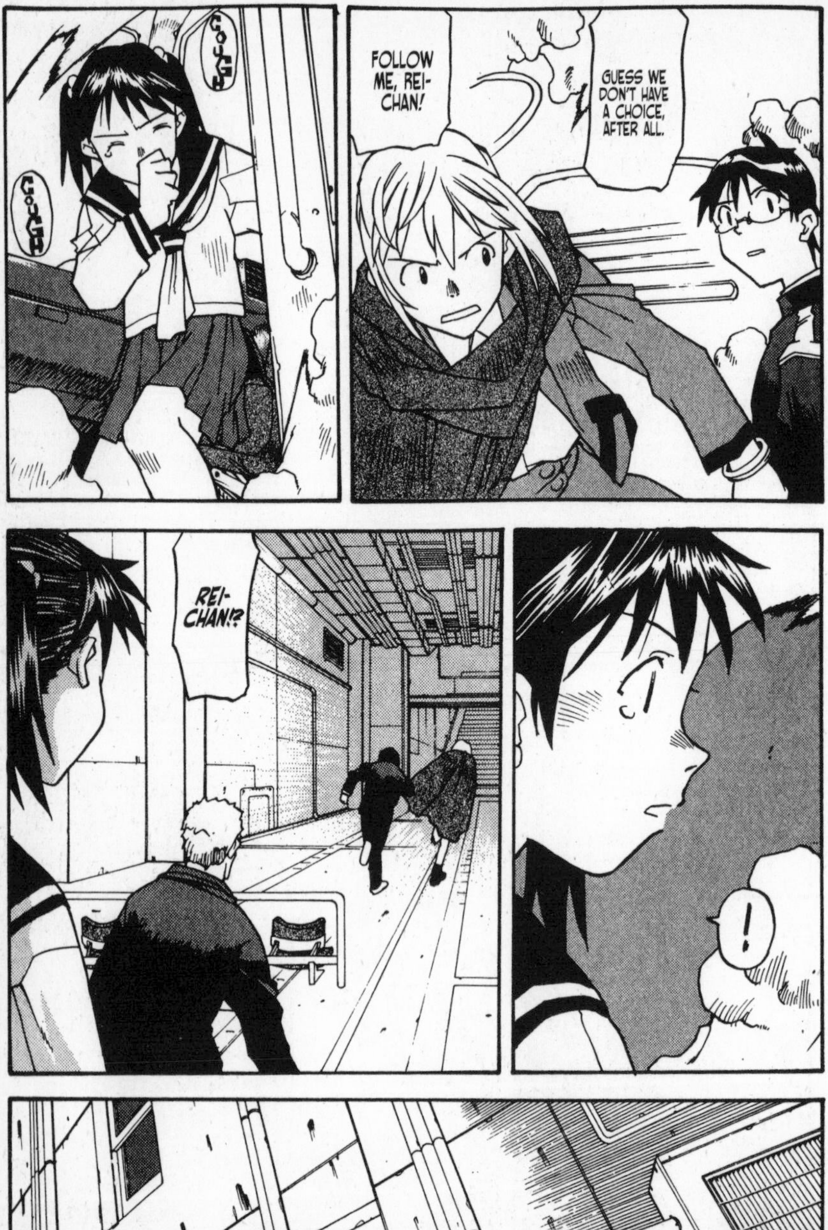
GUESS WE DON'T HAVE A CHOICE, AFTER ALL.
FOLLOW ME, REI-CHAN!
COUGH
COUGH
!
REI-CHAN!?

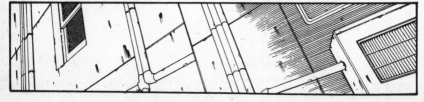

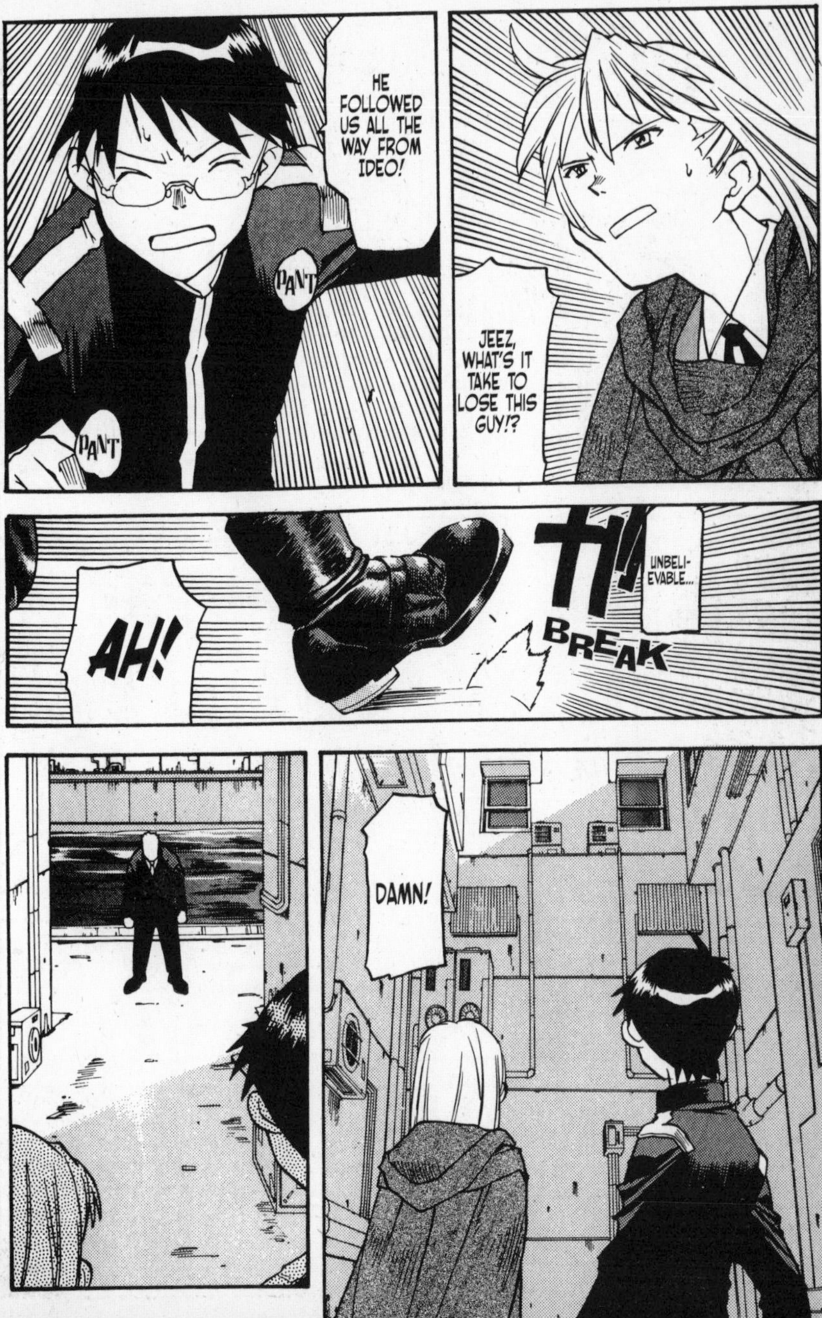
JEEZ, WHAT'S IT TAKE TO LOSE THIS GUY!?
HE FOLLOWED US ALL THE WAY FROM IDEO!
PANT
PANT
UNBELI-EVABLE...
BREAK
AH!
DAMN!

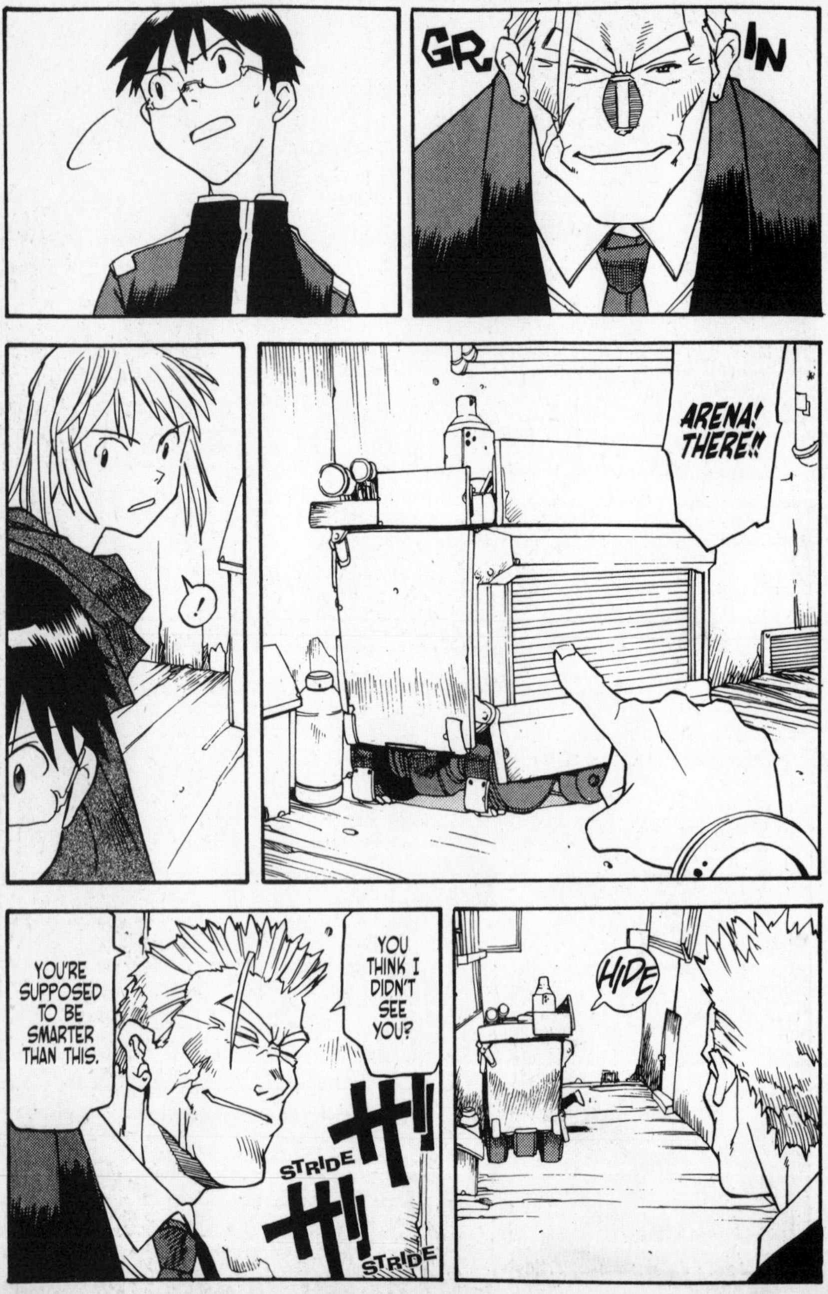

GR
IN
ARENA! THERE!!
!
HIDE
YOU THINK I DIDN'T SEE YOU?
YOU'RE SUPPOSED TO BE SMARTER THAN THIS.
STRIDE
STRIDE

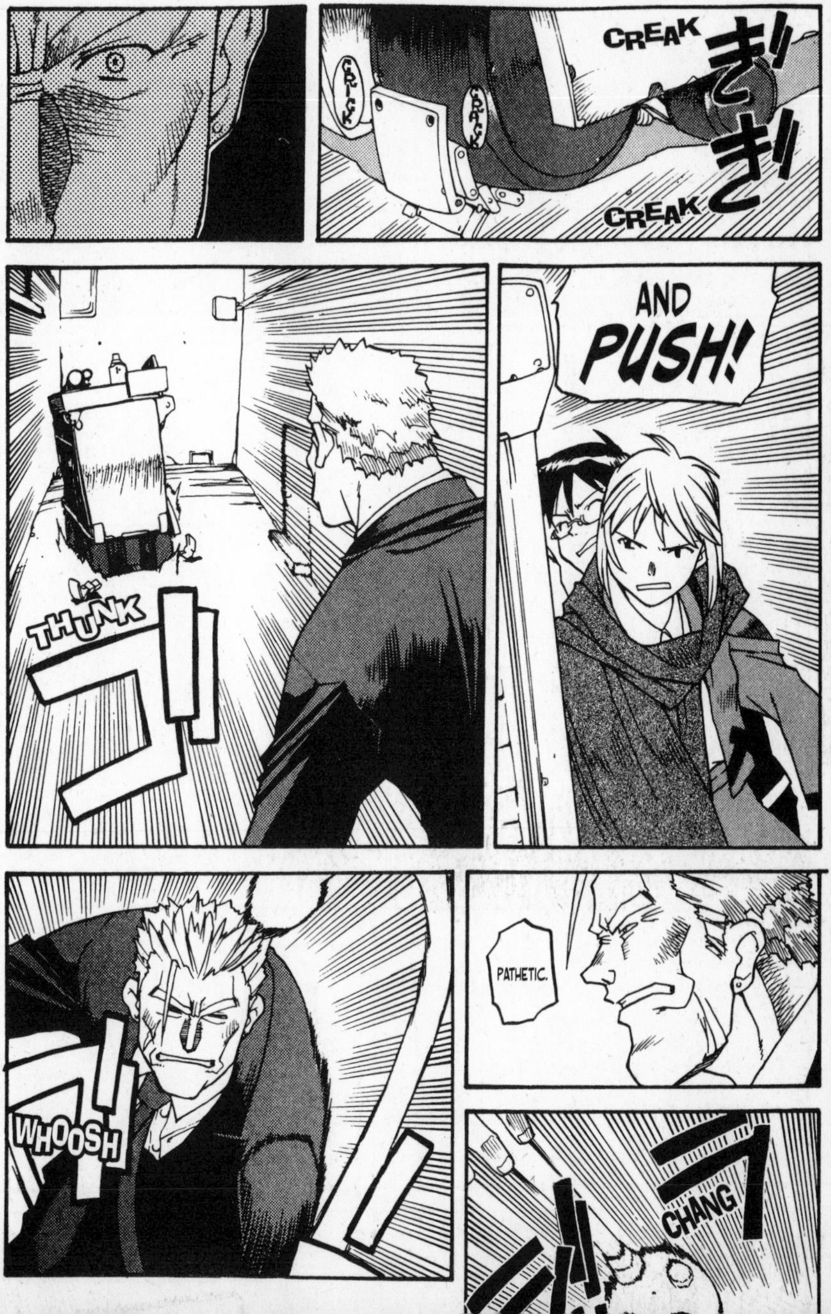
CREAK
CRICK
CRICK
CREAK
AND PUSH!
THUNK
PATHETIC.
CHANG
WHOOSH

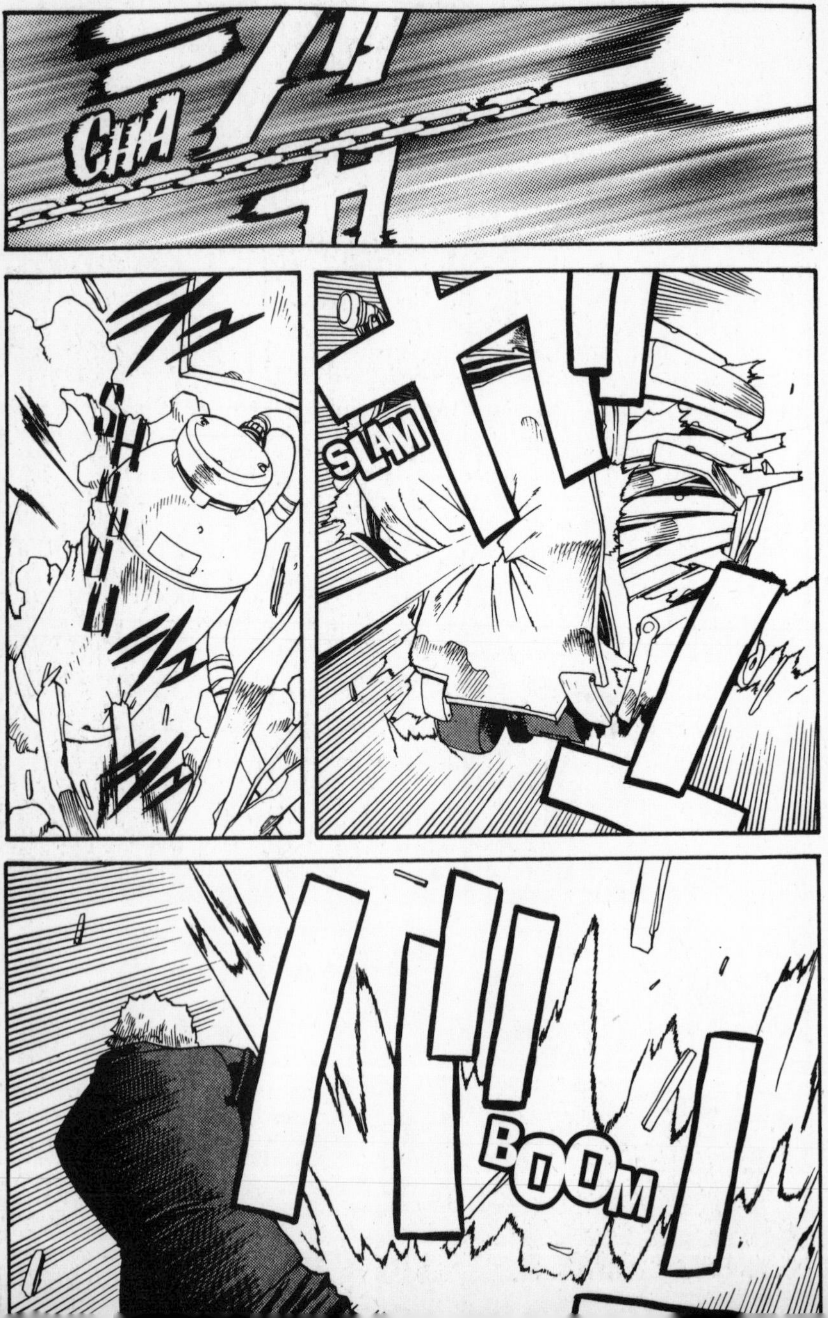
CHA
SLAM
SHUUUU
BOOM

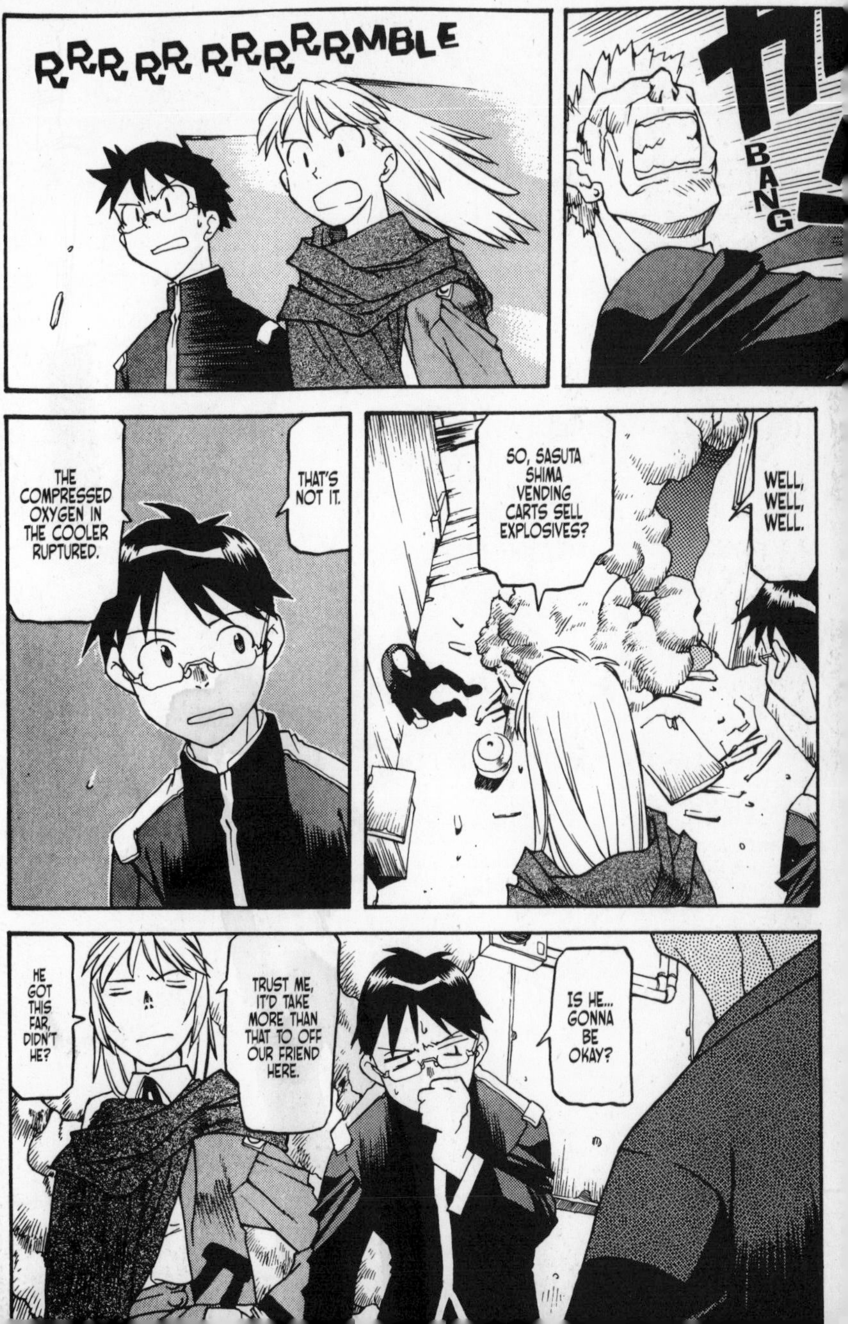
BANG
RRRRRR RRRRRRMBLE
WELL, WELL, WELL.
SO, SASUTA SHIMA VENDING CARTS SELL EXPLOSIVES?
THAT'S NOT IT.
THE COMPRESSED OXYGEN IN THE COOLER RUPTURED.
IS HE... GONNA BE OKAY?
TRUST ME, IT'D TAKE MORE THAN THAT TO OFF OUR FRIEND HERE.
HE GOT THIS FAR, DIDN'T HE?

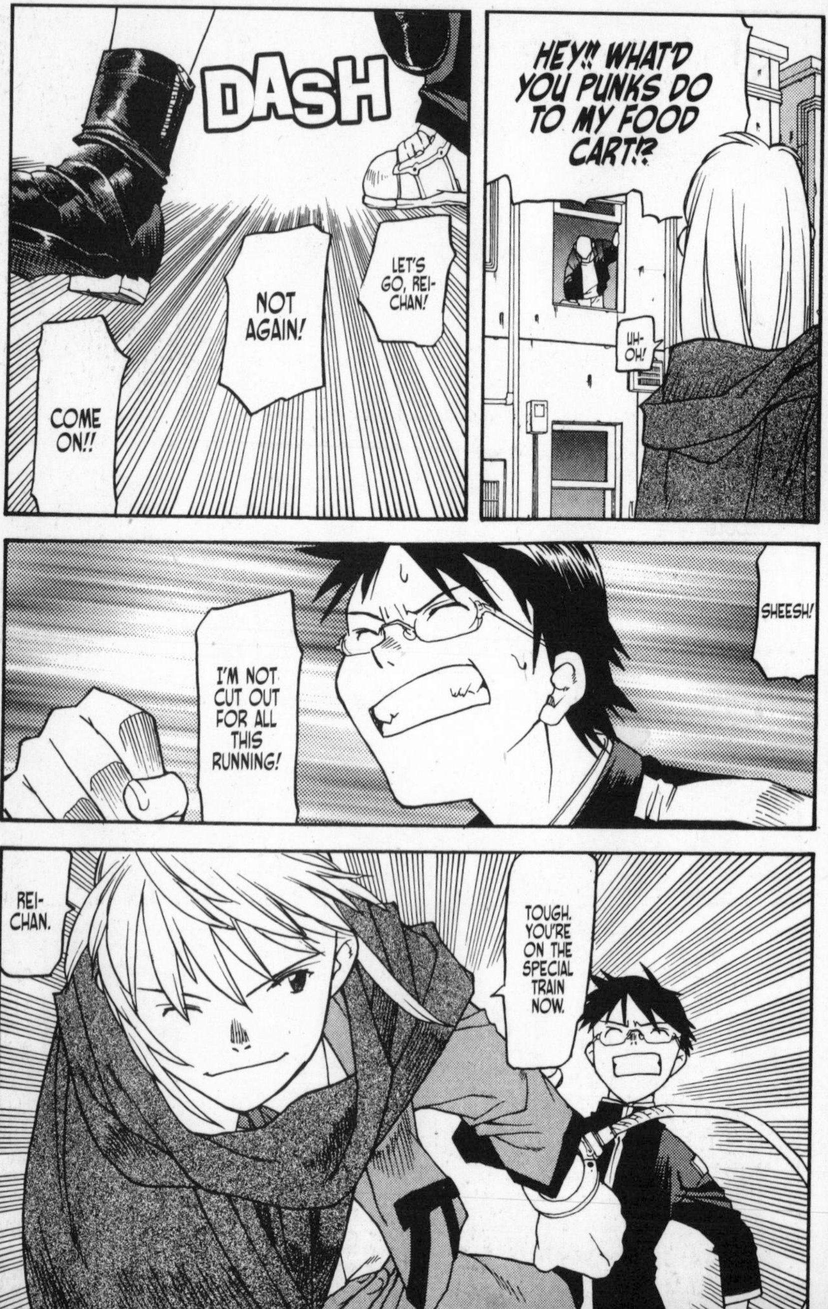
HEY!! WHAT'D YOU PUNKS DO TO MY FOOD CART!?
UH-OH!
DASH
LET'S GO, REI-CHAN!
NOT AGAIN!
COME ON!!
SHEESH!
I'M NOT CUT OUT FOR ALL THIS RUNNING!
TOUGH. YOU'RE ON THE SPECIAL TRAIN NOW.
REI-CHAN.

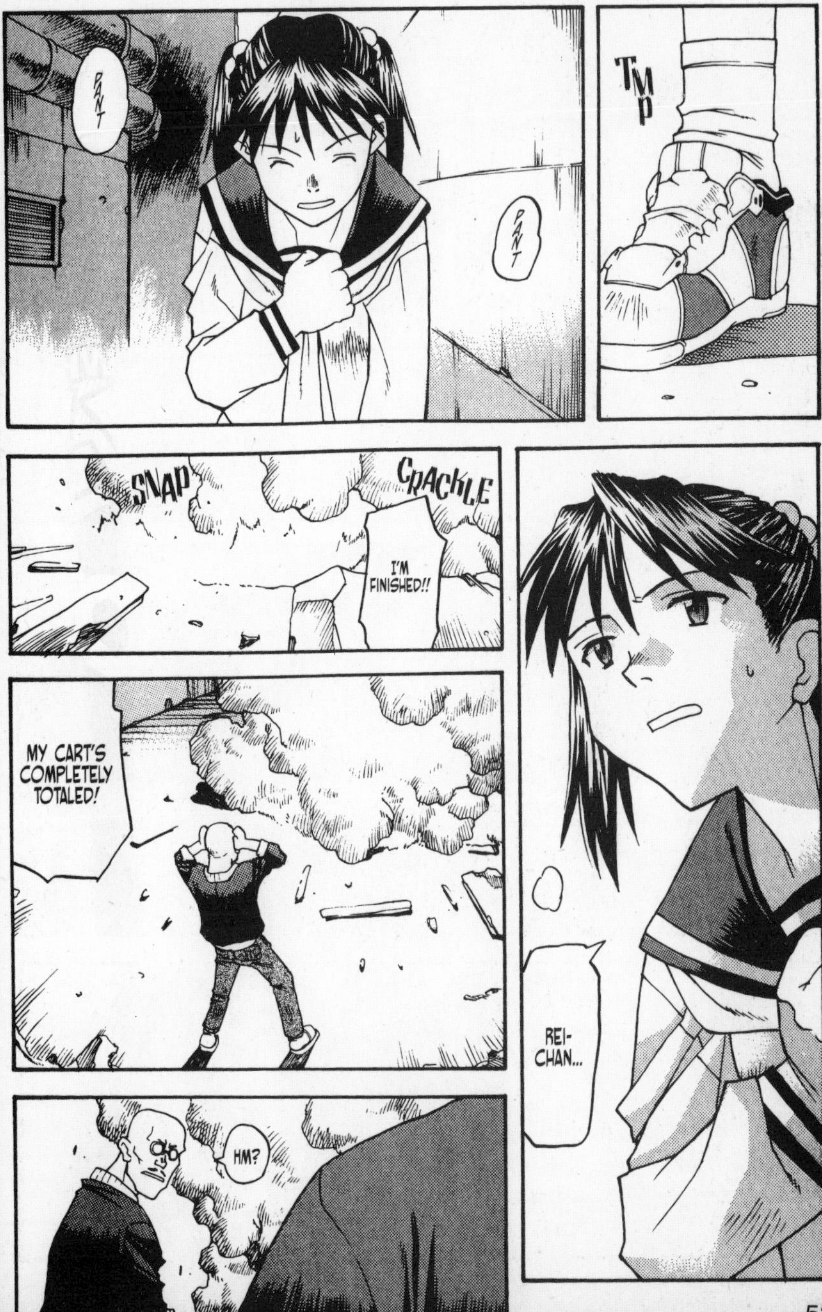
TMP
PANT
PANT
REI-CHAN...
CRACKLE
SNAP
I'M FINISHED!!
MY CART'S COMPLETELY TOTALED!
HM?

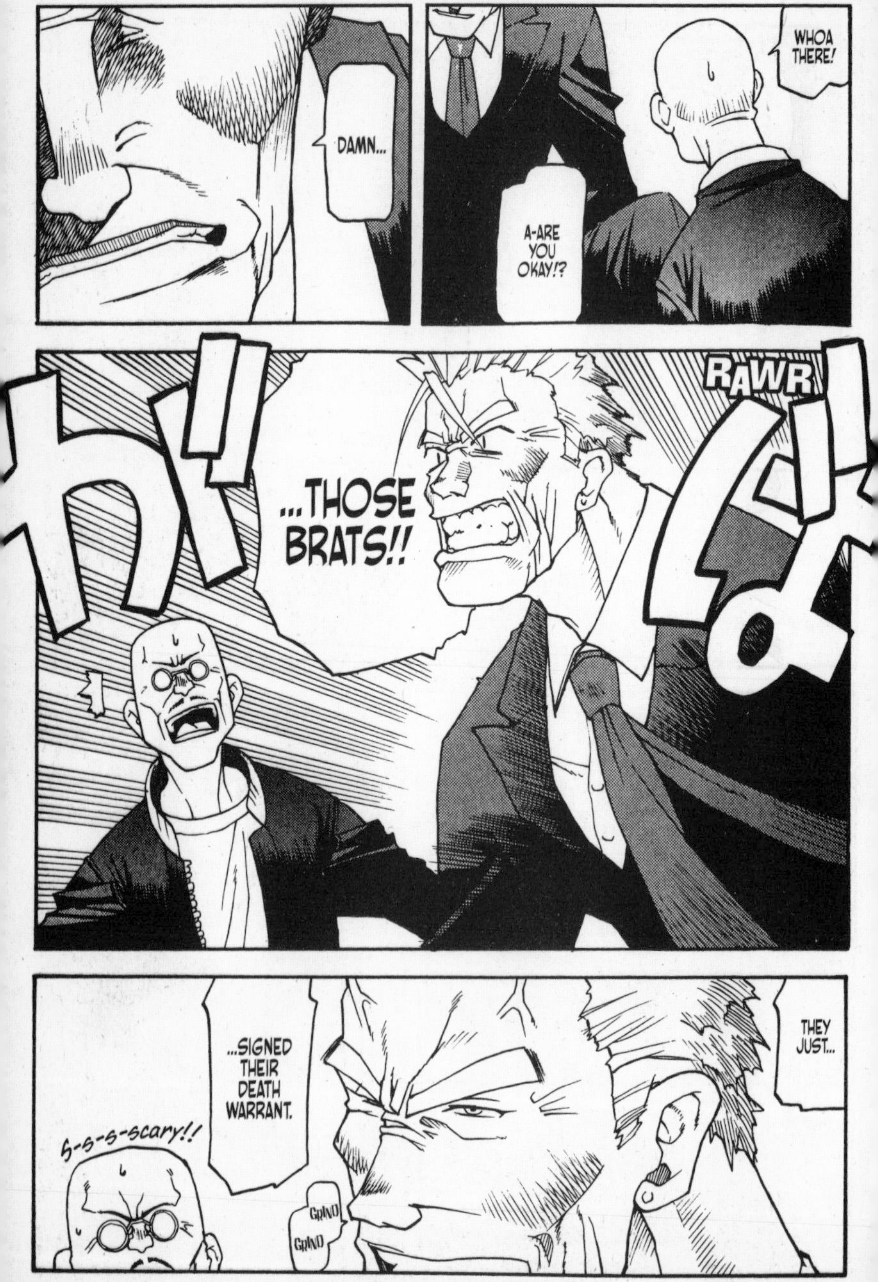
WHOA THERE!
A-ARE YOU OKAY!?
DAMN...
RAWR
...THOSE BRATS!!
THEY JUST...
...SIGNED THEIR DEATH WARRANT.
GRIND
GRIND
s-s-s-scary!!

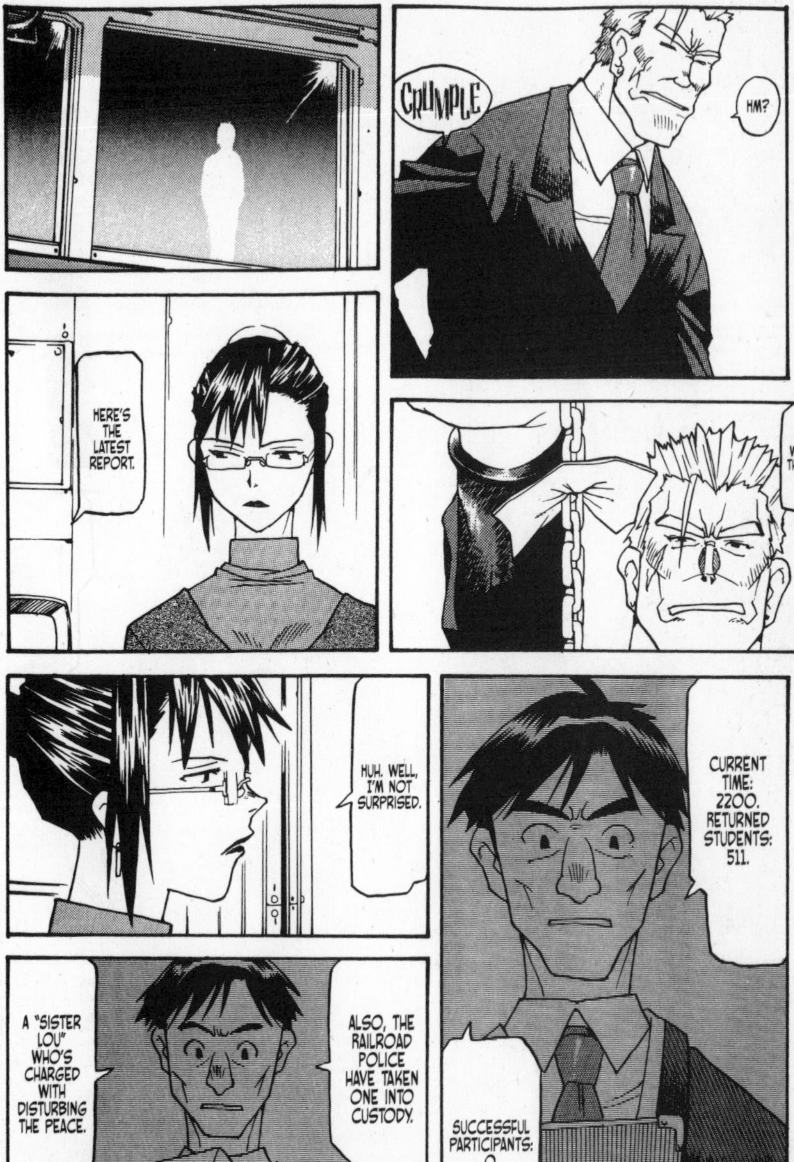
CRUMPLE
HM?
WHAT THE...?
HERE'S THE LATEST REPORT.
CURRENT TIME: 2200. RETURNED STUDENTS: 511.
SUCCESSFUL PARTICIPANTS: 0.
HUH. WELL, I'M NOT SURPRISED.
ALSO, THE RAILROAD POLICE HAVE TAKEN ONE INTO CUSTODY.
A "SISTER LOU" WHO'S CHARGED WITH DISTURBING THE PEACE.

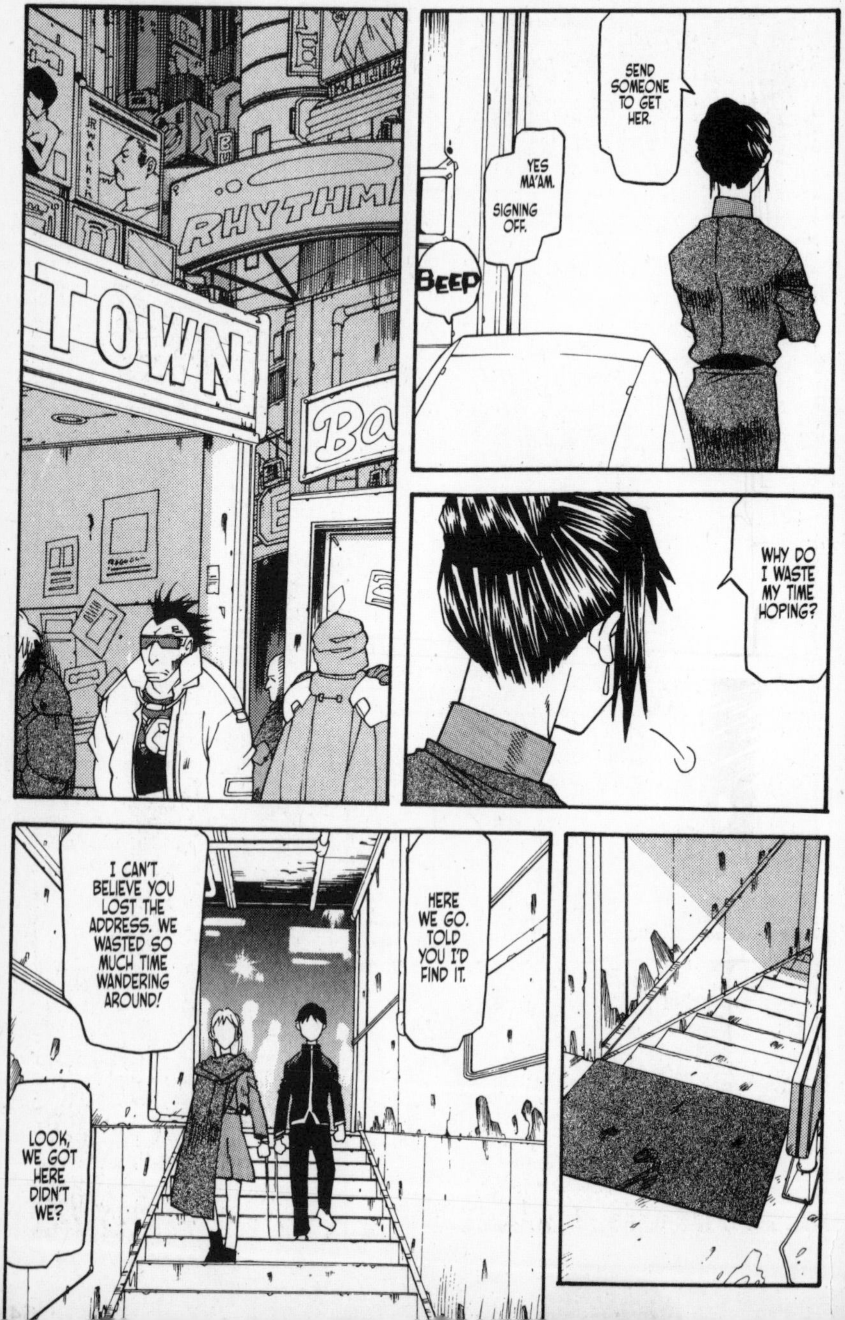
SEND SOMEONE TO GET HER.
YES MA'AM.
SIGNING OFF.
BEEP
WHY DO I WASTE MY TIME HOPING?
RHYTHM
TOWN
HERE WE GO. TOLD YOU I'D FIND IT.
I CAN'T BELIEVE YOU LOST THE ADDRESS. WE WASTED SO MUCH TIME WANDERING AROUND!
LOOK, WE GOT HERE DIDN'T WE?

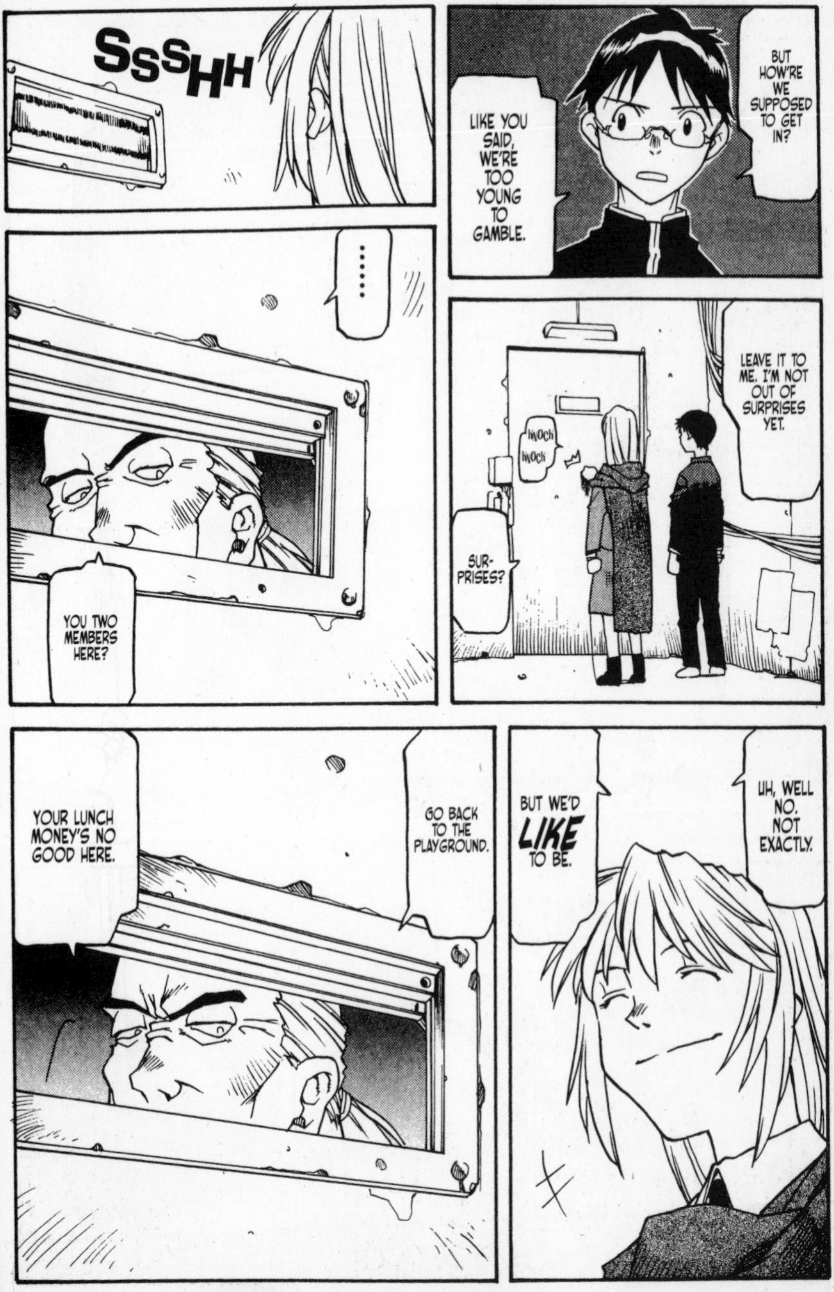
BUT HOW'RE WE SUPPOSED TO GET IN?
LIKE YOU SAID, WE'RE TOO YOUNG TO GAMBLE.
SSSHH
LEAVE IT TO ME. I'M NOT OUT OF SURPRISES YET.
KNOCK KNOCK
SUR-PRISES?
......
YOU TWO MEMBERS HERE?
UH, WELL NO. NOT EXACTLY.
BUT WE'D LIKE TO BE.
GO BACK TO THE PLAYGROUND.
YOUR LUNCH MONEY'S NO GOOD HERE.

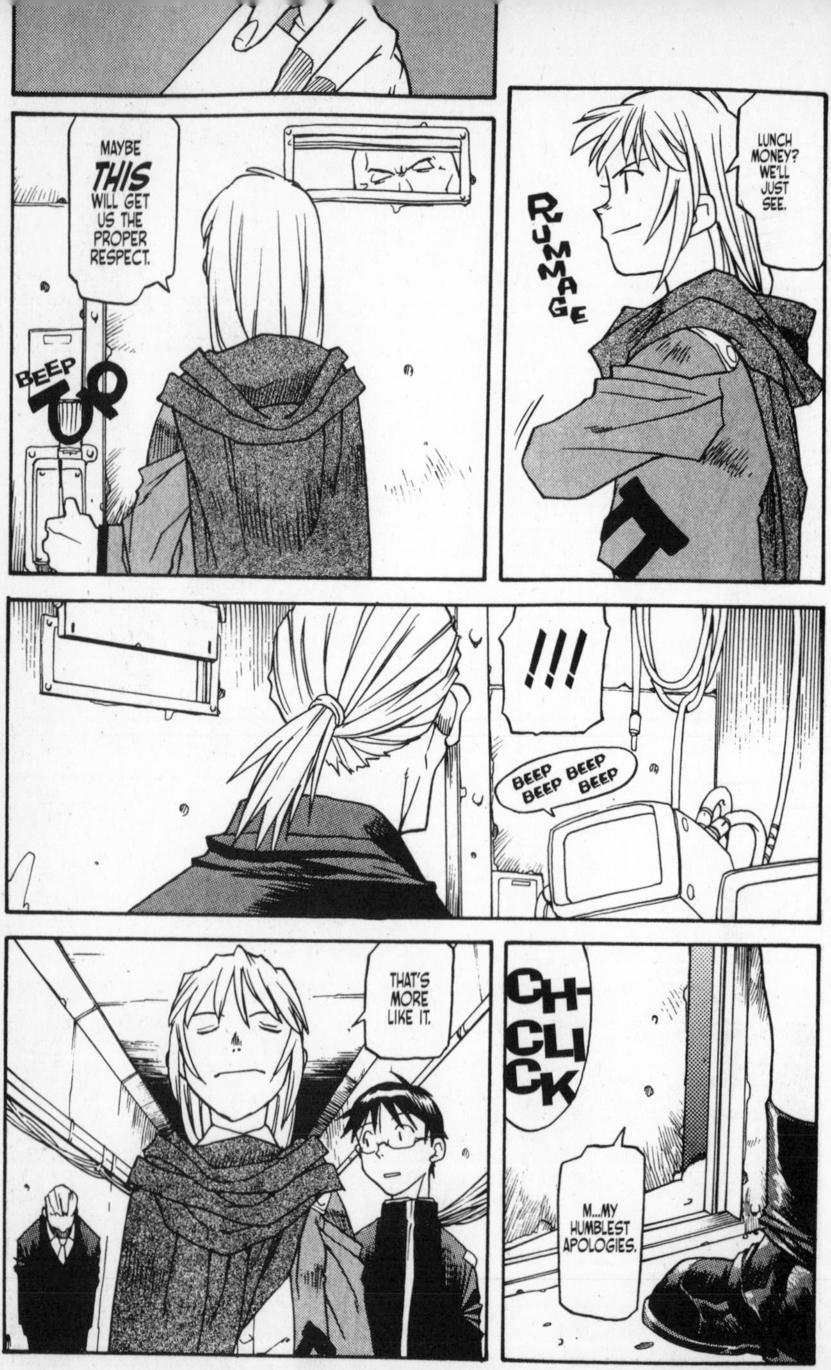
LUNCH MONEY? WE'LL JUST SEE.
RUMMAGE
MAYBE THIS WILL GET US THE PROPER RESPECT.
BEEP
!!!
BEEP BEEP BEEP BEEP
CH-CLICK
M...MY HUMBLEST APOLOGIES.
THAT'S MORE LIKE IT.

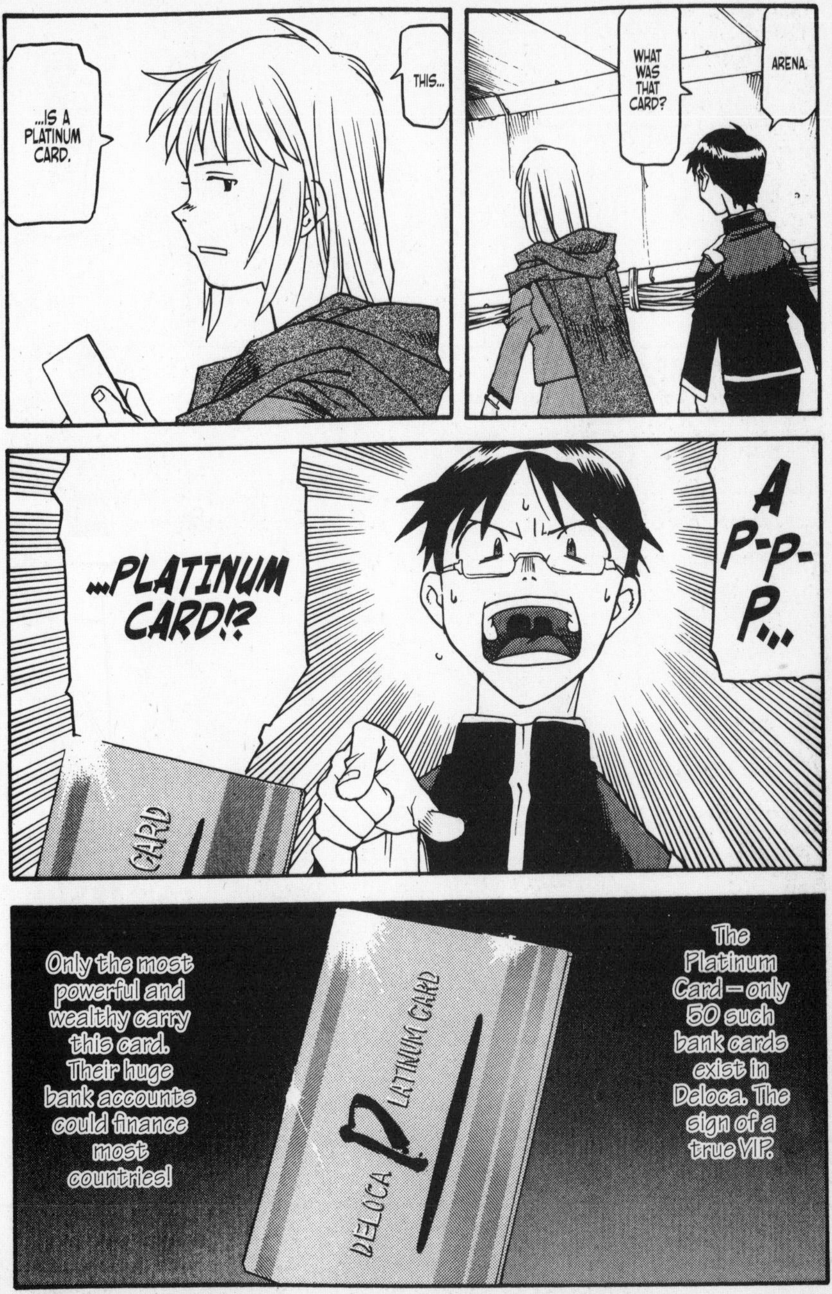
ARENA.
WHAT WAS THAT CARD?
THIS...
...IS A PLATINUM CARD.
A P-P-P...
...PLATINUM CARD!?
CARD
The Platinum Card – only 50 such bank cards exist in Deloca. The sign of a true VIP.
DELOCA PLATINUM CARD
Only the most powerful and wealthy carry this card. Their huge bank accounts could finance most countries!

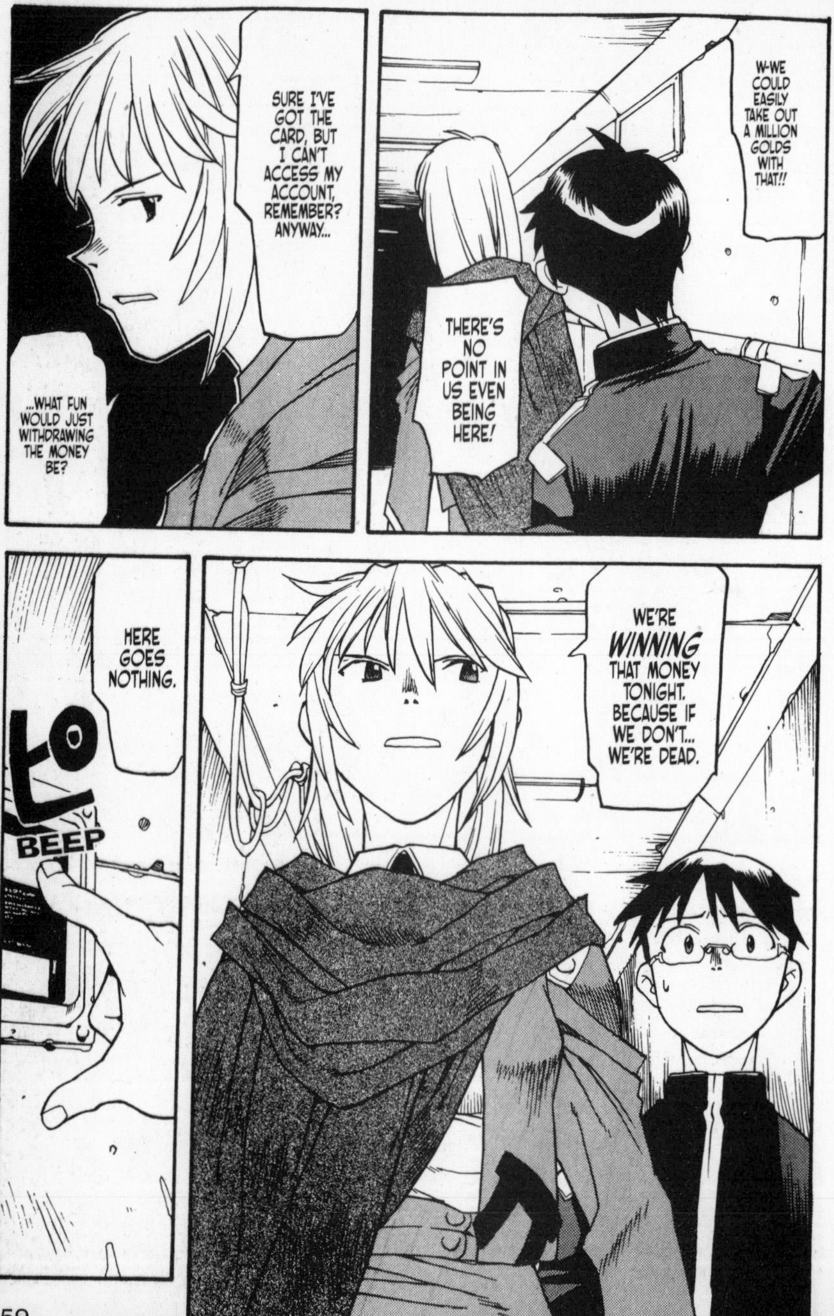
W-WE COULD EASILY TAKE OUT A MILLION GOLDS WITH THAT!!
THERE'S NO POINT IN US EVEN BEING HERE!
SURE I'VE GOT THE CARD, BUT I CAN'T ACCESS MY ACCOUNT, REMEMBER? ANYWAY...
...WHAT FUN WOULD JUST WITHDRAWING THE MONEY BE?
WE'RE *WINNING* THAT MONEY TONIGHT. BECAUSE IF WE DON'T... WE'RE DEAD.
HERE GOES NOTHING.
BEEP

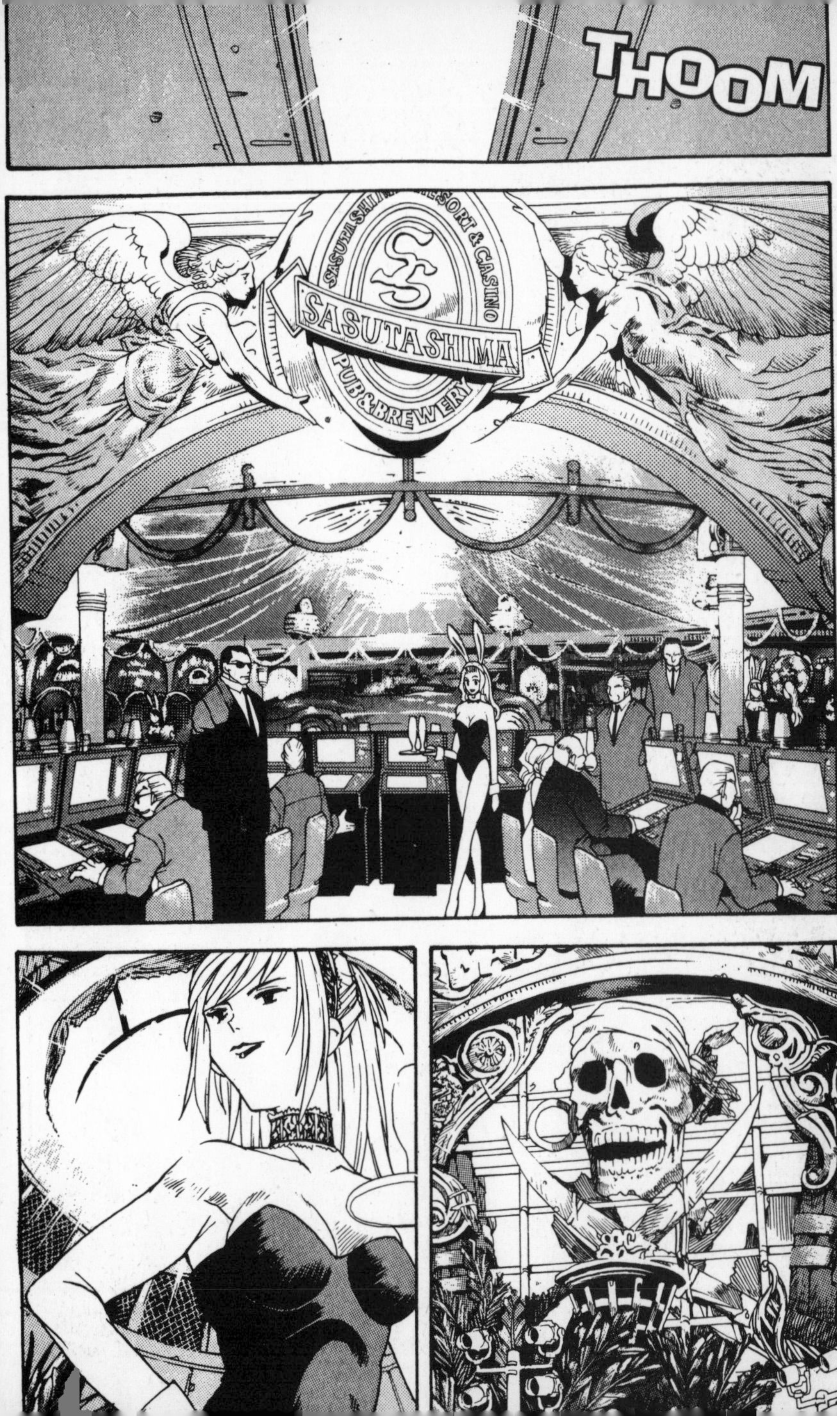
THOOM
SASUTASHIMA
PUB&BREWERY

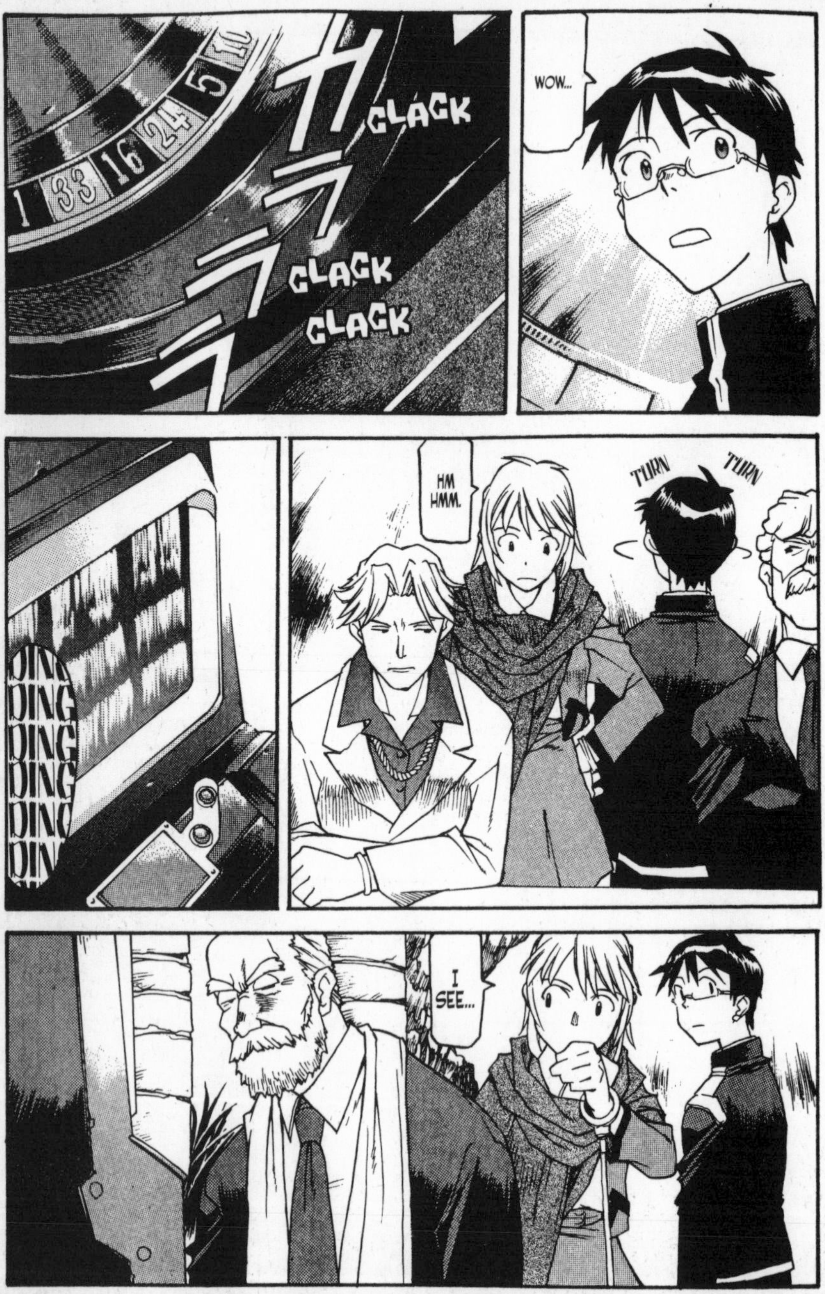
WOW...
カラララ
CLACK
CLACK
CLACK
HM HMM.
TURN
TURN
DING
DING
DING
DING
DING
I SEE...

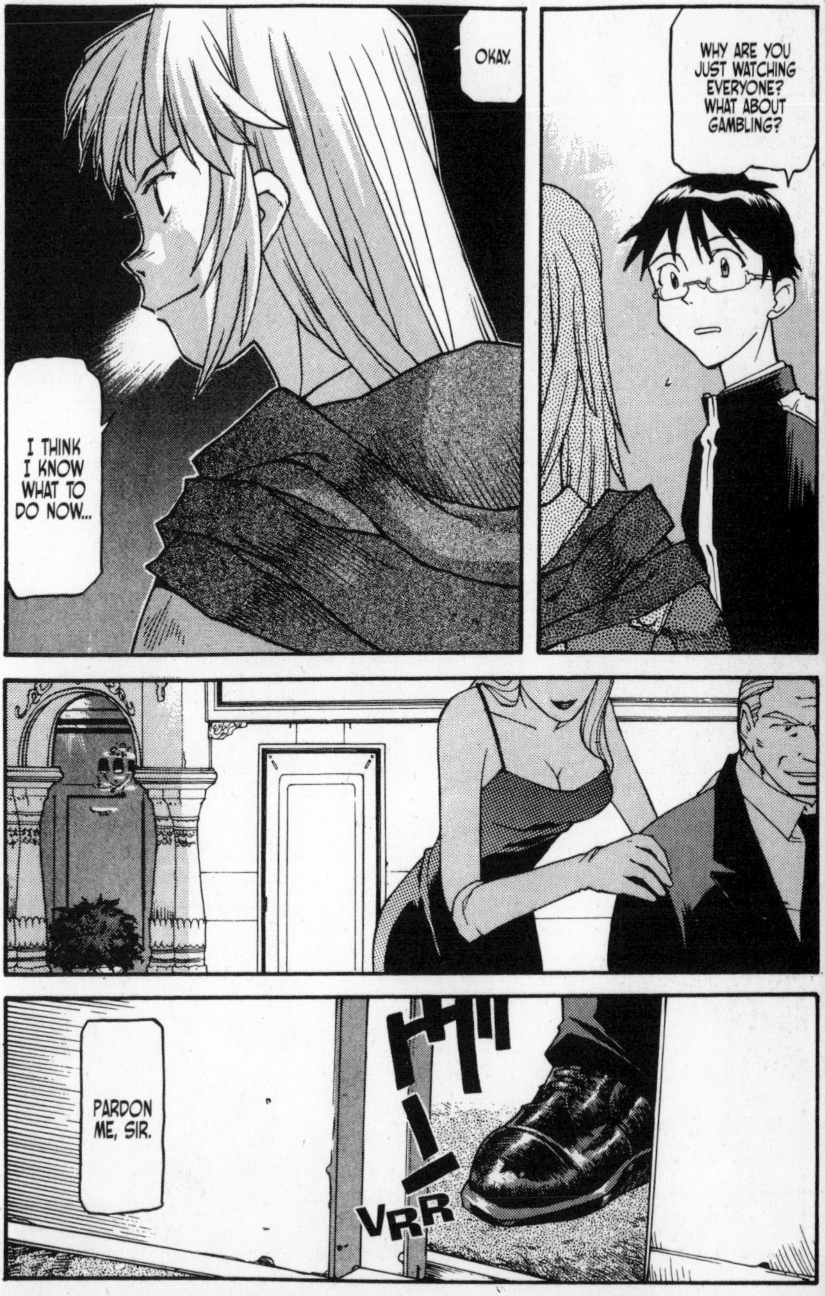
WHY ARE YOU JUST WATCHING EVERYONE? WHAT ABOUT GAMBLING?
OKAY.
I THINK I KNOW WHAT TO DO NOW...
PARDON ME, SIR.
VRR

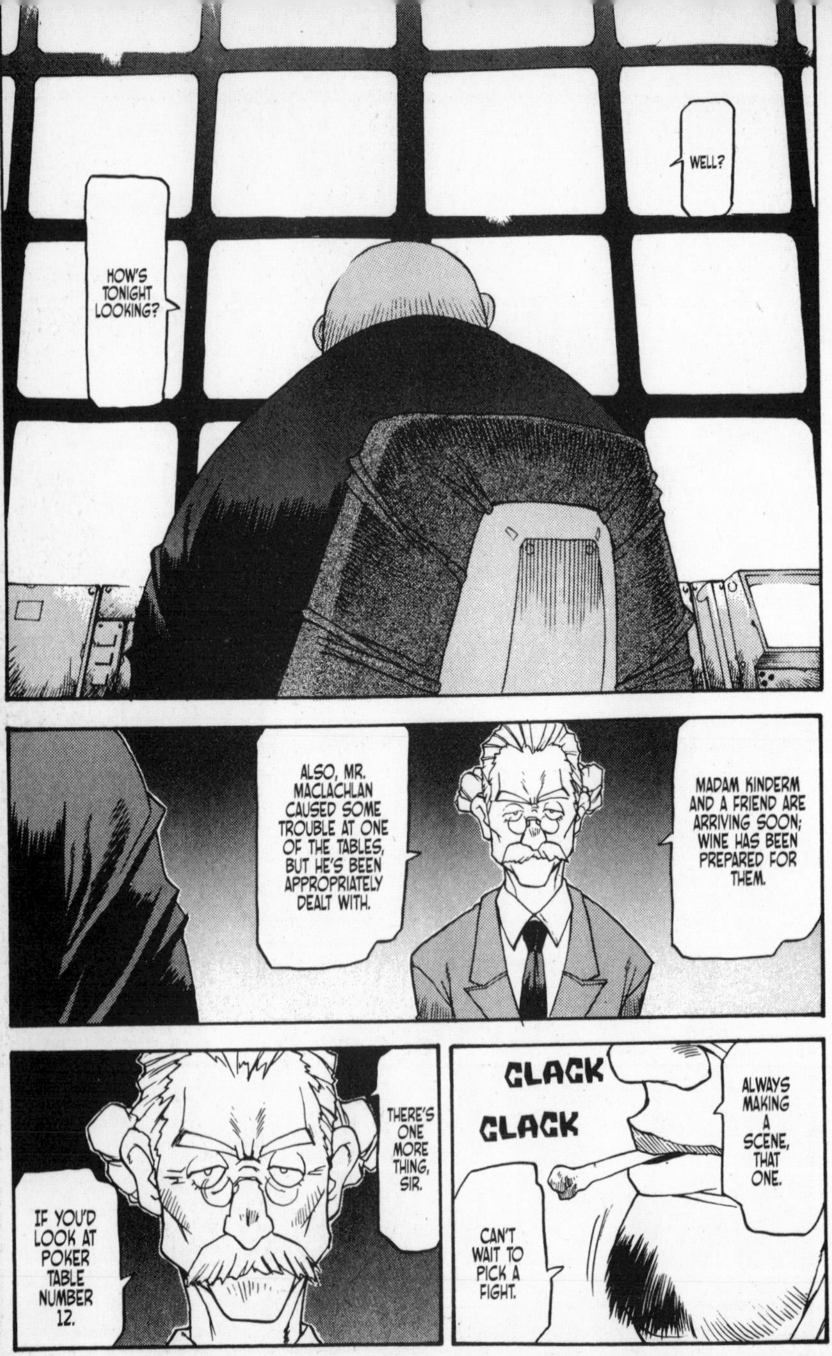
WELL?
HOW'S TONIGHT LOOKING?
MADAM KINDERM AND A FRIEND ARE ARRIVING SOON; WINE HAS BEEN PREPARED FOR THEM.
ALSO, MR. MACLACHLAN CAUSED SOME TROUBLE AT ONE OF THE TABLES, BUT HE'S BEEN APPROPRIATELY DEALT WITH.
ALWAYS MAKING A SCENE, THAT ONE.
CLACK
CLACK
CAN'T WAIT TO PICK A FIGHT.
THERE'S ONE MORE THING, SIR.
IF YOU'D LOOK AT POKER TABLE NUMBER 12.

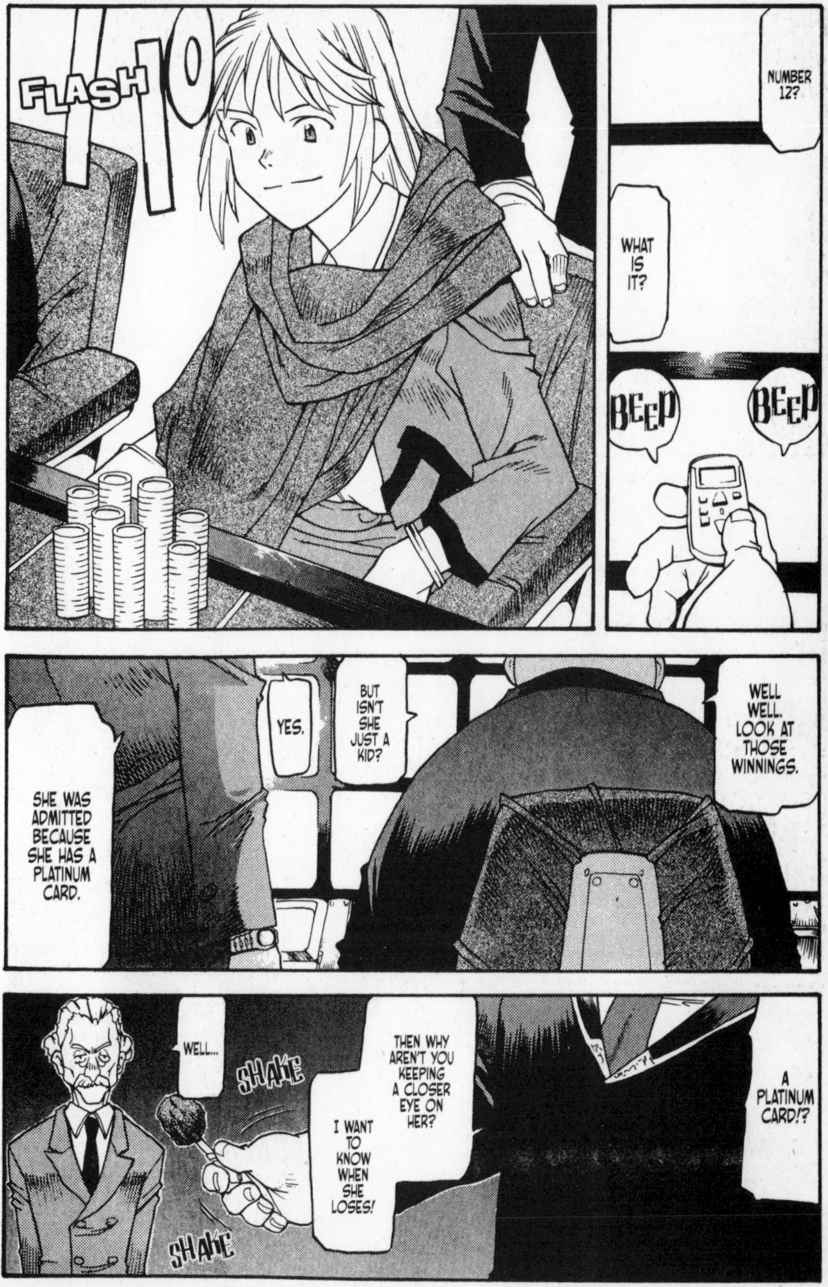
NUMBER 12?
WHAT IS IT?
BEEP
BEEP
FLASH
WELL WELL. LOOK AT THOSE WINNINGS.
BUT ISN'T SHE JUST A KID?
YES.
SHE WAS ADMITTED BECAUSE SHE HAS A PLATINUM CARD.
A PLATINUM CARD!?
THEN WHY AREN'T YOU KEEPING A CLOSER EYE ON HER?
I WANT TO KNOW WHEN SHE LOSES!
SHAKE
WELL...
SHAKE

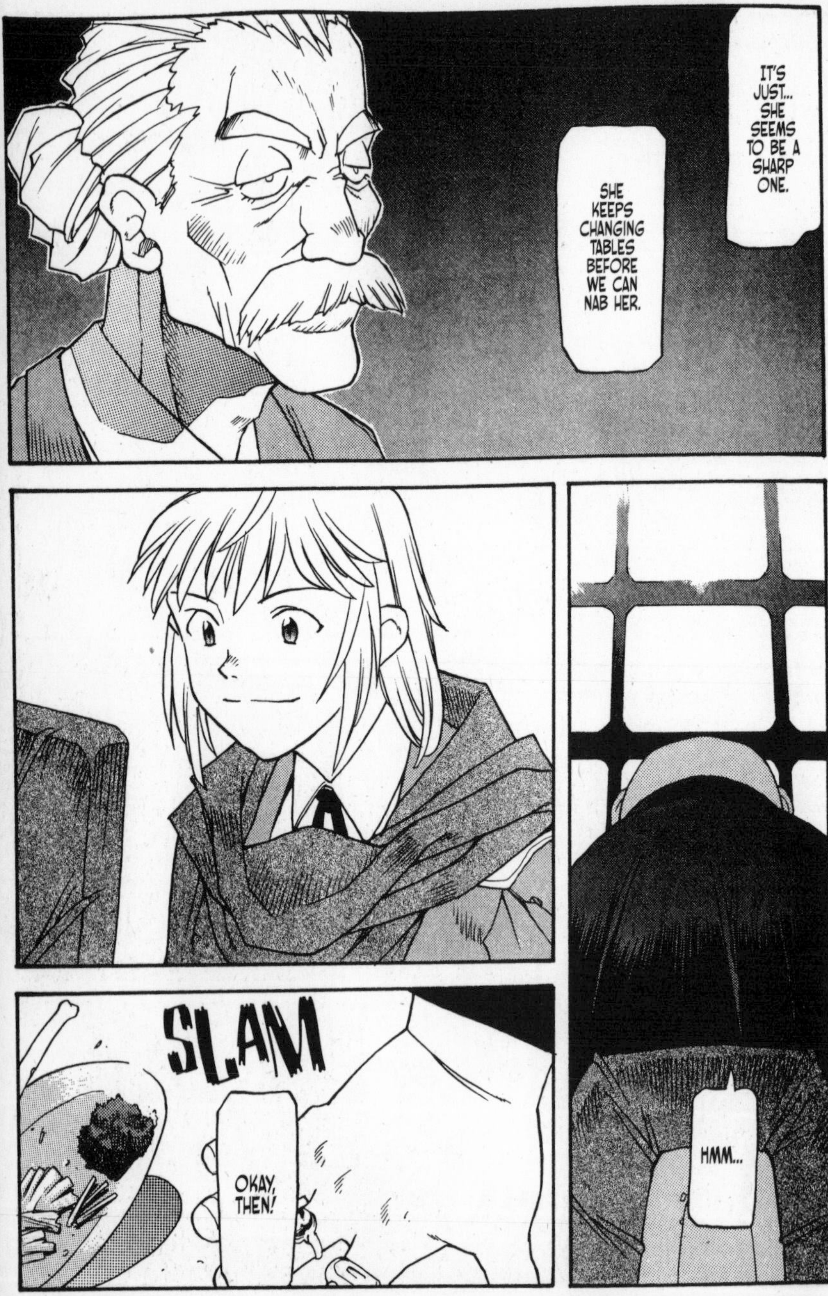
IT'S JUST... SHE SEEMS TO BE A SHARP ONE.
SHE KEEPS CHANGING TABLES BEFORE WE CAN NAB HER.
HMM...
SLAM
OKAY, THEN!

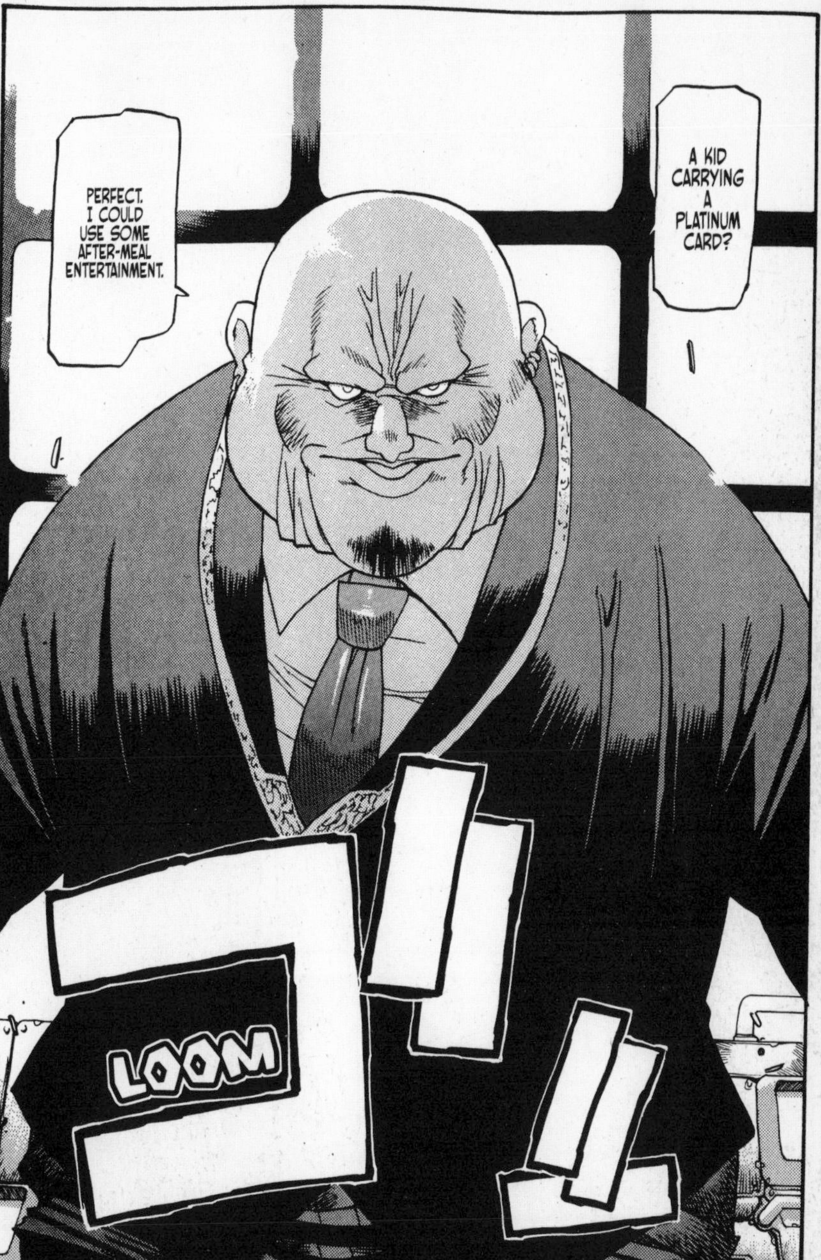
A KID CARRYING A PLATINUM CARD?
PERFECT. I COULD USE SOME AFTER-MEAL ENTERTAINMENT.
LOOM

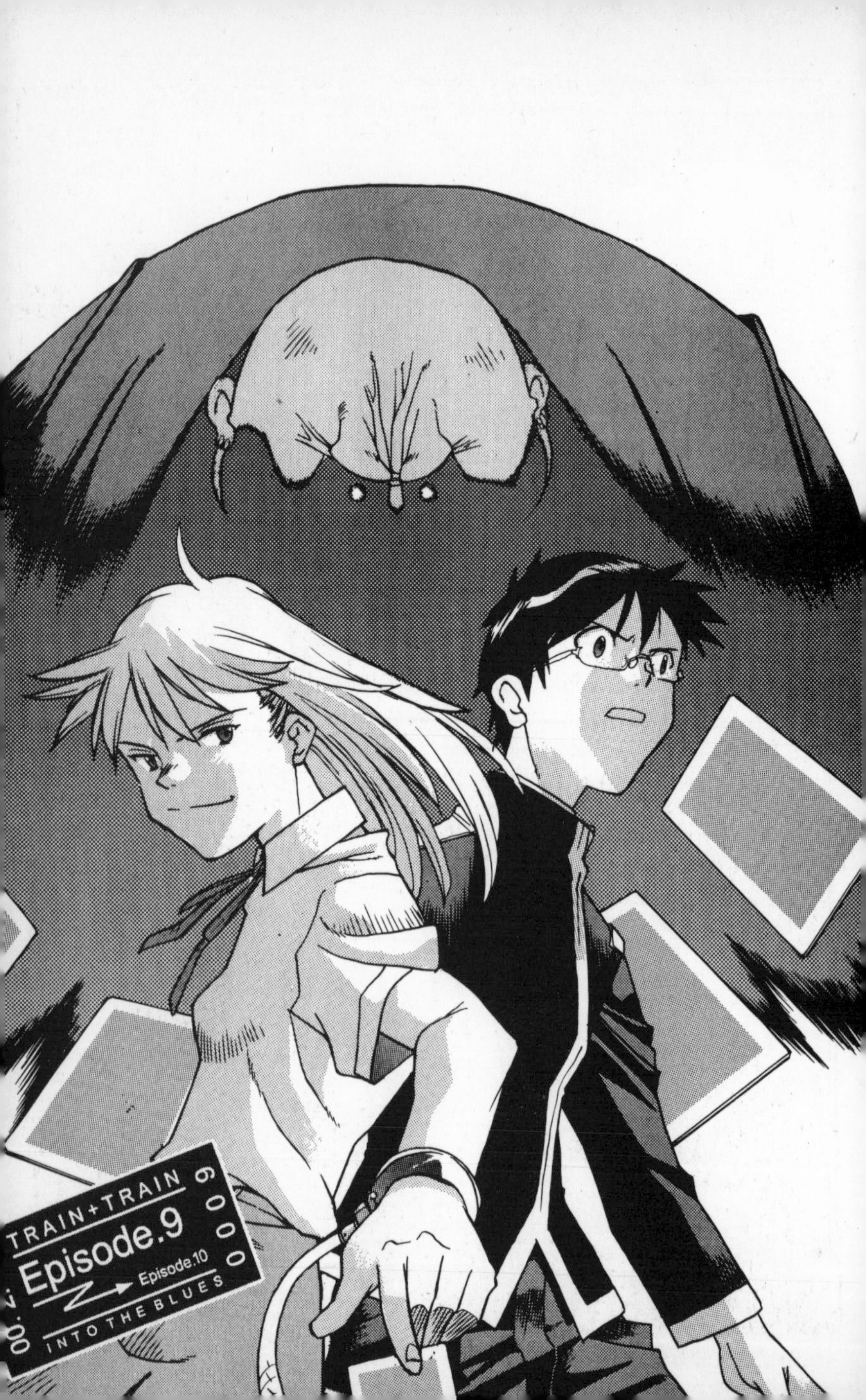
TRAIN+TRAIN
Episode.9
Episode.10
INTO THE BLUES
6000

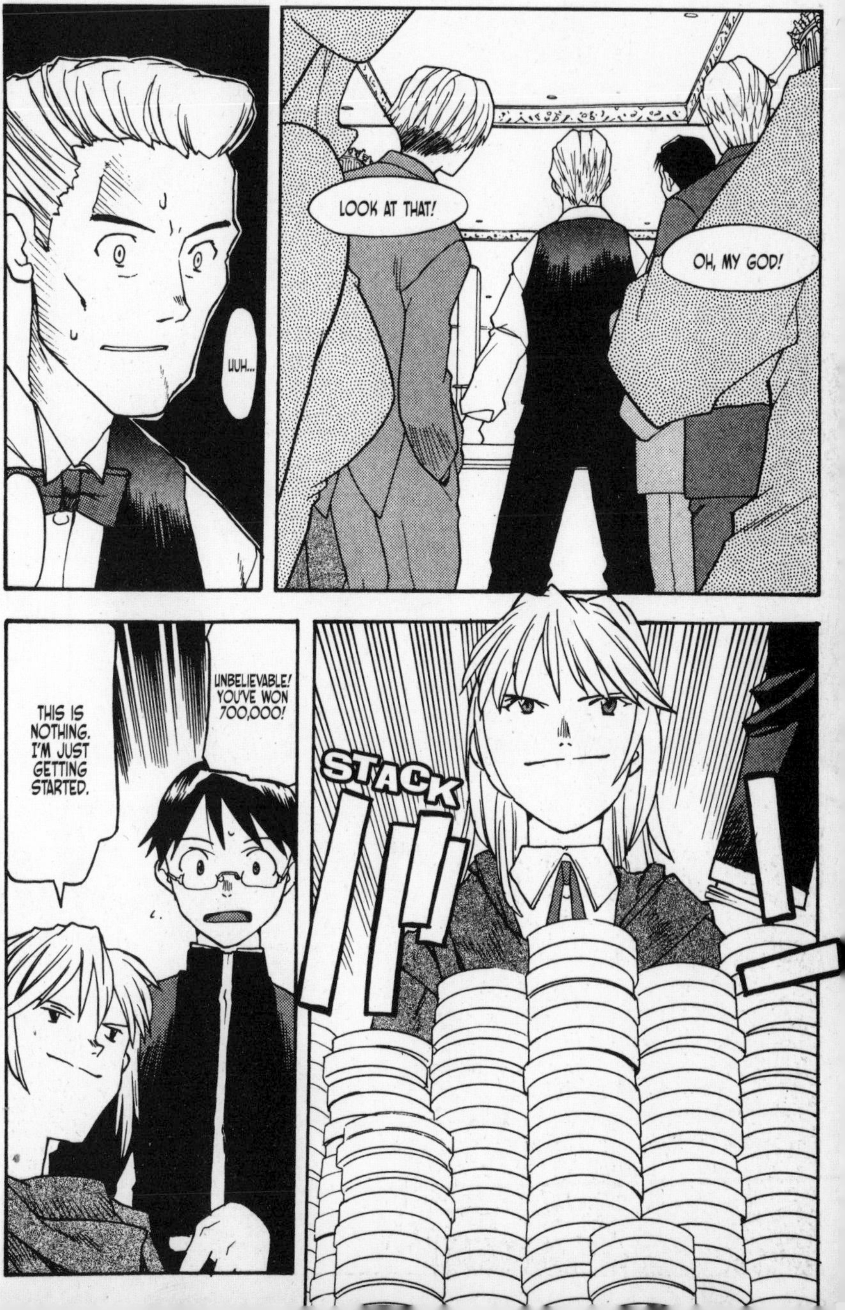
LOOK AT THAT!
OH, MY GOD!
UUH...
STACK
UNBELIEVABLE! YOU'VE WON 700,000!
THIS IS NOTHING. I'M JUST GETTING STARTED.

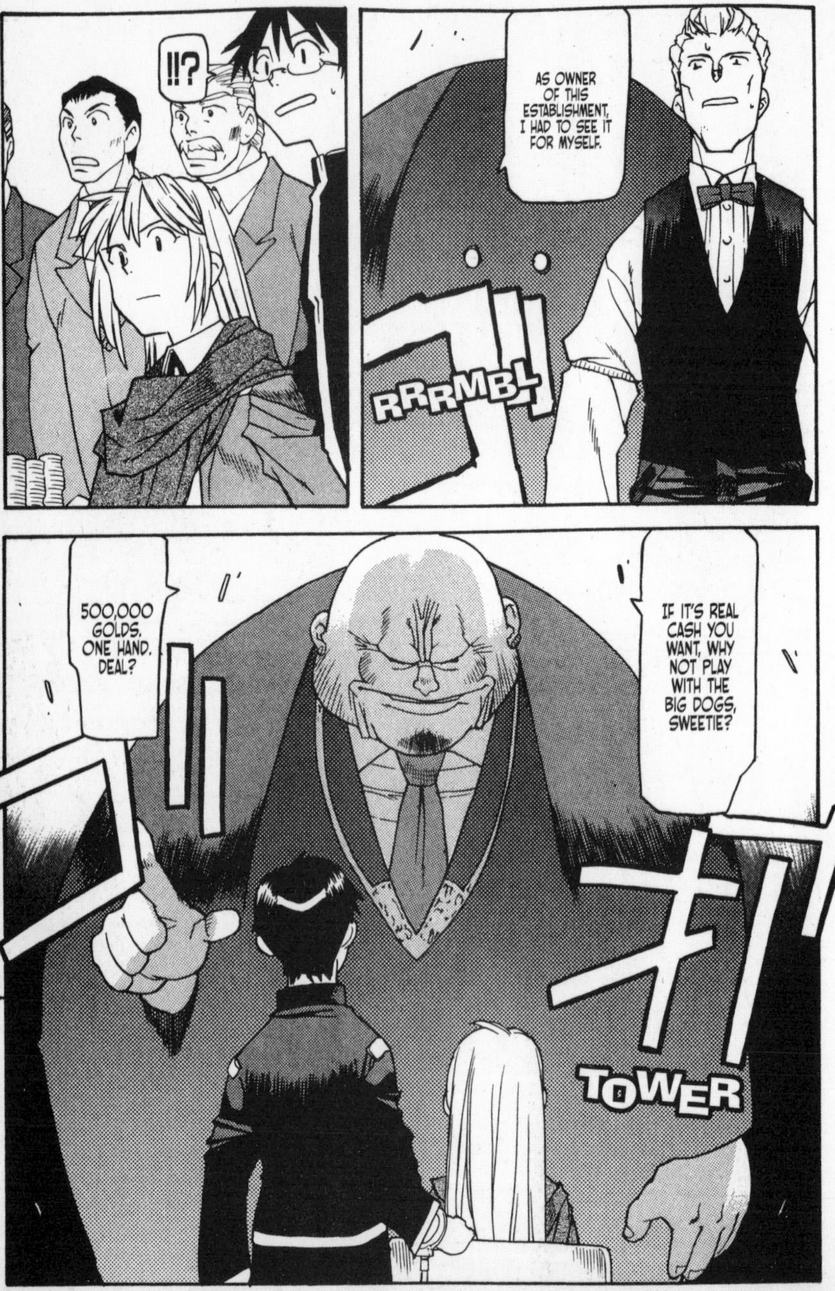
AS OWNER OF THIS ESTABLISHMENT, I HAD TO SEE IT FOR MYSELF.
RRRMBL
!!?
IF IT'S REAL CASH YOU WANT, WHY NOT PLAY WITH THE BIG DOGS, SWEETIE?
500,000 GOLDS. ONE HAND. DEAL?
TOWER

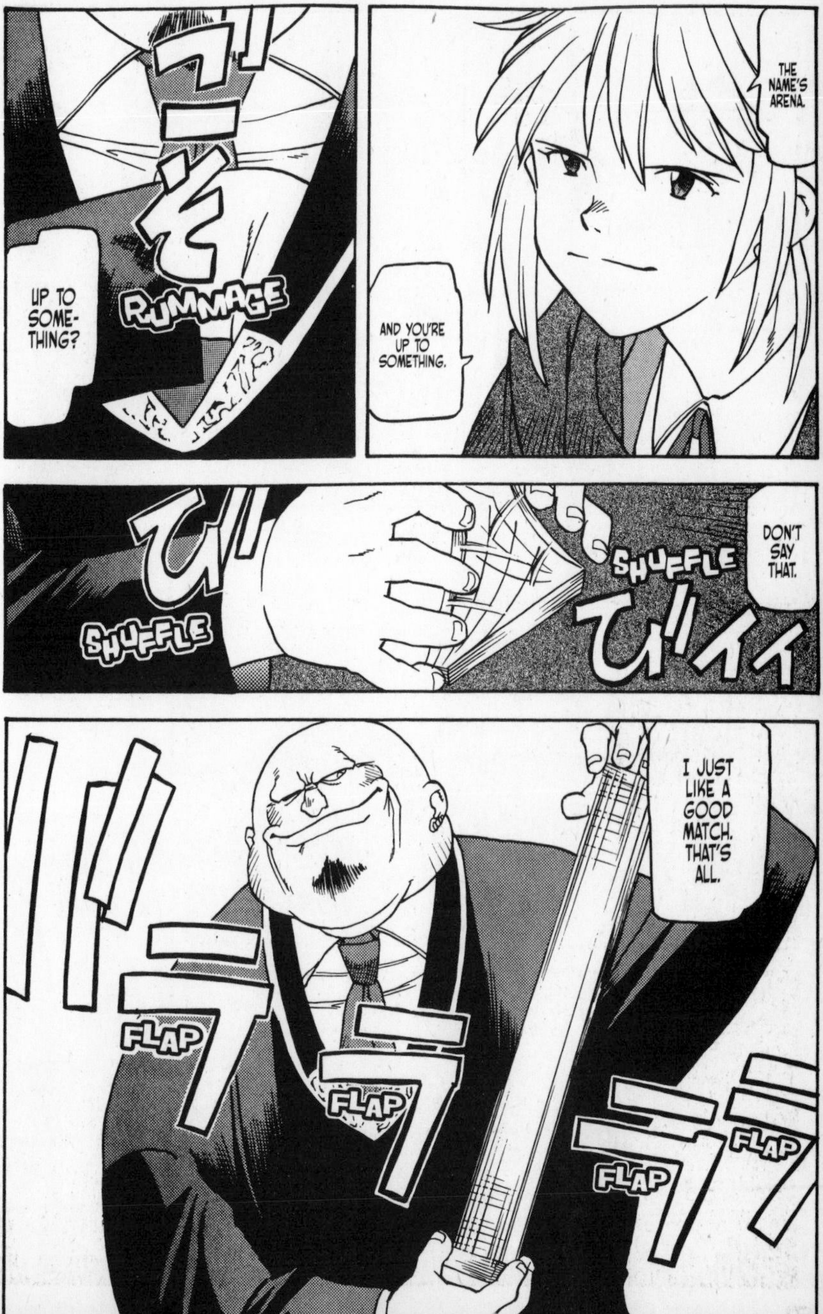
THE NAME'S ARENA.
AND YOU'RE UP TO SOMETHING.
UP TO SOME-THING?
RUMMAGE
DON'T SAY THAT.
SHUFFLE
SHUFFLE
I JUST LIKE A GOOD MATCH. THAT'S ALL.
FLAP
FLAP
FLAP
FLAP

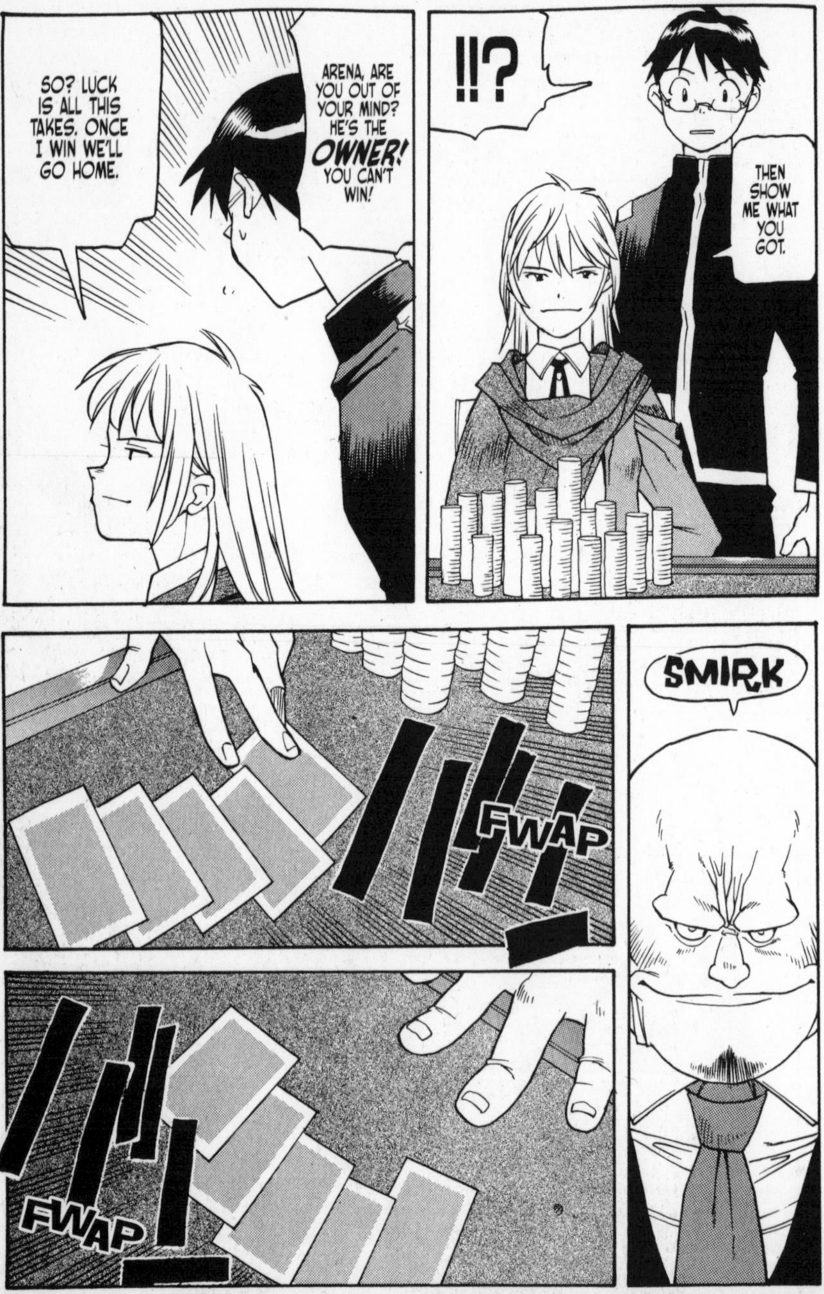
ARENA, ARE YOU OUT OF YOUR MIND? HE'S THE OWNER! YOU CAN'T WIN!
SO? LUCK IS ALL THIS TAKES. ONCE I WIN WE'LL GO HOME.
!!?
THEN SHOW ME WHAT YOU GOT.
FWAP
FWAP
SMIRK

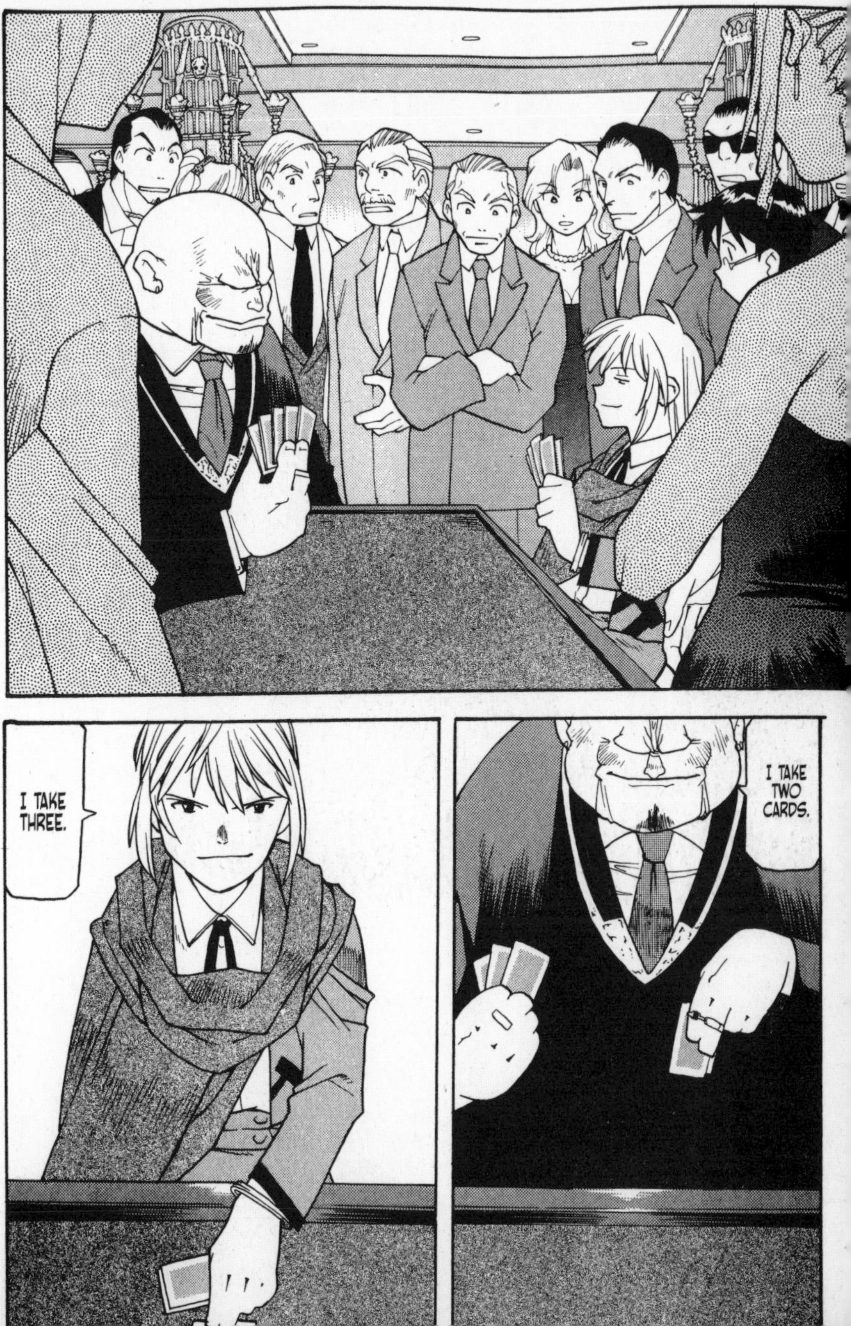
I TAKE TWO CARDS.
I TAKE THREE.

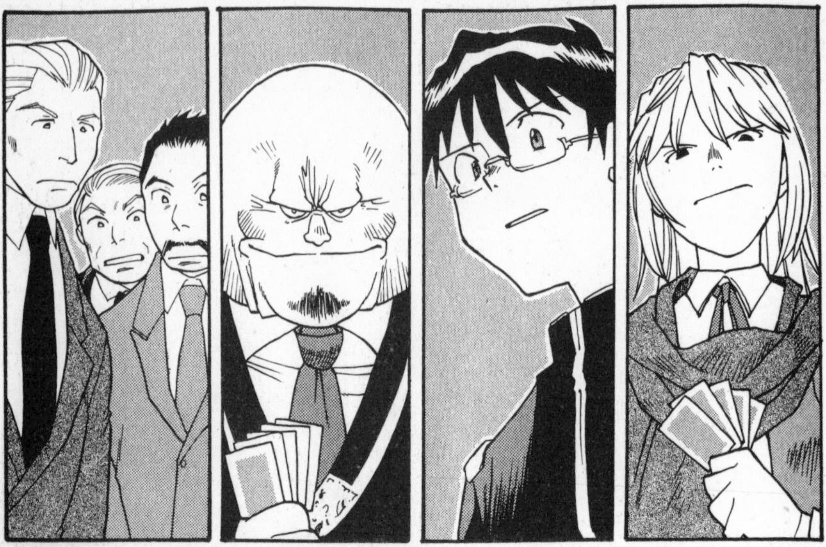

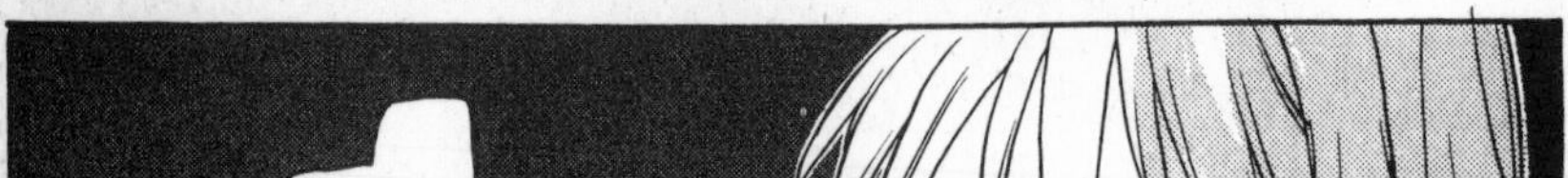
......CALL*.

*A poker move in which you place an amount of chips in the pot equal to the previous bet.

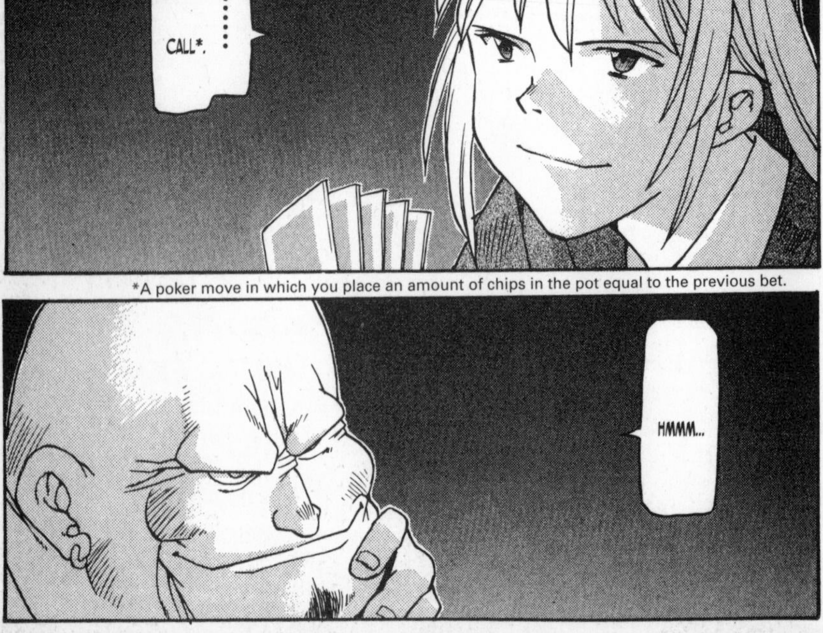
HMMM...

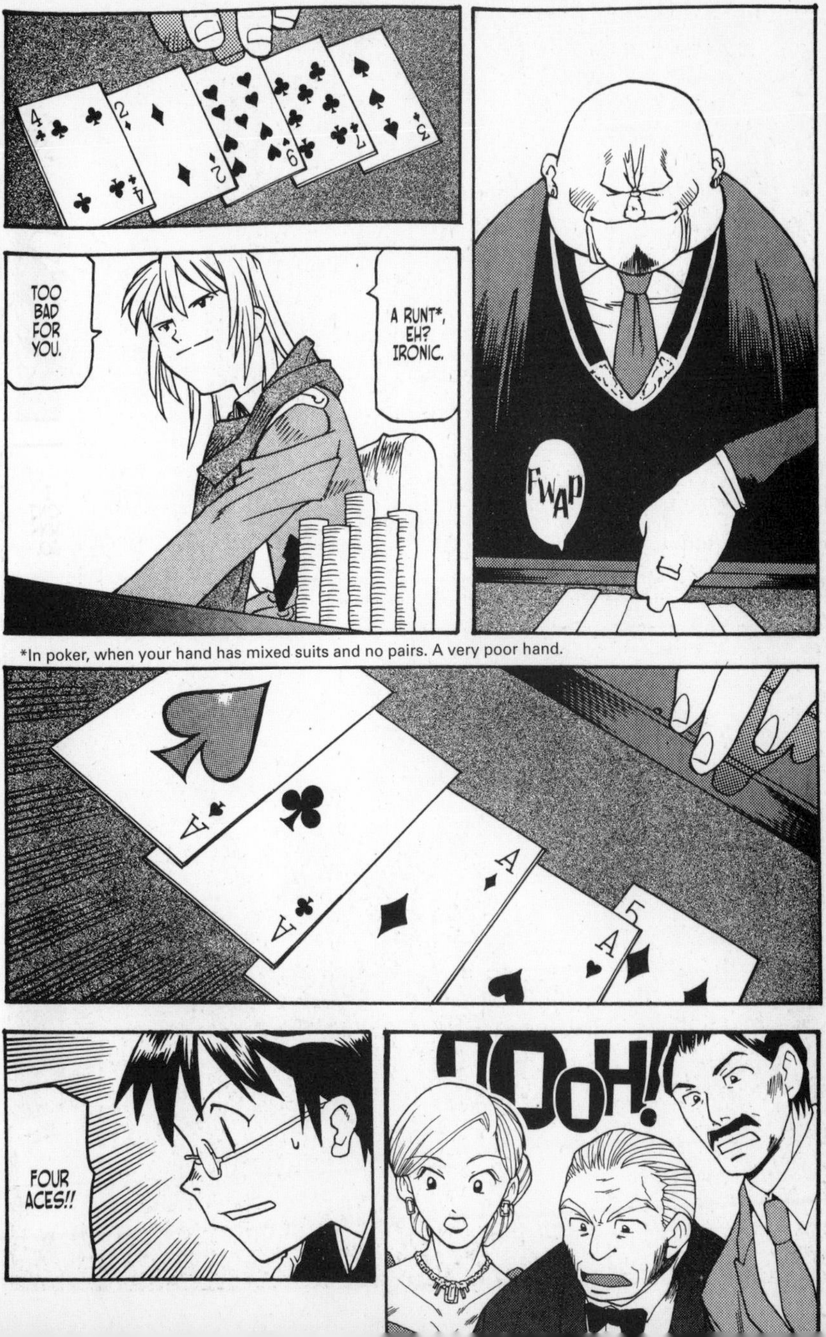
FWAP
A RUNT*, EH? IRONIC.
TOO BAD FOR YOU.
OOOH!
FOUR ACES!!
*In poker, when your hand has mixed suits and no pairs. A very poor hand.

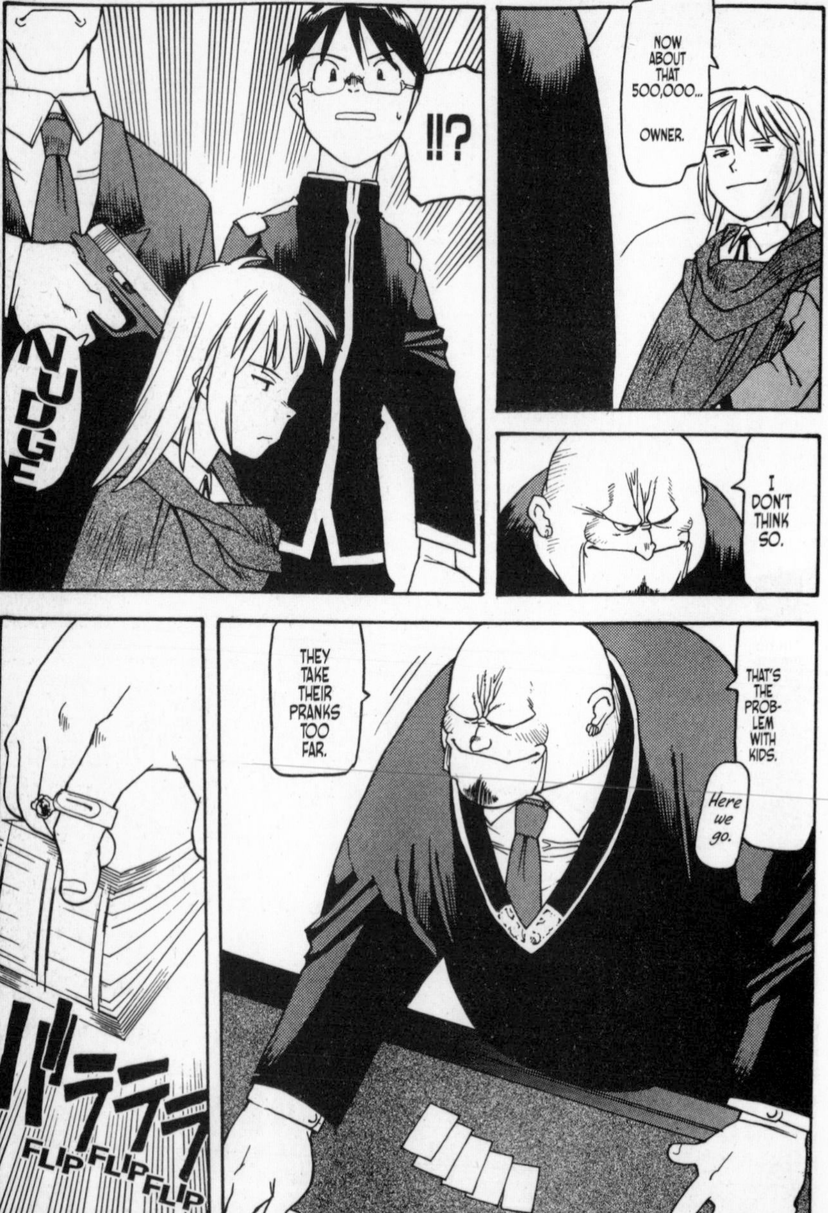
NOW ABOUT THAT 500,000...
OWNER.
I DON'T THINK SO.
!!?
NUDGE
THAT'S THE PROB-LEM WITH KIDS.
THEY TAKE THEIR PRANKS TOO FAR.
Here we go.
パラララ
FLIPFLIPFLIP

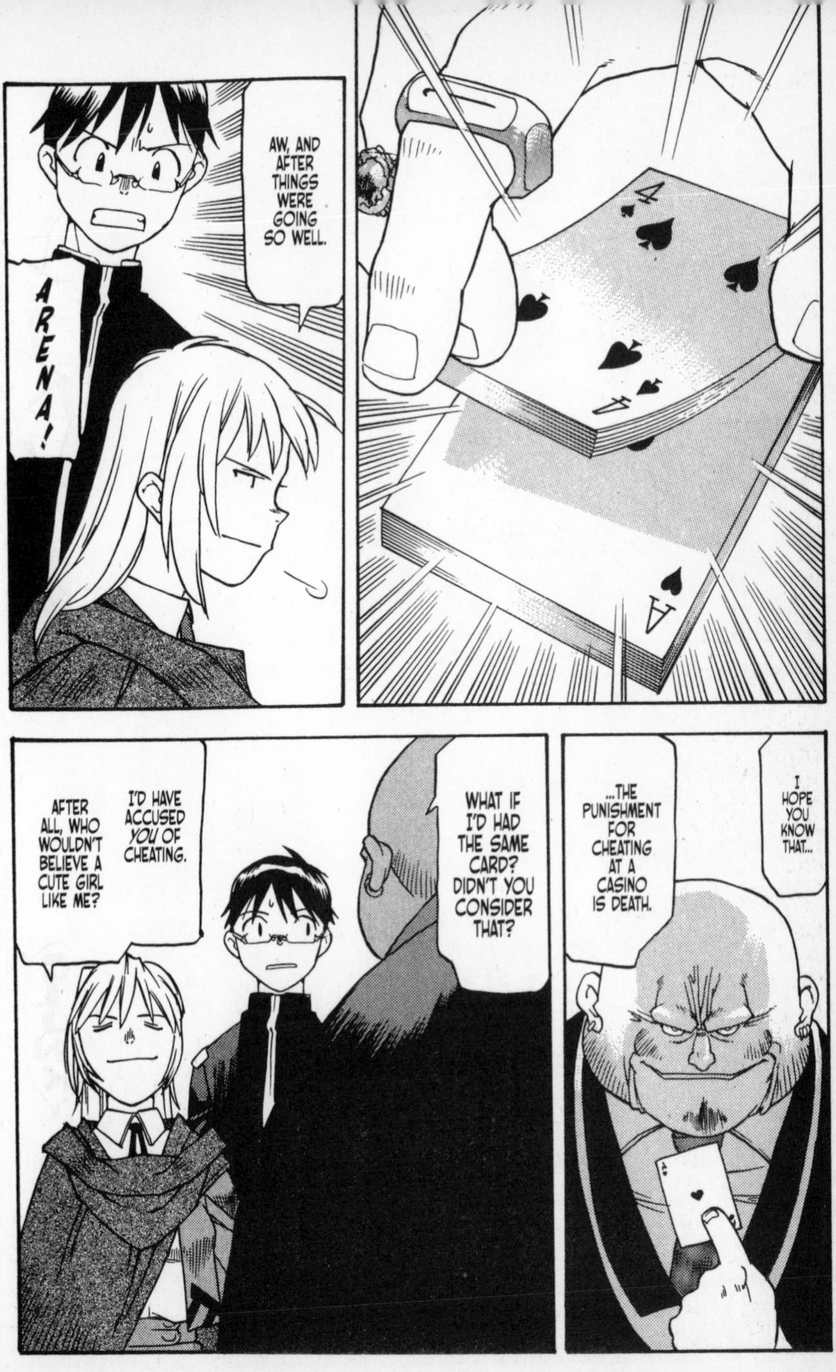
AW, AND AFTER THINGS WERE GOING SO WELL.
ARENA!
I HOPE YOU KNOW THAT...
...THE PUNISHMENT FOR CHEATING AT A CASINO IS DEATH.
WHAT IF I'D HAD THE SAME CARD? DIDN'T YOU CONSIDER THAT?
I'D HAVE ACCUSED *YOU* OF CHEATING.
AFTER ALL, WHO WOULDN'T BELIEVE A CUTE GIRL LIKE ME?

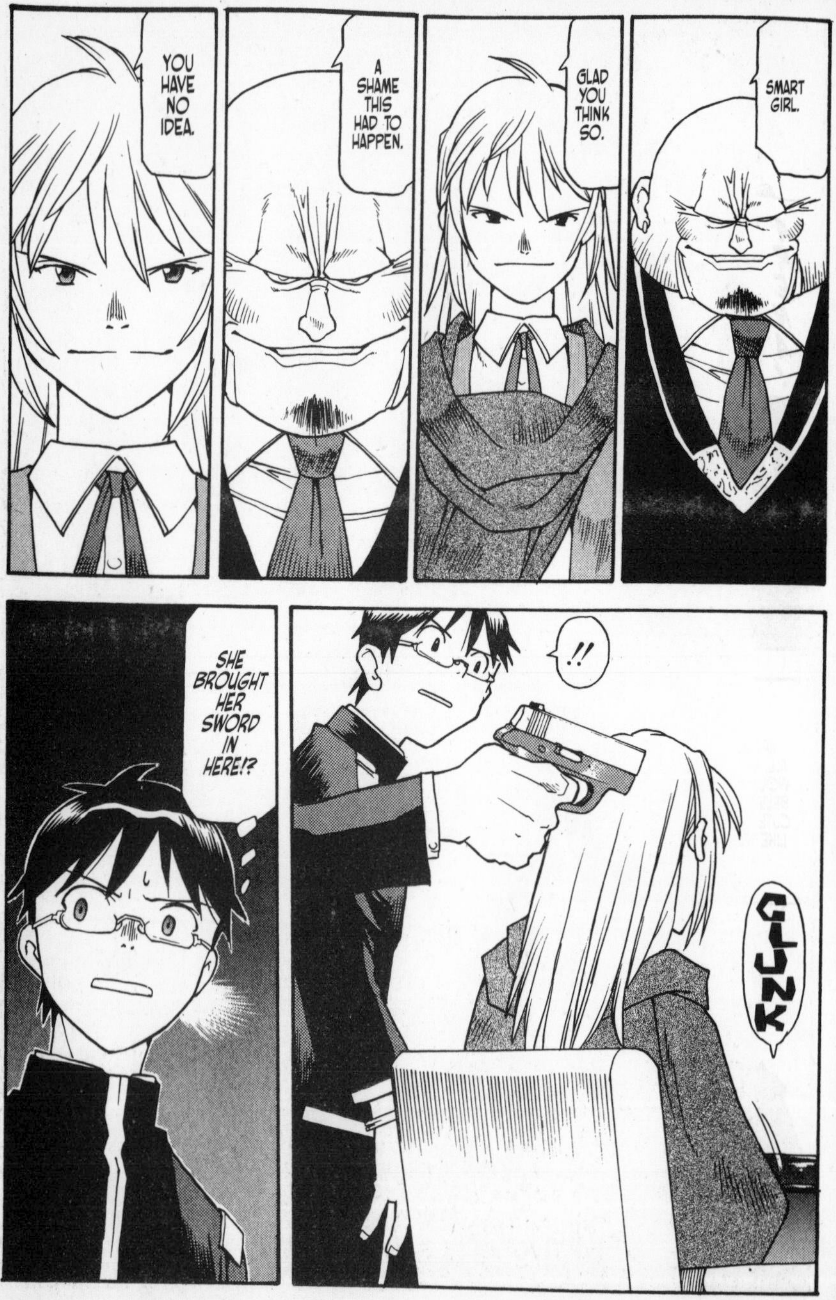
SMART GIRL.
GLAD YOU THINK SO.
A SHAME THIS HAD TO HAPPEN.
YOU HAVE NO IDEA.
!!
CLUNK
SHE BROUGHT HER SWORD IN HERE!?

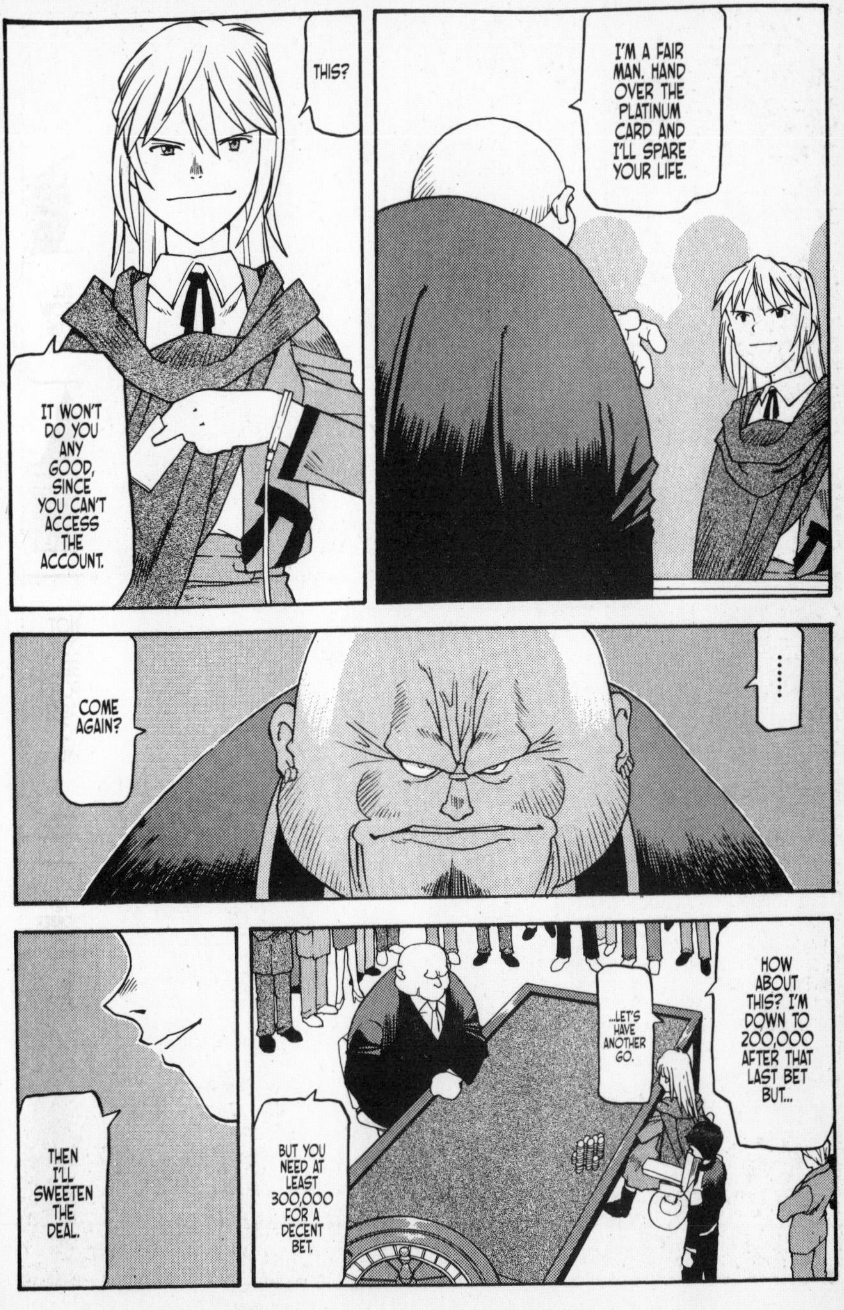
I'M A FAIR MAN. HAND OVER THE PLATINUM CARD AND I'LL SPARE YOUR LIFE.
THIS?
IT WON'T DO YOU ANY GOOD, SINCE YOU CAN'T ACCESS THE ACCOUNT.
......
COME AGAIN?
HOW ABOUT THIS? I'M DOWN TO 200,000 AFTER THAT LAST BET BUT...
...LET'S HAVE ANOTHER GO.
BUT YOU NEED AT LEAST 300,000 FOR A DECENT BET.
THEN I'LL SWEETEN THE DEAL.

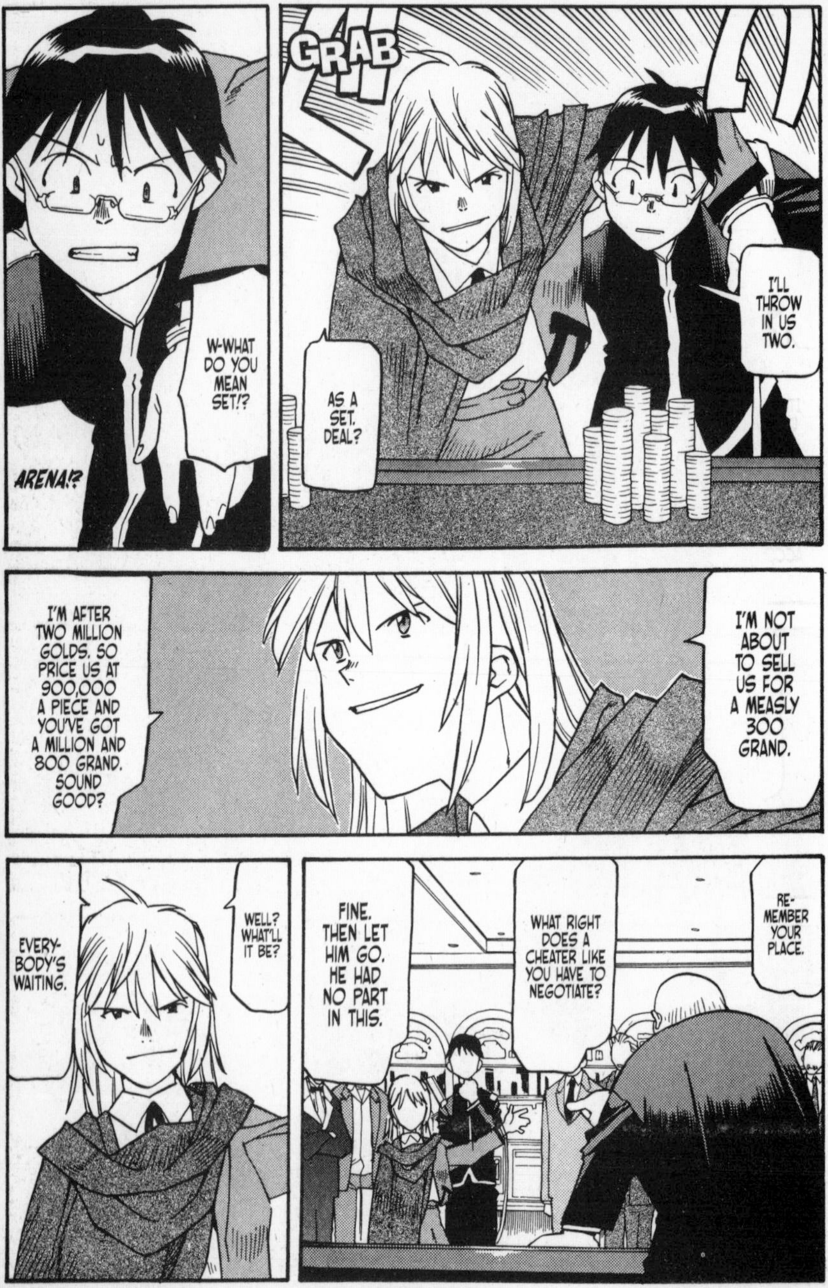
GRAB
I'LL THROW IN US TWO.
AS A SET. DEAL?
W-WHAT DO YOU MEAN SET!?
ARENA!?
I'M NOT ABOUT TO SELL US FOR A MEASLY 300 GRAND.
I'M AFTER TWO MILLION GOLDS. SO PRICE US AT 900,000 A PIECE AND YOU'VE GOT A MILLION AND 800 GRAND. SOUND GOOD?
RE-MEMBER YOUR PLACE.
WHAT RIGHT DOES A CHEATER LIKE YOU HAVE TO NEGOTIATE?
FINE. THEN LET HIM GO. HE HAD NO PART IN THIS.
WELL? WHAT'LL IT BE?
EVERY-BODY'S WAITING.

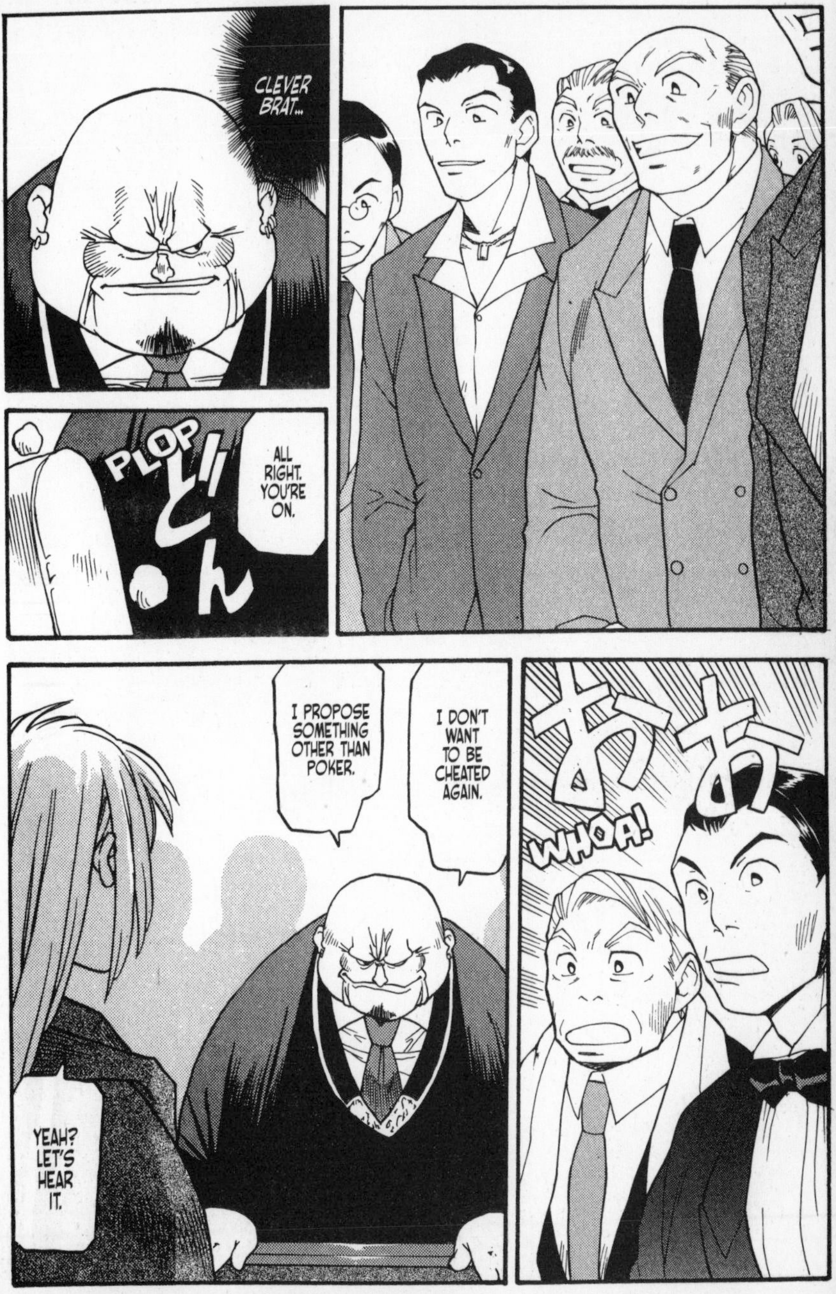
CLEVER BRAT...
ALL RIGHT. YOU'RE ON.
PLOP
どん
おお
WHOA!
I DON'T WANT TO BE CHEATED AGAIN.
I PROPOSE SOMETHING OTHER THAN POKER.
YEAH? LET'S HEAR IT.

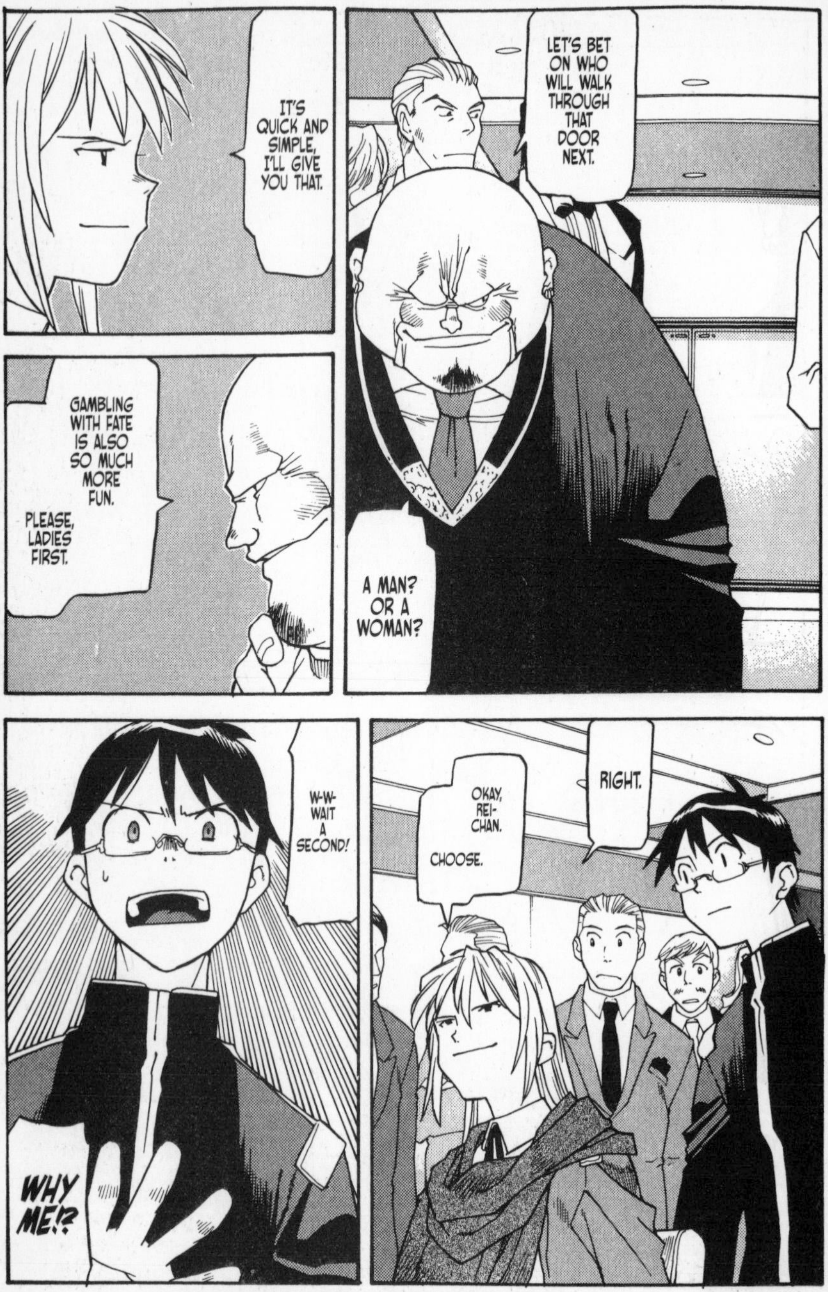
LET'S BET ON WHO WILL WALK THROUGH THAT DOOR NEXT.
A MAN? OR A WOMAN?
IT'S QUICK AND SIMPLE, I'LL GIVE YOU THAT.
GAMBLING WITH FATE IS ALSO SO MUCH MORE FUN.
PLEASE, LADIES FIRST.
RIGHT.
OKAY, REI-CHAN.
CHOOSE.
W-W-WAIT A SECOND!
WHY ME!?

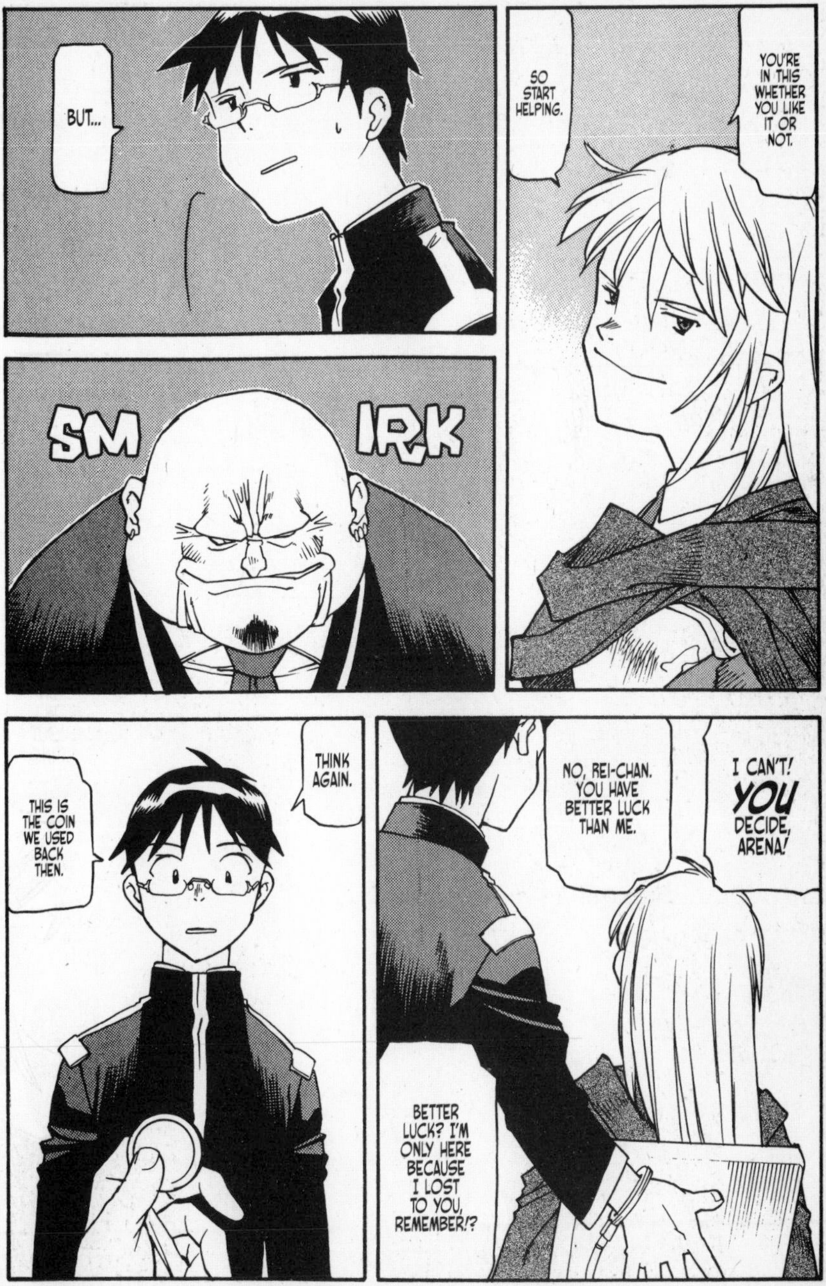
YOU'RE IN THIS WHETHER YOU LIKE IT OR NOT.
SO START HELPING.
BUT...
SM IRK
I CAN'T! ***YOU*** DECIDE, ARENA!
NO, REI-CHAN. YOU HAVE BETTER LUCK THAN ME.
BETTER LUCK? I'M ONLY HERE BECAUSE I LOST TO YOU, REMEMBER!?
THINK AGAIN.
THIS IS THE COIN WE USED BACK THEN.

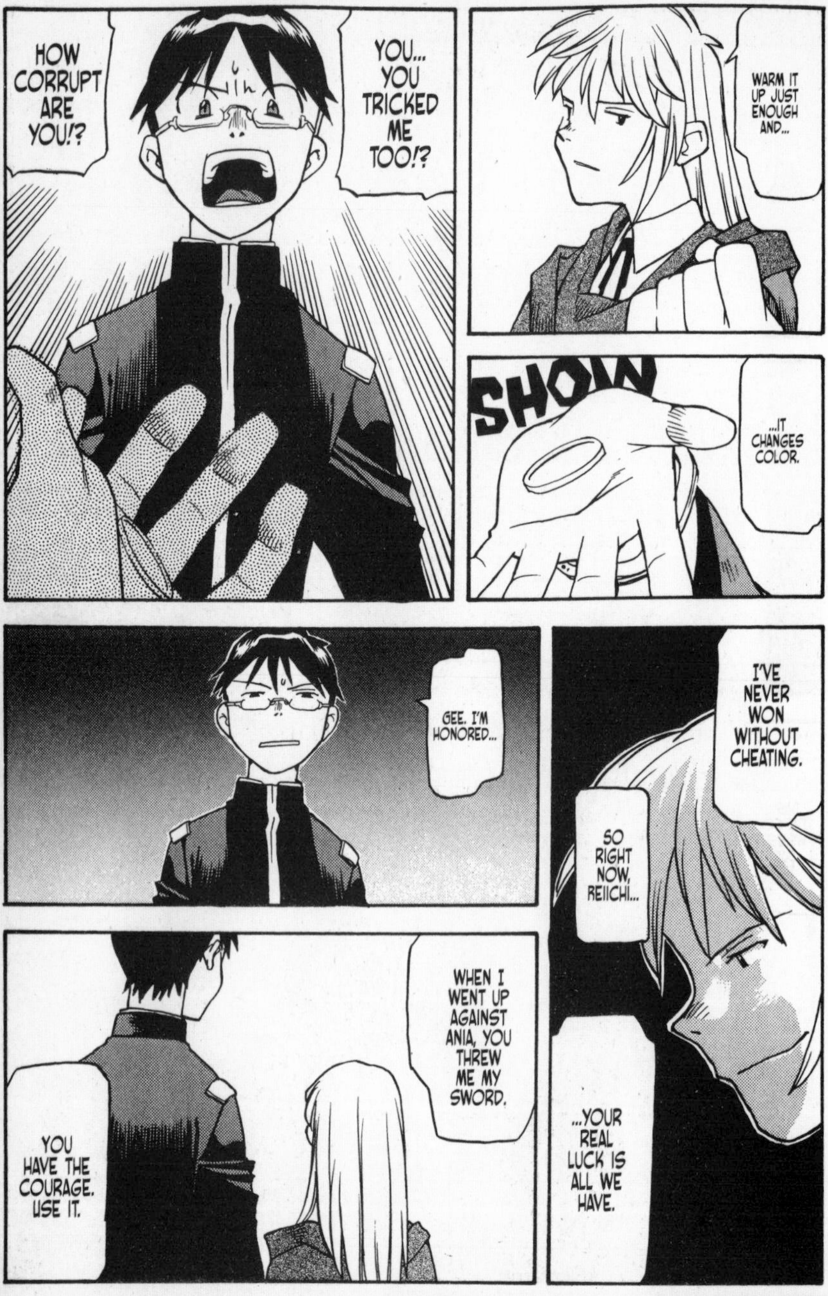
WARM IT UP JUST ENOUGH AND...
SHOW
...IT CHANGES COLOR.
YOU... YOU TRICKED ME TOO!?
HOW CORRUPT ARE YOU!?
I'VE NEVER WON WITHOUT CHEATING.
SO RIGHT NOW, REIICHI...
...YOUR REAL LUCK IS ALL WE HAVE.
GEE. I'M HONORED...
WHEN I WENT UP AGAINST ANIA, YOU THREW ME MY SWORD.
YOU HAVE THE COURAGE. USE IT.

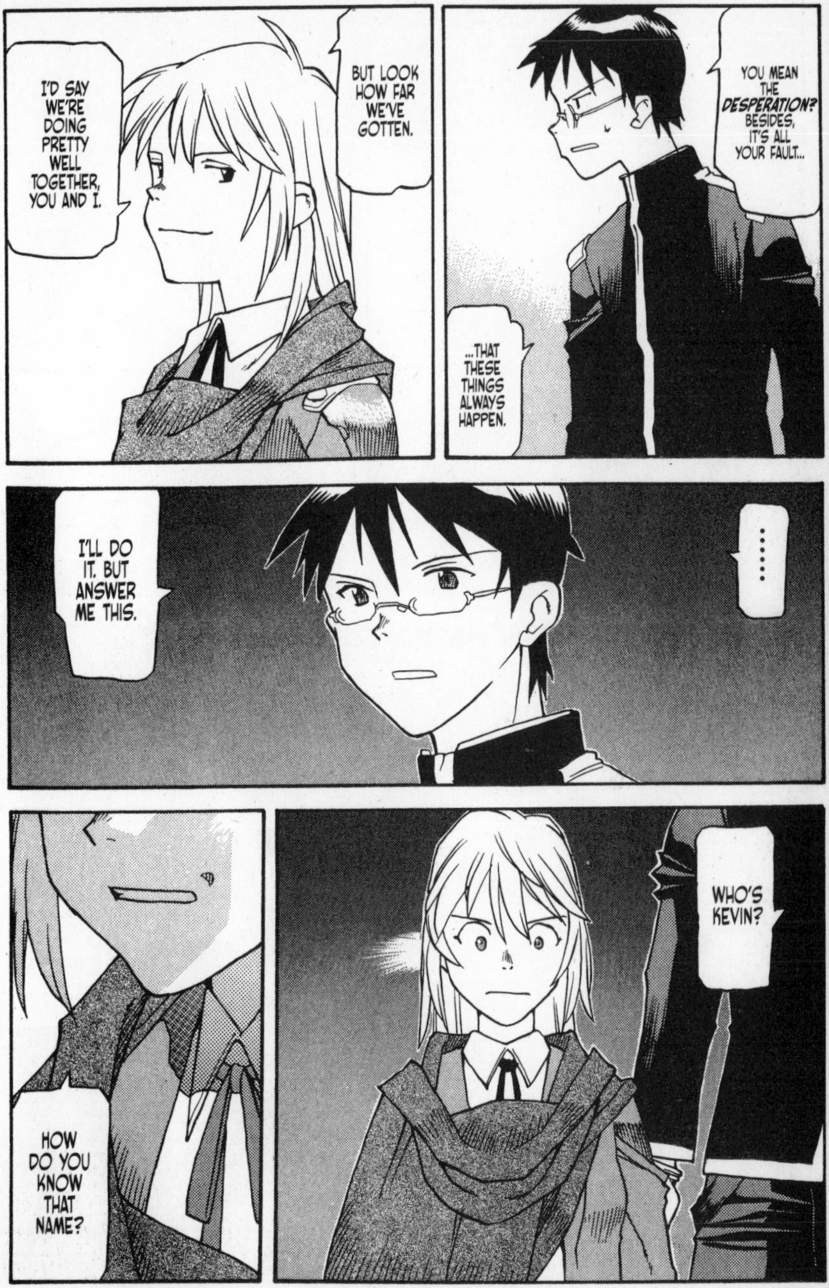
YOU MEAN THE *DESPERATION?* BESIDES, IT'S ALL YOUR FAULT...
...THAT THESE THINGS ALWAYS HAPPEN.
BUT LOOK HOW FAR WE'VE GOTTEN.
I'D SAY WE'RE DOING PRETTY WELL TOGETHER, YOU AND I.
......
I'LL DO IT. BUT ANSWER ME THIS.
WHO'S KEVIN?
HOW DO YOU KNOW THAT NAME?

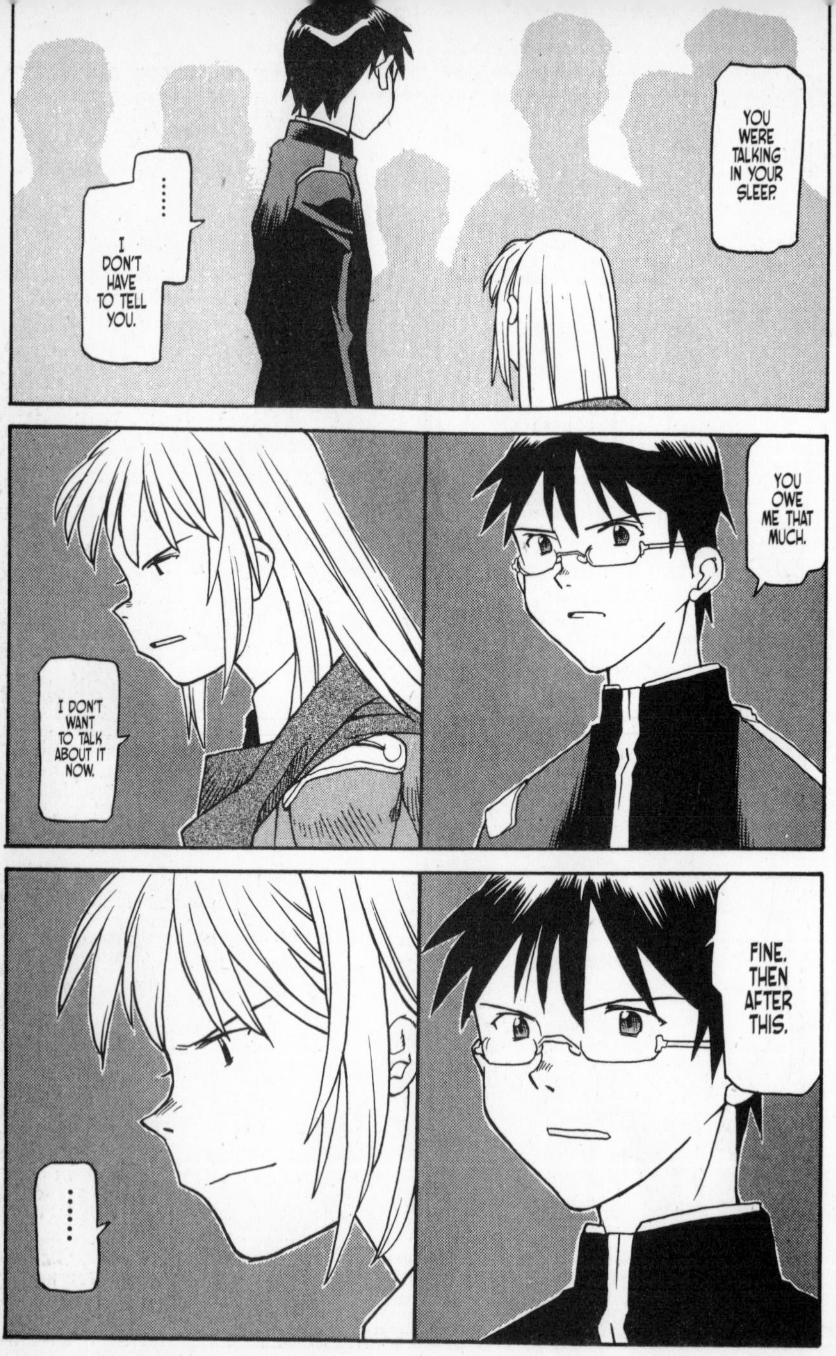
YOU WERE TALKING IN YOUR SLEEP.
......
I DON'T HAVE TO TELL YOU.
YOU OWE ME THAT MUCH.
I DON'T WANT TO TALK ABOUT IT NOW.
FINE. THEN AFTER THIS.
......

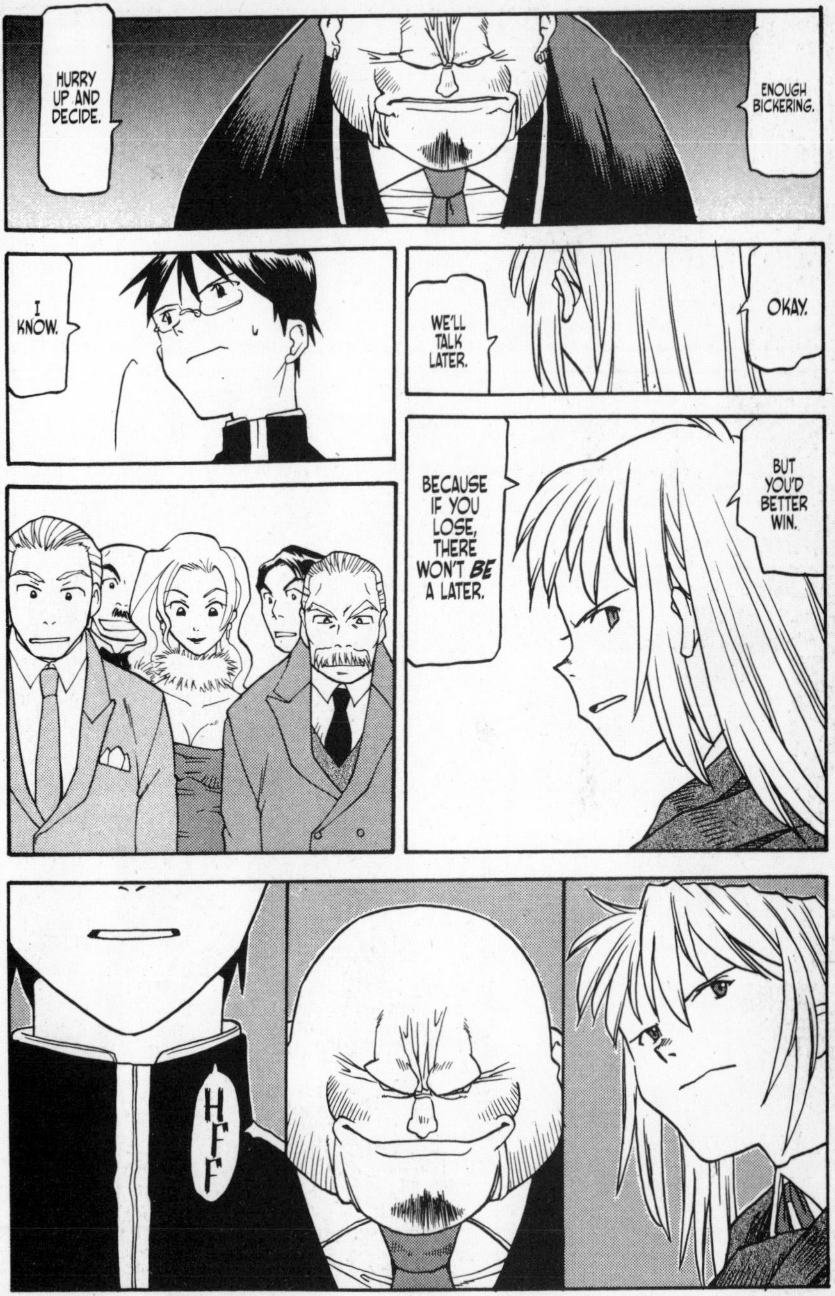
ENOUGH BICKERING.
HURRY UP AND DECIDE.
OKAY.
WE'LL TALK LATER.
I KNOW.
BUT YOU'D BETTER WIN.
BECAUSE IF YOU LOSE, THERE WON'T *BE* A LATER.
HFF

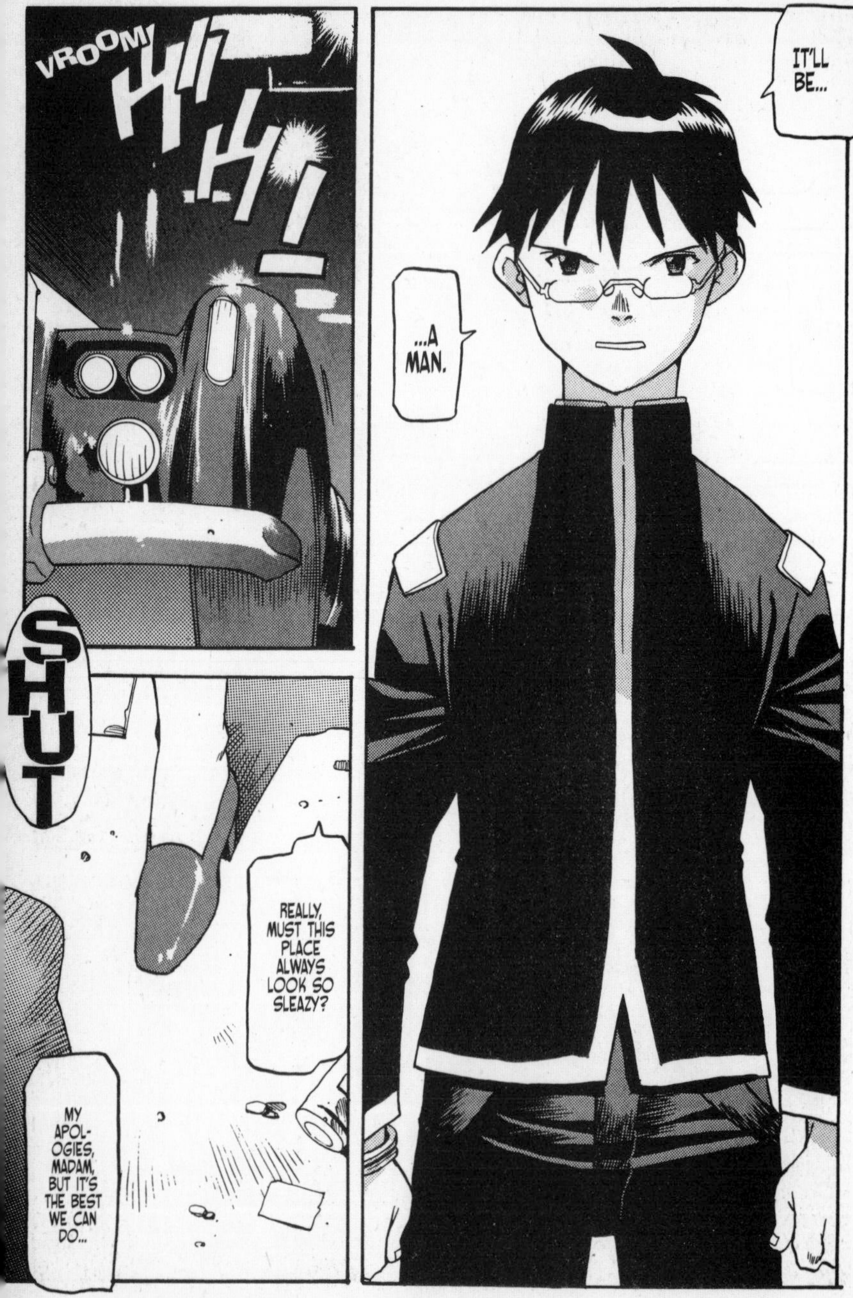
IT'LL BE...
...A MAN.
VROOM
SHUT
REALLY, MUST THIS PLACE ALWAYS LOOK SO SLEAZY?
MY APOLOGIES, MADAM, BUT IT'S THE BEST WE CAN DO...

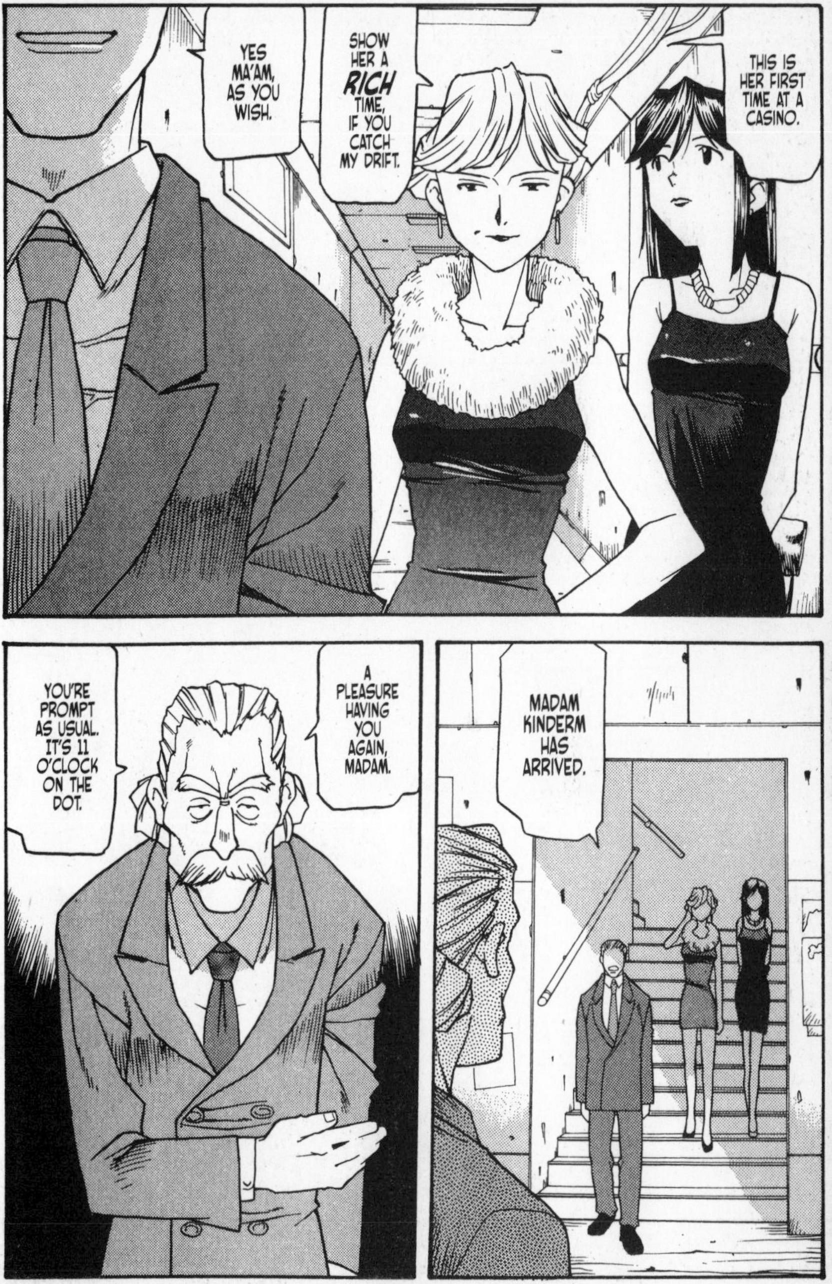
THIS IS HER FIRST TIME AT A CASINO.
SHOW HER A **RICH** TIME, IF YOU CATCH MY DRIFT.
YES MA'AM, AS YOU WISH.
MADAM KINDERM HAS ARRIVED.
A PLEASURE HAVING YOU AGAIN, MADAM.
YOU'RE PROMPT AS USUAL. IT'S 11 O'CLOCK ON THE DOT.

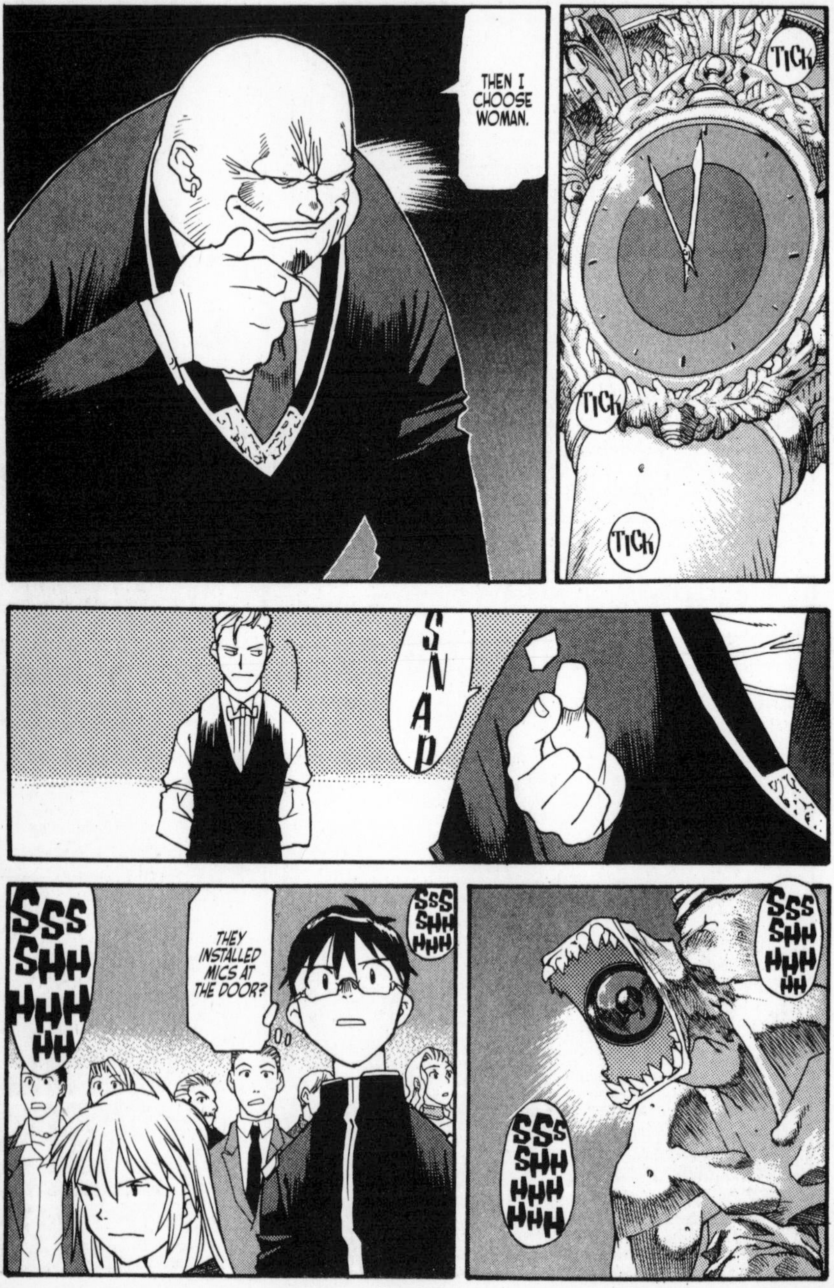
TICK
TICK
TICK
THEN I CHOOSE WOMAN.
SNAP
SSSSHHHHHHHH
SSSSHHHHHHHHH
SSSSHHHHH
THEY INSTALLED MICS AT THE DOOR?
SSSSHHHHHHHH

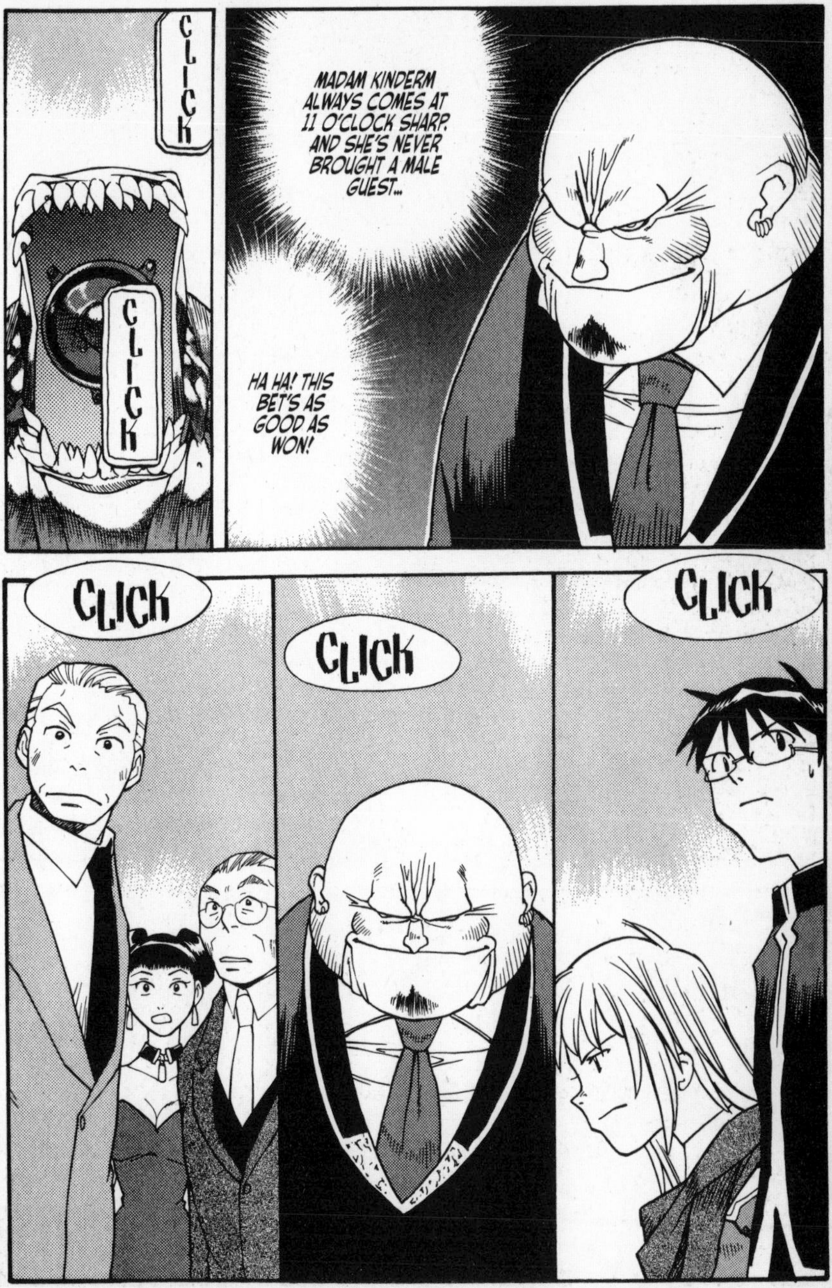
MADAM KINDERM ALWAYS COMES AT 11 O'CLOCK SHARP. AND SHE'S NEVER BROUGHT A MALE GUEST...
HA HA! THIS BET'S AS GOOD AS WON!
CLICK
CLICK
CLICK
CLICK
CLICK

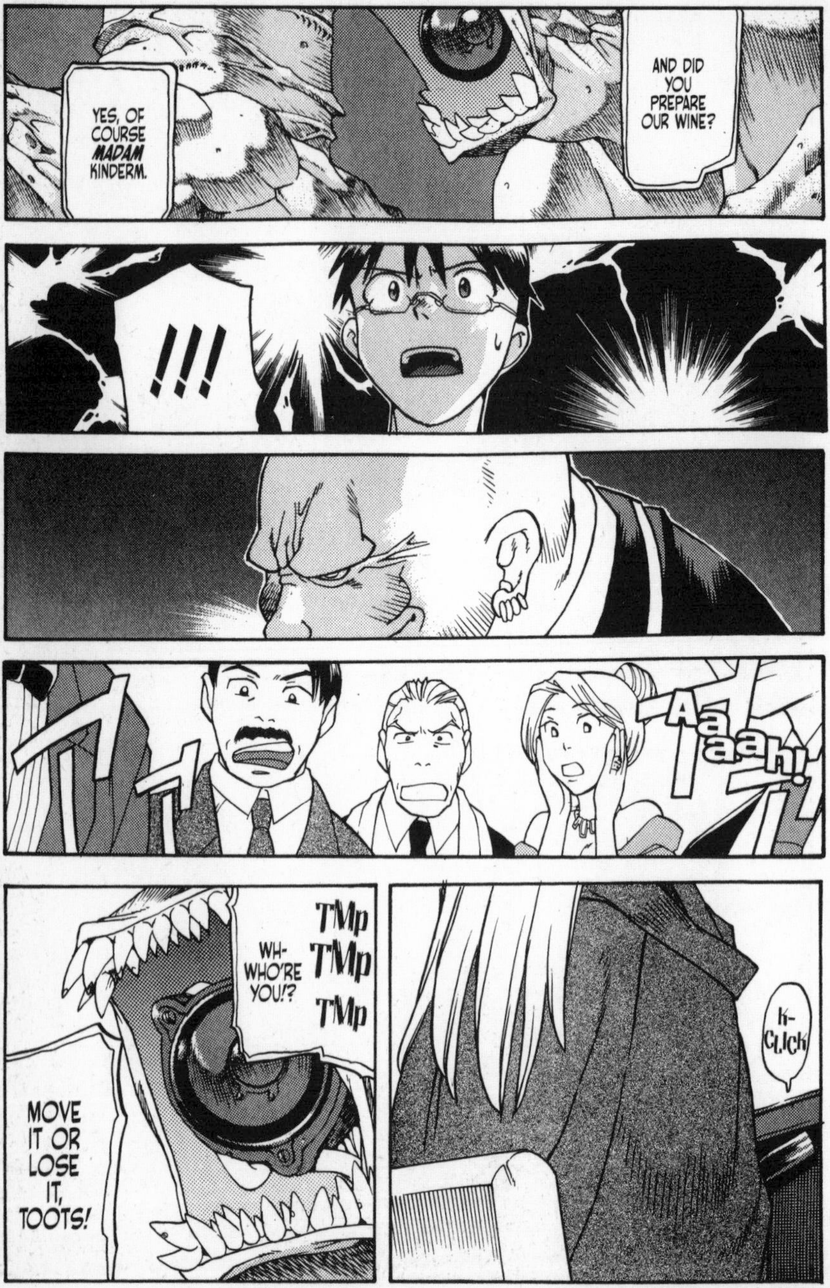
AND DID YOU PREPARE OUR WINE?
YES, OF COURSE MADAM KINDERM.
!!!
Aaaah!
K-CLICK
TMp TMp TMp
WH- WHO'RE YOU!?
MOVE IT OR LOSE IT, TOOTS!

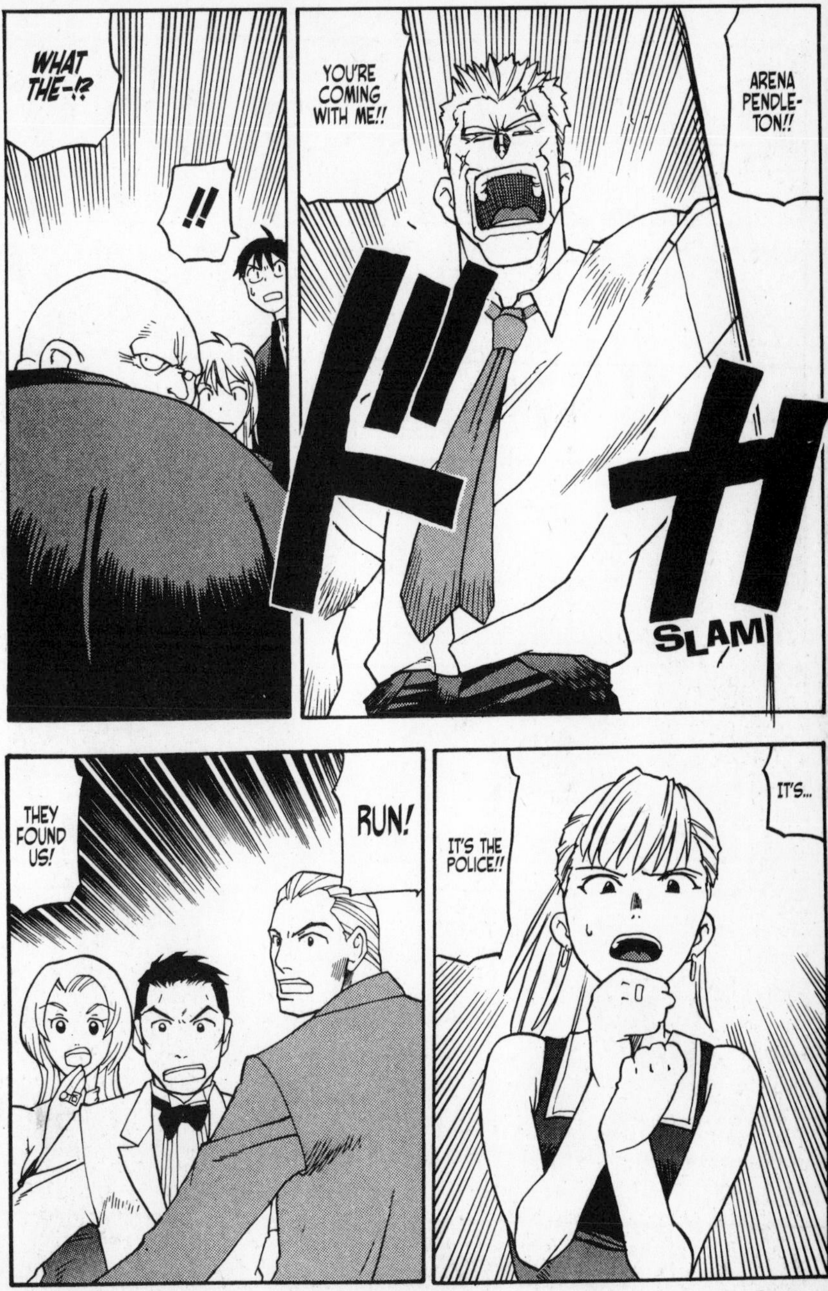

ARENA PENDLE-TON!!
YOU'RE COMING WITH ME!!
ドカ
SLAM
WHAT THE-!?
!!
IT'S...
IT'S THE POLICE!!
RUN!
THEY FOUND US!

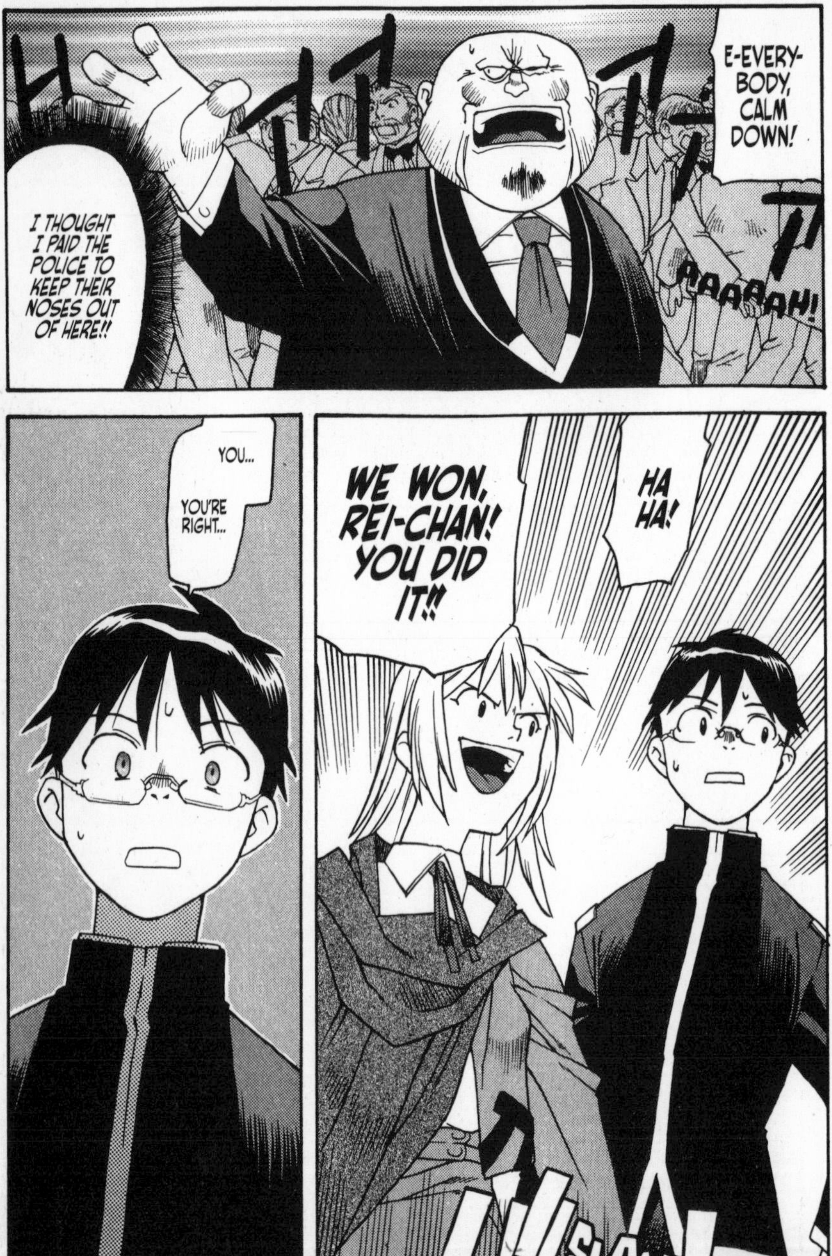
E-EVERY-BODY, CALM DOWN!
AAAAAH!
I THOUGHT I PAID THE POLICE TO KEEP THEIR NOSES OUT OF HERE!!
HA HA!
WE WON, REI-CHAN! YOU DID IT!!
SLAM
YOU...
YOU'RE RIGHT...

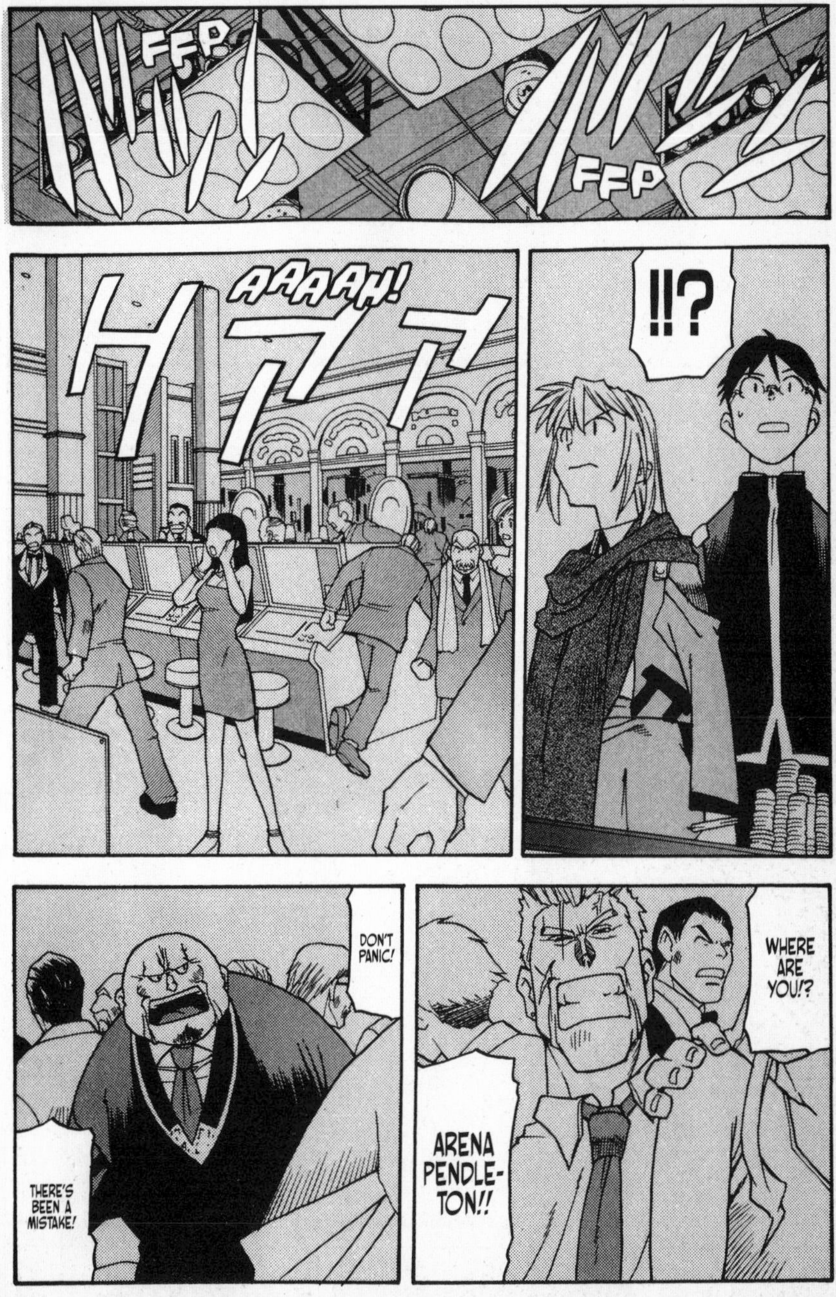
FFP
FFP
!!?
AAAAH!
WHERE ARE YOU!?
ARENA PENDLE-TON!!
DON'T PANIC!
THERE'S BEEN A MISTAKE!

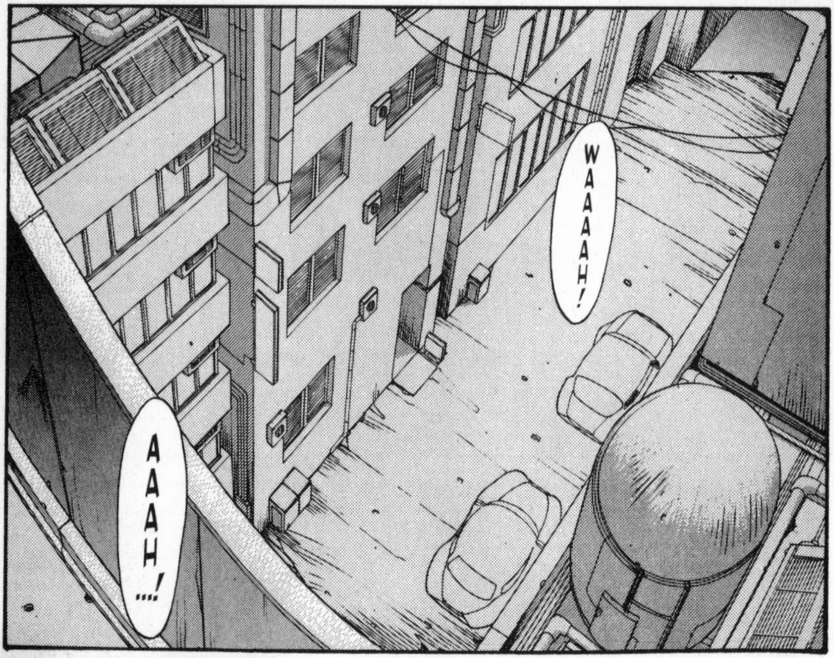
WAAAAAH!
AAAAH...!

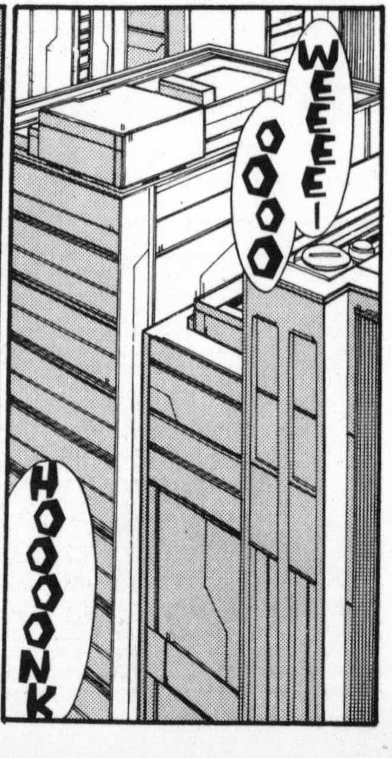
WEEEI
OOOO
HOOOONK

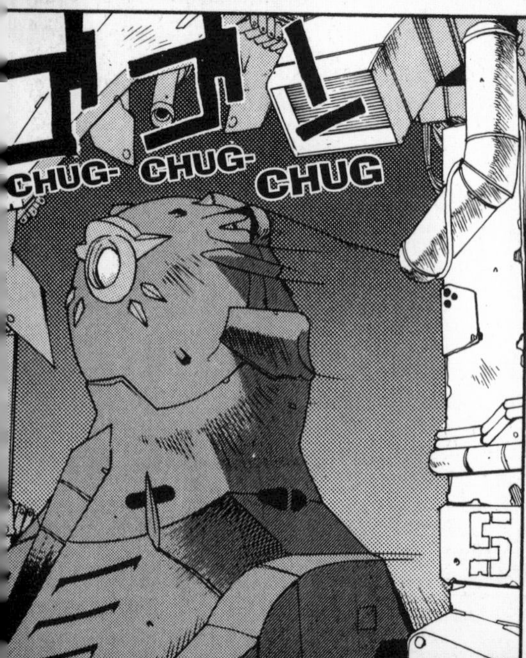
CHUG- CHUG- CHUG

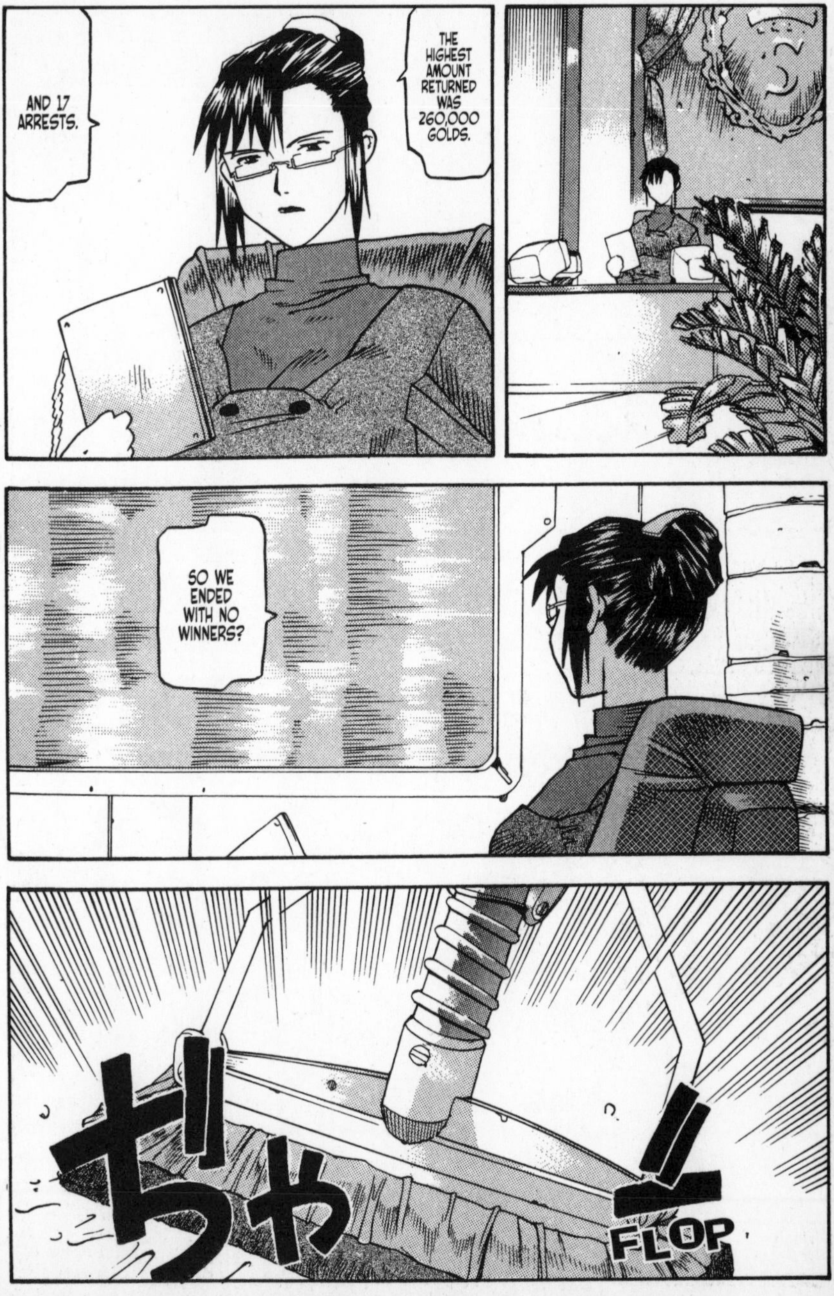
THE HIGHEST AMOUNT RETURNED WAS 260,000 GOLDS.
AND 17 ARRESTS.
SO WE ENDED WITH NO WINNERS?
FLOP

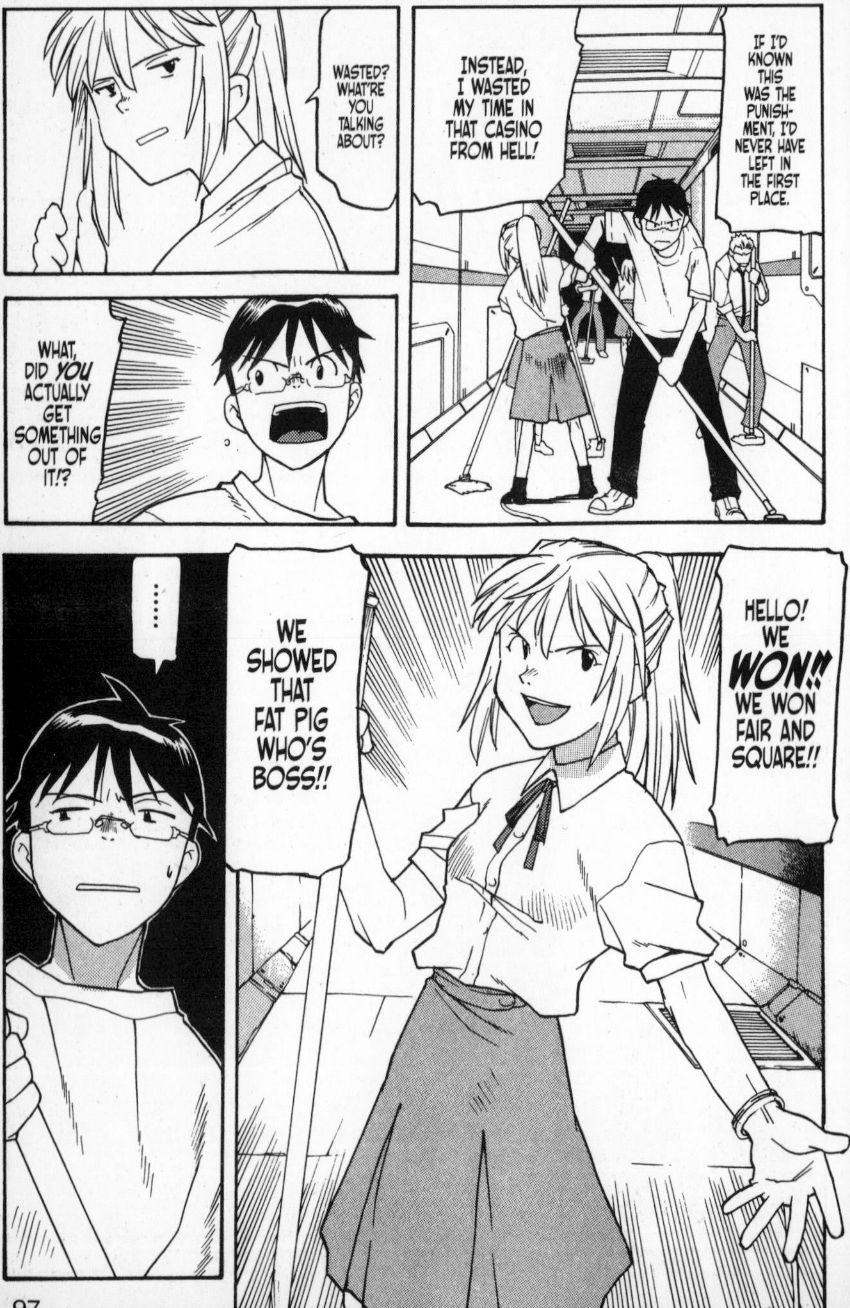
IF I'D KNOWN THIS WAS THE PUNISHMENT, I'D NEVER HAVE LEFT IN THE FIRST PLACE.
INSTEAD, I WASTED MY TIME IN THAT CASINO FROM HELL!
WASTED? WHAT'RE YOU TALKING ABOUT?
WHAT, DID YOU ACTUALLY GET SOMETHING OUT OF IT!?
HELLO! WE WON!! WE WON FAIR AND SQUARE!!
WE SHOWED THAT FAT PIG WHO'S BOSS!!
......!

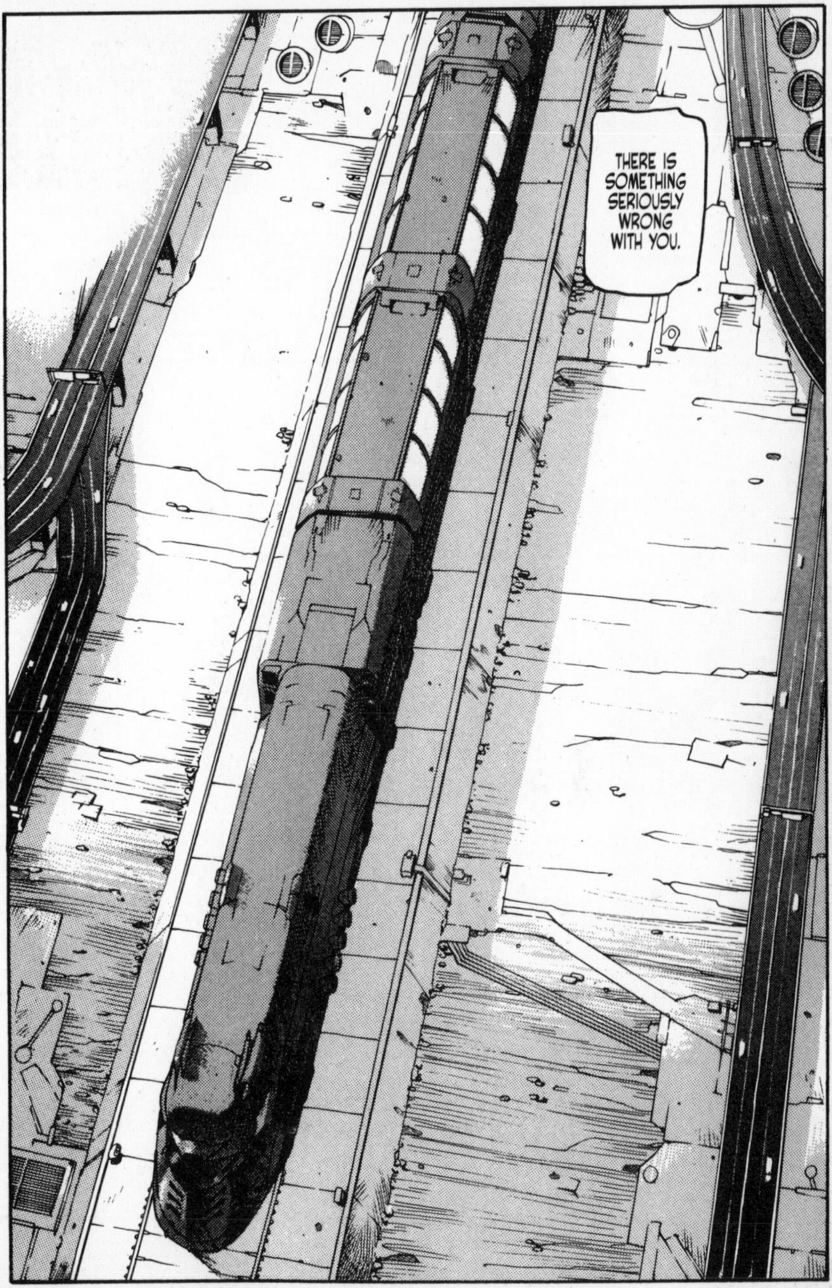
THERE IS SOMETHING SERIOUSLY WRONG WITH YOU.

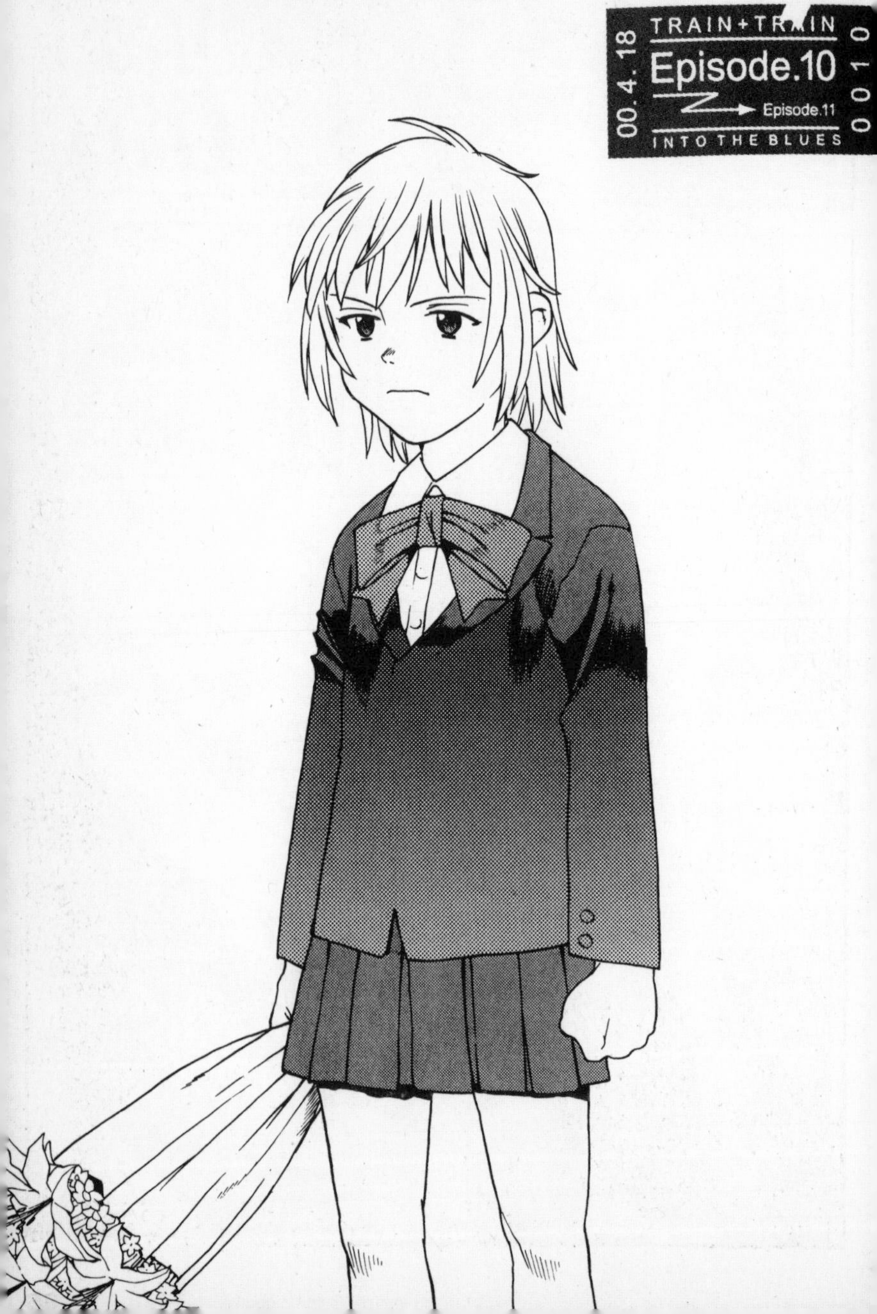
00.4.18
TRAIN+TRAIN
Episode.10
Episode.11
INTO THE BLUES
0010

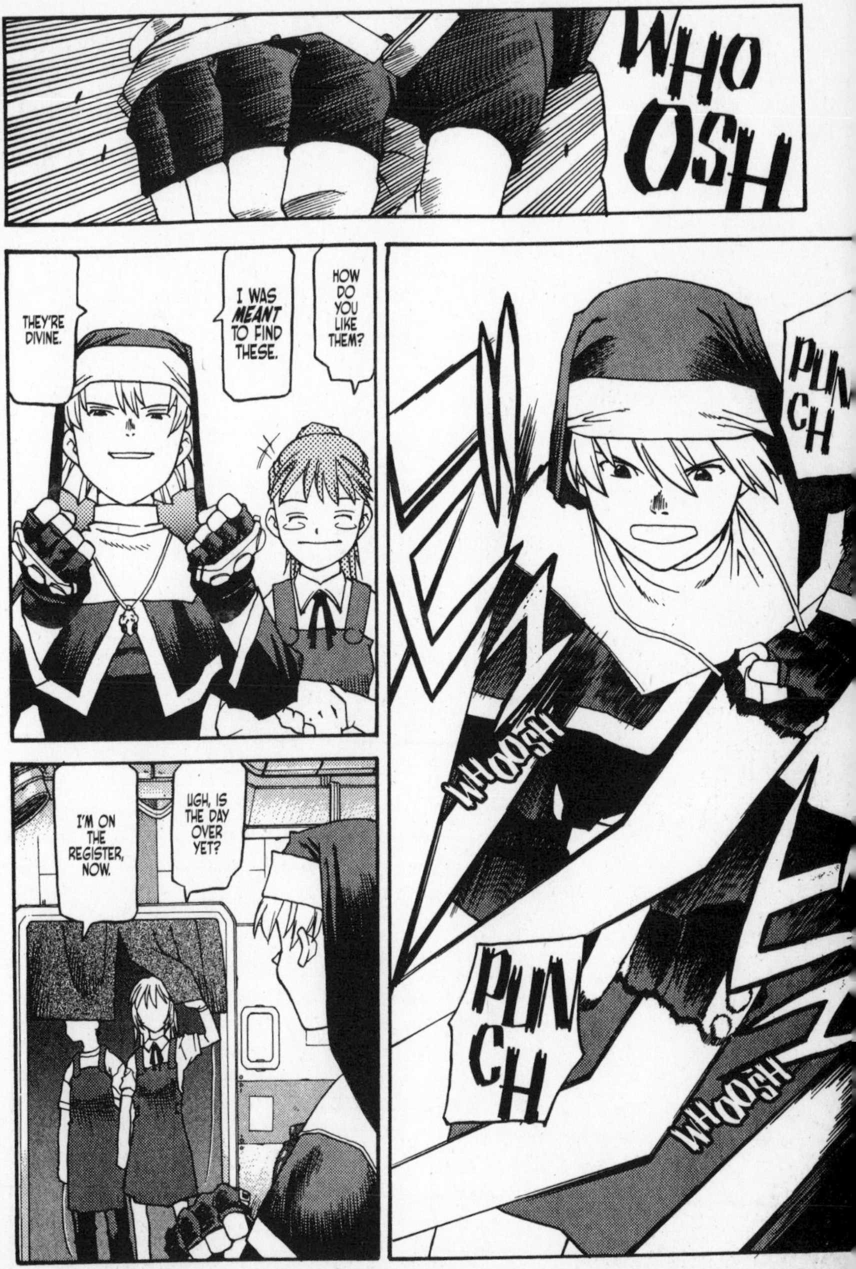
WHOOSH
PUNCH
WHOOSH
PUNCH
WHOOSH
HOW DO YOU LIKE THEM?
I WAS *MEANT* TO FIND THESE.
THEY'RE DIVINE.
UGH, IS THE DAY OVER YET?
I'M ON THE REGISTER, NOW.

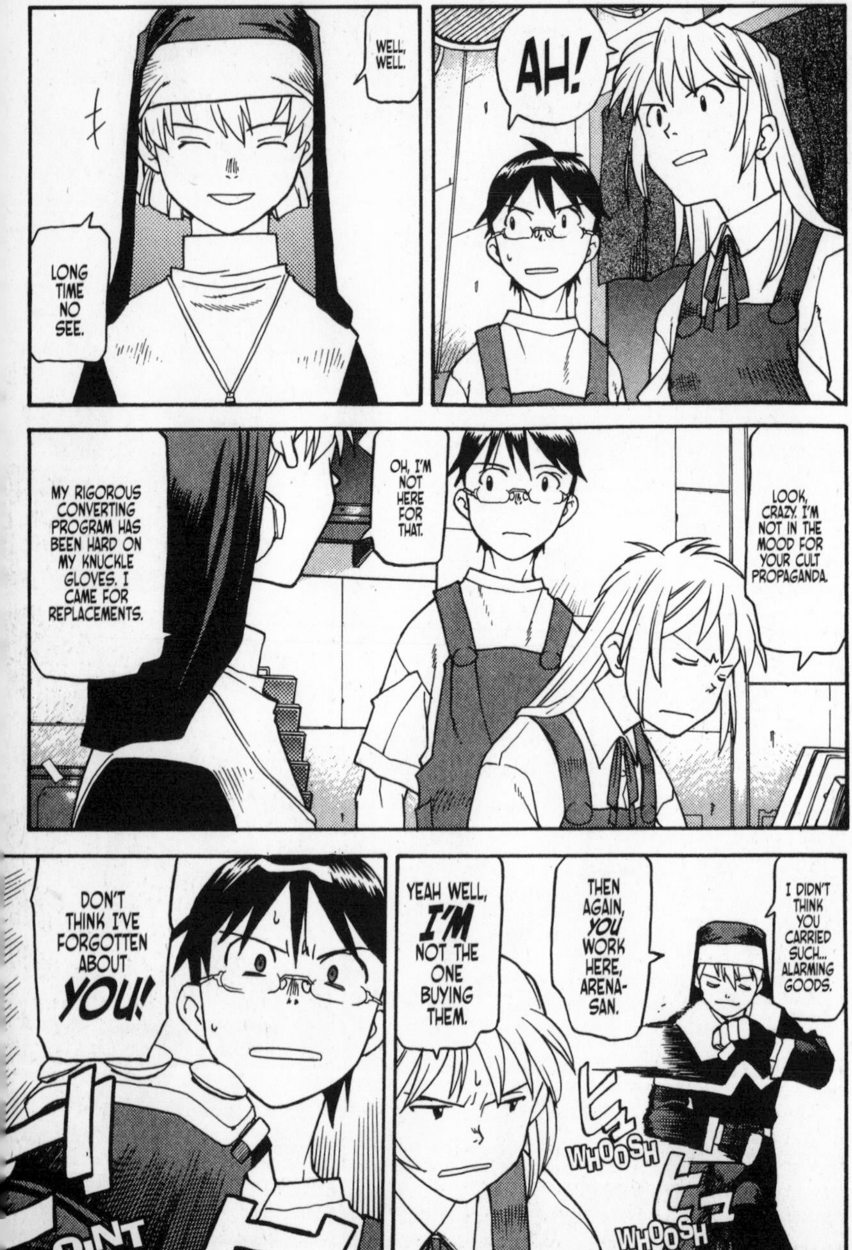
AH!
WELL, WELL.
LONG TIME NO SEE.
LOOK, CRAZY. I'M NOT IN THE MOOD FOR YOUR CULT PROPAGANDA.
OH, I'M NOT HERE FOR THAT.
MY RIGOROUS CONVERTING PROGRAM HAS BEEN HARD ON MY KNUCKLE GLOVES. I CAME FOR REPLACEMENTS.
I DIDN'T THINK YOU CARRIED SUCH... ALARMING GOODS.
THEN AGAIN, YOU WORK HERE, ARENA-SAN.
YEAH WELL, I'M NOT THE ONE BUYING THEM.
WHOOSH
WHOOSH
DON'T THINK I'VE FORGOTTEN ABOUT YOU!
POINT

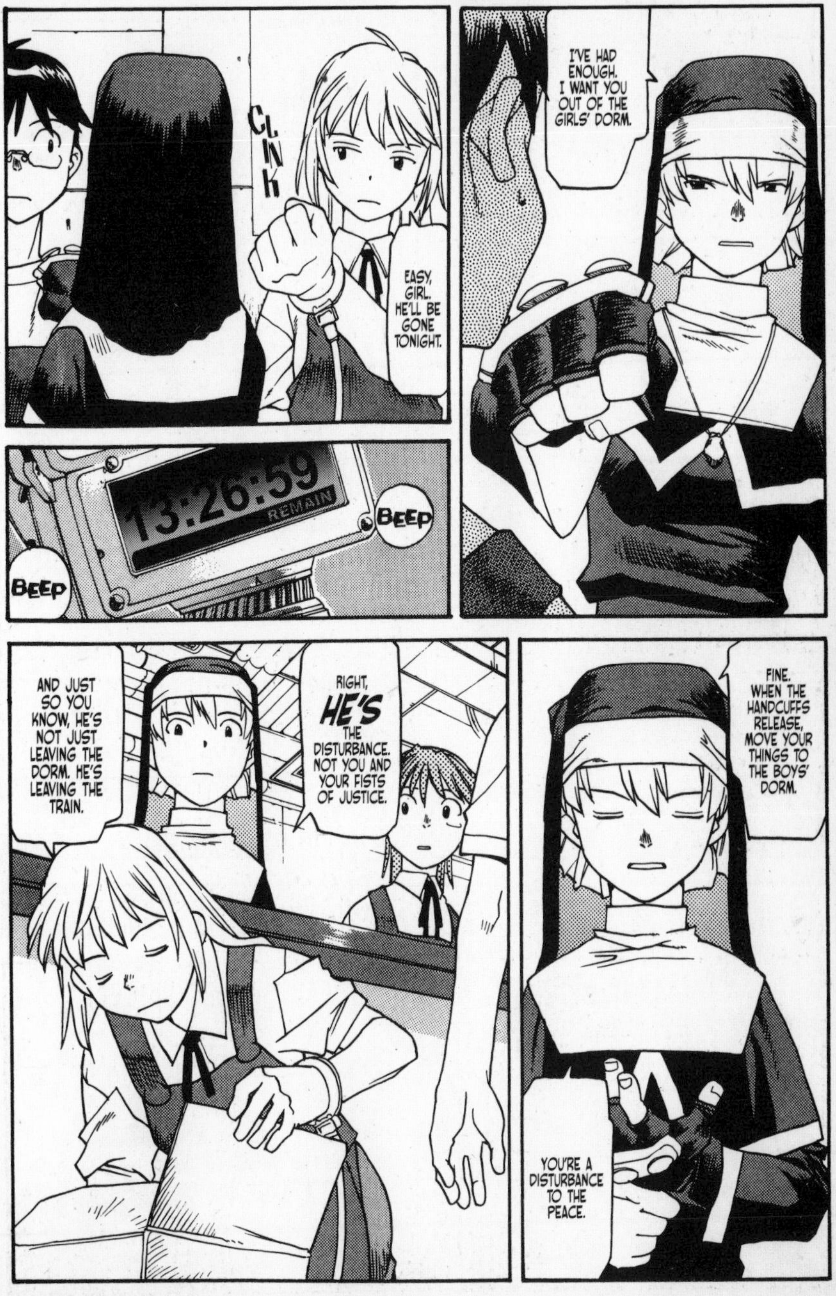
I'VE HAD ENOUGH. I WANT YOU OUT OF THE GIRLS' DORM.
CLINK
EASY, GIRL. HE'LL BE GONE TONIGHT.
13:26:59
REMAIN
BEEP
BEEP
FINE. WHEN THE HANDCUFFS RELEASE, MOVE YOUR THINGS TO THE BOYS' DORM.
YOU'RE A DISTURBANCE TO THE PEACE.
RIGHT, HE'S THE DISTURBANCE. NOT YOU AND YOUR FISTS OF JUSTICE.
AND JUST SO YOU KNOW, HE'S NOT JUST LEAVING THE DORM. HE'S LEAVING THE TRAIN.

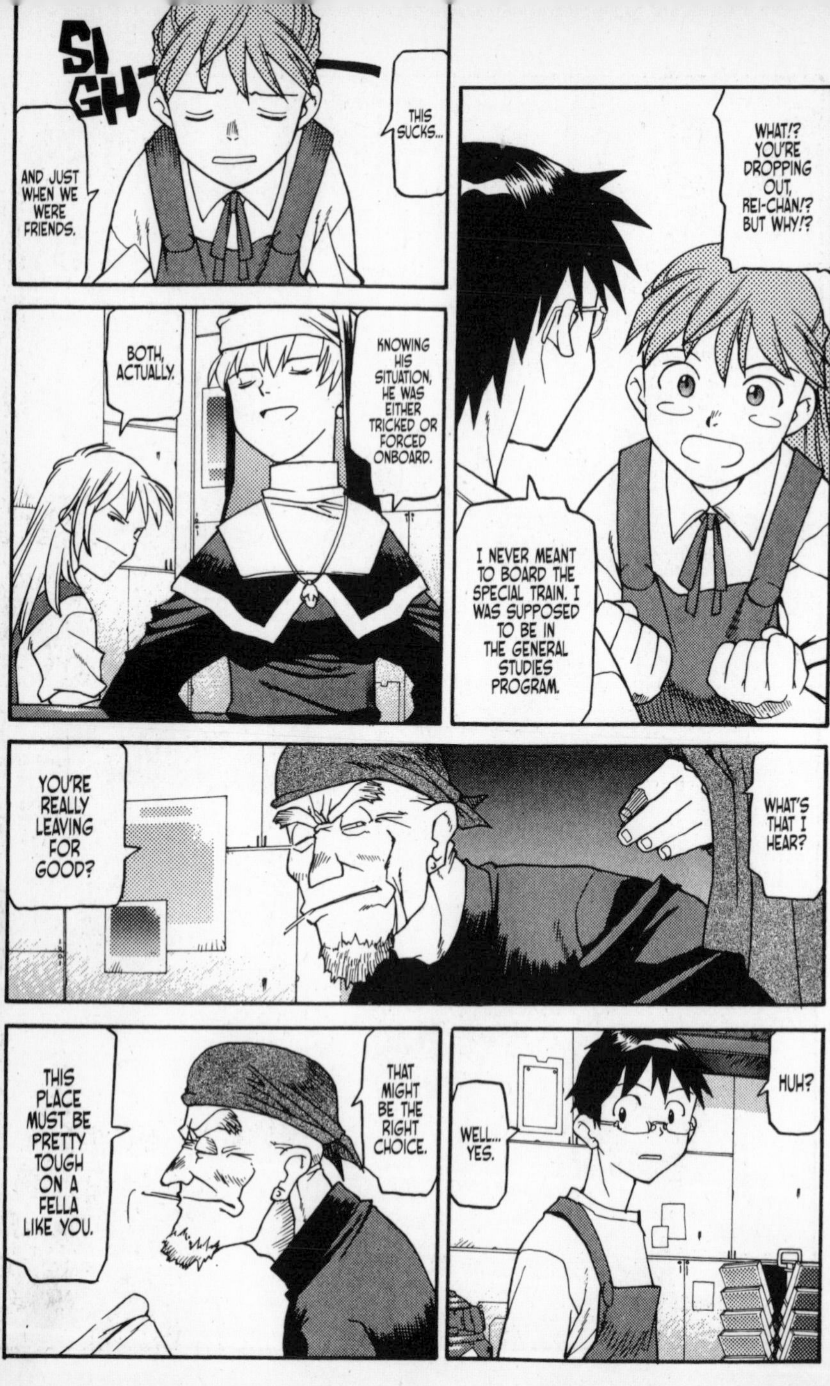
WHAT!? YOU'RE DROPPING OUT, REI-CHAN!? BUT WHY!?
I NEVER MEANT TO BOARD THE SPECIAL TRAIN. I WAS SUPPOSED TO BE IN THE GENERAL STUDIES PROGRAM.
THIS SUCKS...
SIGH-
AND JUST WHEN WE WERE FRIENDS.
KNOWING HIS SITUATION, HE WAS EITHER TRICKED OR FORCED ONBOARD.
BOTH, ACTUALLY.
WHAT'S THAT I HEAR?
YOU'RE REALLY LEAVING FOR GOOD?
HUH?
WELL... YES.
THAT MIGHT BE THE RIGHT CHOICE.
THIS PLACE MUST BE PRETTY TOUGH ON A FELLA LIKE YOU.

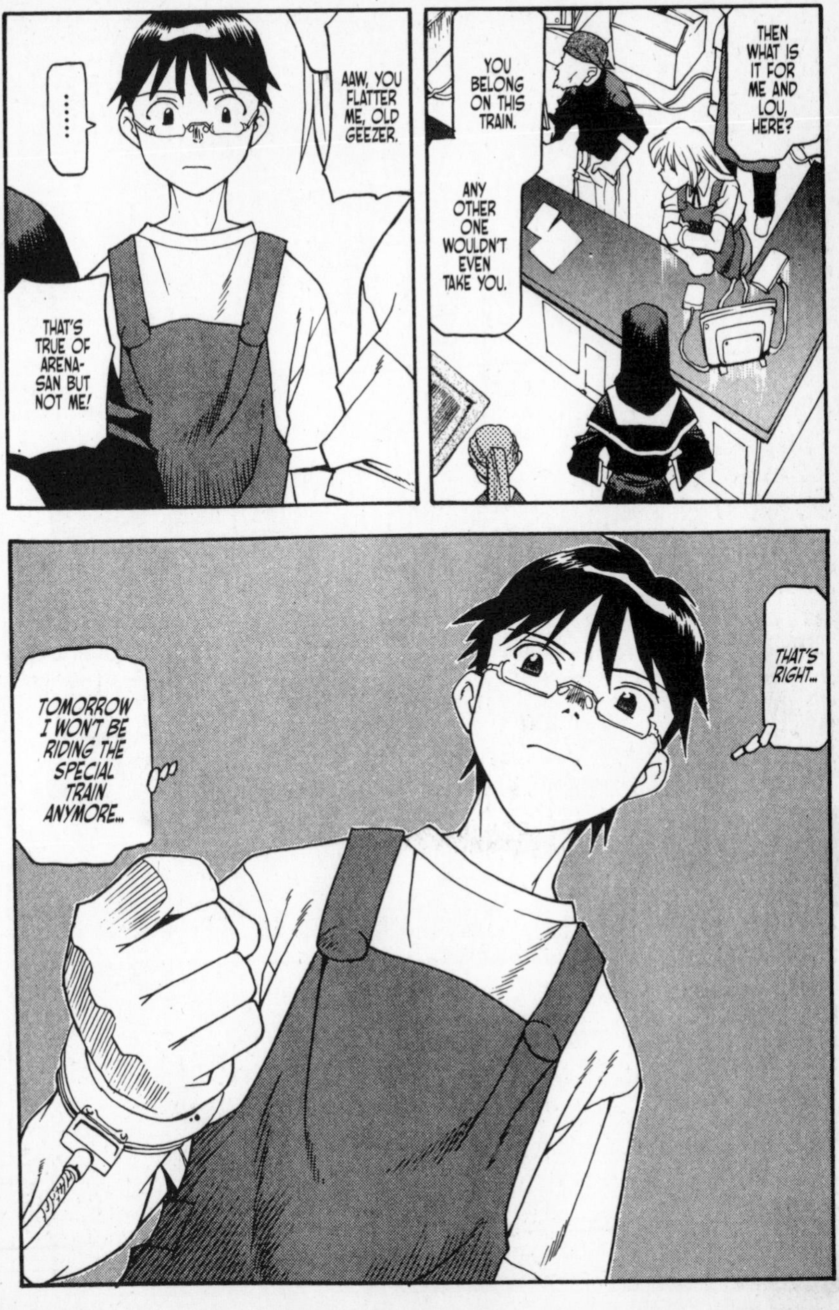
THEN WHAT IS IT FOR ME AND LOU, HERE?
YOU BELONG ON THIS TRAIN.
ANY OTHER ONE WOULDN'T EVEN TAKE YOU.
AAW, YOU FLATTER ME, OLD GEEZER.
......
THAT'S TRUE OF ARENA-SAN BUT NOT ME!
THAT'S RIGHT...
TOMORROW I WON'T BE RIDING THE SPECIAL TRAIN ANYMORE...

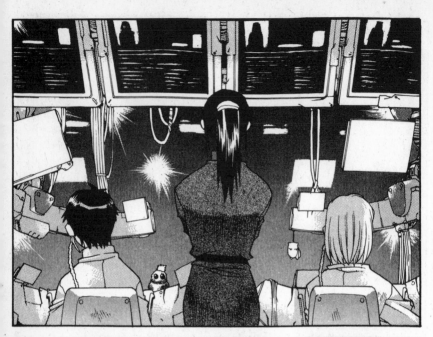

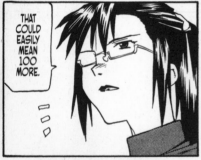

THAT COULD EASILY MEAN 100 MORE.

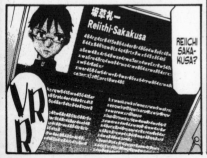

坂割礼一
Reiichi-Sakakusa

484rg4sr84t5s864s4er8r486odw8o6c48n
844x846tqw8tz4q4drtx8w×645s86445
a86w48r4r548waadrwa3erx4wed×r8w545t
xwa8rd8rqd4we84rwe4rrwe84rrwa84rr
xw84r84er
Xwar4584er4r w4r4rw4r86w46rw864trw48

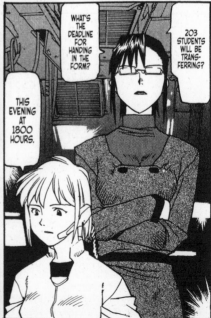

WHAT'S THE DEADLINE FOR HANDING IN THE FORM?

203 STUDENTS WILL BE TRANS-FERRING?

THIS EVENING AT 1800 HOURS.

REIICHI SAKA-KUSA?

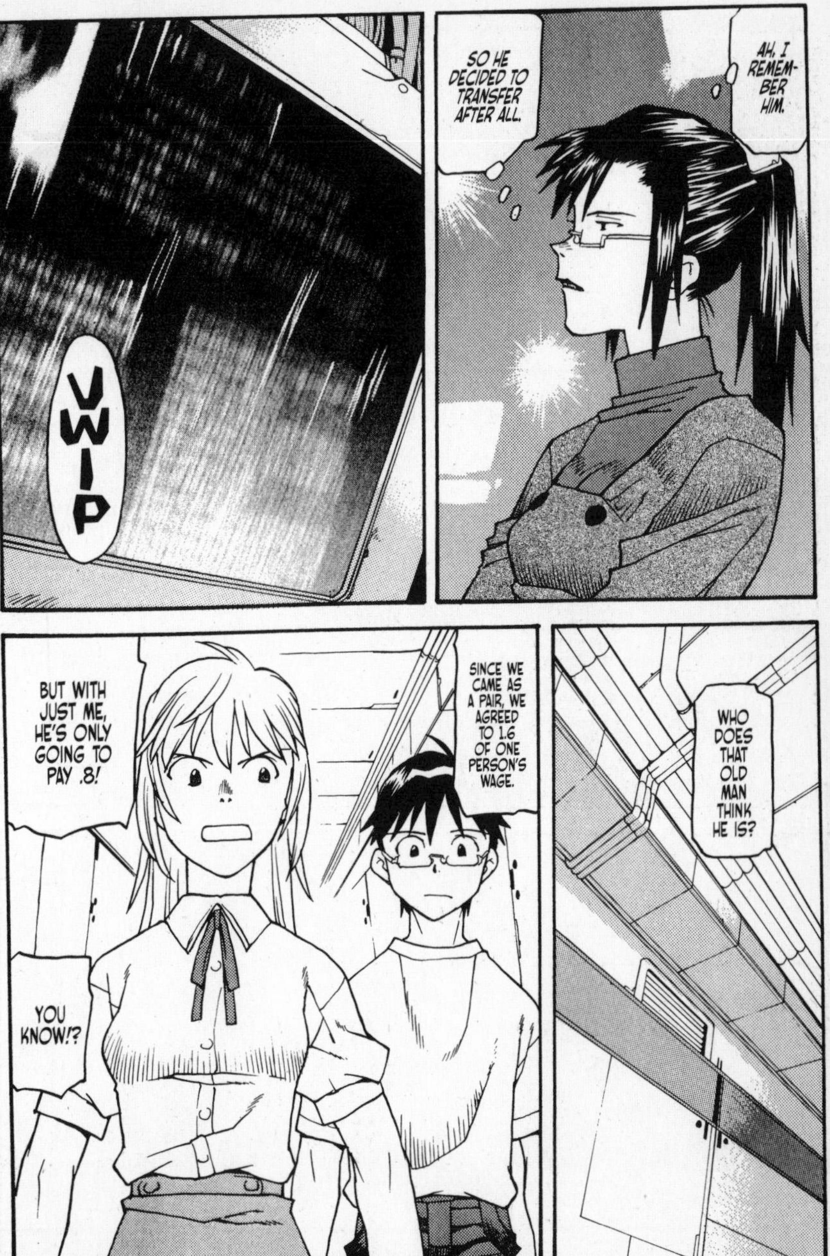
AH, I REMEMBER HIM.
SO HE DECIDED TO TRANSFER AFTER ALL.
VWIP
WHO DOES THAT OLD MAN THINK HE IS?
SINCE WE CAME AS A PAIR, WE AGREED TO 1.6 OF ONE PERSON'S WAGE.
BUT WITH JUST ME, HE'S ONLY GOING TO PAY .8!
YOU KNOW!?

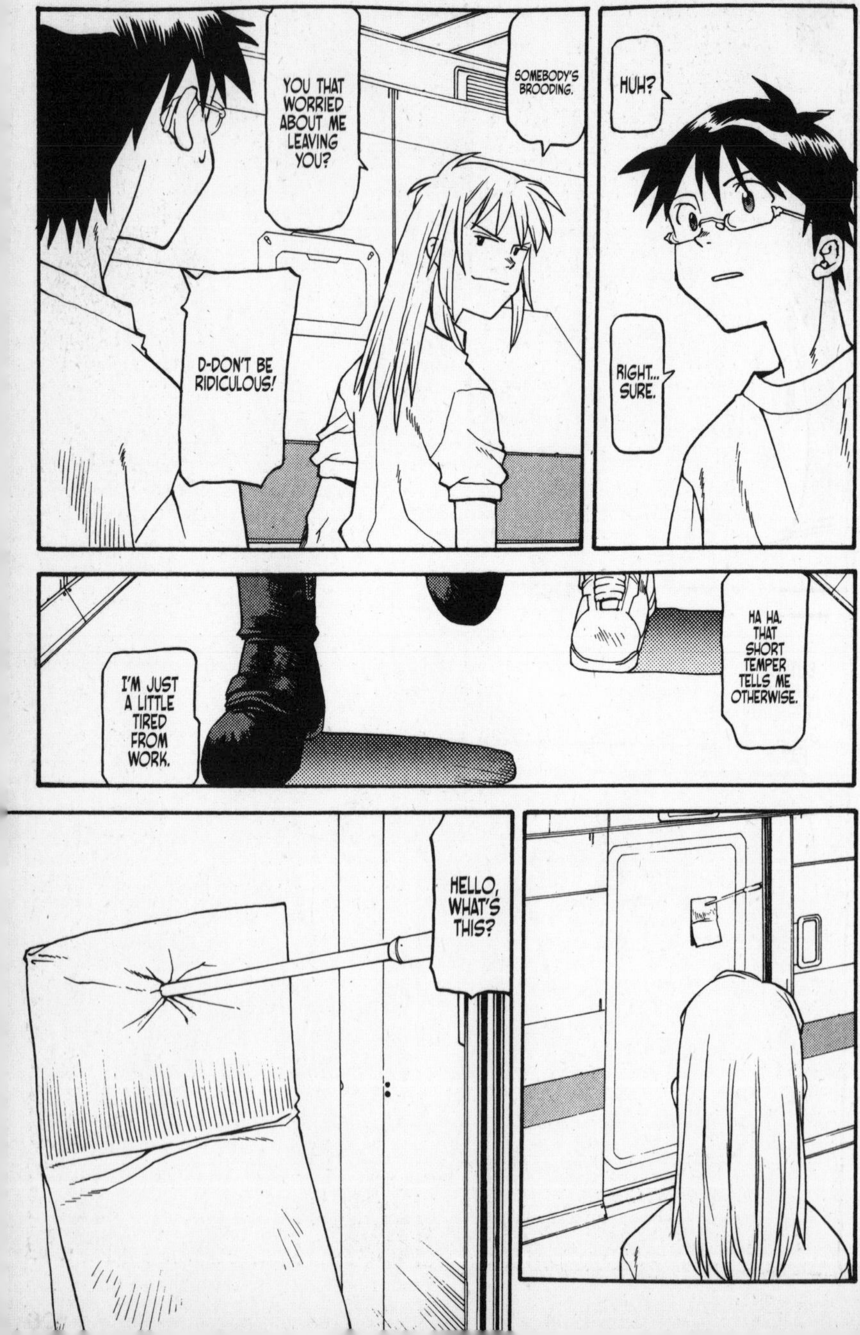
HUH?
RIGHT... SURE.
SOMEBODY'S BROODING.
YOU THAT WORRIED ABOUT ME LEAVING YOU?
D-DON'T BE RIDICULOUS!
HA HA. THAT SHORT TEMPER TELLS ME OTHERWISE.
I'M JUST A LITTLE TIRED FROM WORK.
HELLO, WHAT'S THIS?

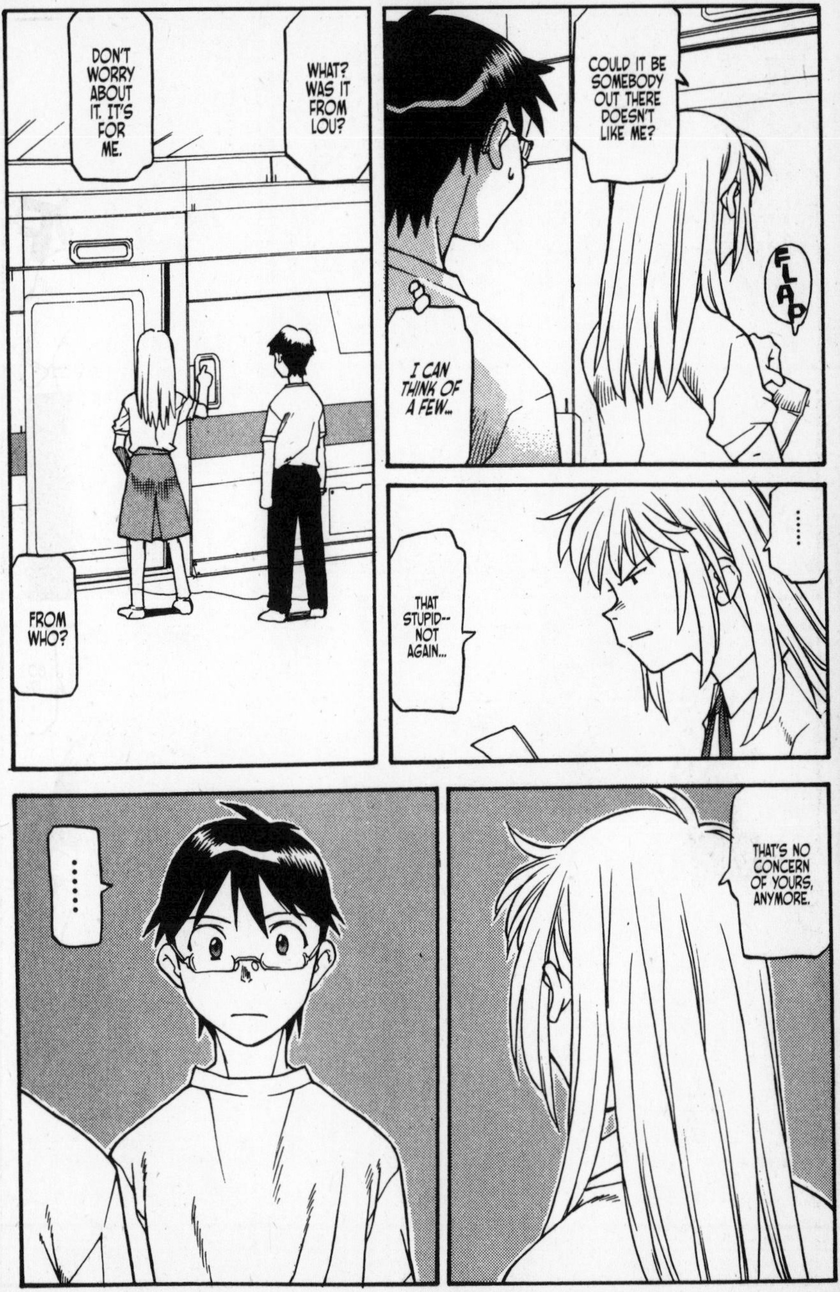
COULD IT BE SOMEBODY OUT THERE DOESN'T LIKE ME?
FLAP
I CAN THINK OF A FEW...
......
THAT STUPID-- NOT AGAIN...
WHAT? WAS IT FROM LOU?
DON'T WORRY ABOUT IT. IT'S FOR ME.
FROM WHO?
THAT'S NO CONCERN OF YOURS, ANYMORE.
......

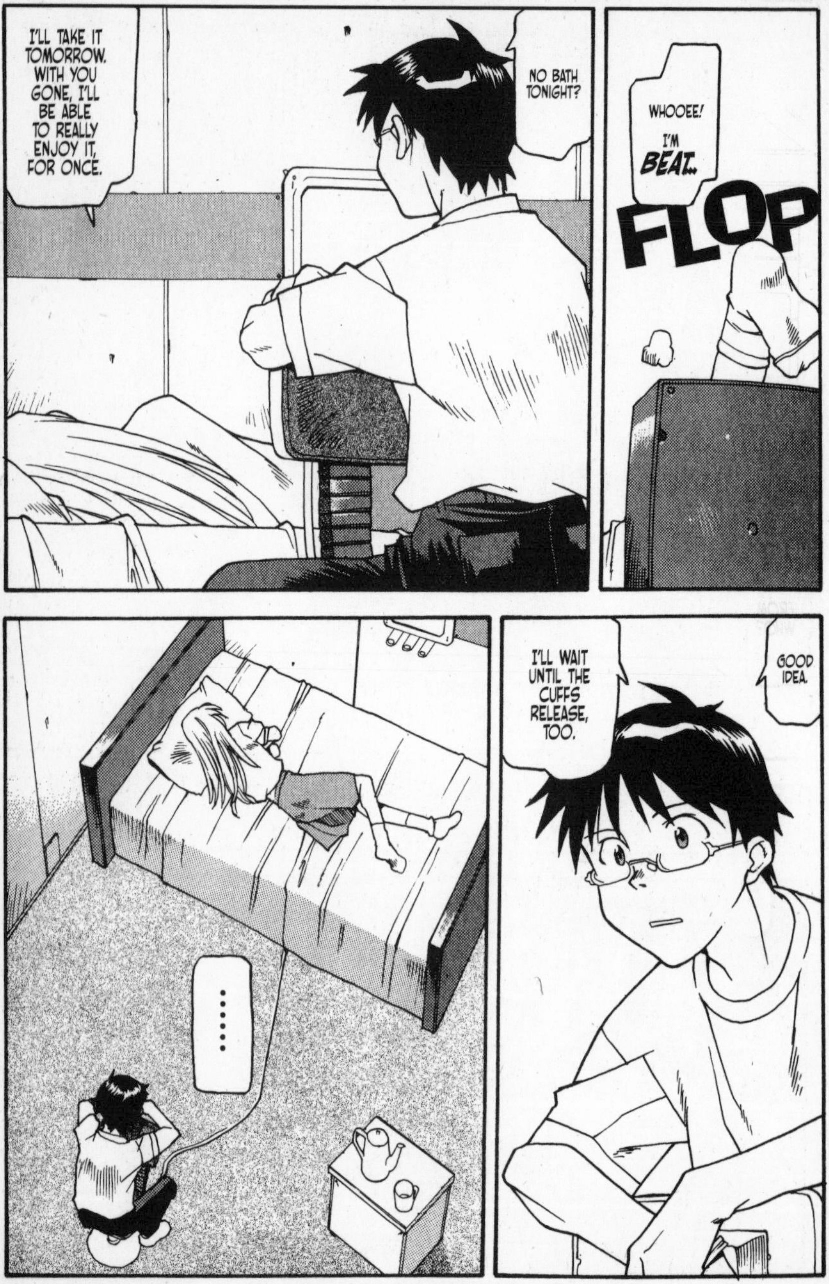
WHOOEE! I'M BEAT...
FLOP
NO BATH TONIGHT?
I'LL TAKE IT TOMORROW. WITH YOU GONE, I'LL BE ABLE TO REALLY ENJOY IT, FOR ONCE.
GOOD IDEA.
I'LL WAIT UNTIL THE CUFFS RELEASE, TOO.
......

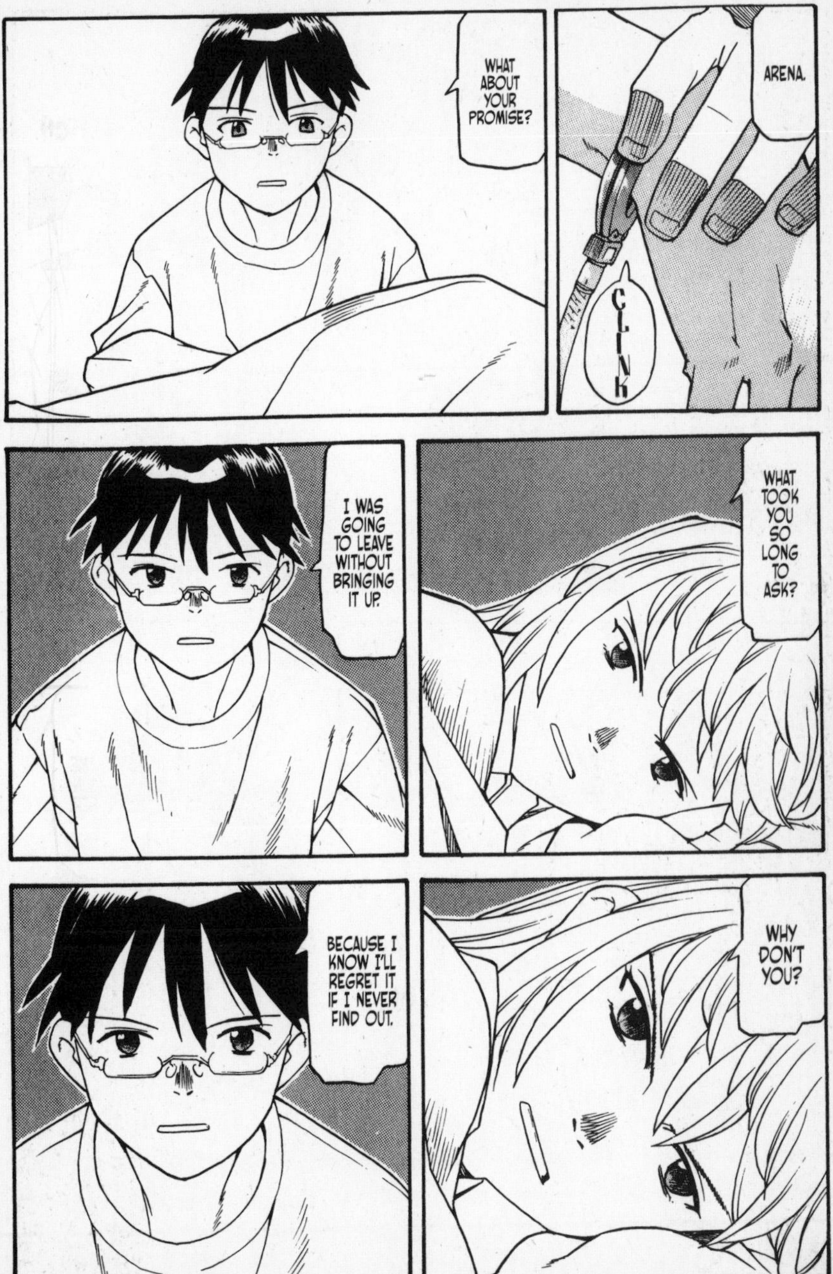
ARENA.
CLINK
WHAT ABOUT YOUR PROMISE?
WHAT TOOK YOU SO LONG TO ASK?
I WAS GOING TO LEAVE WITHOUT BRINGING IT UP.
WHY DON'T YOU?
BECAUSE I KNOW I'LL REGRET IT IF I NEVER FIND OUT.

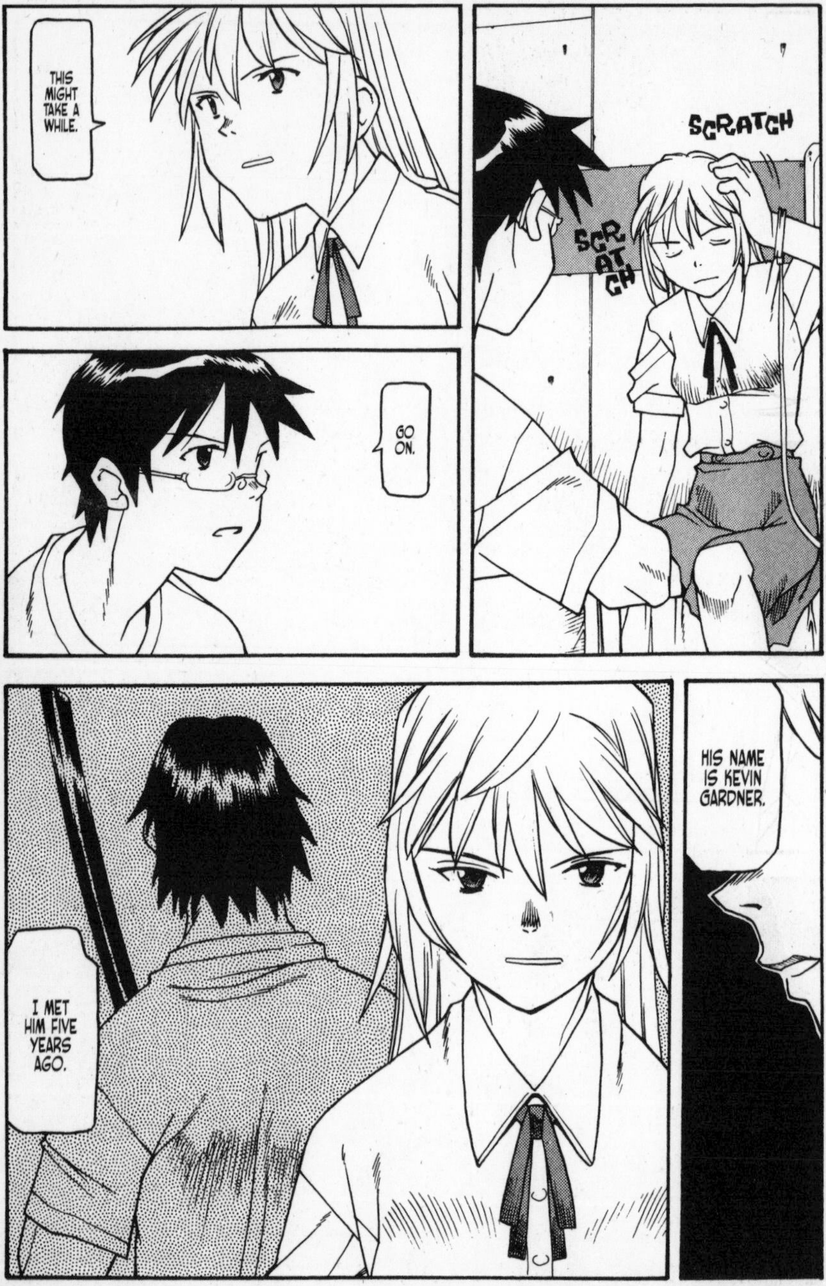
SCRATCH
SCRATCH
THIS MIGHT TAKE A WHILE.
GO ON.
HIS NAME IS KEVIN GARDNER.
I MET HIM FIVE YEARS AGO.

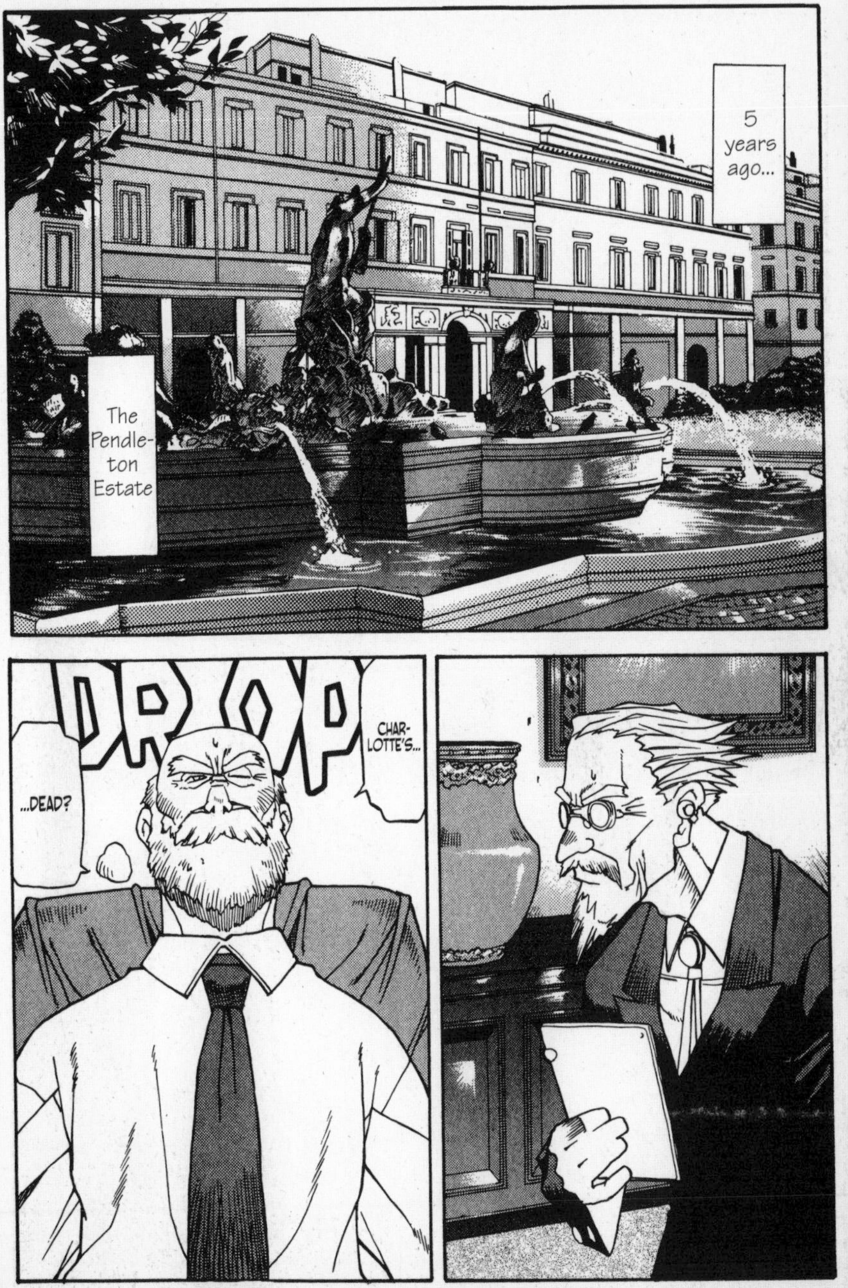
5 years ago...
The Pendleton Estate
CHARLOTTE'S...
DROP
...DEAD?

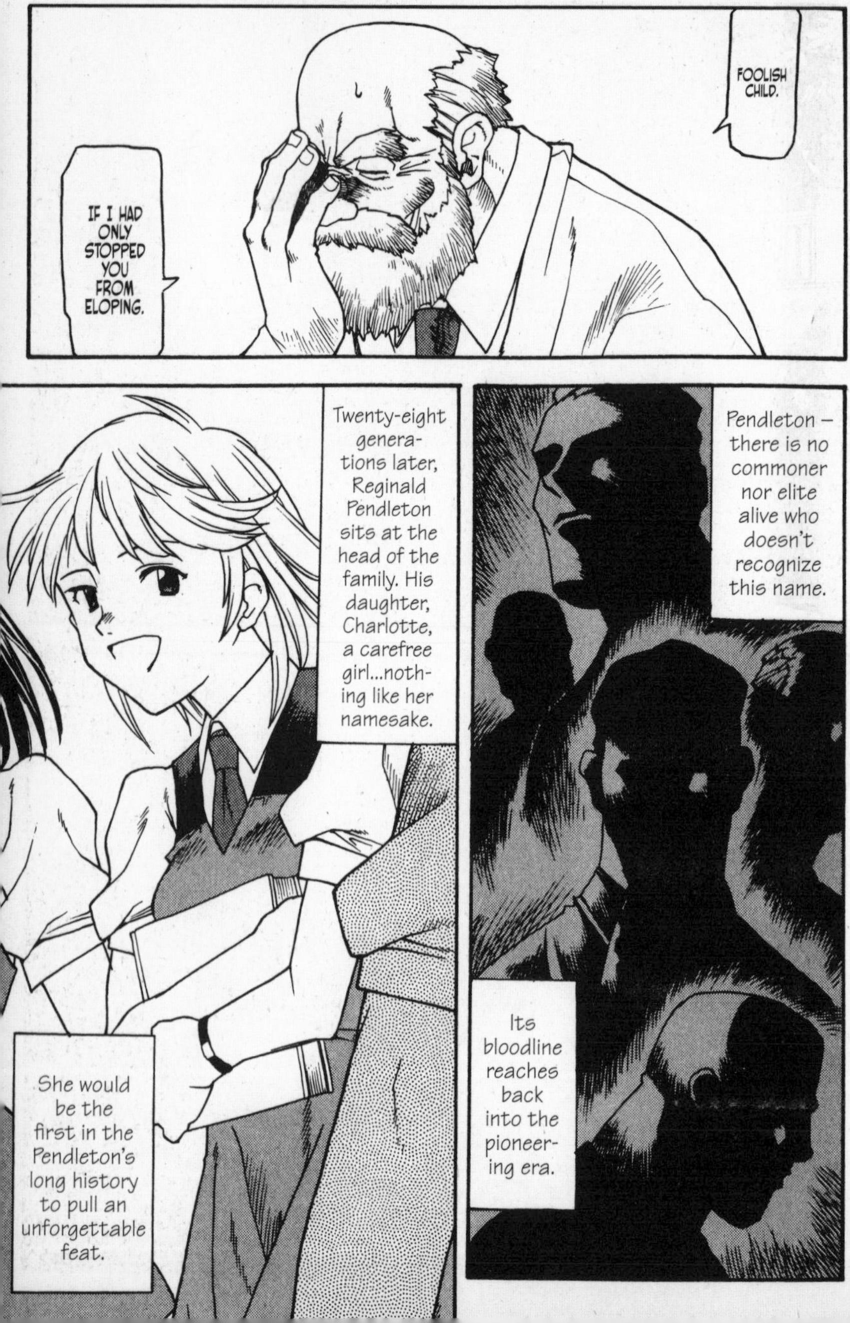
FOOLISH CHILD.
IF I HAD ONLY STOPPED YOU FROM ELOPING.
Pendleton – there is no commoner nor elite alive who doesn't recognize this name.
Its bloodline reaches back into the pioneering era.
Twenty-eight generations later, Reginald Pendleton sits at the head of the family. His daughter, Charlotte, a carefree girl...nothing like her namesake.
She would be the first in the Pendleton's long history to pull an unforgettable feat.

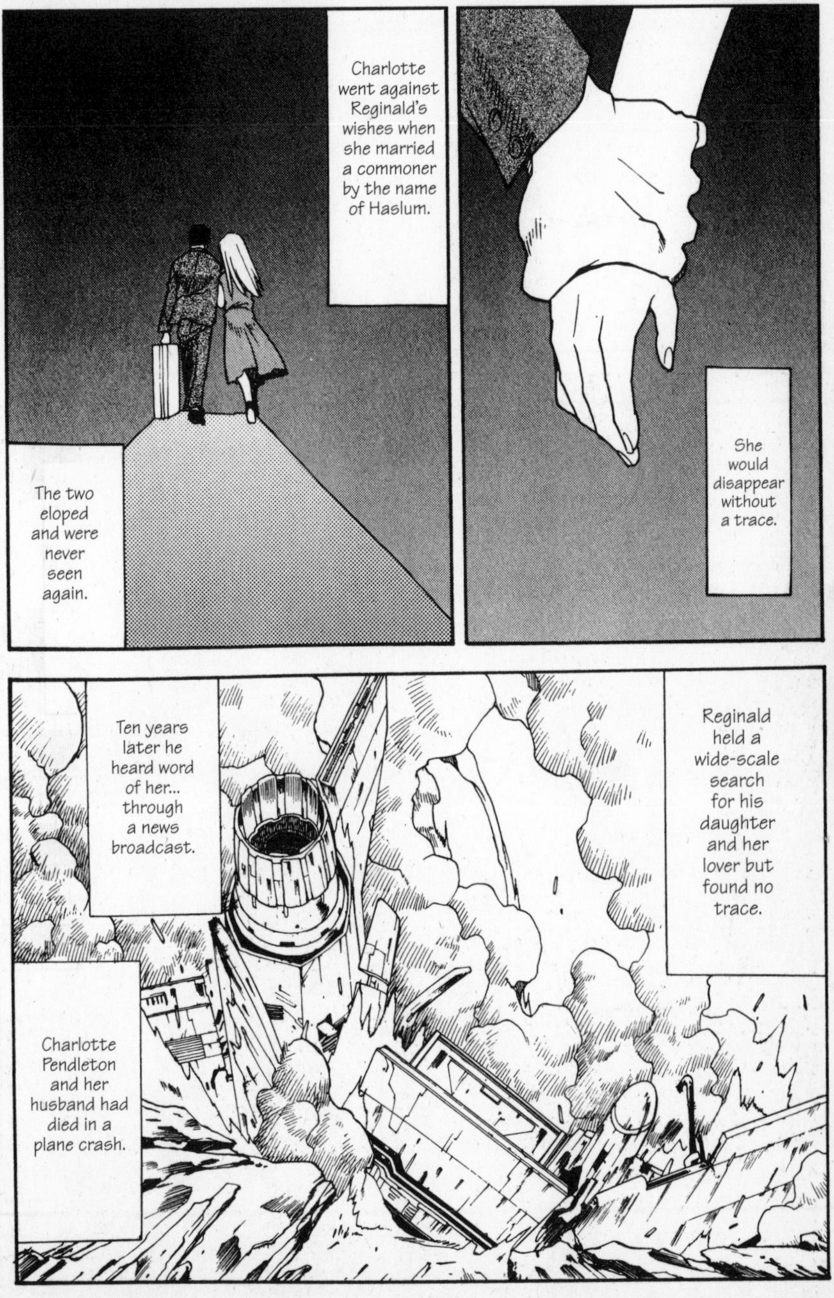
She would disappear without a trace.
Charlotte went against Reginald's wishes when she married a commoner by the name of Haslum.
The two eloped and were never seen again.
Reginald held a wide-scale search for his daughter and her lover but found no trace.
Ten years later he heard word of her... through a news broadcast.
Charlotte Pendleton and her husband had died in a plane crash.

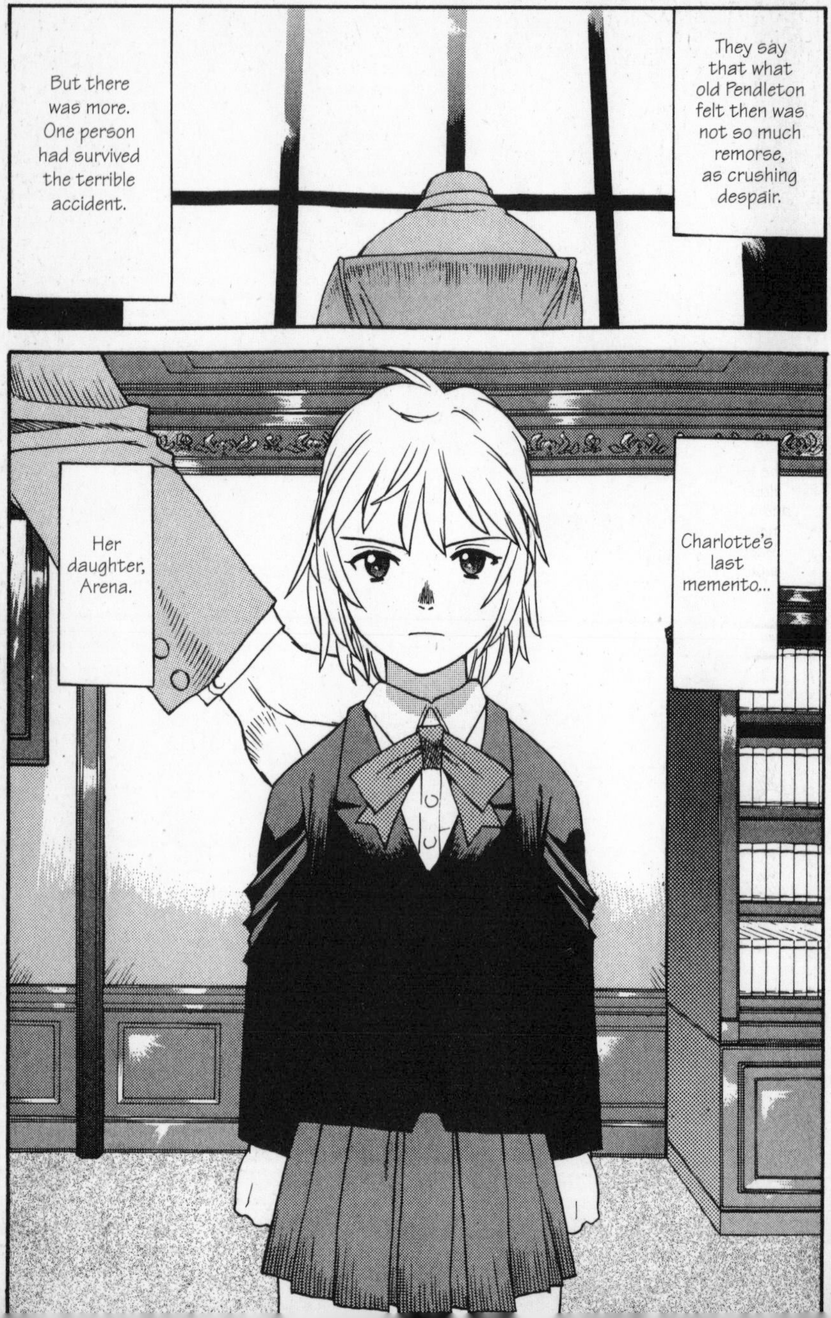
They say that what old Pendleton felt then was not so much remorse, as crushing despair.
But there was more. One person had survived the terrible accident.
Charlotte's last memento...
Her daughter, Arena.

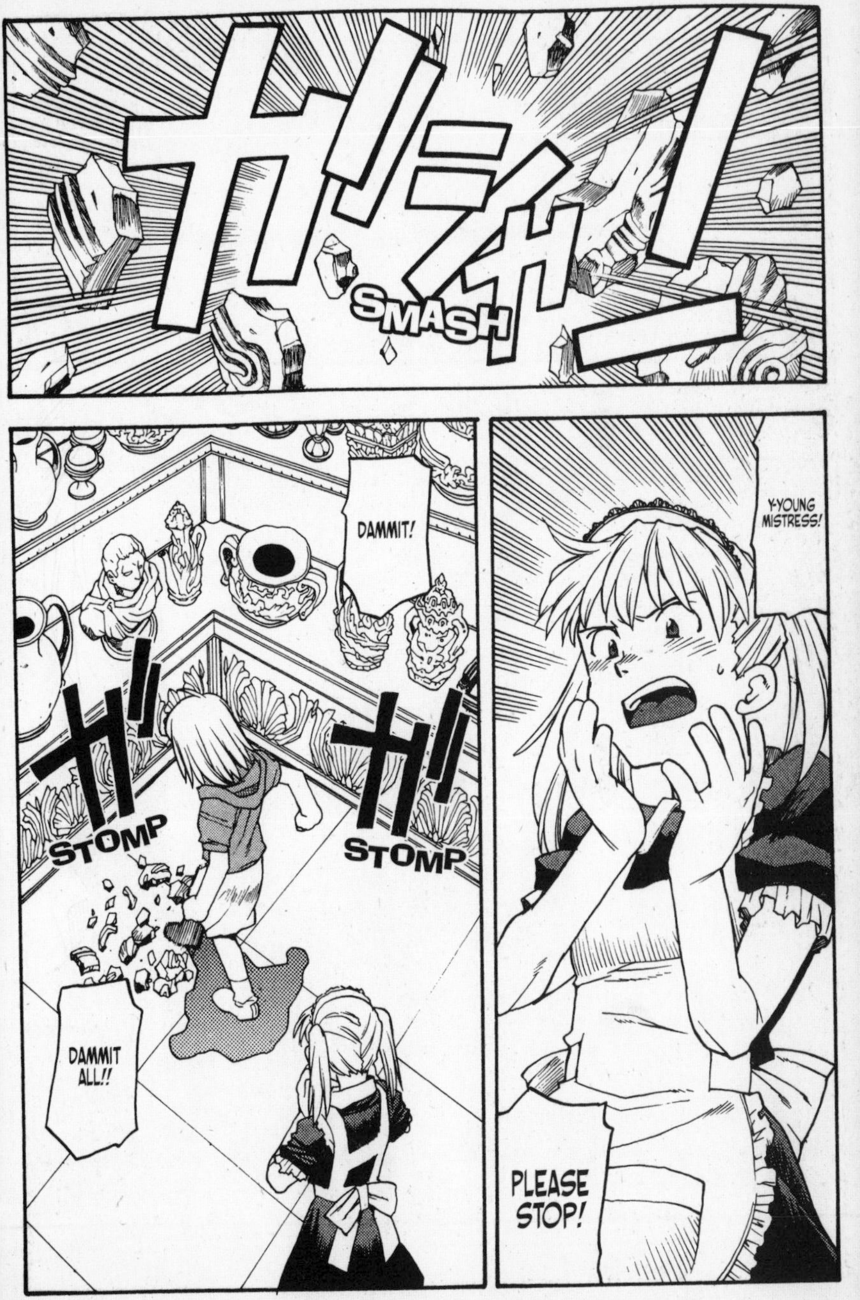
SMASH
Y-YOUNG MISTRESS!
PLEASE STOP!
DAMMIT!
STOMP
STOMP
DAMMIT ALL!!

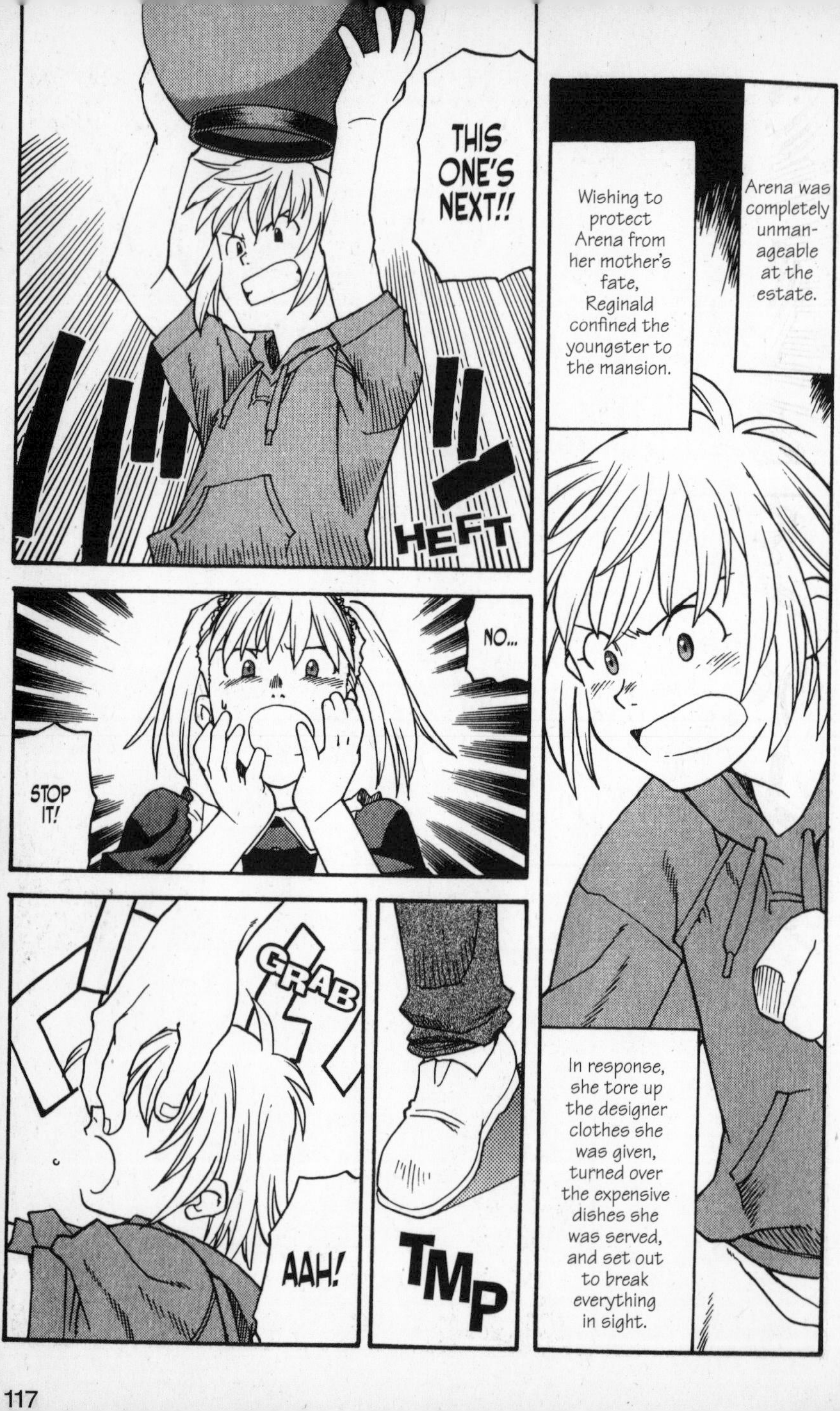

Arena was completely unman-ageable at the estate.
Wishing to protect Arena from her mother's fate, Reginald confined the youngster to the mansion.
In response, she tore up the designer clothes she was given, turned over the expensive dishes she was served, and set out to break everything in sight.
THIS ONE'S NEXT!!
HEFT
NO...
STOP IT!
TMP
GRAB
AAH!

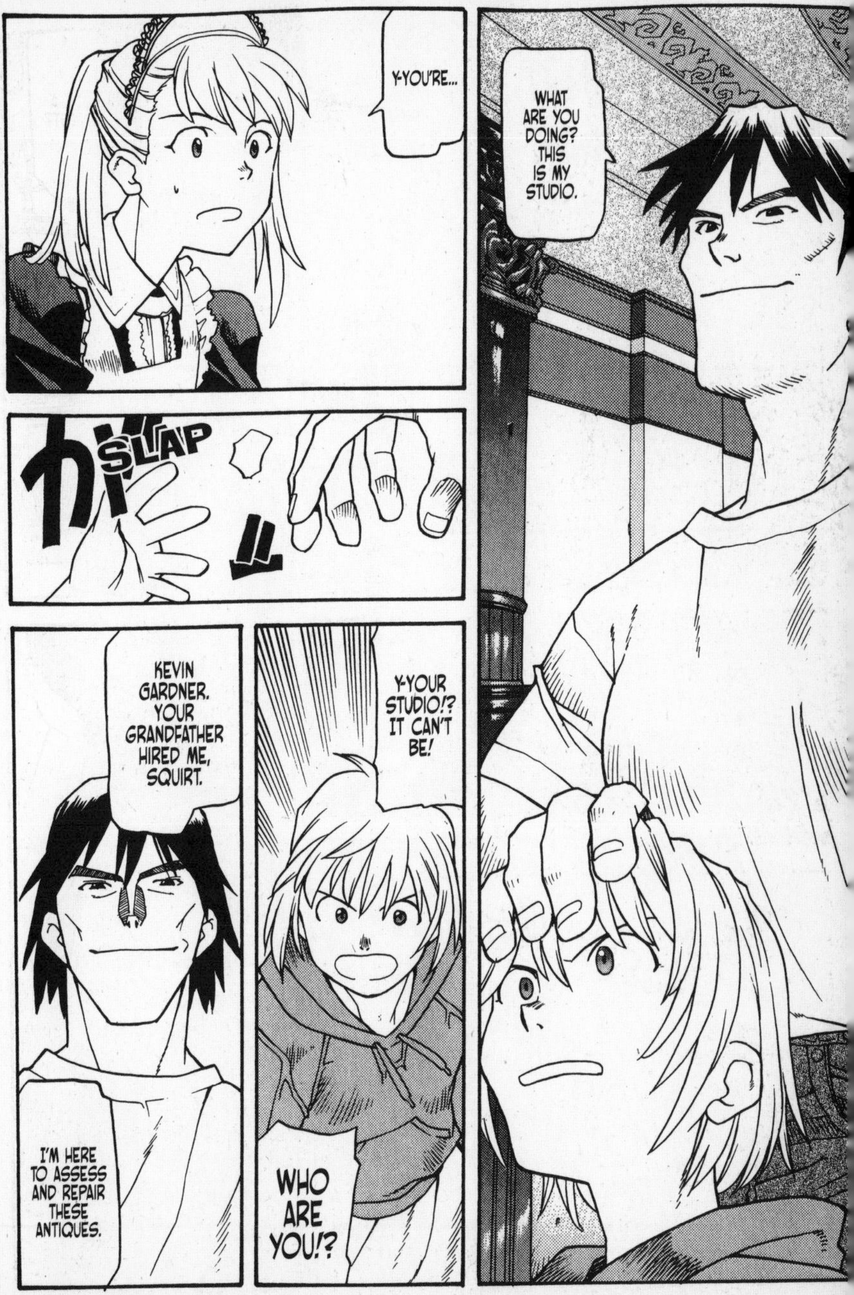
WHAT ARE YOU DOING? THIS IS MY STUDIO.
Y-YOU'RE...
SLAP
Y-YOUR STUDIO!? IT CAN'T BE!
WHO ARE YOU!?
KEVIN GARDNER. YOUR GRANDFATHER HIRED ME, SQUIRT.
I'M HERE TO ASSESS AND REPAIR THESE ANTIQUES.

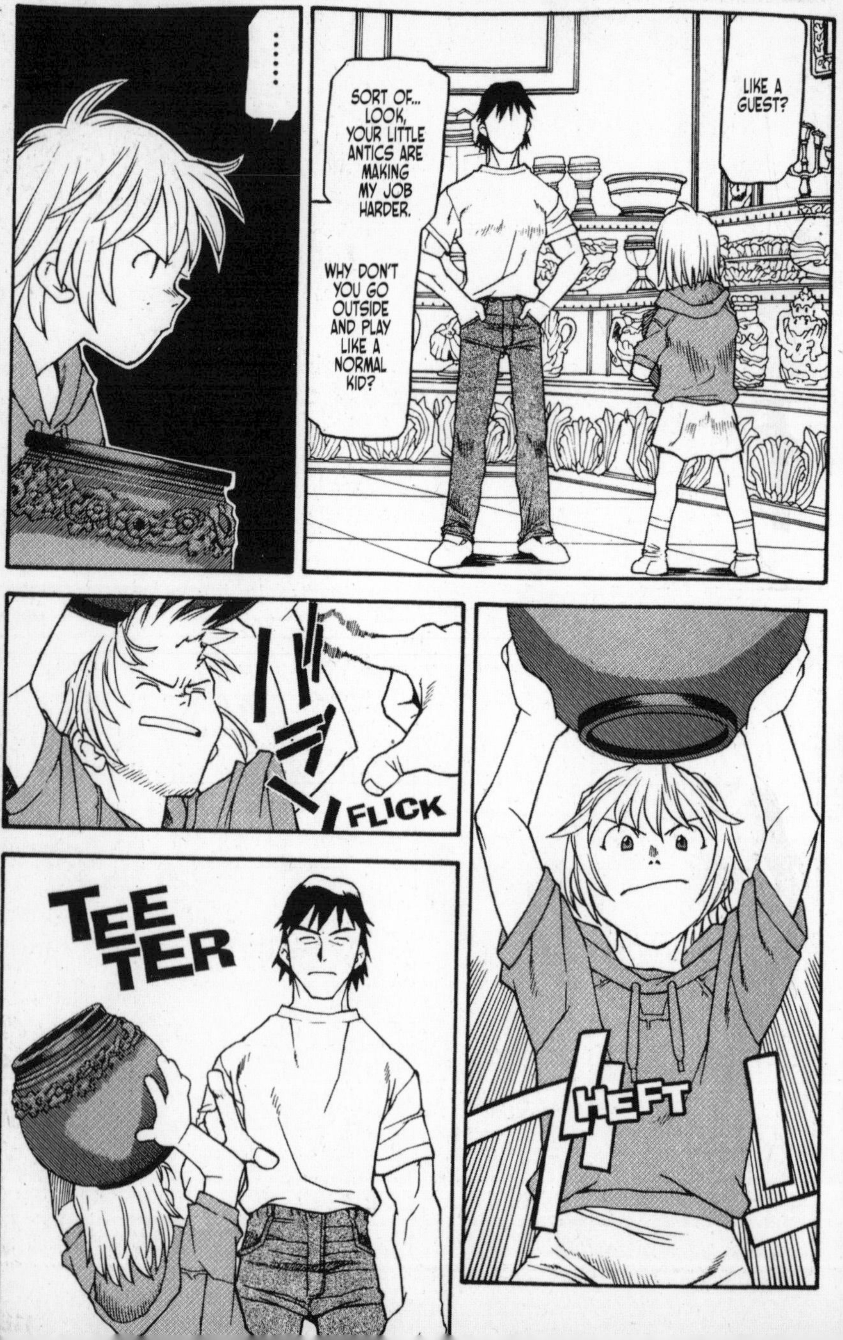
LIKE A GUEST?
SORT OF... LOOK, YOUR LITTLE ANTICS ARE MAKING MY JOB HARDER.
WHY DON'T YOU GO OUTSIDE AND PLAY LIKE A NORMAL KID?
......
HEFT
FLICK
TEETER

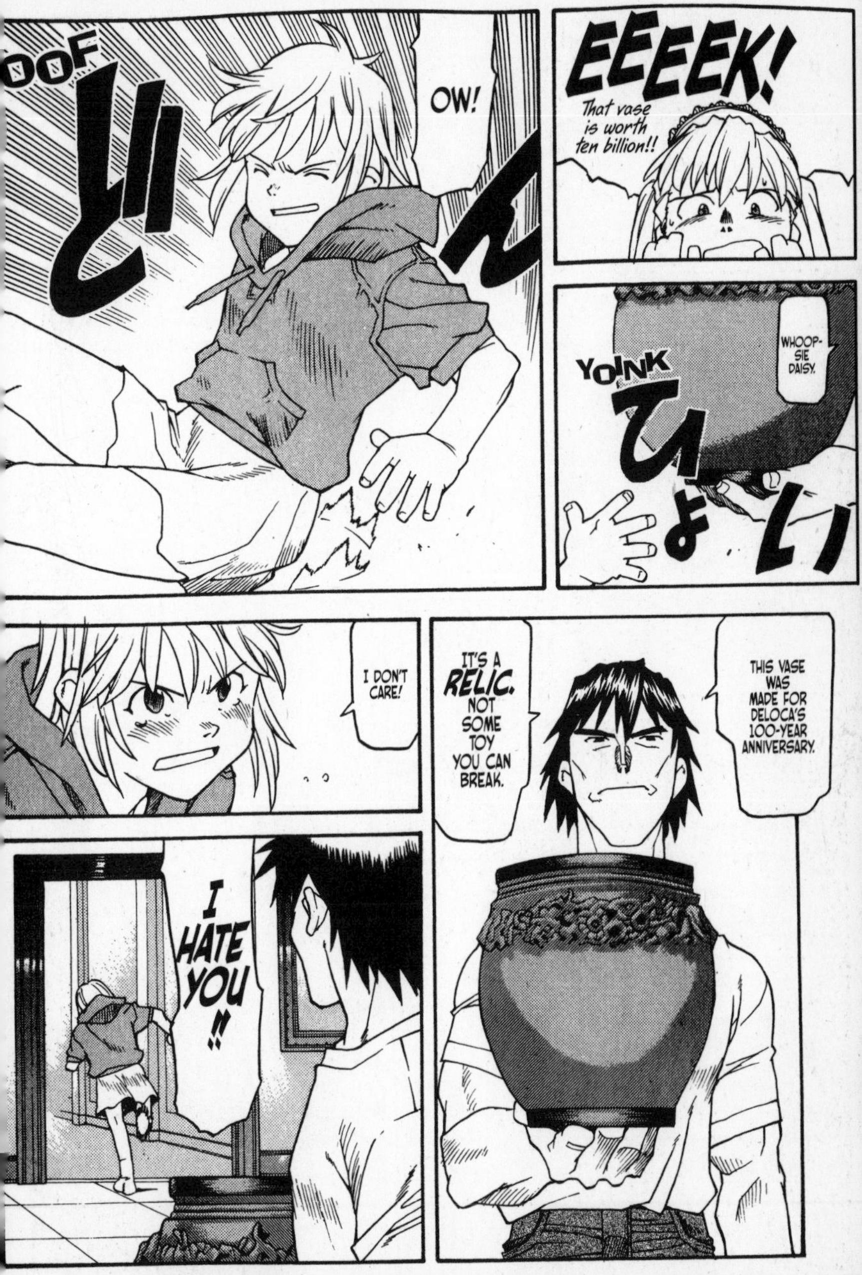
EEEEK!
That vase is worth ten billion!!
YOINK
ひょい
WHOOP-SIE DAISY.
OW!
OOF
THIS VASE WAS MADE FOR DELOCA'S 100-YEAR ANNIVERSARY.
IT'S A RELIC. NOT SOME TOY YOU CAN BREAK.
I DON'T CARE!
I HATE YOU!!

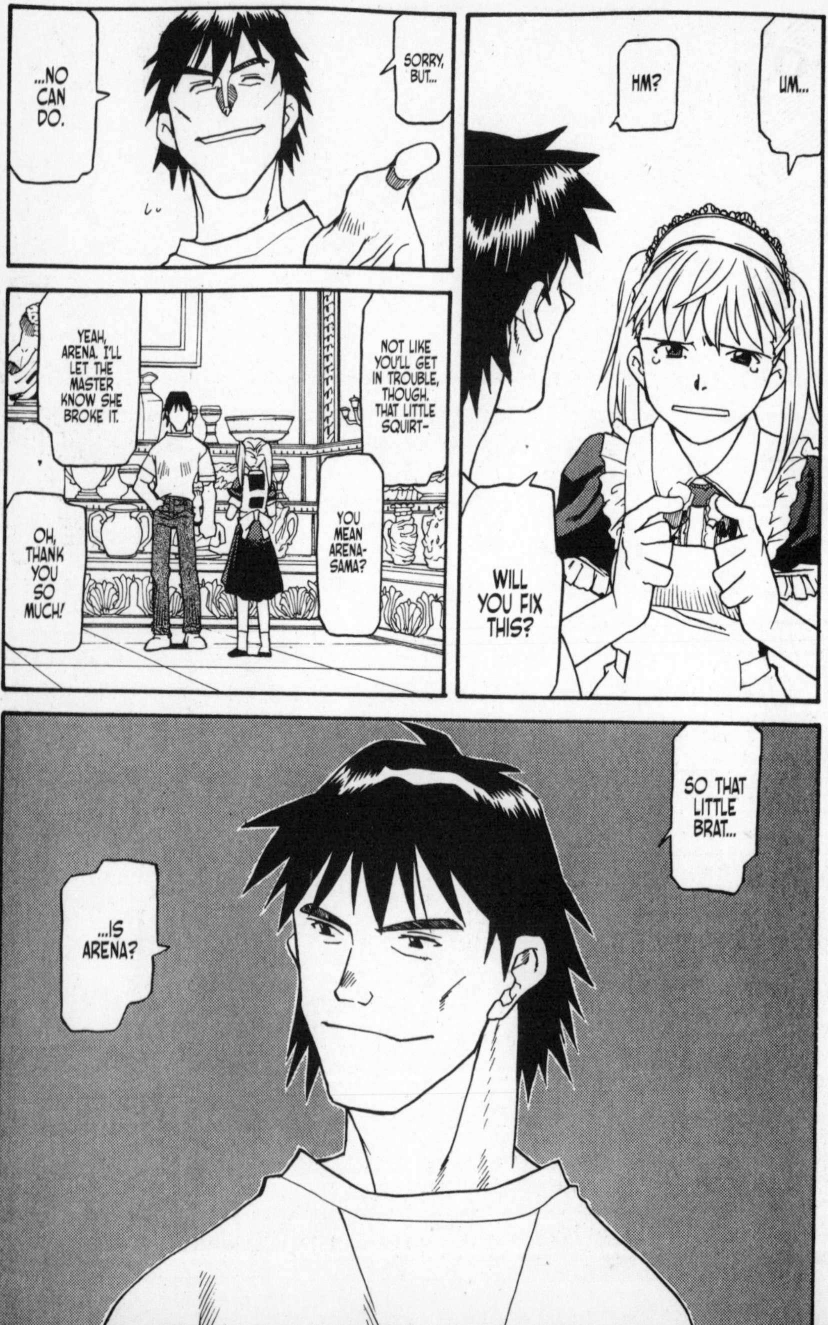
UM...
HM?
WILL YOU FIX THIS?
SORRY, BUT...
...NO CAN DO.
NOT LIKE YOU'LL GET IN TROUBLE, THOUGH. THAT LITTLE SQUIRT-
YOU MEAN ARENA-SAMA?
YEAH, ARENA. I'LL LET THE MASTER KNOW SHE BROKE IT.
OH, THANK YOU SO MUCH!
SO THAT LITTLE BRAT...
...IS ARENA?

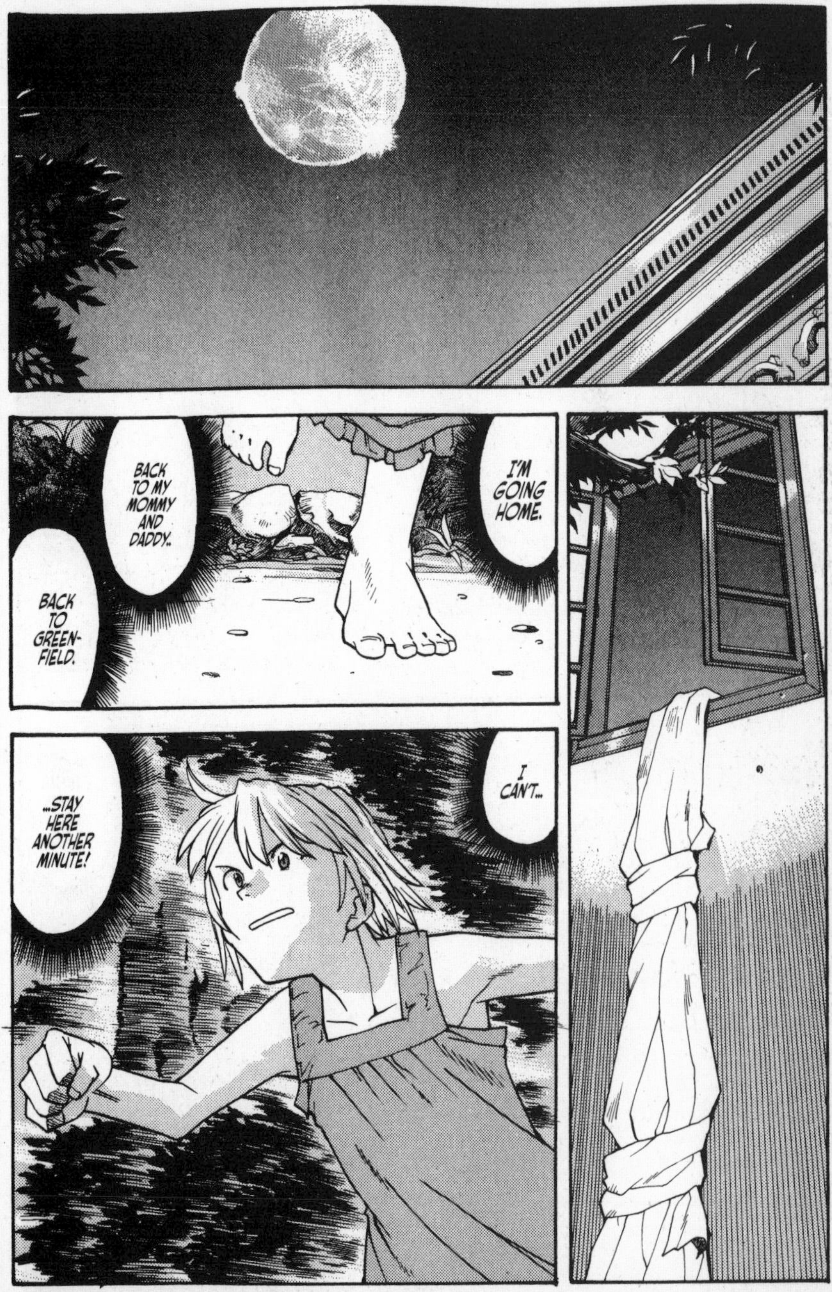
I'M GOING HOME.
BACK TO MY MOMMY AND DADDY..
BACK TO GREEN-FIELD.
I CAN'T...
...STAY HERE ANOTHER MINUTE!

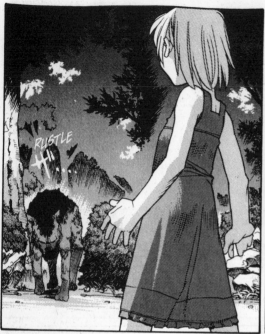

RUSTLE

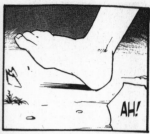

AH!

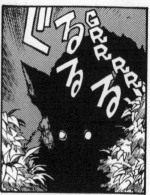

GRRRR

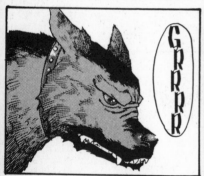

GRRRR

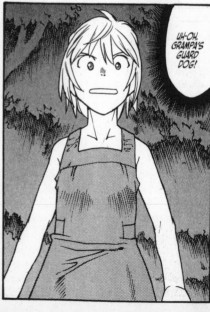

UH-OH. GRAMPA'S GUARD DOG!

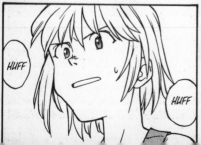

HUFF

HUFF

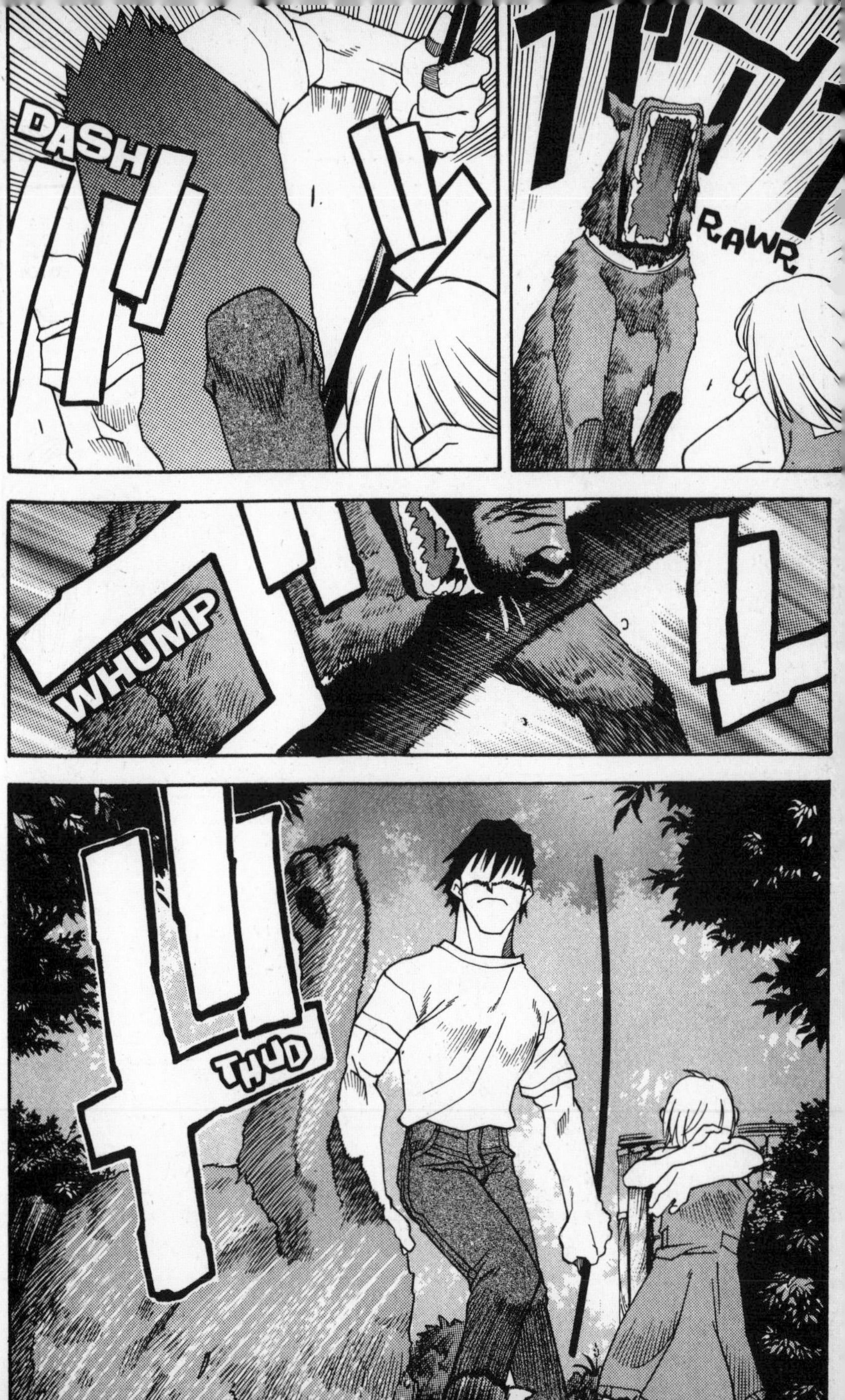
RAWR
DASH
WHUMP
THUD

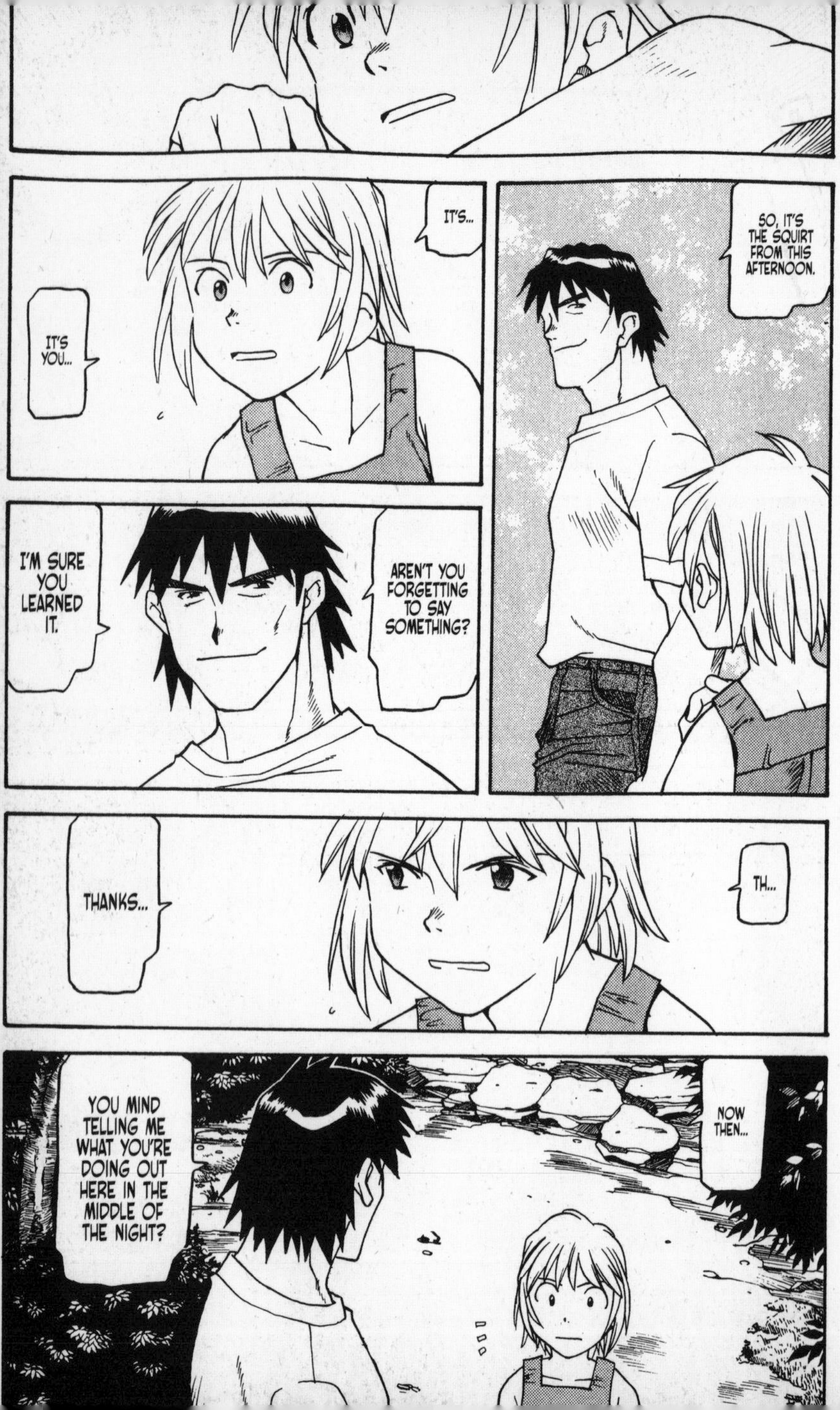
SO, IT'S THE SQUIRT FROM THIS AFTERNOON.
IT'S...
IT'S YOU...
AREN'T YOU FORGETTING TO SAY SOMETHING?
I'M SURE YOU LEARNED IT.
TH...
THANKS...
NOW THEN...
YOU MIND TELLING ME WHAT YOU'RE DOING OUT HERE IN THE MIDDLE OF THE NIGHT?

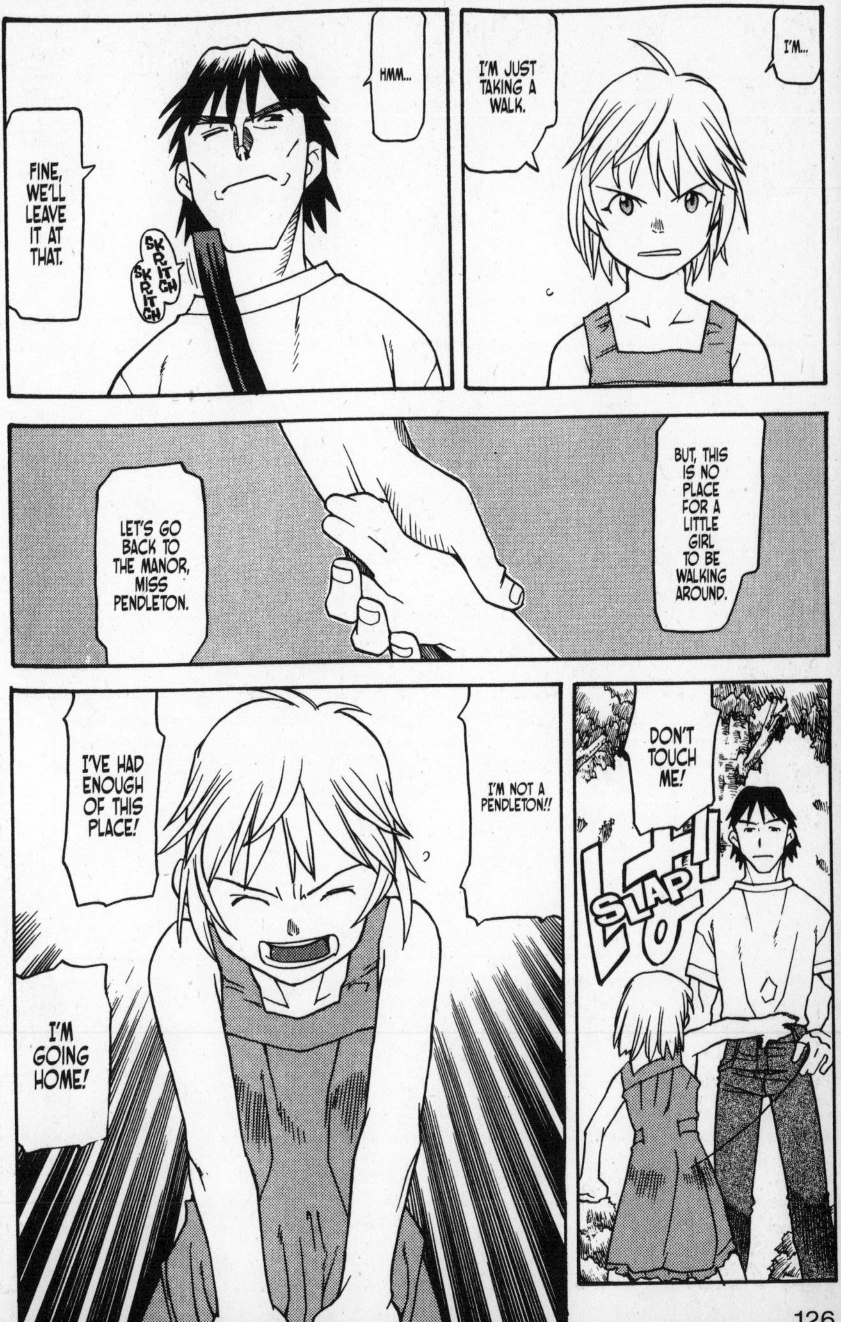
I'M...
I'M JUST TAKING A WALK.
HMM...
FINE, WE'LL LEAVE IT AT THAT.
SKRITCH SKRITCH
BUT, THIS IS NO PLACE FOR A LITTLE GIRL TO BE WALKING AROUND.
LET'S GO BACK TO THE MANOR, MISS PENDLETON.
DON'T TOUCH ME!
SLAP
I'M NOT A PENDLETON!!
I'VE HAD ENOUGH OF THIS PLACE!
I'M GOING HOME!

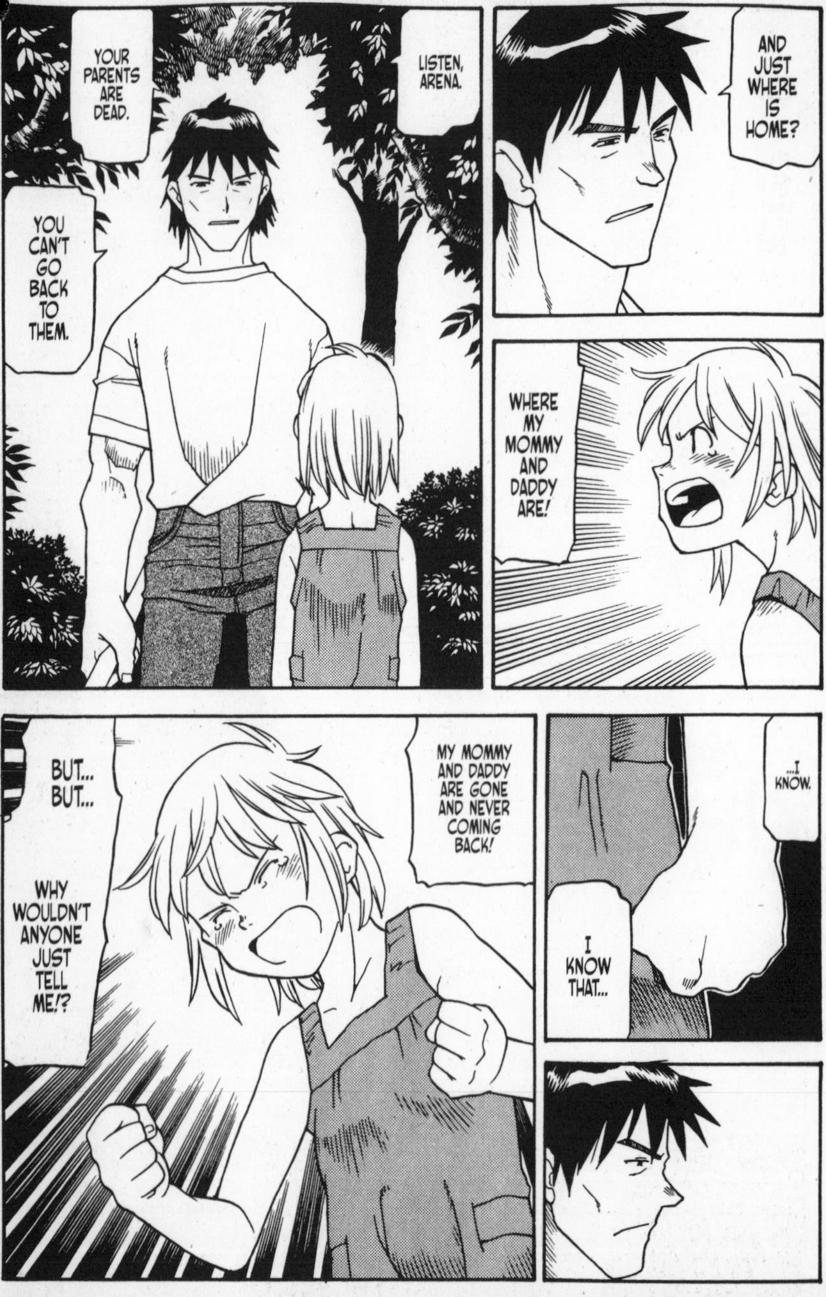
AND JUST WHERE IS HOME?
WHERE MY MOMMY AND DADDY ARE!
LISTEN, ARENA.
YOUR PARENTS ARE DEAD.
YOU CAN'T GO BACK TO THEM.
...I KNOW.
I KNOW THAT...
MY MOMMY AND DADDY ARE GONE AND NEVER COMING BACK!
BUT... BUT...
WHY WOULDN'T ANYONE JUST TELL ME!?

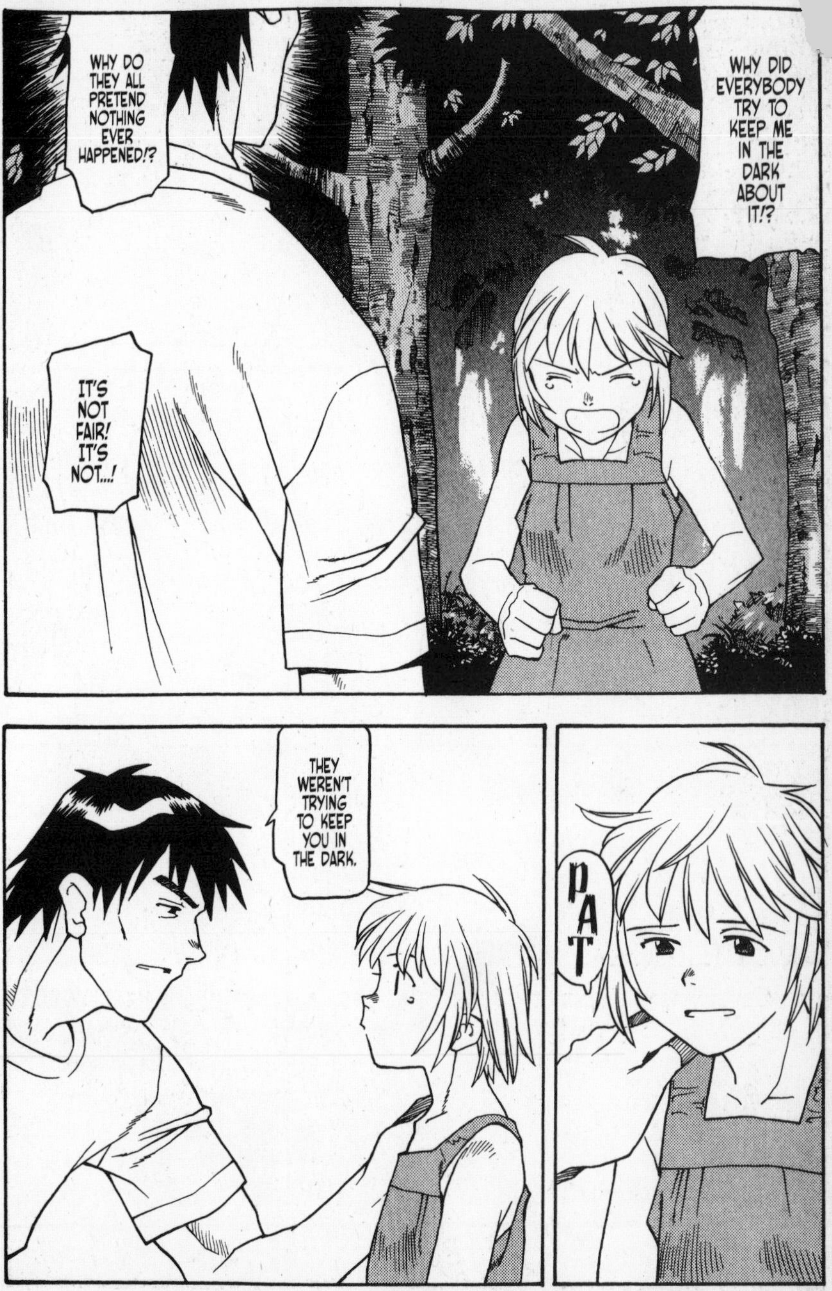
WHY DID EVERYBODY TRY TO KEEP ME IN THE DARK ABOUT IT!?
WHY DO THEY ALL PRETEND NOTHING EVER HAPPENED!?
IT'S NOT FAIR! IT'S NOT...!
PAT
THEY WEREN'T TRYING TO KEEP YOU IN THE DARK.

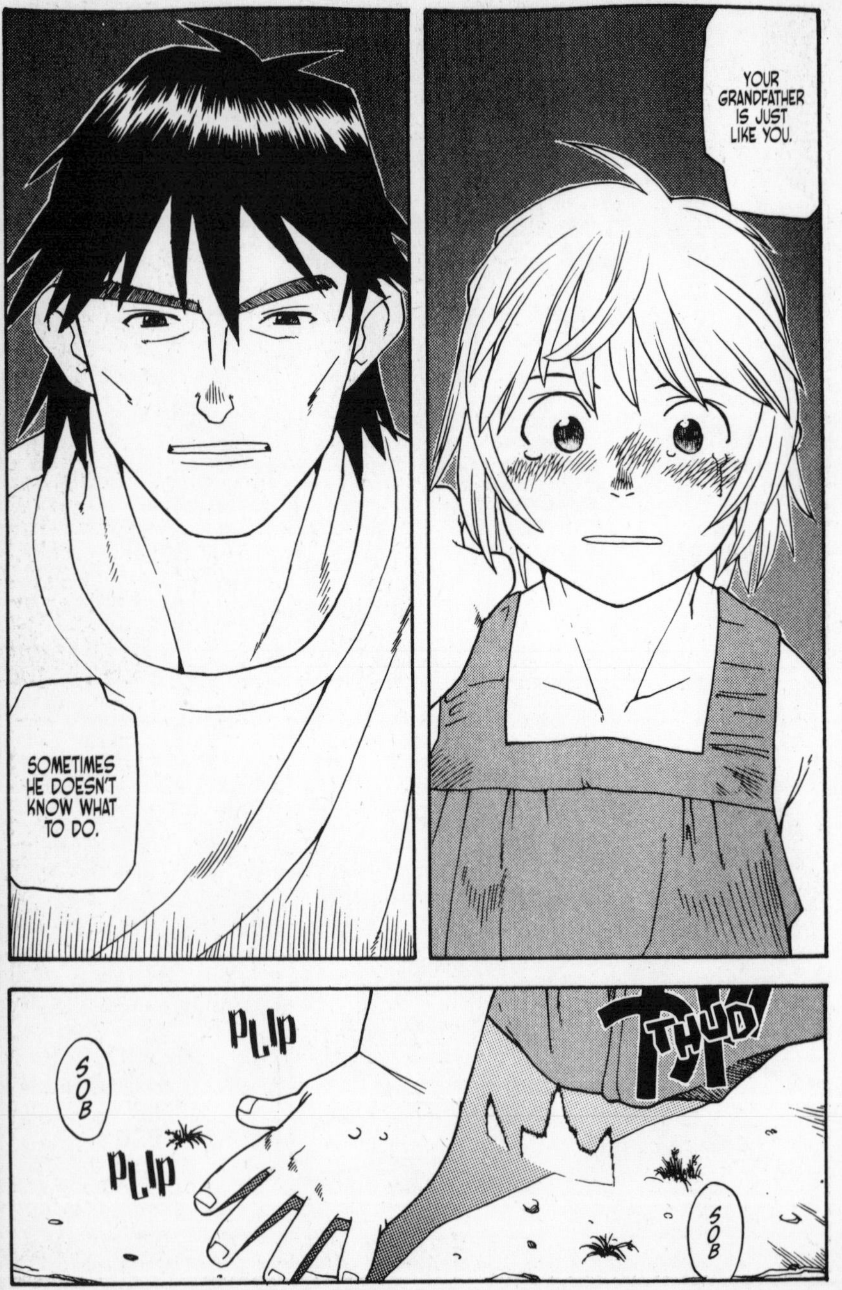
YOUR GRANDFATHER IS JUST LIKE YOU.
SOMETIMES HE DOESN'T KNOW WHAT TO DO.
THUD
SOB
PLIP
SOB
PLIP

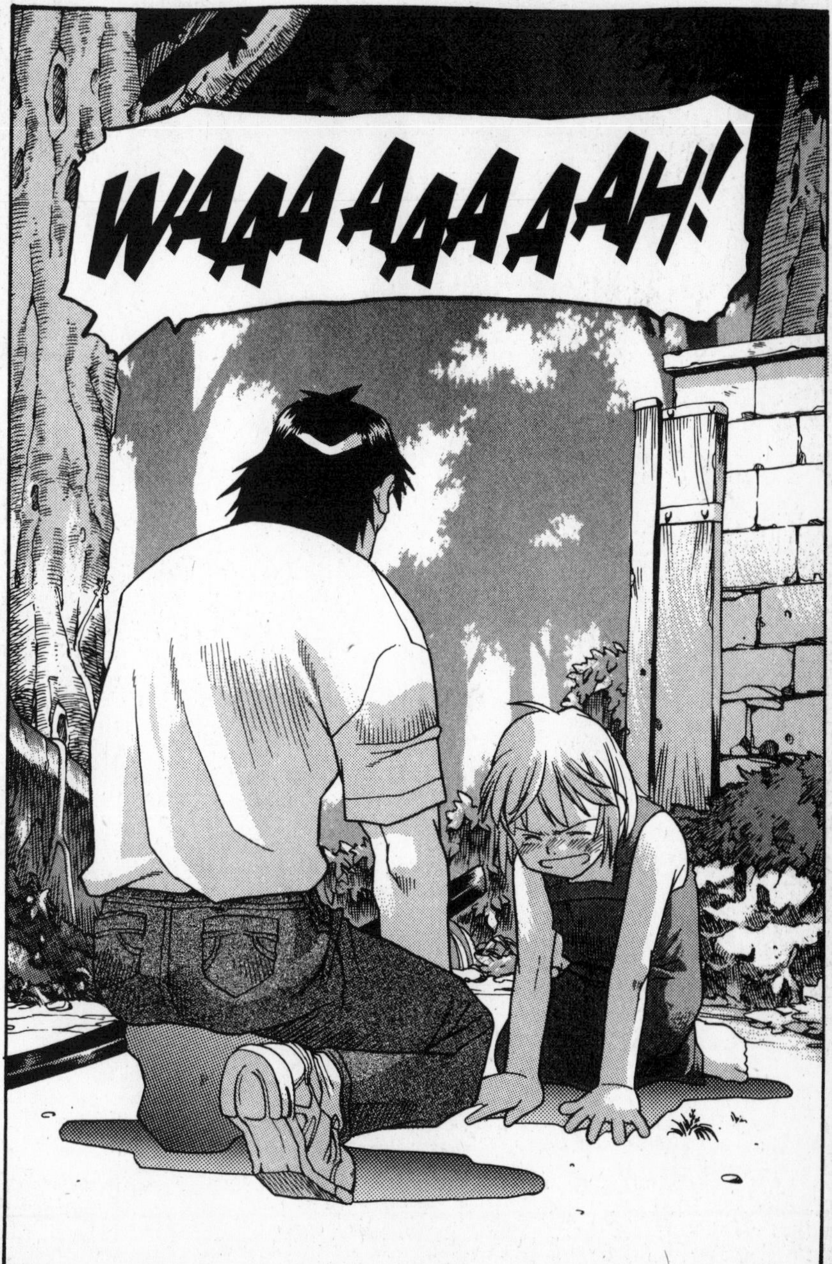
WAAAAAAAAAH!

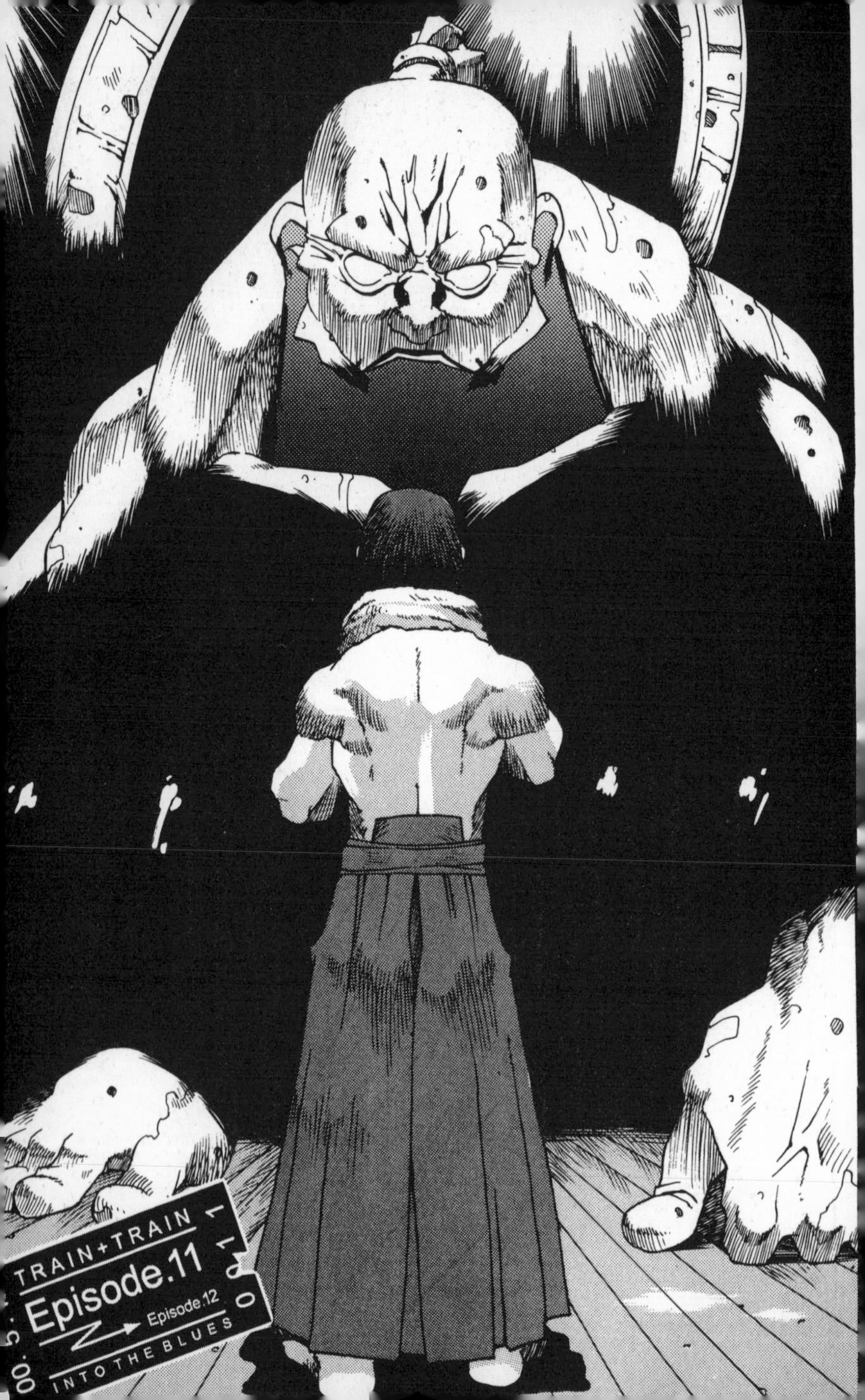
TRAIN+TRAIN
Episode.11
Episode.12
INTO THE BLUES

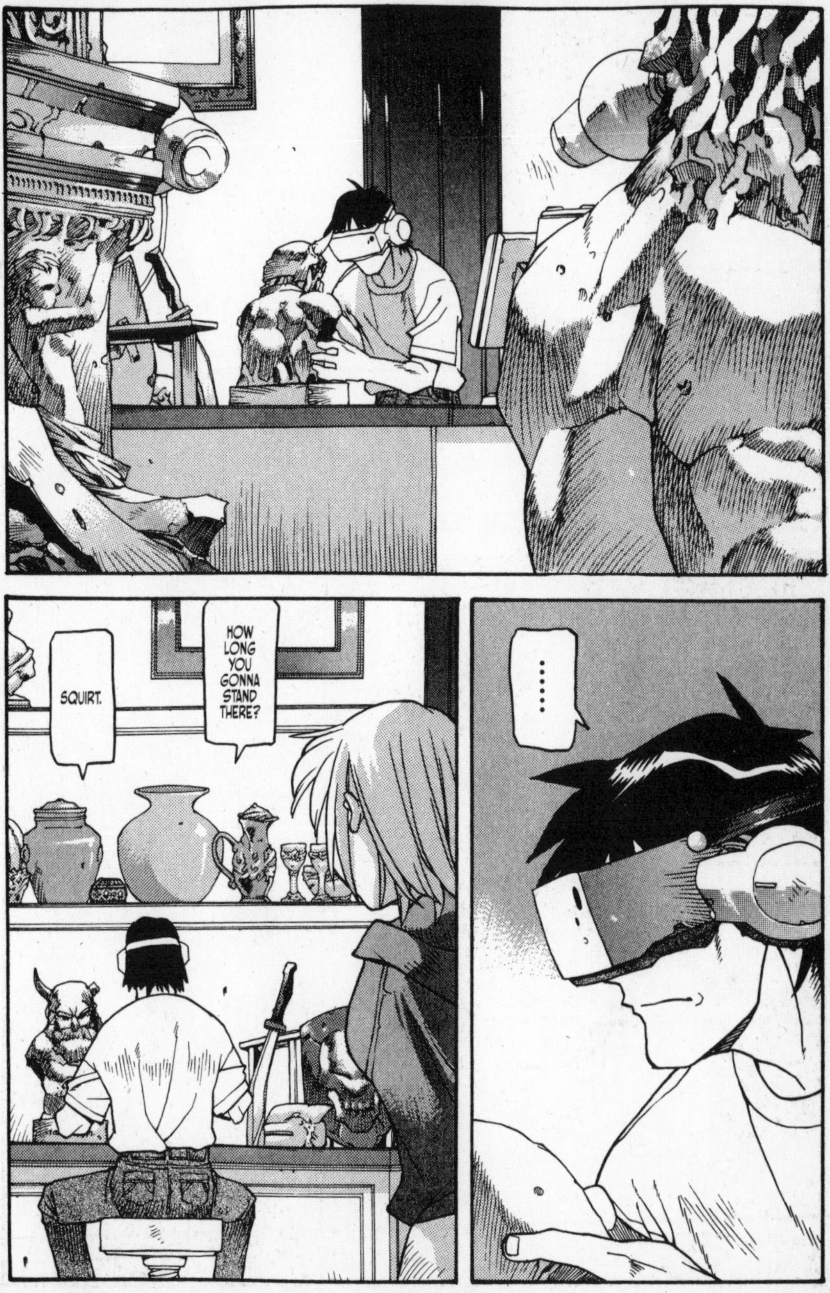
……
HOW LONG YOU GONNA STAND THERE?
SQUIRT.

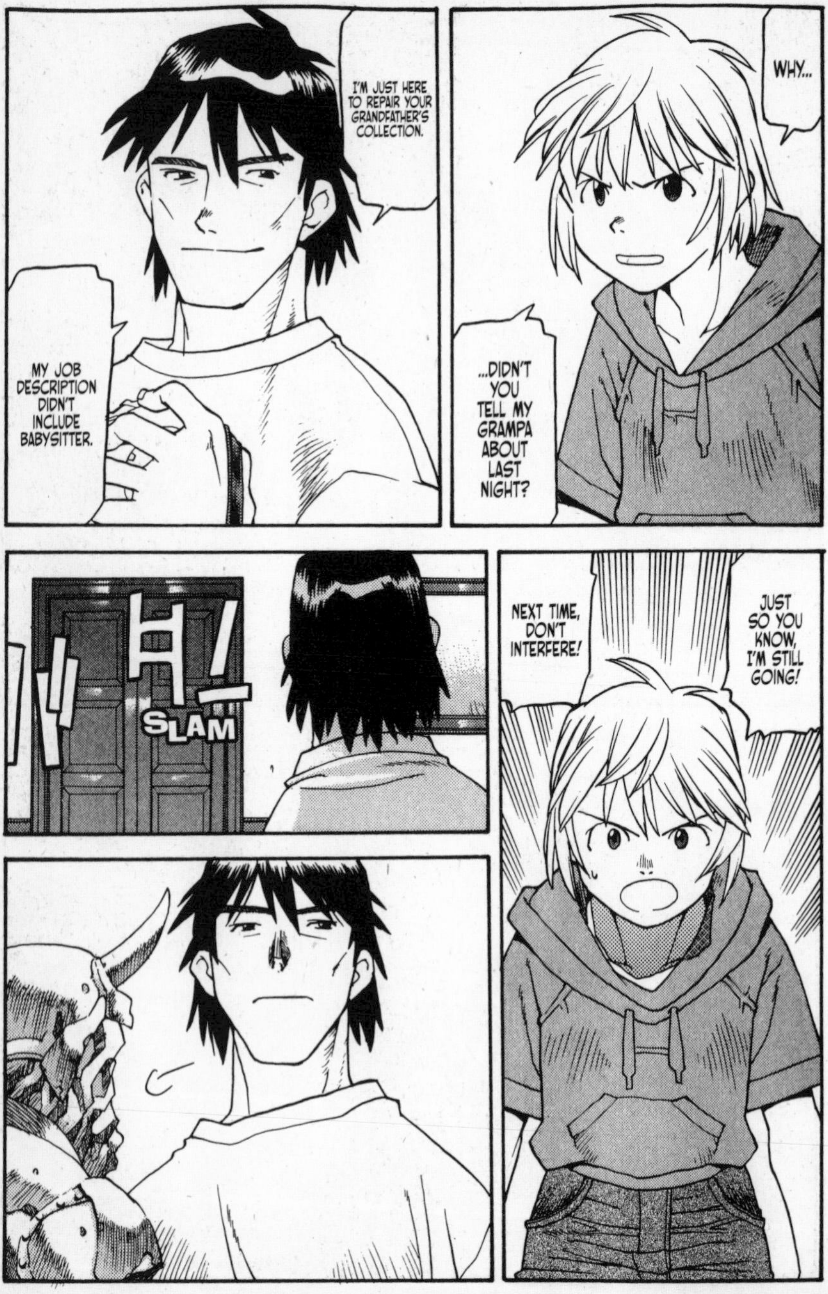
WHY...
...DIDN'T YOU TELL MY GRAMPA ABOUT LAST NIGHT?
I'M JUST HERE TO REPAIR YOUR GRANDFATHER'S COLLECTION.
MY JOB DESCRIPTION DIDN'T INCLUDE BABYSITTER.
JUST SO YOU KNOW, I'M STILL GOING!
NEXT TIME, DON'T INTERFERE!
SLAM

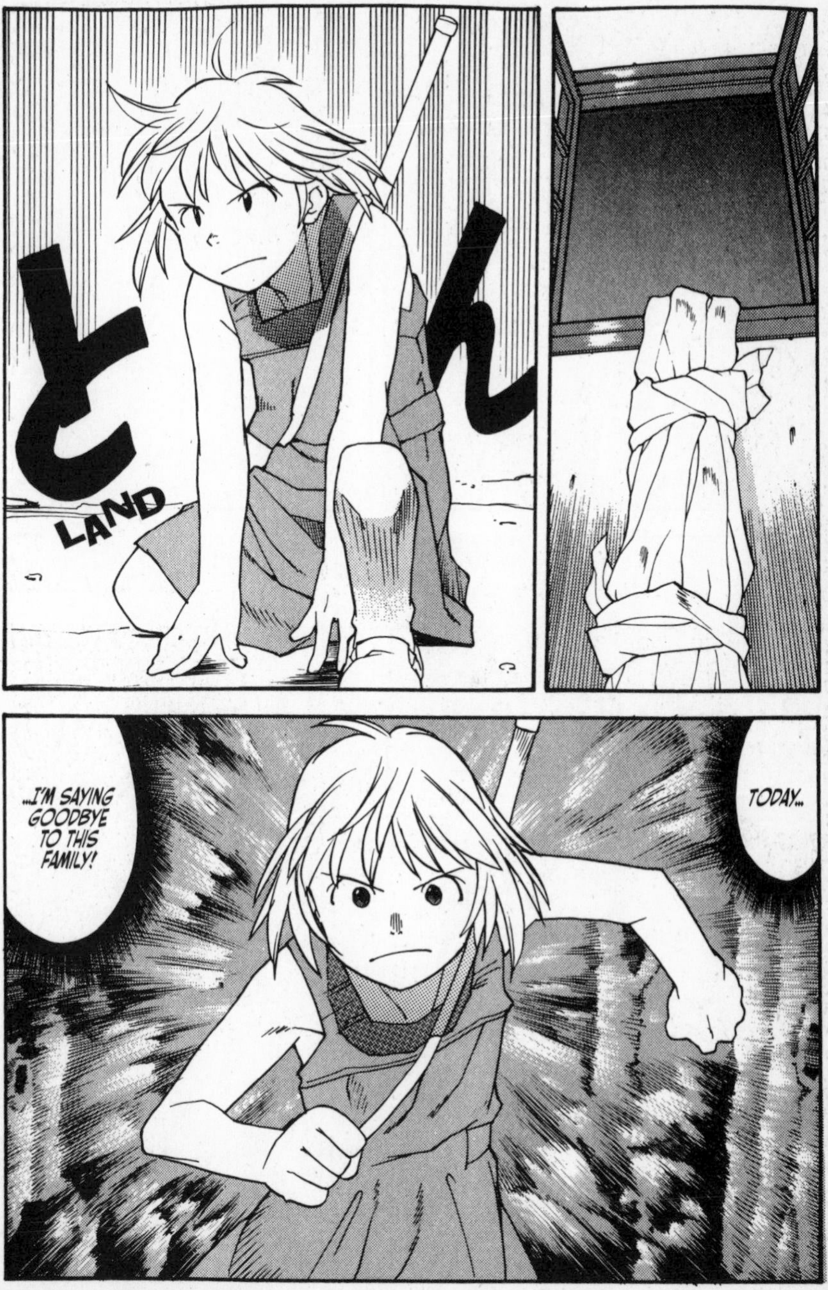
とん
LAND
TODAY...
...I'M SAYING GOODBYE TO THIS FAMILY!

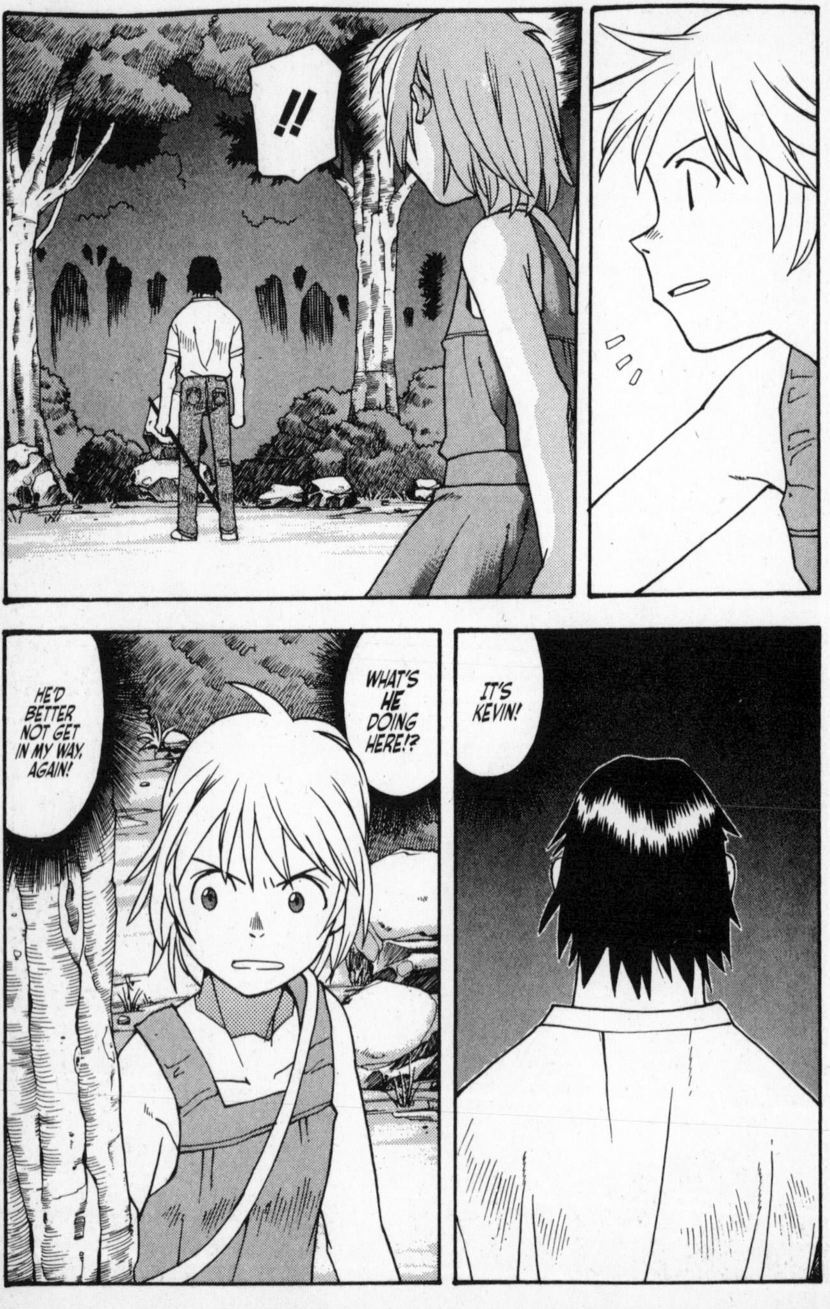
!!
IT'S KEVIN!
WHAT'S HE DOING HERE!?
HE'D BETTER NOT GET IN MY WAY. AGAIN!

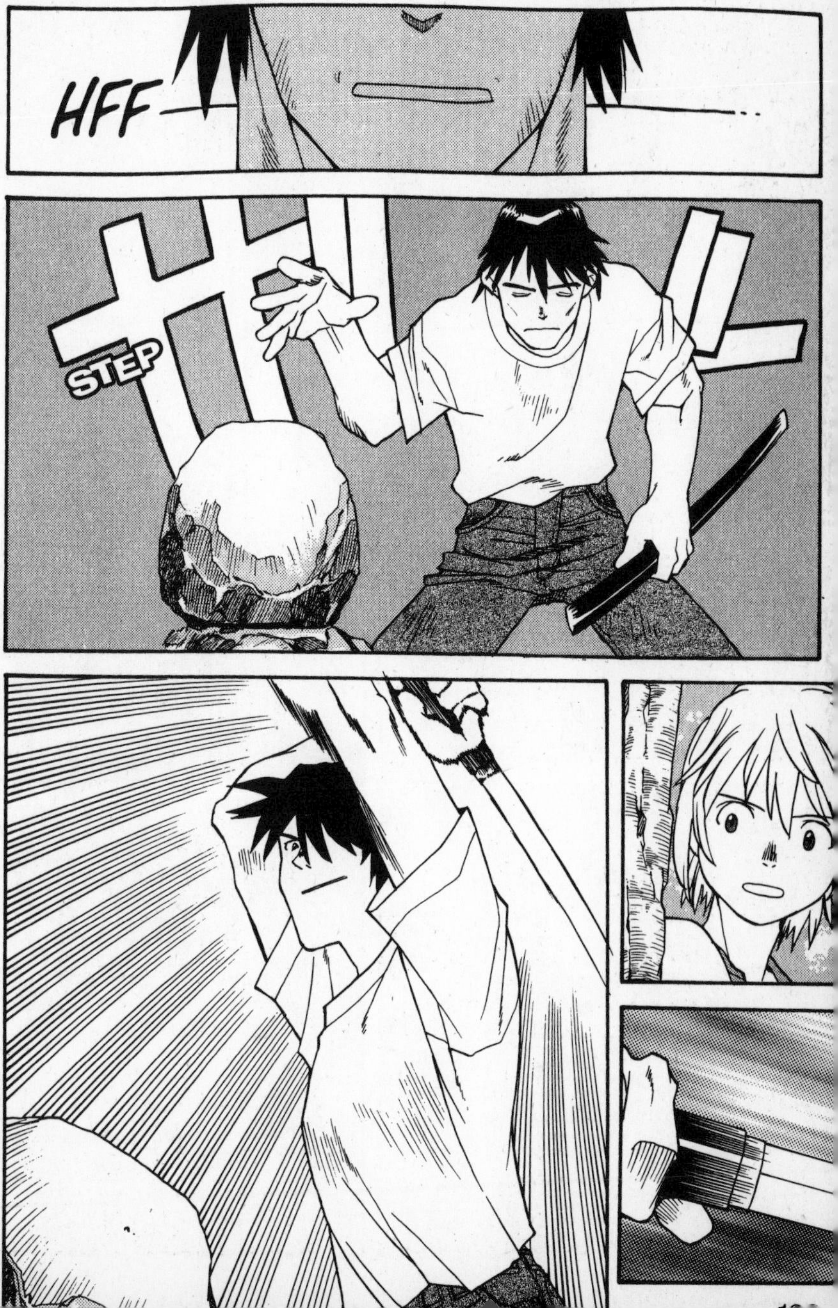
HFF
STEP

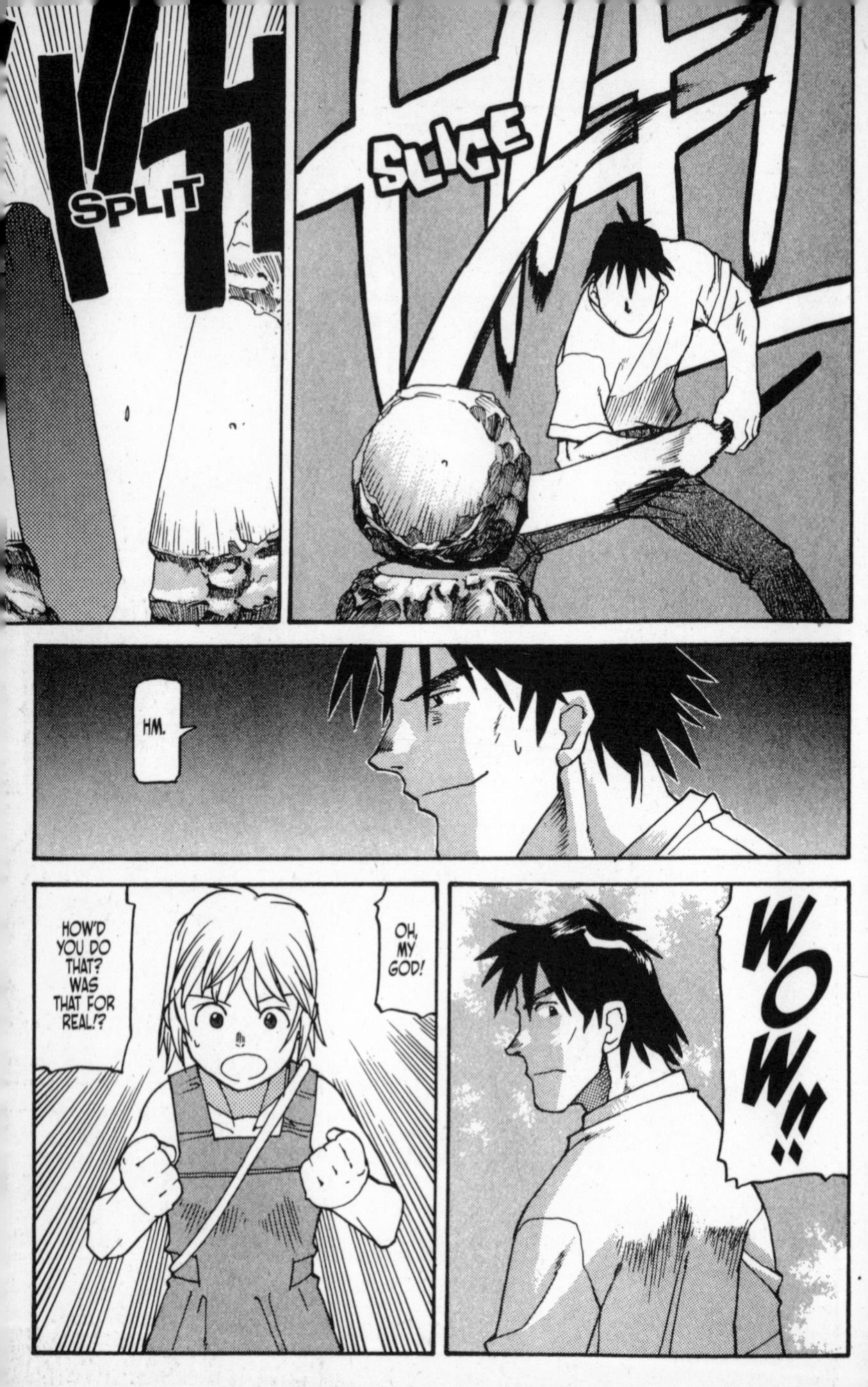
SLICE
SPLIT
HM.
WOW!!
OH, MY GOD!
HOW'D YOU DO THAT? WAS THAT FOR REAL!?

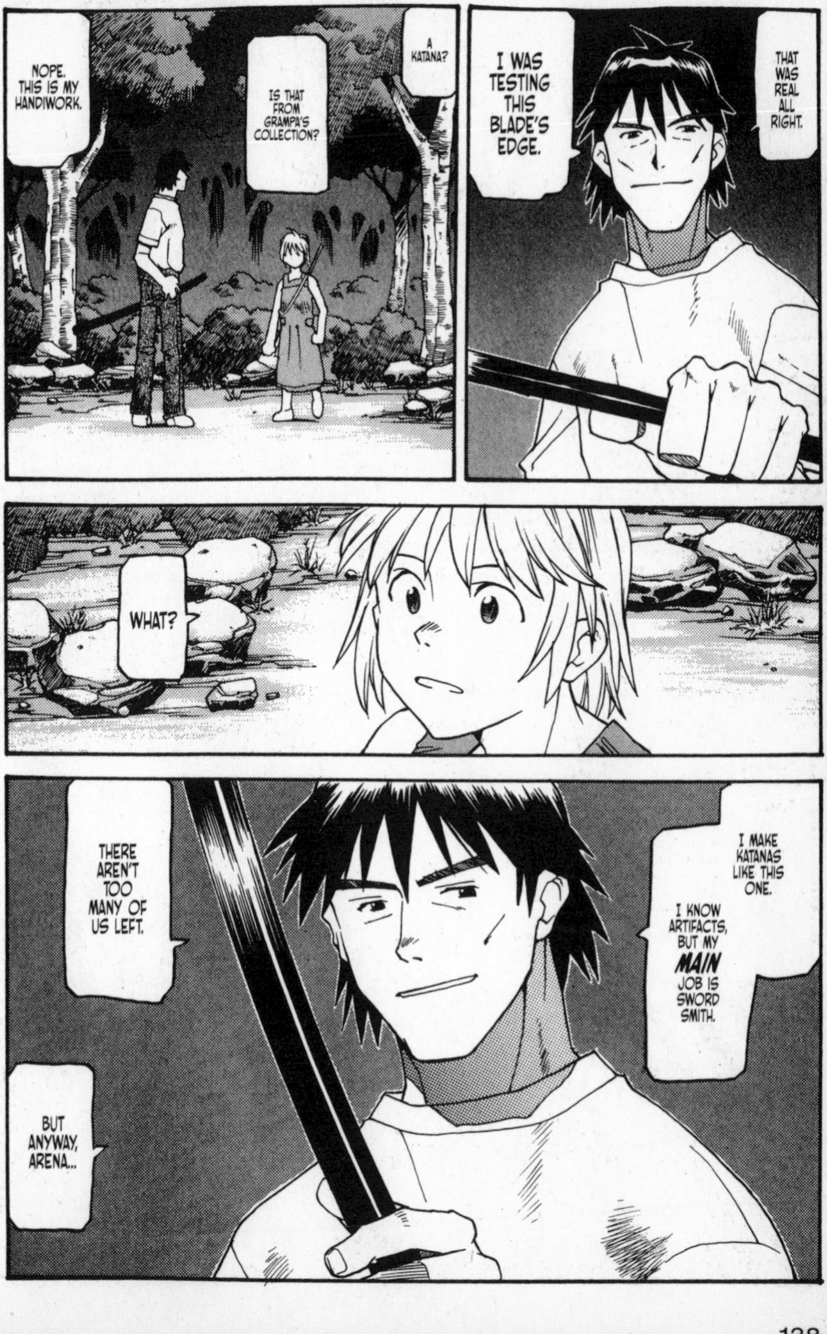
THAT WAS REAL ALL RIGHT.
I WAS TESTING THIS BLADE'S EDGE.
A KATANA?
IS THAT FROM GRAMPA'S COLLECTION?
NOPE. THIS IS MY HANDIWORK.
WHAT?
I MAKE KATANAS LIKE THIS ONE.
I KNOW ARTIFACTS, BUT MY MAIN JOB IS SWORD SMITH.
THERE AREN'T TOO MANY OF US LEFT.
BUT ANYWAY, ARENA...

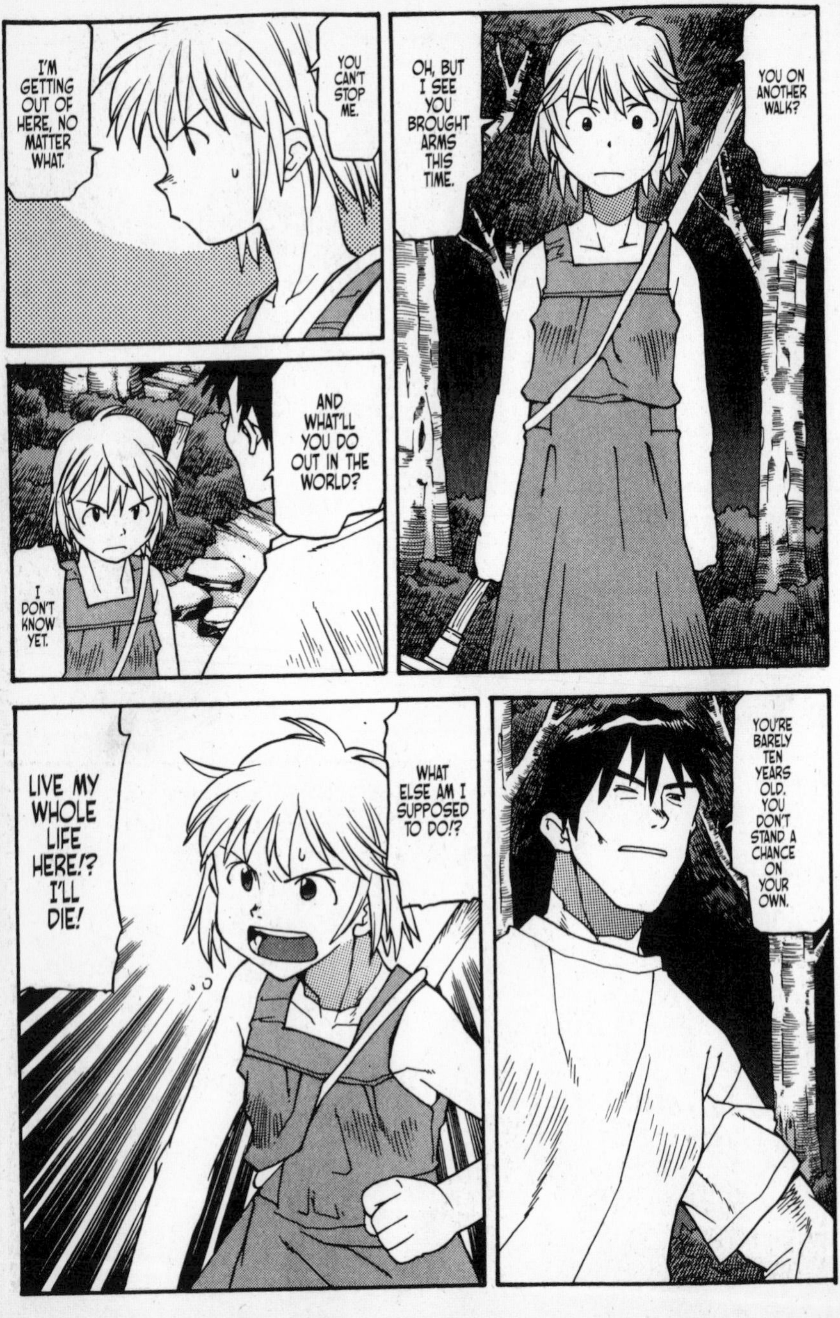
YOU ON ANOTHER WALK?
OH, BUT I SEE YOU BROUGHT ARMS THIS TIME.
YOU CAN'T STOP ME.
I'M GETTING OUT OF HERE, NO MATTER WHAT.
AND WHAT'LL YOU DO OUT IN THE WORLD?
I DON'T KNOW YET.
YOU'RE BARELY TEN YEARS OLD. YOU DON'T STAND A CHANCE ON YOUR OWN.
WHAT ELSE AM I SUPPOSED TO DO!?
LIVE MY WHOLE LIFE HERE!? I'LL DIE!

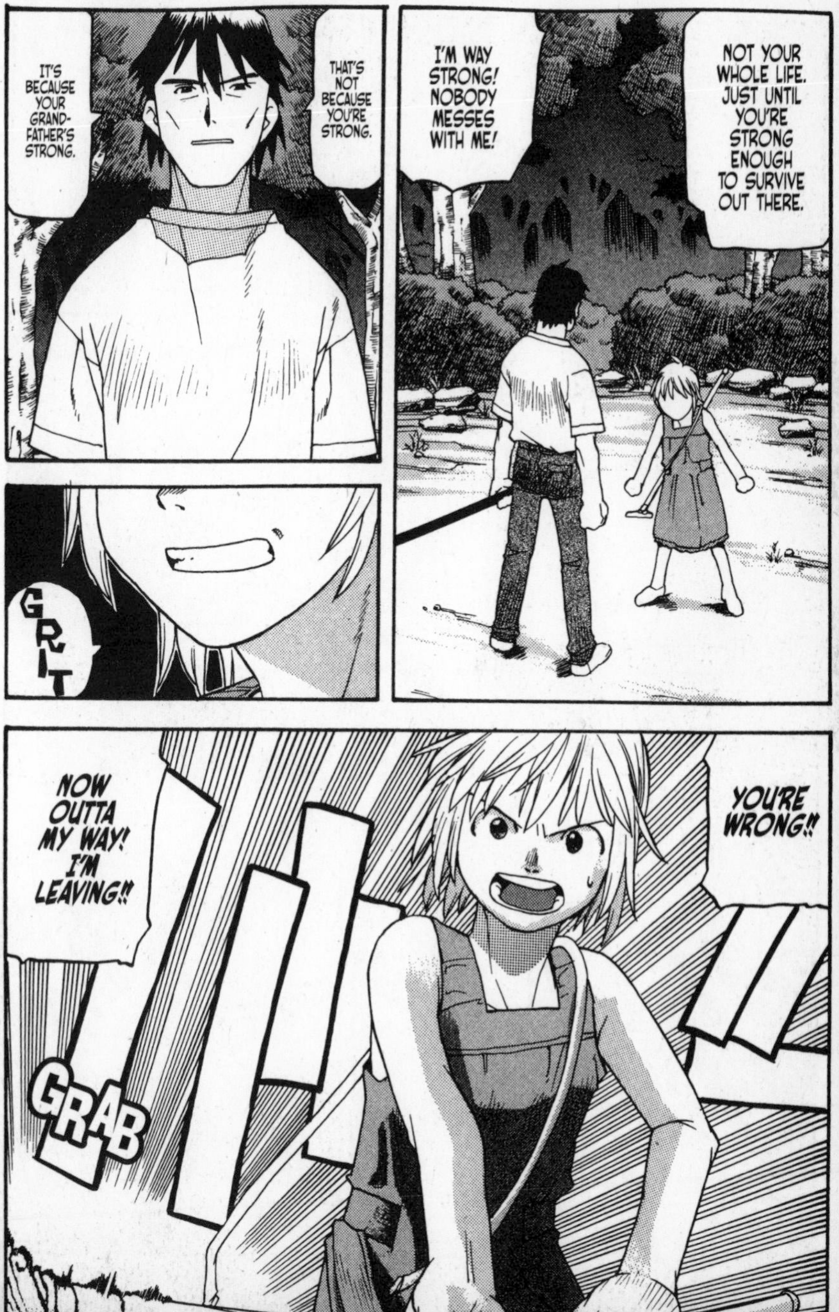
NOT YOUR WHOLE LIFE. JUST UNTIL YOU'RE STRONG ENOUGH TO SURVIVE OUT THERE.
I'M WAY STRONG! NOBODY MESSES WITH ME!
THAT'S NOT BECAUSE YOU'RE STRONG.
IT'S BECAUSE YOUR GRAND-FATHER'S STRONG.
GRIT
YOU'RE WRONG!!
NOW OUTTA MY WAY! I'M LEAVING!!
GRAB

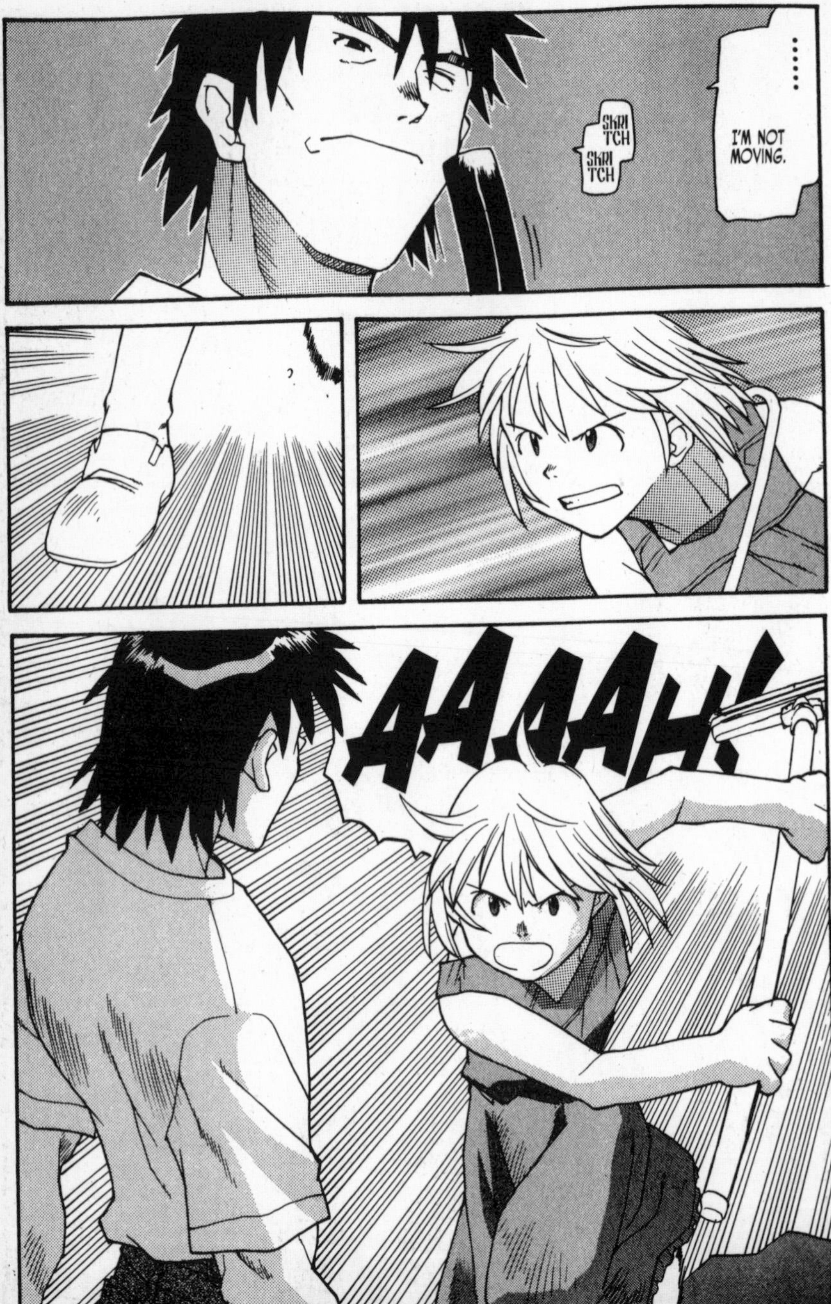
......
I'M NOT MOVING.
SKRITCH SKRITCH
AAAAH!

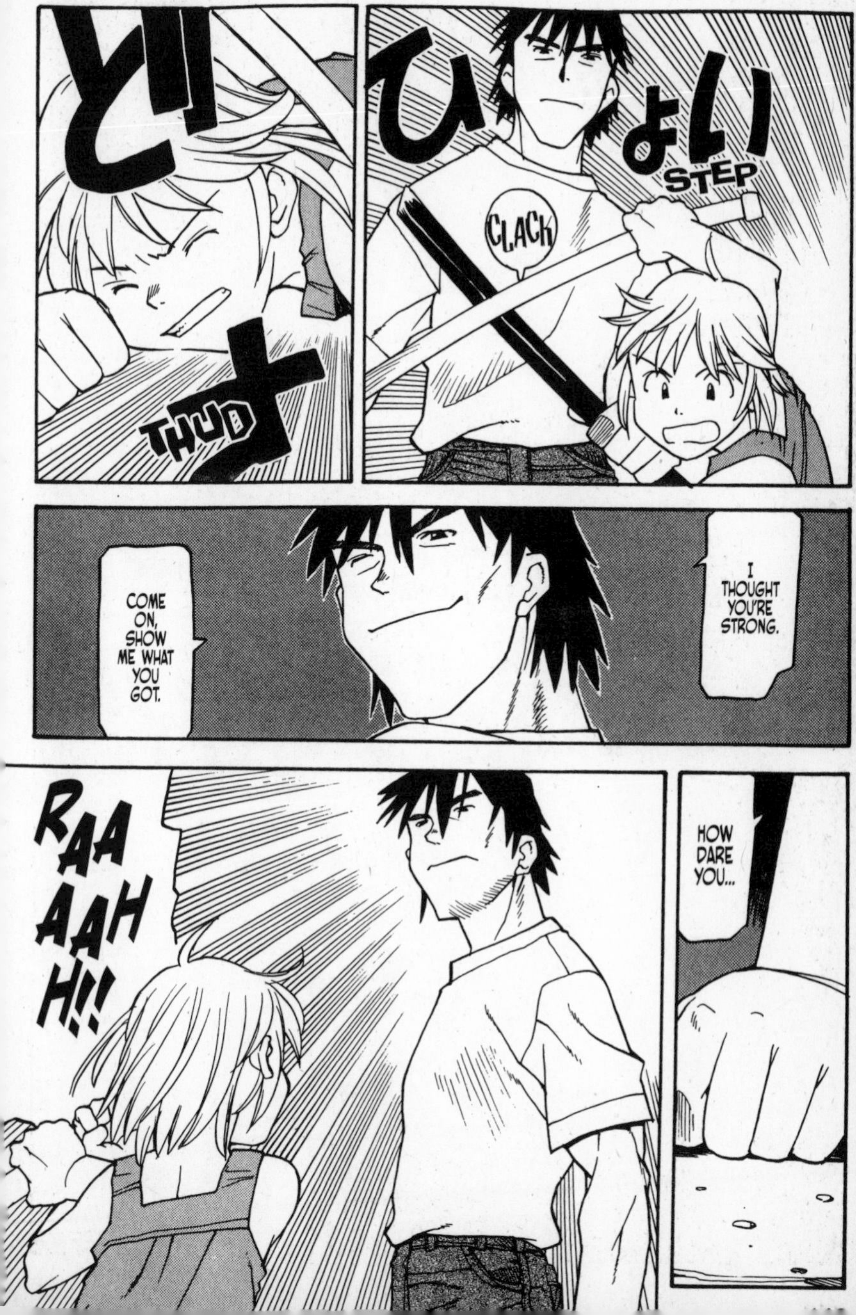
ひょい
STEP
CLACK
ど!
THUD
I THOUGHT YOU'RE STRONG.
COME ON, SHOW ME WHAT YOU GOT.
HOW DARE YOU...
RAAAAAAH!!

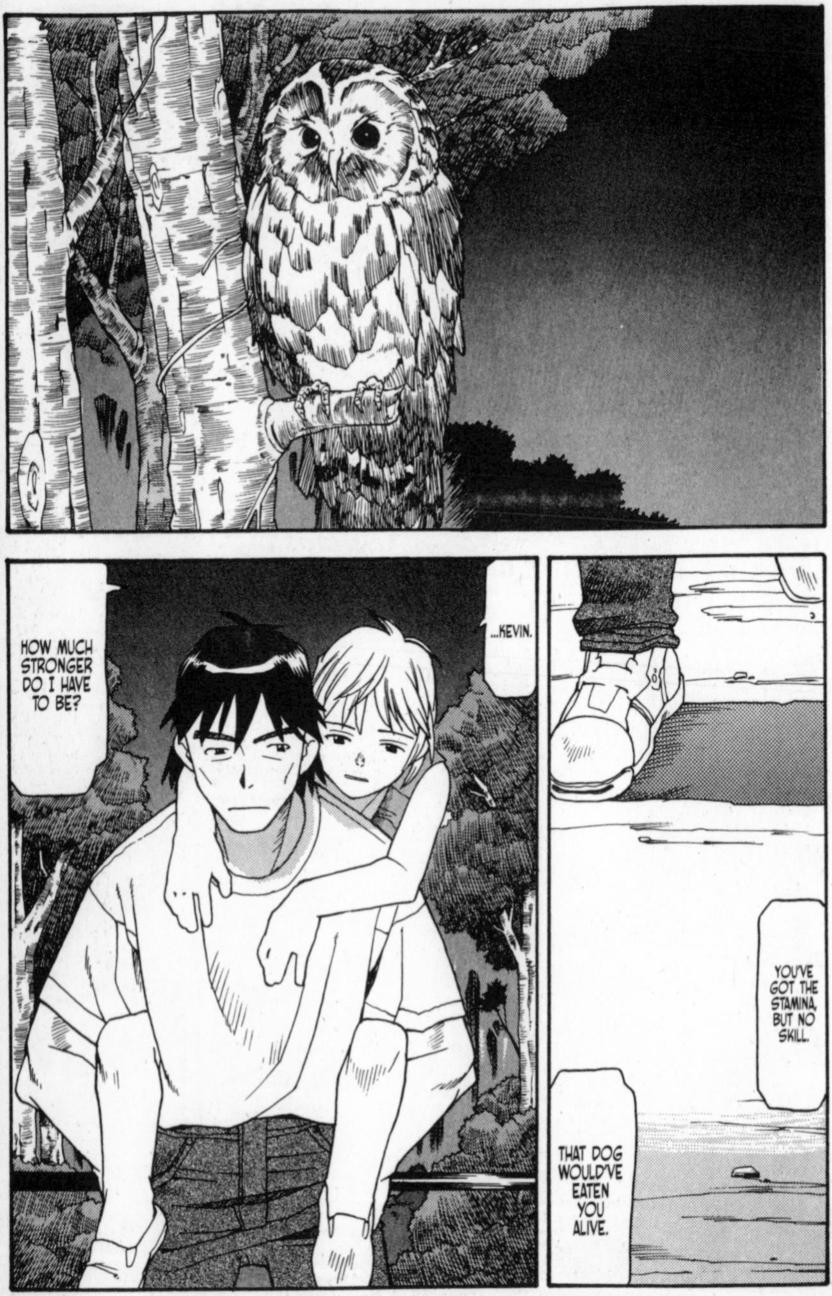
YOU'VE GOT THE STAMINA, BUT NO SKILL.
THAT DOG WOULD'VE EATEN YOU ALIVE.
...KEVIN.
HOW MUCH STRONGER DO I HAVE TO BE?

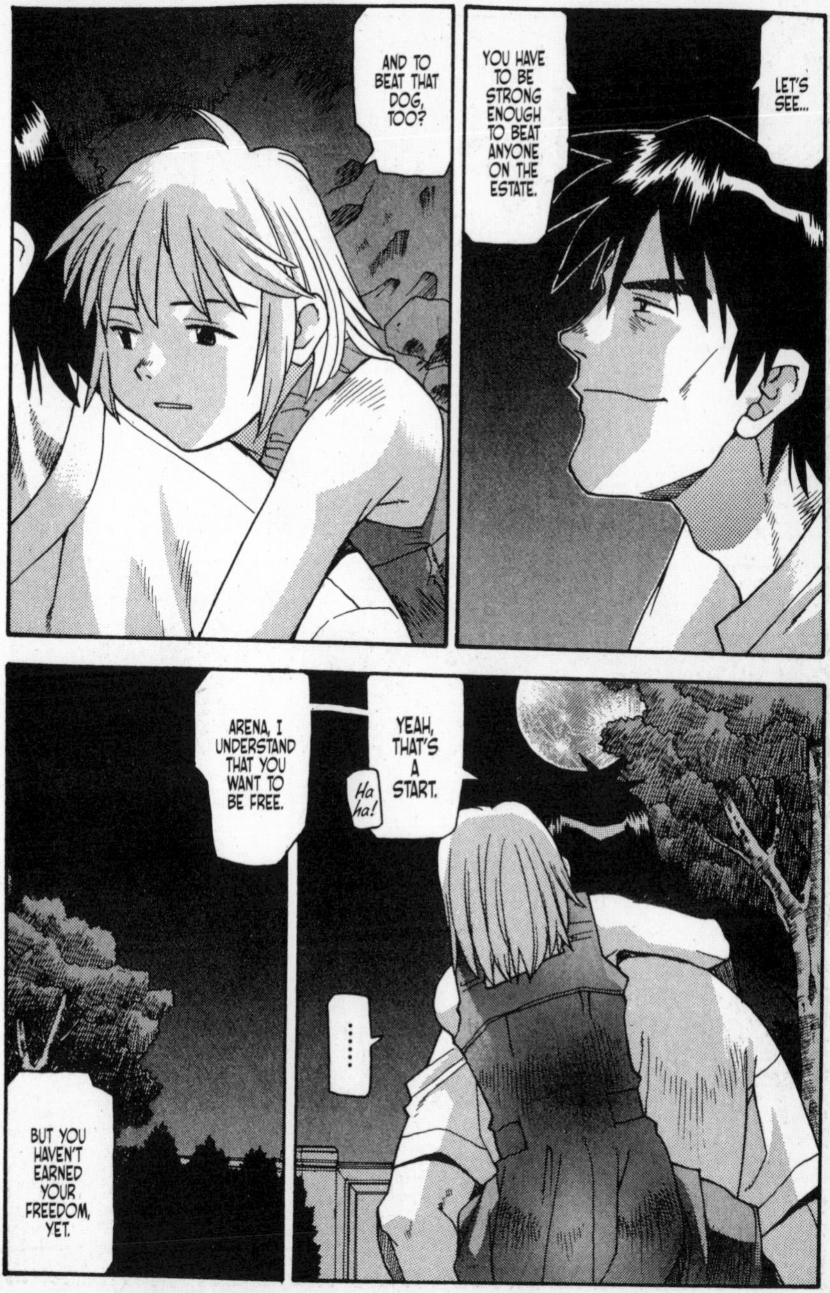
LET'S SEE...
YOU HAVE TO BE STRONG ENOUGH TO BEAT ANYONE ON THE ESTATE.
AND TO BEAT THAT DOG, TOO?
YEAH, THAT'S A START.
Ha ha!
ARENA, I UNDERSTAND THAT YOU WANT TO BE FREE.
......
BUT YOU HAVEN'T EARNED YOUR FREEDOM, YET.

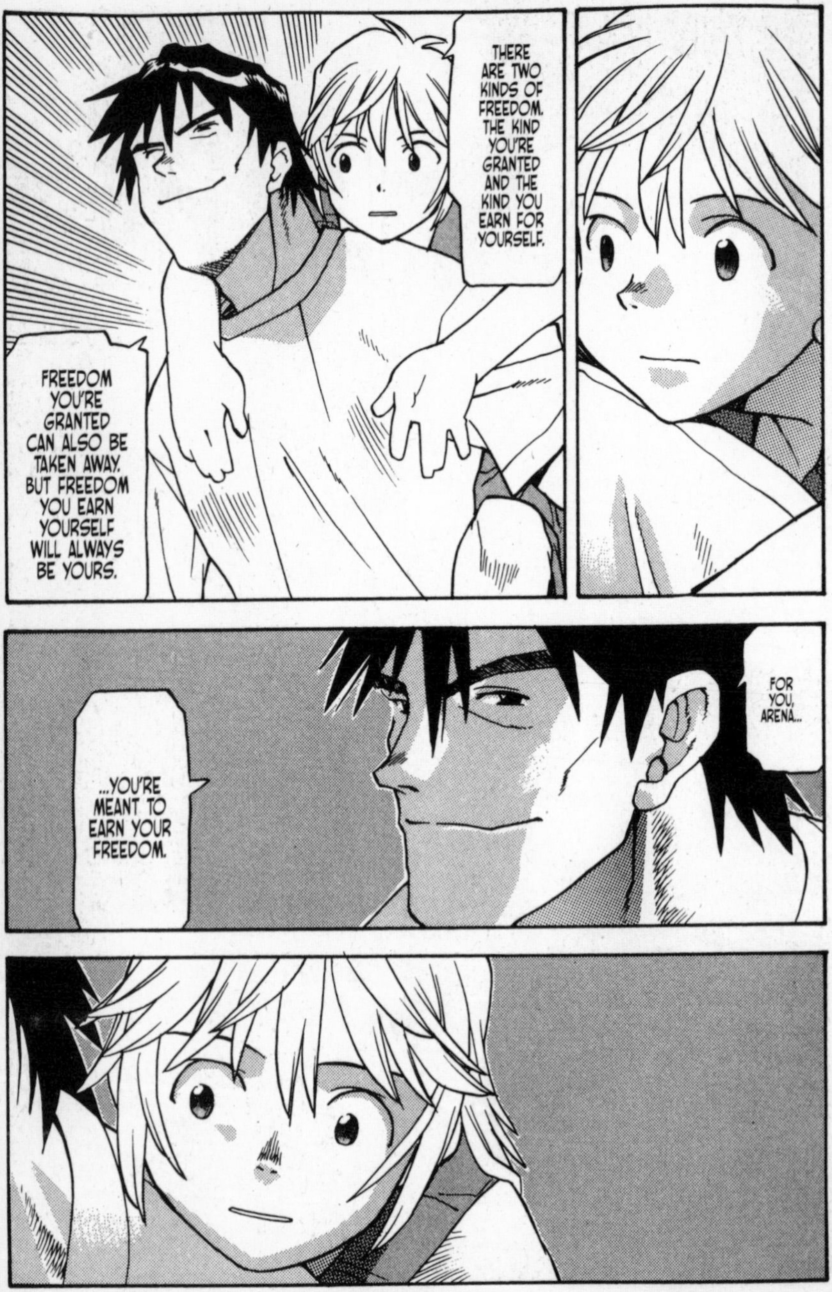
THERE ARE TWO KINDS OF FREEDOM. THE KIND YOU'RE GRANTED AND THE KIND YOU EARN FOR YOURSELF.
FREEDOM YOU'RE GRANTED CAN ALSO BE TAKEN AWAY. BUT FREEDOM YOU EARN YOURSELF WILL ALWAYS BE YOURS.
FOR YOU, ARENA...
...YOU'RE MEANT TO EARN YOUR FREEDOM.

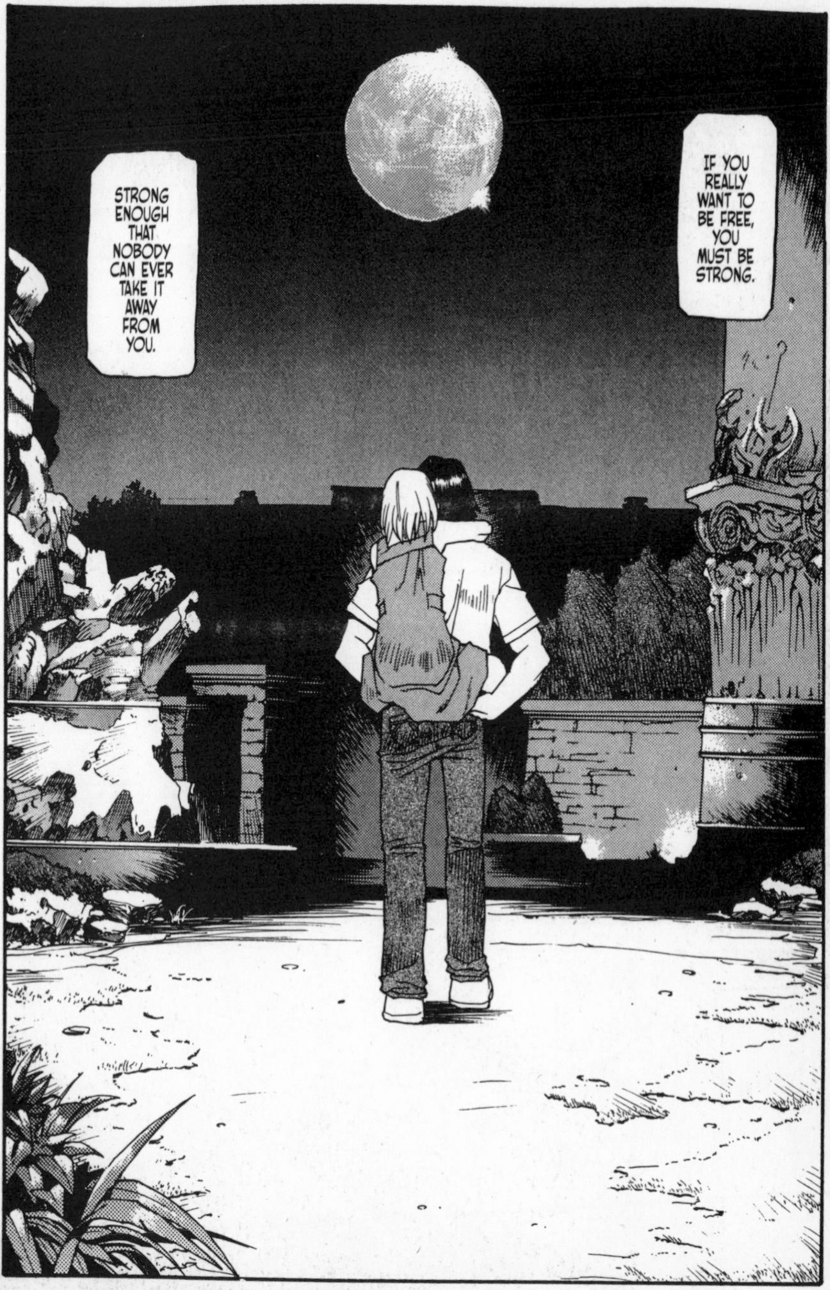
IF YOU REALLY WANT TO BE FREE, YOU MUST BE STRONG.
STRONG ENOUGH THAT NOBODY CAN EVER TAKE IT AWAY FROM YOU.

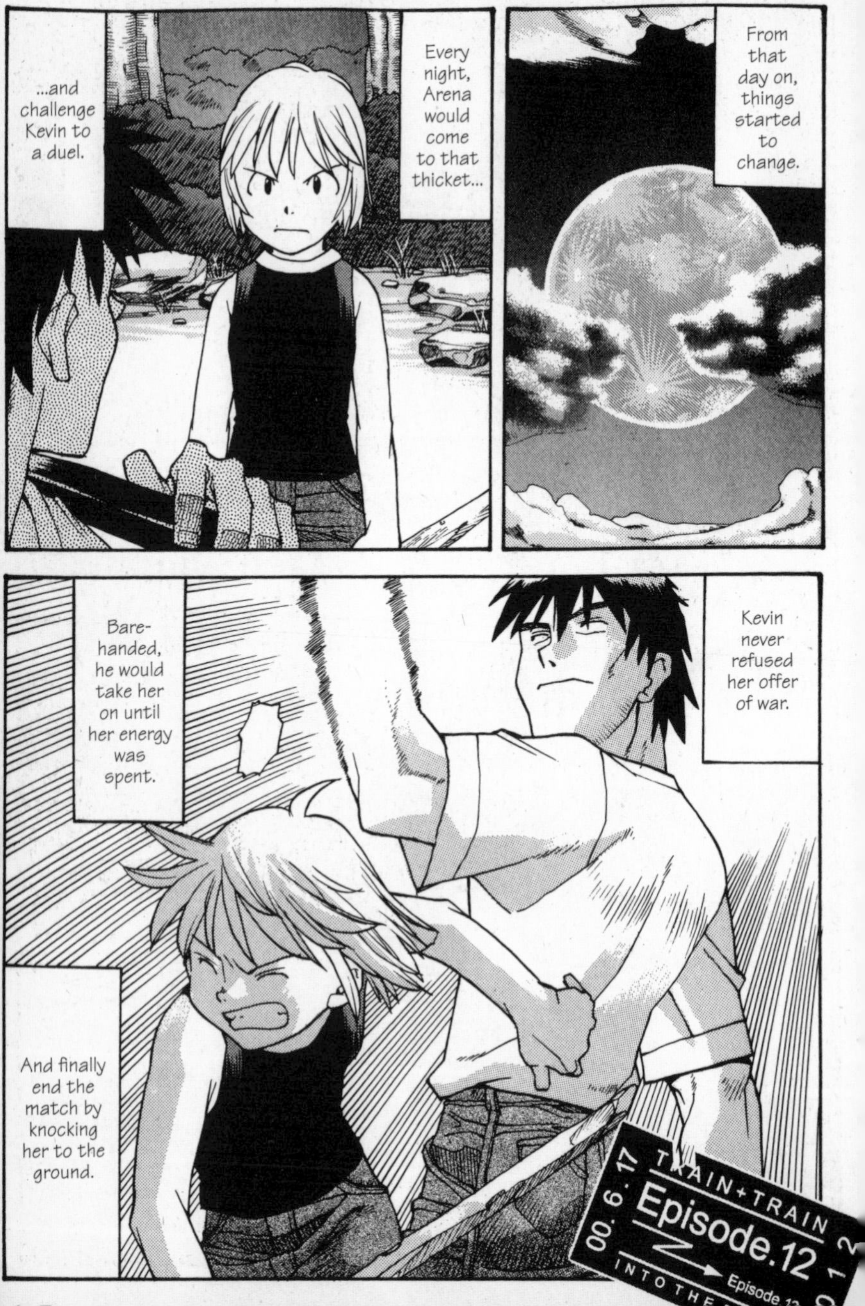

From that day on, things started to change.
Every night, Arena would come to that thicket...
...and challenge Kevin to a duel.
Kevin never refused her offer of war.
Bare-handed, he would take her on until her energy was spent.
And finally end the match by knocking her to the ground.
00. 6. 17
TRAIN+TRAIN
Episode.12

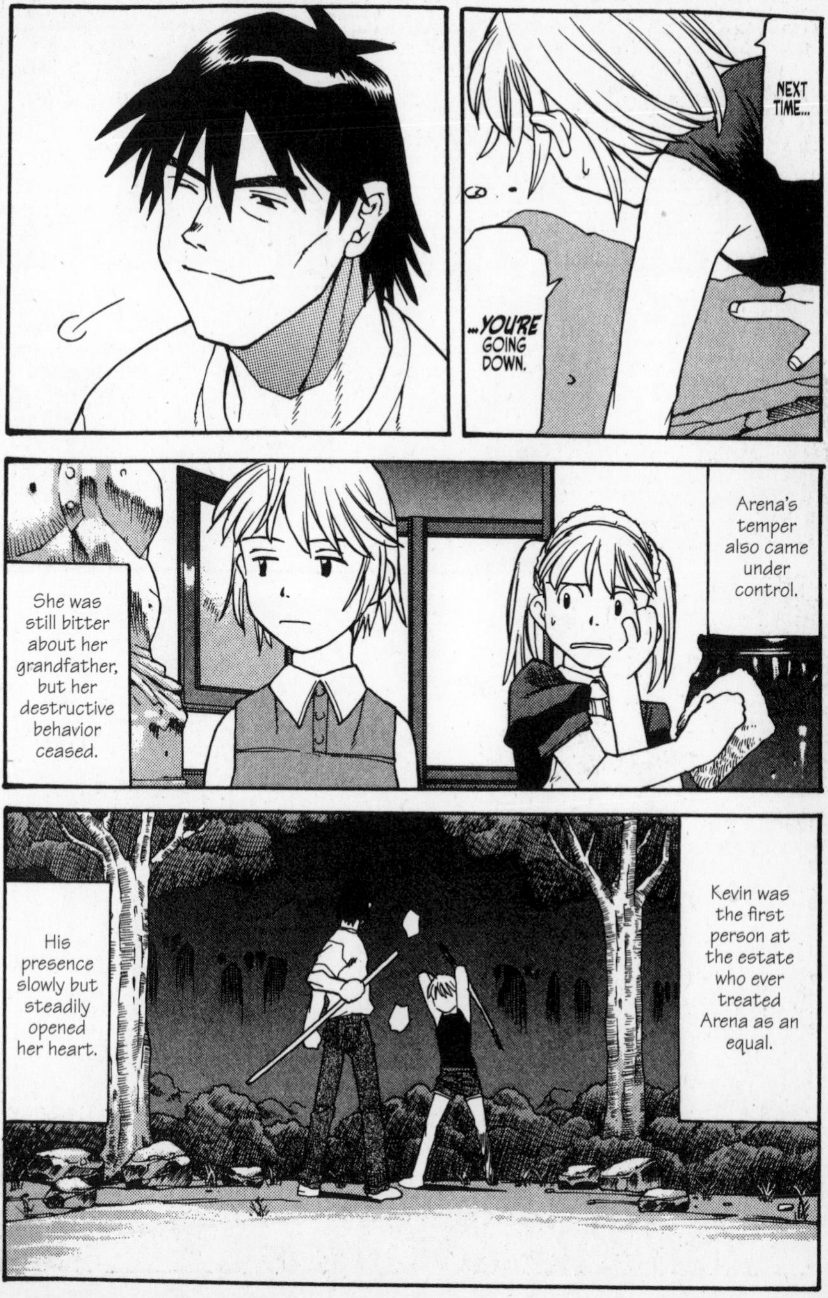
NEXT TIME...
...YOU'RE GOING DOWN.
Arena's temper also came under control.
She was still bitter about her grandfather, but her destructive behavior ceased.
Kevin was the first person at the estate who ever treated Arena as an equal.
His presence slowly but steadily opened her heart.

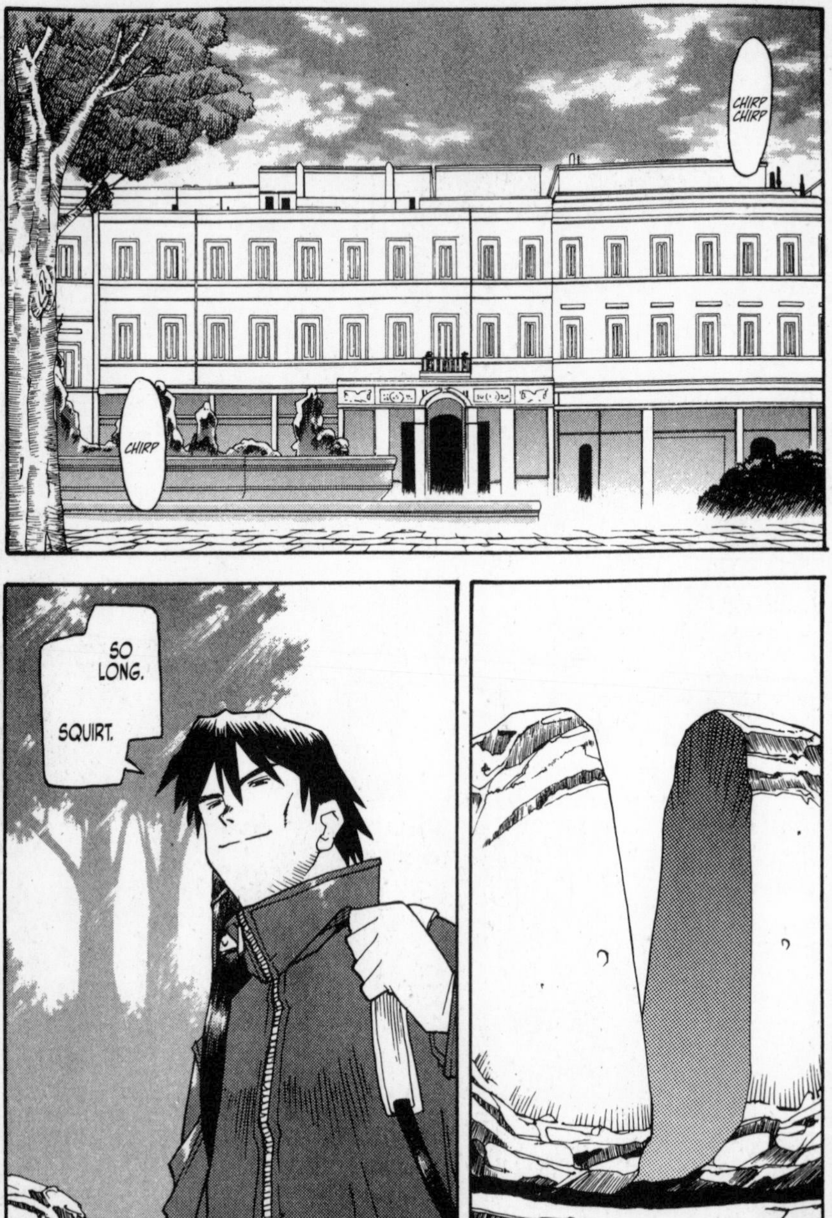
CHIRP CHIRP
CHIRP
SO LONG.
SQUIRT.

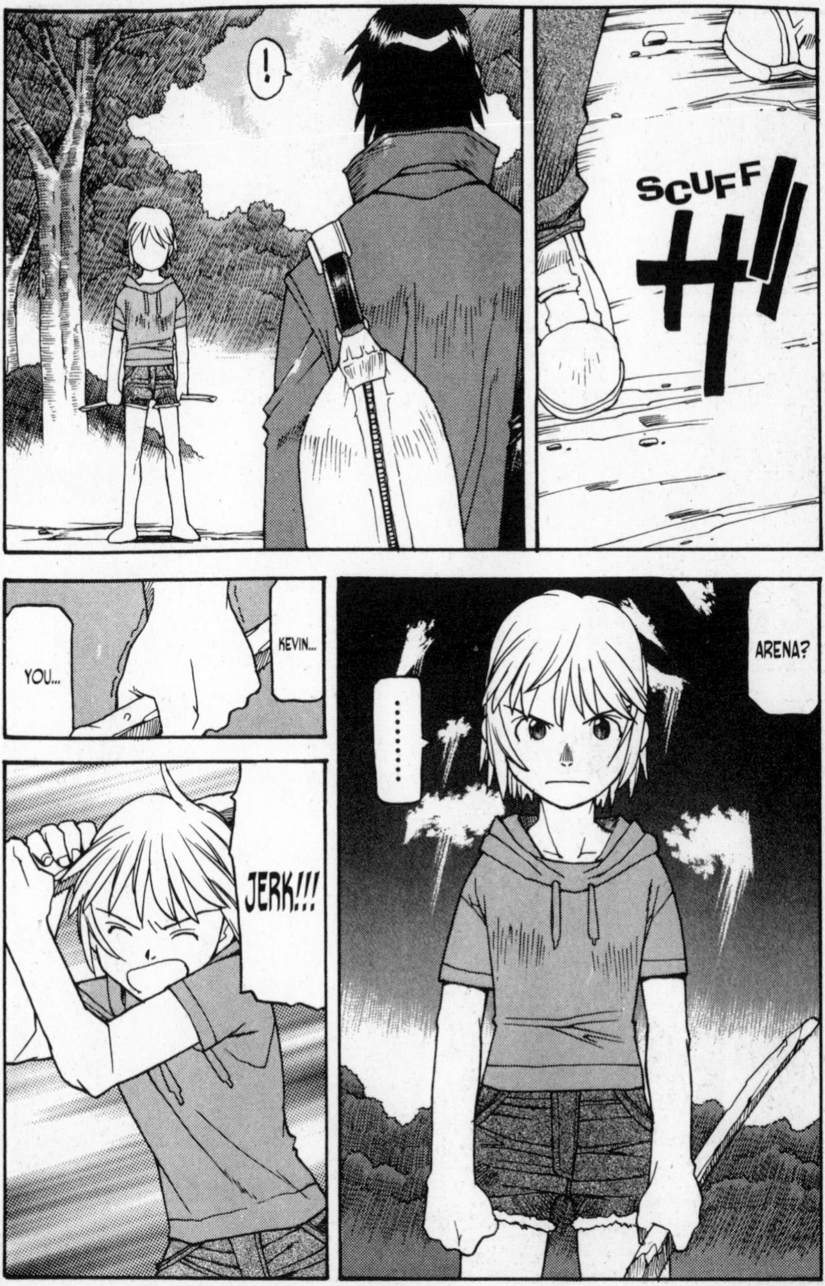
SCUFF
!
ARENA?
....
KEVIN...
YOU...
JERK!!!

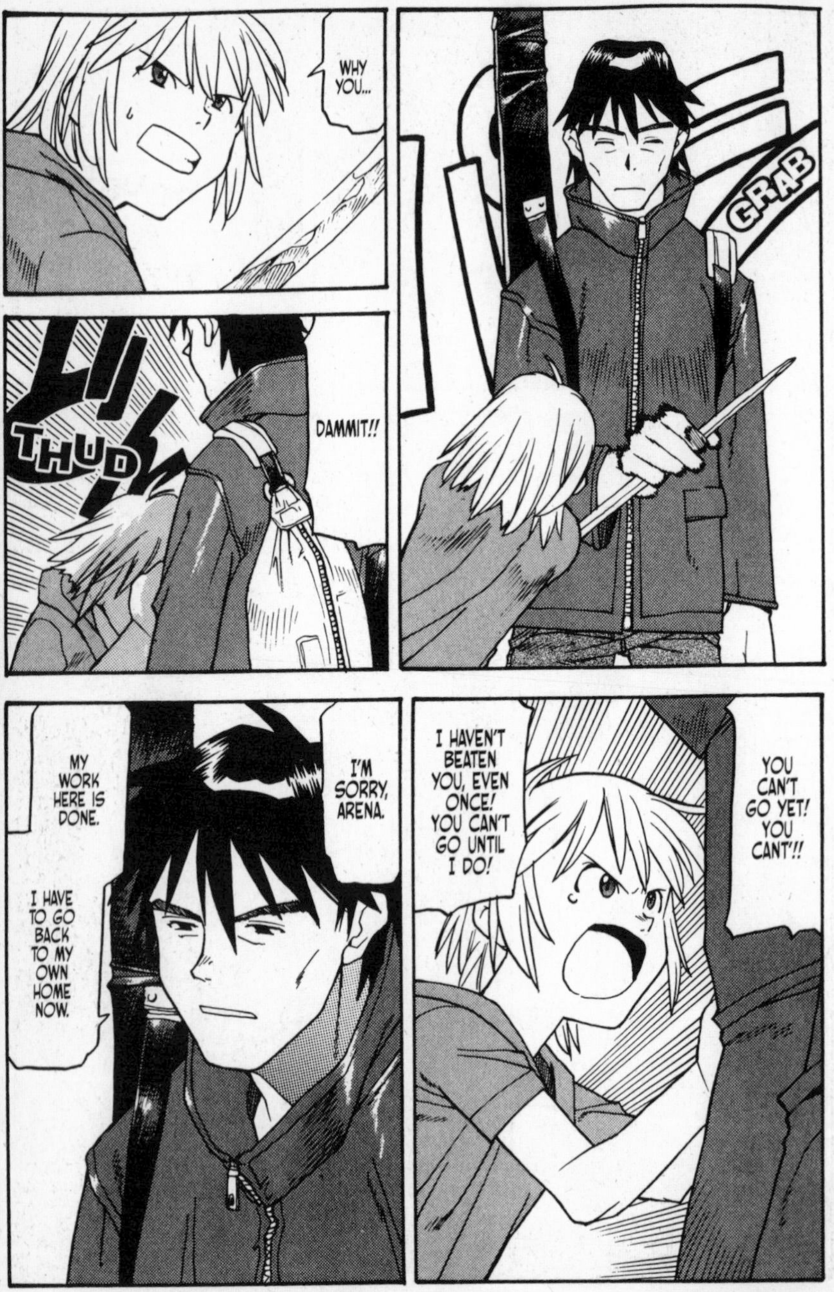
GRAB
WHY YOU...
DAMMIT!!
THUD
YOU CAN'T GO YET! YOU CANT'!!
I HAVEN'T BEATEN YOU, EVEN ONCE! YOU CAN'T GO UNTIL I DO!
I'M SORRY, ARENA.
MY WORK HERE IS DONE.
I HAVE TO GO BACK TO MY OWN HOME NOW.

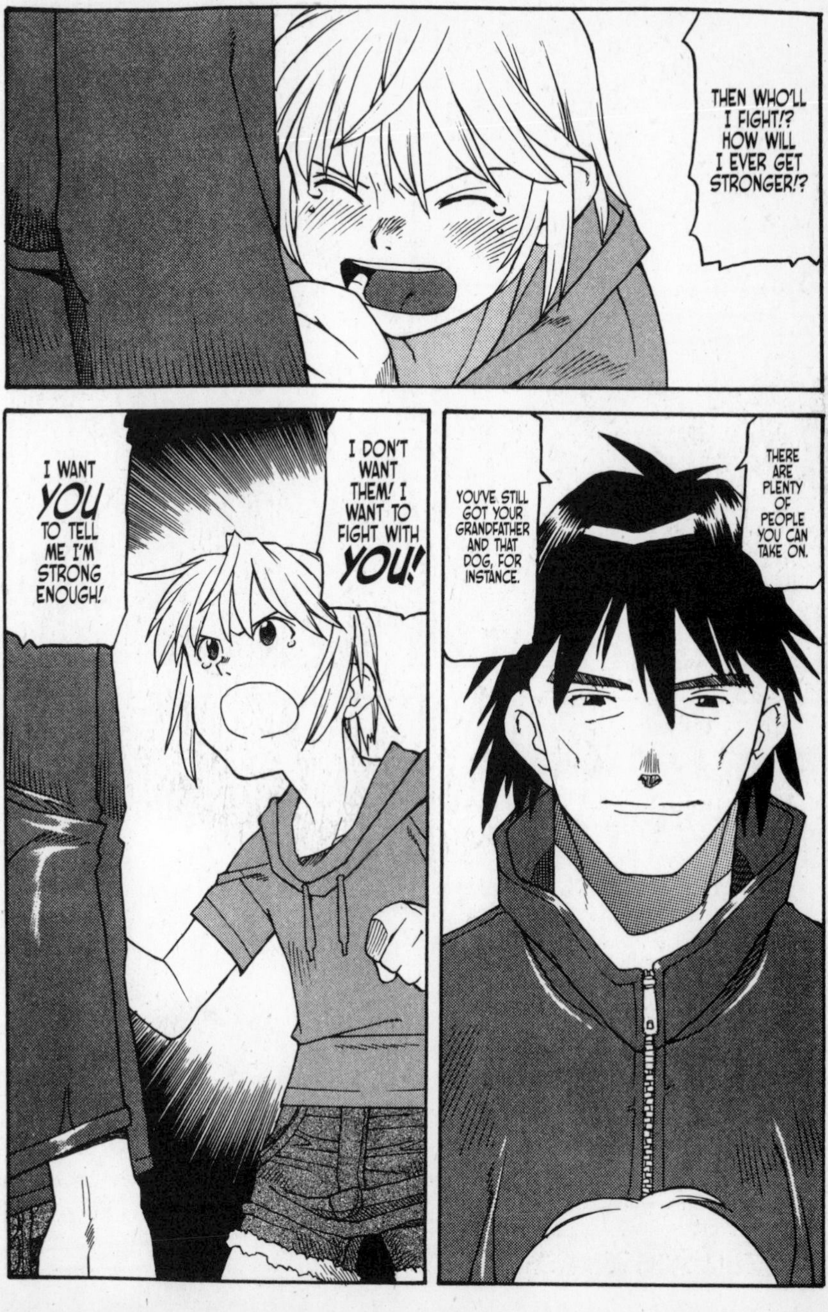
THEN WHO'LL I FIGHT!? HOW WILL I EVER GET STRONGER!?
THERE ARE PLENTY OF PEOPLE YOU CAN TAKE ON.
YOU'VE STILL GOT YOUR GRANDFATHER AND THAT DOG, FOR INSTANCE.
I DON'T WANT THEM! I WANT TO FIGHT WITH YOU!
I WANT YOU TO TELL ME I'M STRONG ENOUGH!

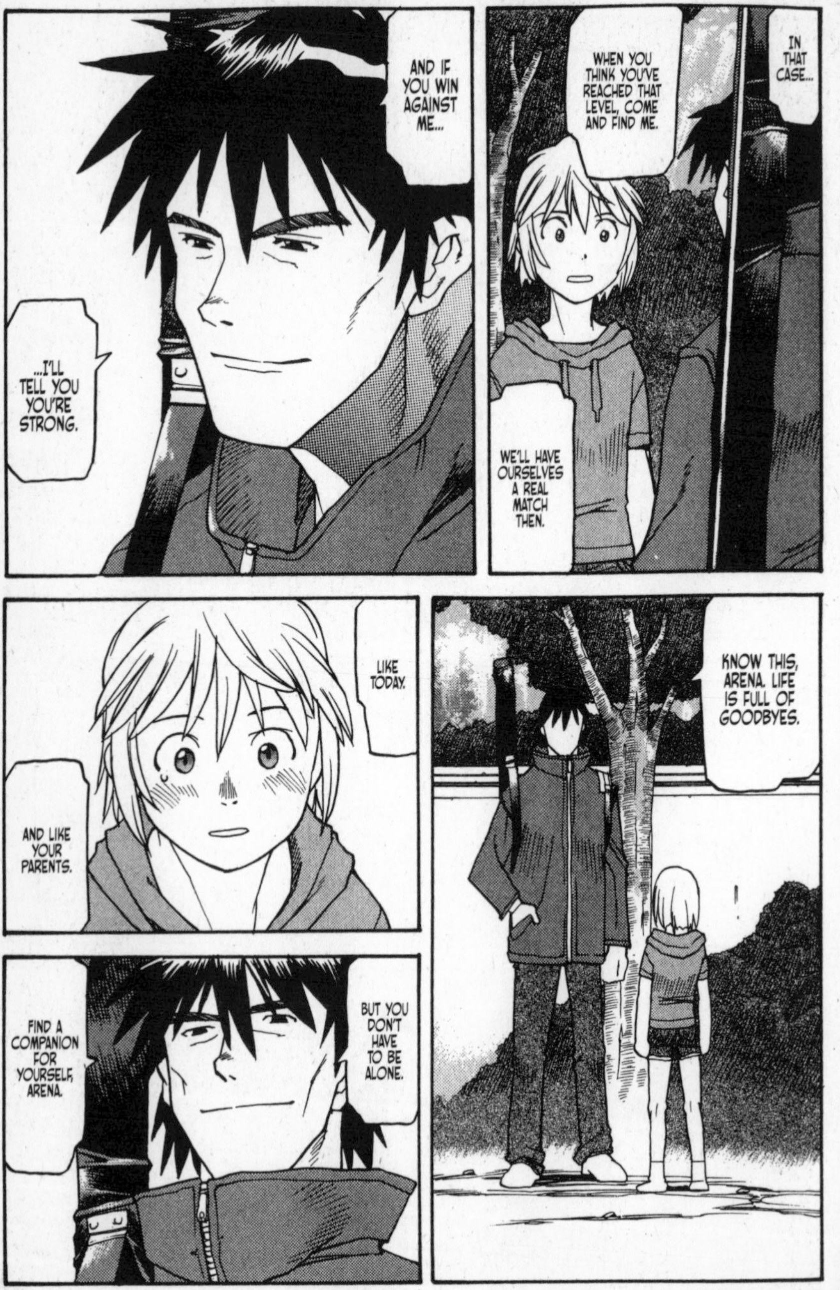
IN THAT CASE...
WHEN YOU THINK YOU'VE REACHED THAT LEVEL, COME AND FIND ME.
WE'LL HAVE OURSELVES A REAL MATCH THEN.
AND IF YOU WIN AGAINST ME...
...I'LL TELL YOU YOU'RE STRONG.
KNOW THIS, ARENA. LIFE IS FULL OF GOODBYES.
!
LIKE TODAY.
AND LIKE YOUR PARENTS.
BUT YOU DON'T HAVE TO BE ALONE.
FIND A COMPANION FOR YOURSELF, ARENA.

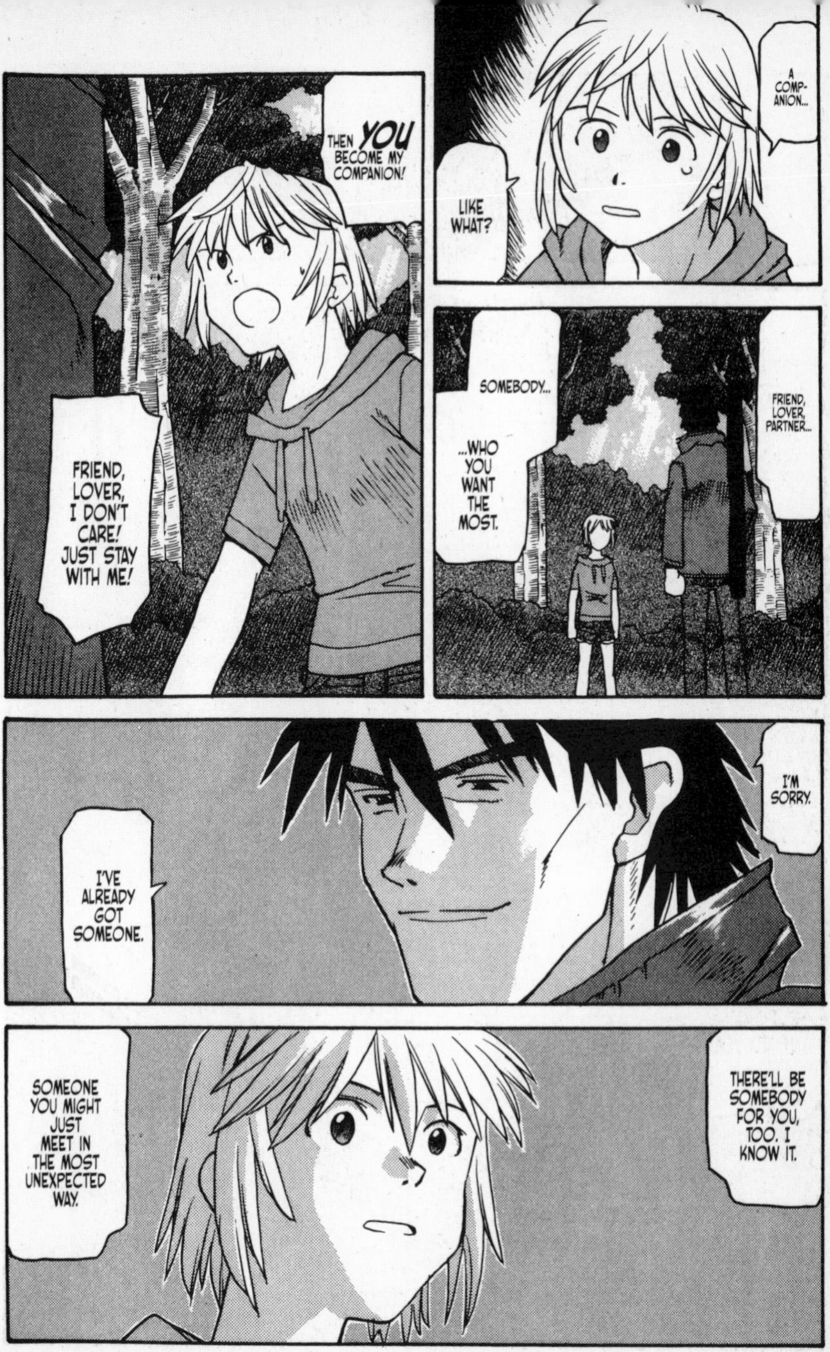

A COMPANION...
LIKE WHAT?
FRIEND, LOVER, PARTNER...
SOMEBODY...
...WHO YOU WANT THE MOST.
THEN YOU BECOME MY COMPANION!
FRIEND, LOVER, I DON'T CARE! JUST STAY WITH ME!
I'M SORRY.
I'VE ALREADY GOT SOMEONE.
THERE'LL BE SOMEBODY FOR YOU, TOO. I KNOW IT.
SOMEONE YOU MIGHT JUST MEET IN THE MOST UNEXPECTED WAY.

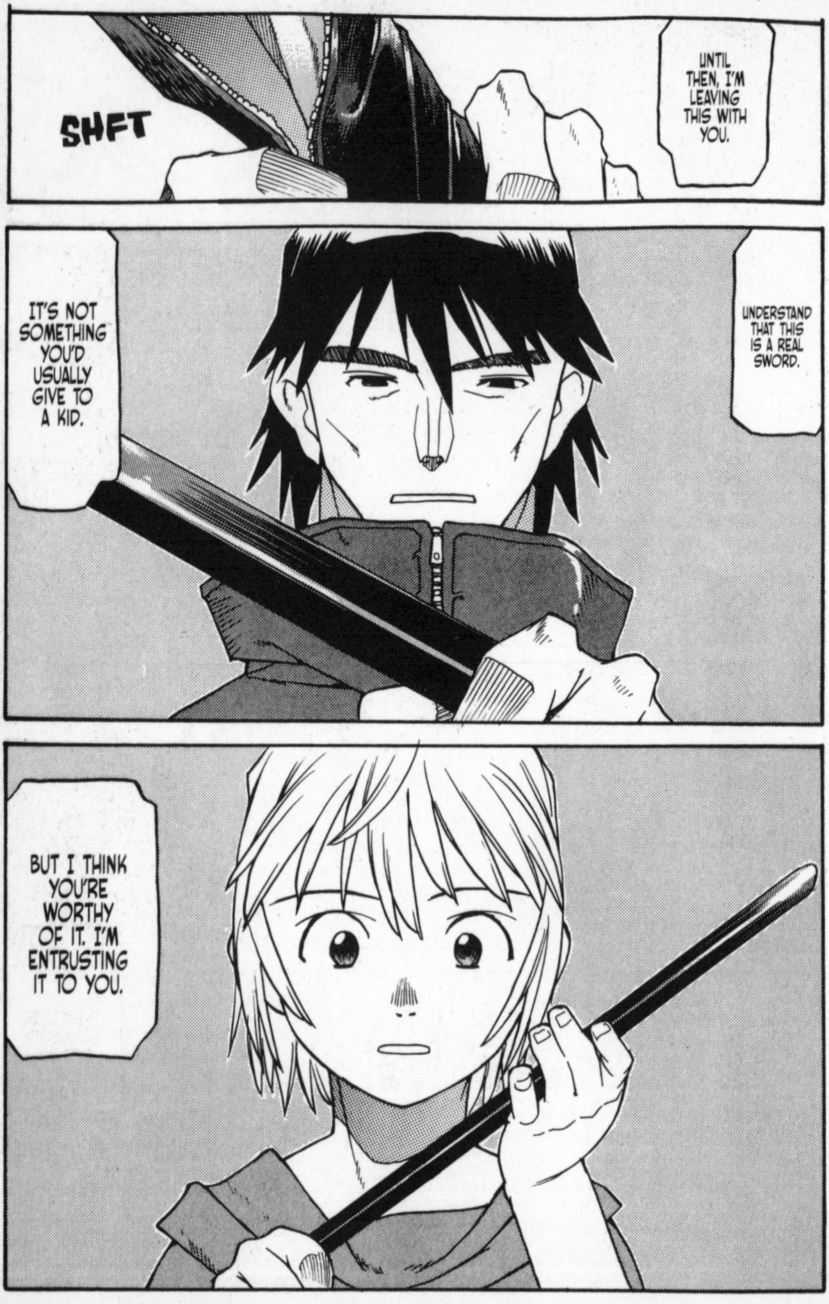
UNTIL THEN, I'M LEAVING THIS WITH YOU.
SHFT
UNDERSTAND THAT THIS IS A REAL SWORD.
IT'S NOT SOMETHING YOU'D USUALLY GIVE TO A KID.
BUT I THINK YOU'RE WORTHY OF IT. I'M ENTRUSTING IT TO YOU.

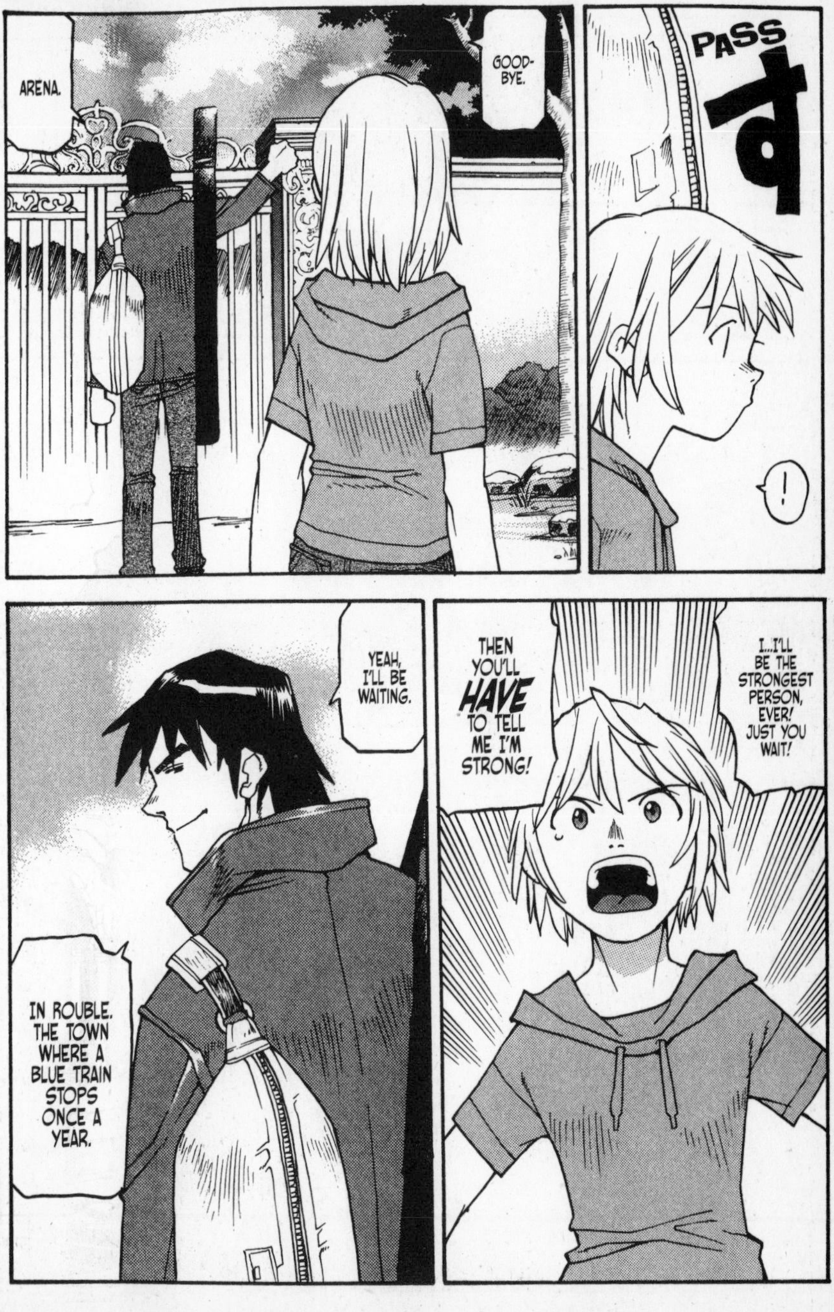
PASS
す
!
GOOD-BYE.
ARENA.
I...I'LL BE THE STRONGEST PERSON, EVER! JUST YOU WAIT!
THEN YOU'LL HAVE TO TELL ME I'M STRONG!
YEAH, I'LL BE WAITING.
IN ROUBLE. THE TOWN WHERE A BLUE TRAIN STOPS ONCE A YEAR.

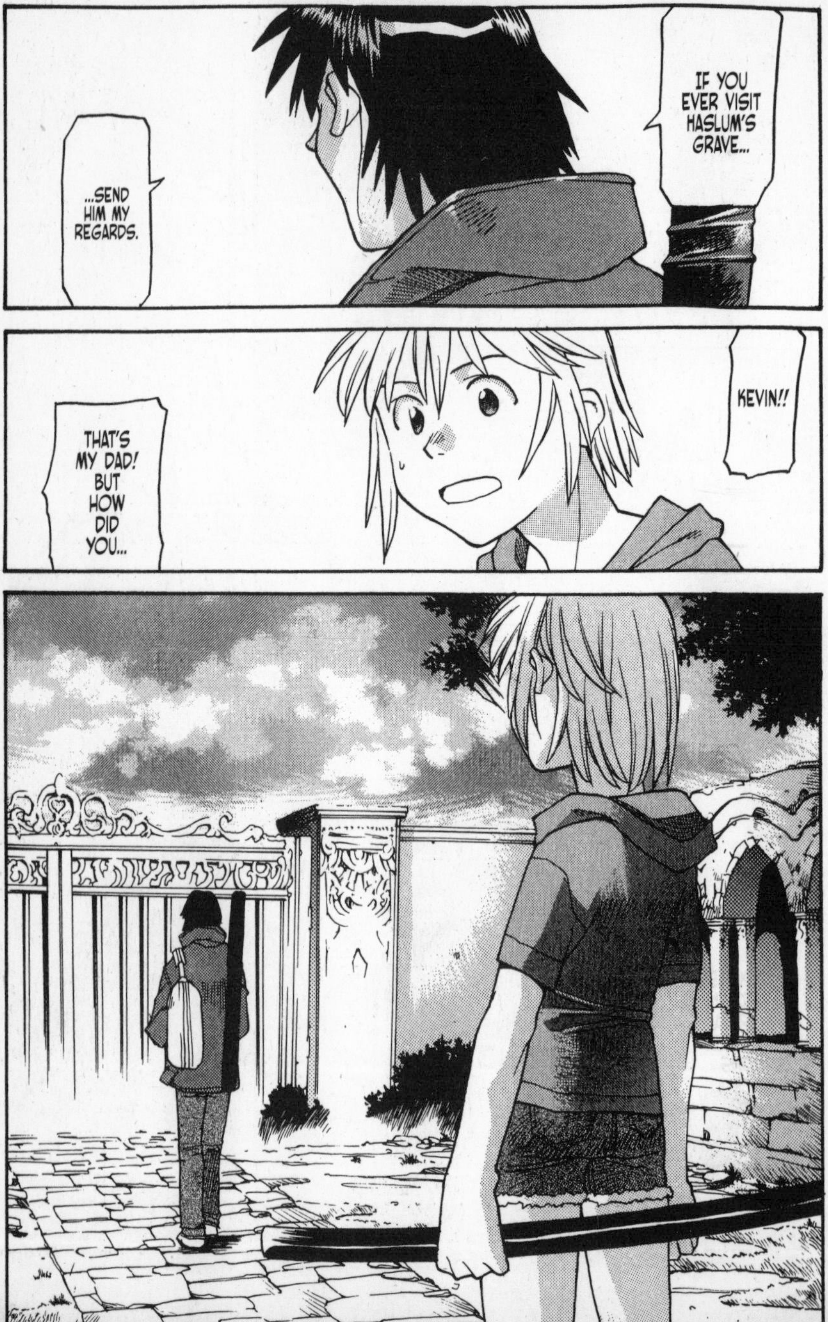
IF YOU EVER VISIT HASLUM'S GRAVE...
...SEND HIM MY REGARDS.
KEVIN!!
THAT'S MY DAD! BUT HOW DID YOU...

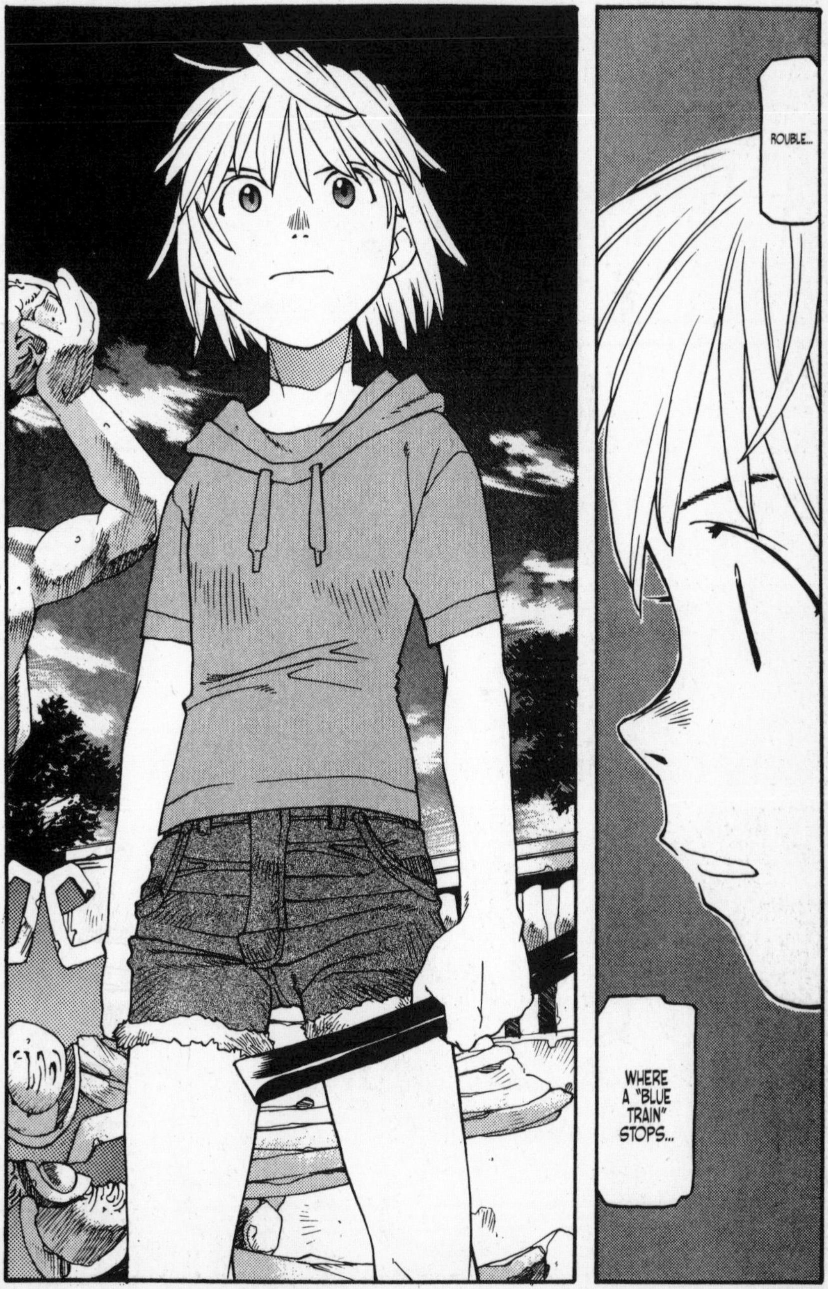
ROUBLE...
WHERE A "BLUE TRAIN" STOPS...

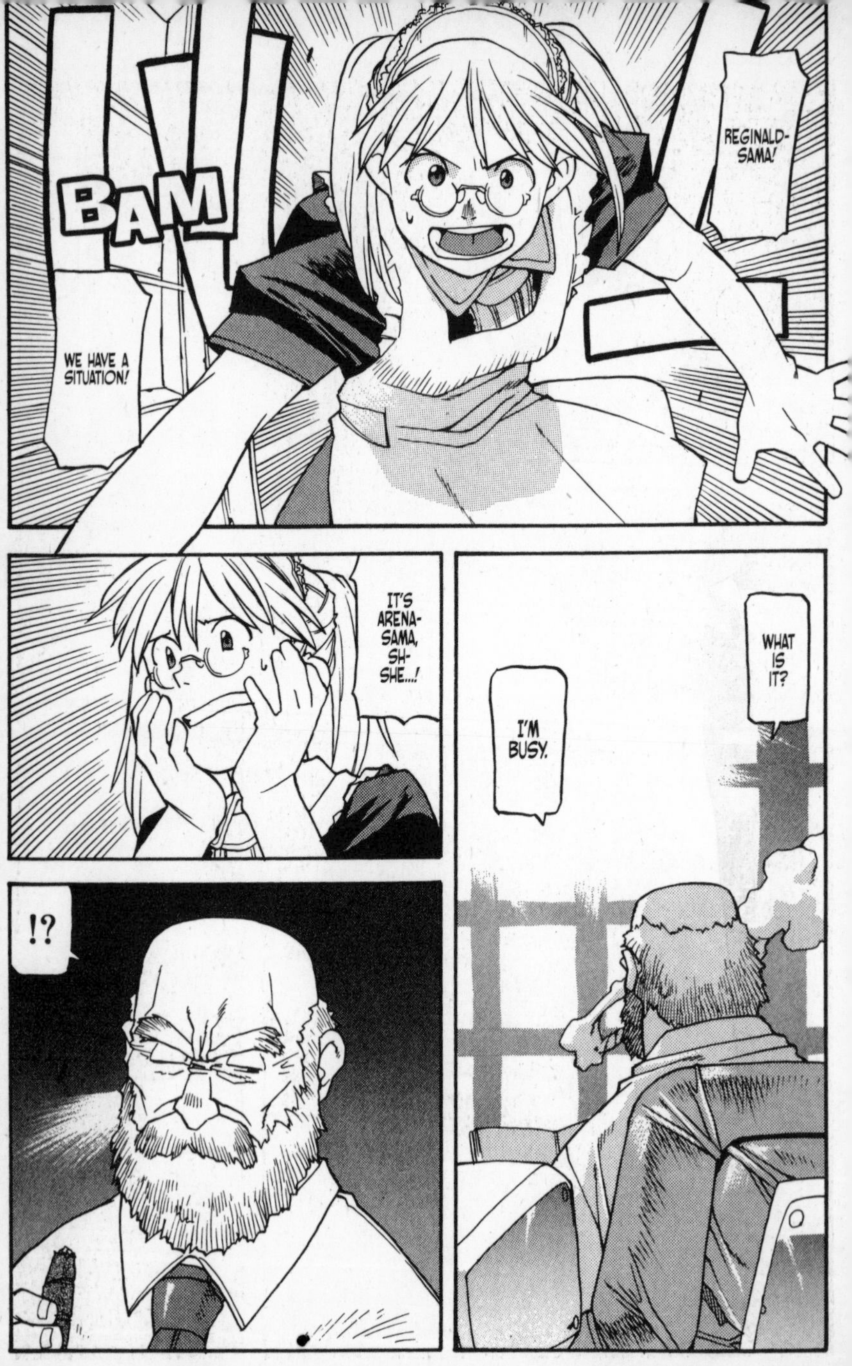
REGINALD-SAMA!
BAM
WE HAVE A SITUATION!
WHAT IS IT?
I'M BUSY.
IT'S ARENA-SAMA, SH-SHE...!
!?

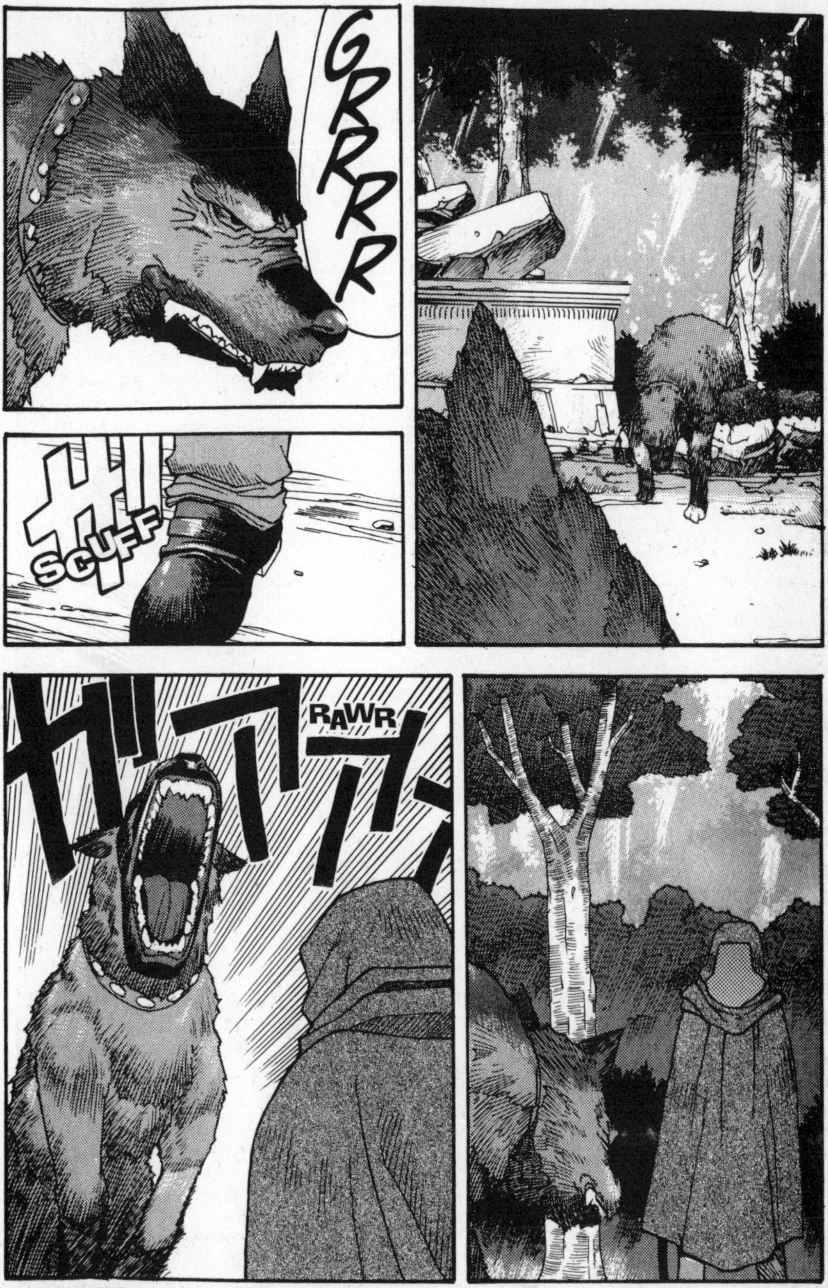
GRRRR
SCUFF
RAWR

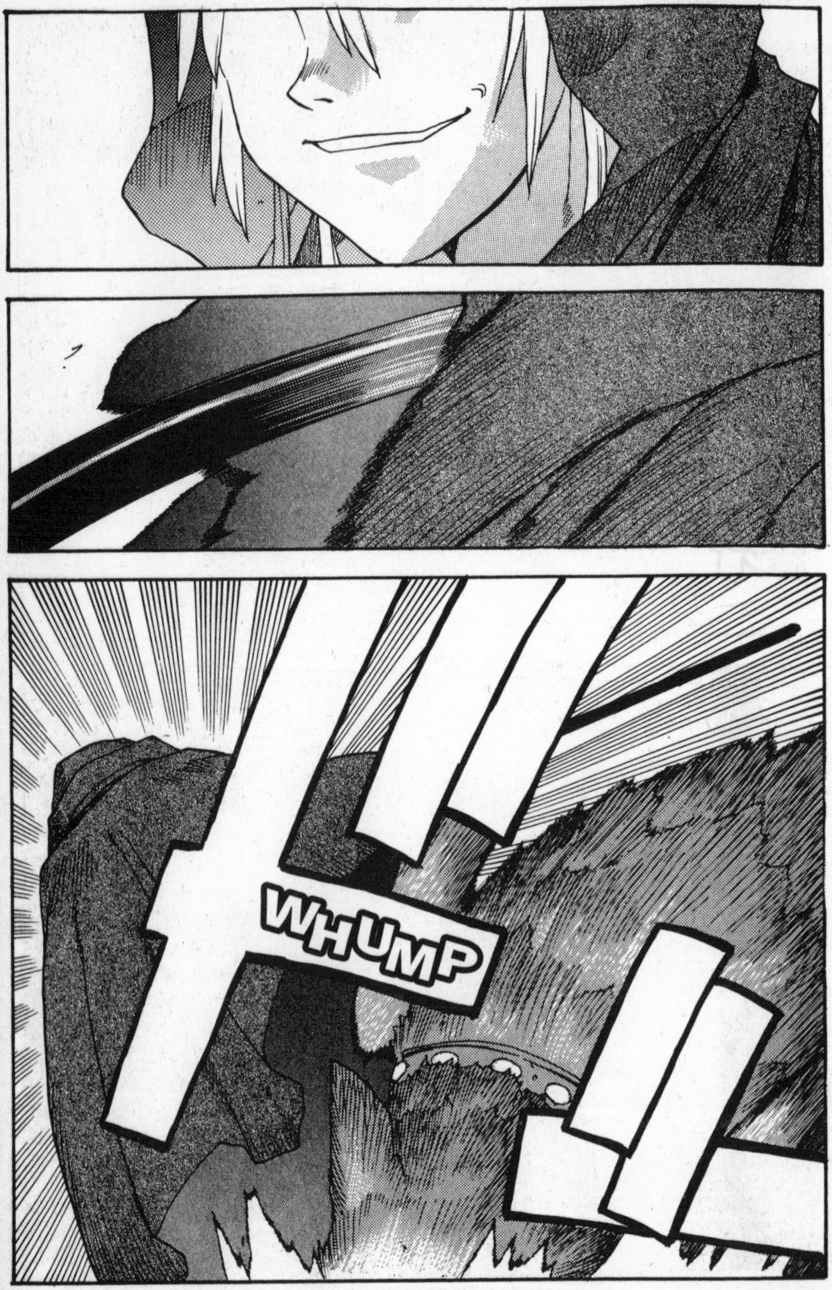
WHUMP

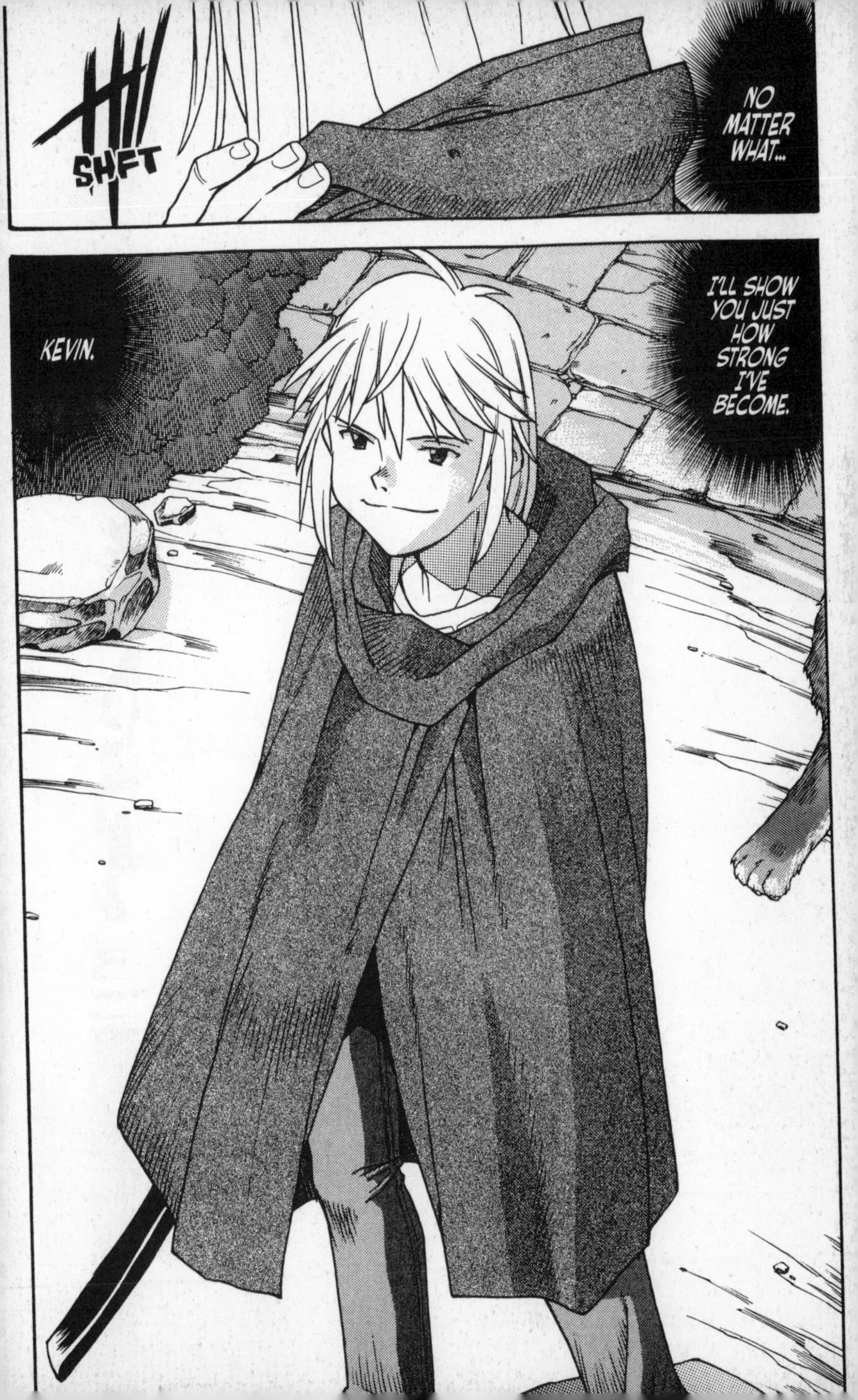
NO MATTER WHAT...
SHFT
I'LL SHOW YOU JUST HOW STRONG I'VE BECOME.
KEVIN.

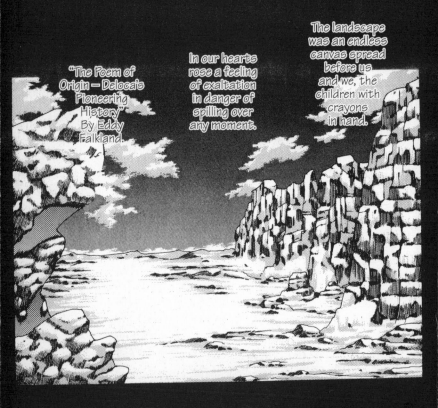

The landscape was an endless canvas spread before us and we, the children with crayons in hand.
In our hearts rose a feeling of exaltation in danger of spilling over any moment.
"The Poem of Origin – Deloca's Pioneering History" By Eddy Falkland.

00. 7. 18
TRAIN+TRAIN
Episode.13
→ Episode.14
INTO THE BLUES
0013

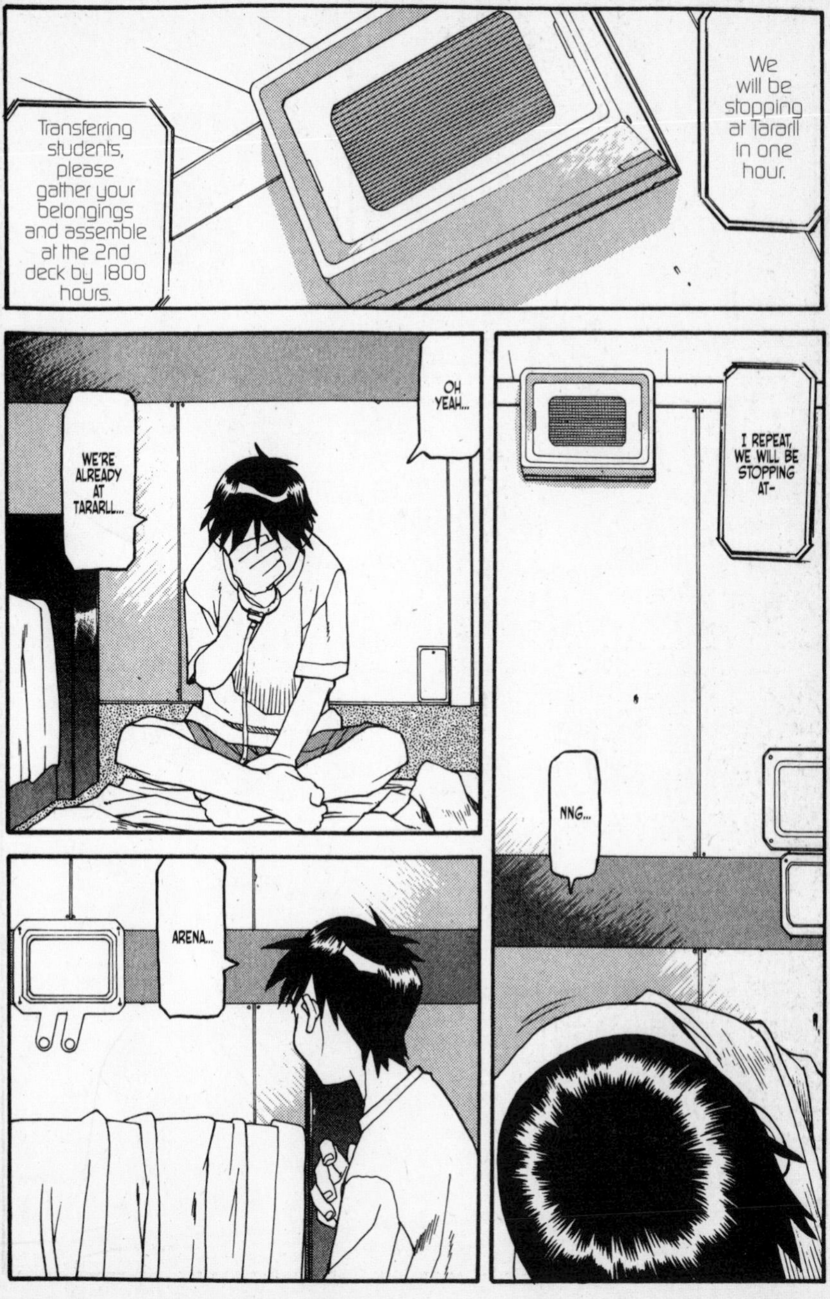
We will be stopping at Tararll in one hour.
Transferring students, please gather your belongings and assemble at the 2nd deck by 1800 hours.
I REPEAT, WE WILL BE STOPPING AT-
NNG...
OH YEAH...
WE'RE ALREADY AT TARARLL...
ARENA...

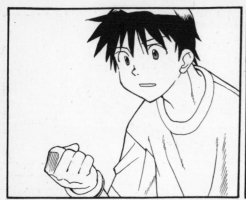

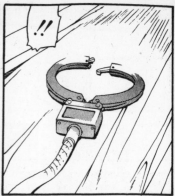

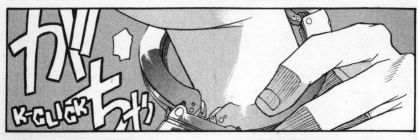

K-GLICK

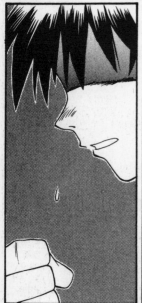

...CAME OFF.

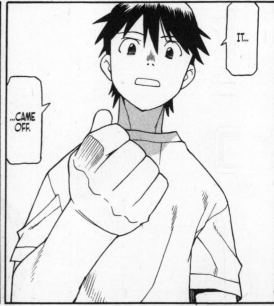

IT...

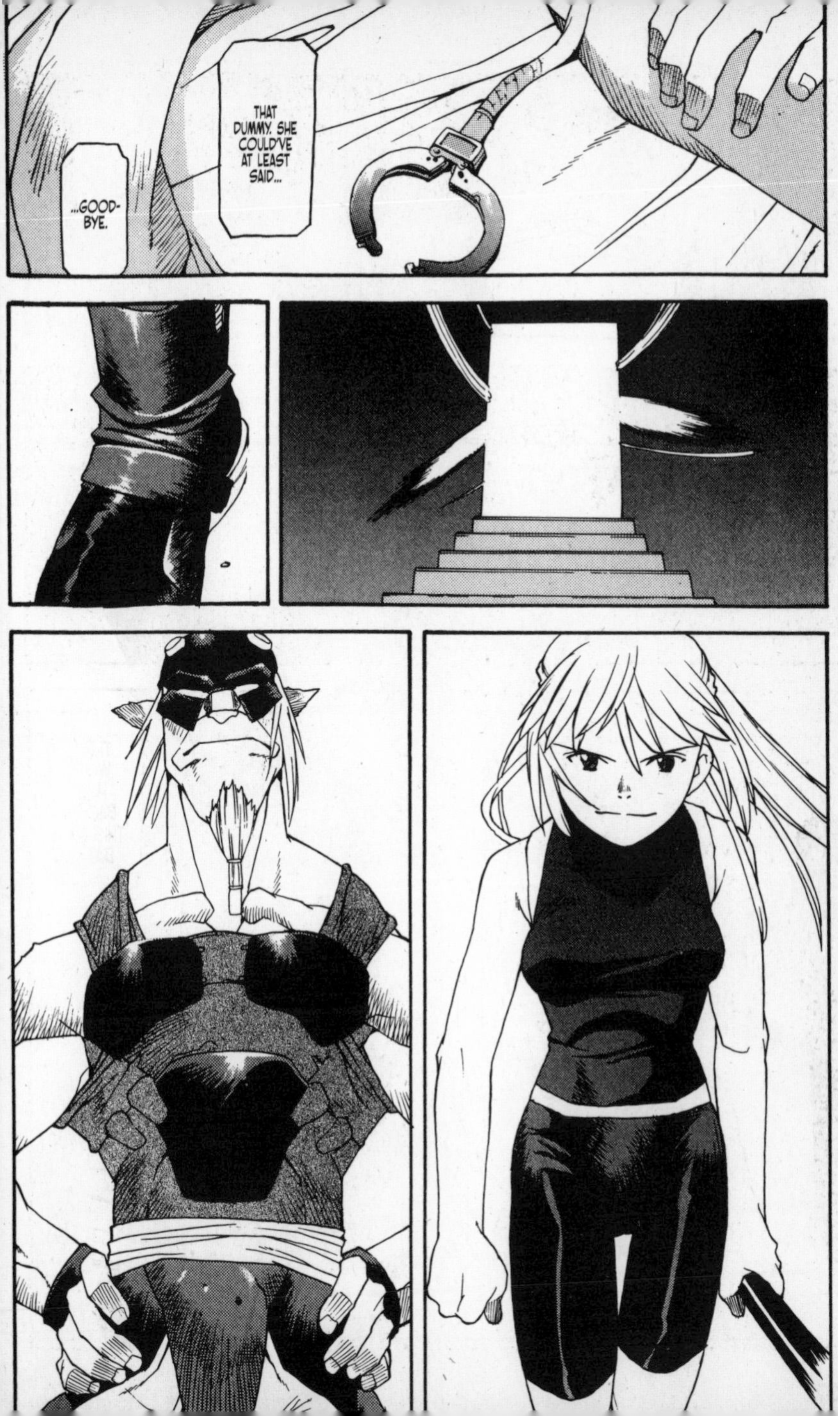
THAT DUMMY. SHE COULD'VE AT LEAST SAID...
...GOOD-BYE.

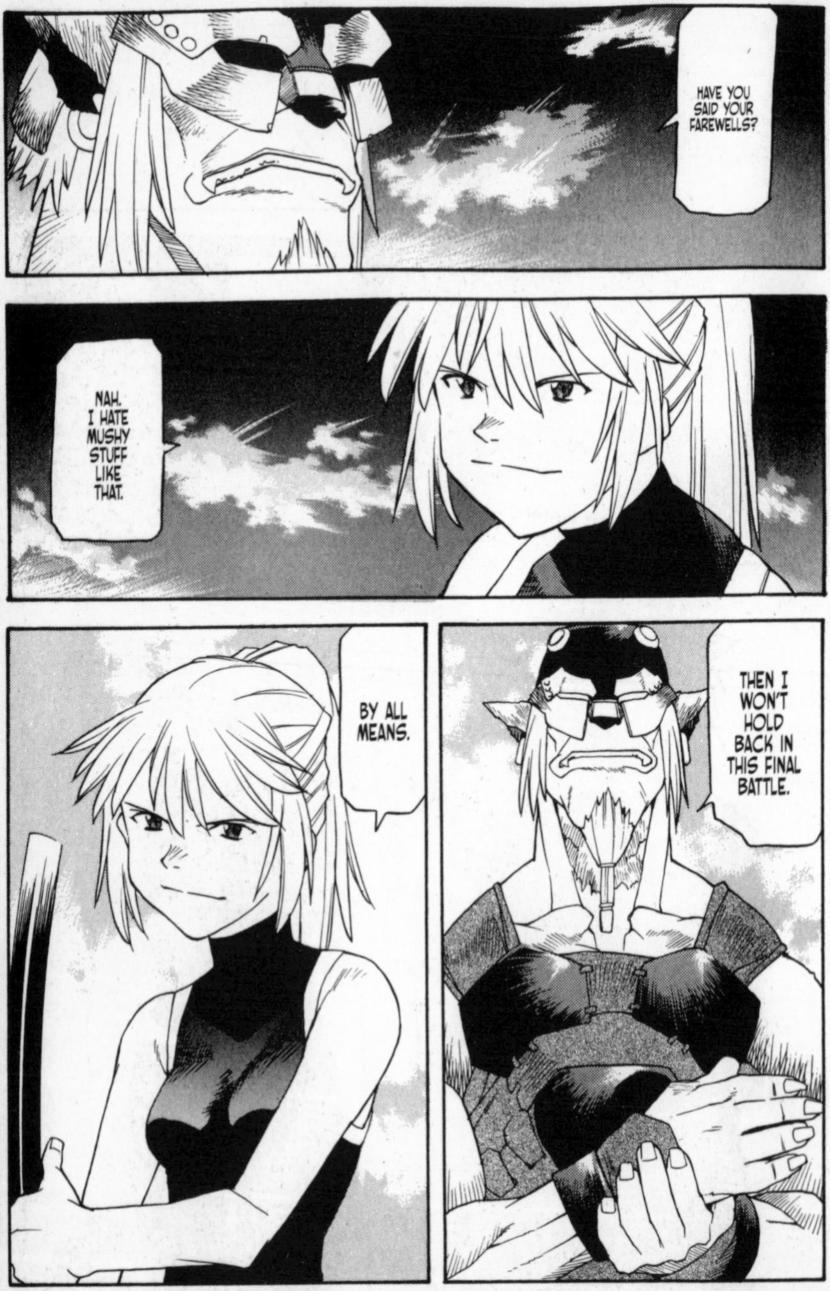
HAVE YOU SAID YOUR FAREWELLS?
NAH. I HATE MUSHY STUFF LIKE THAT.
THEN I WON'T HOLD BACK IN THIS FINAL BATTLE.
BY ALL MEANS.

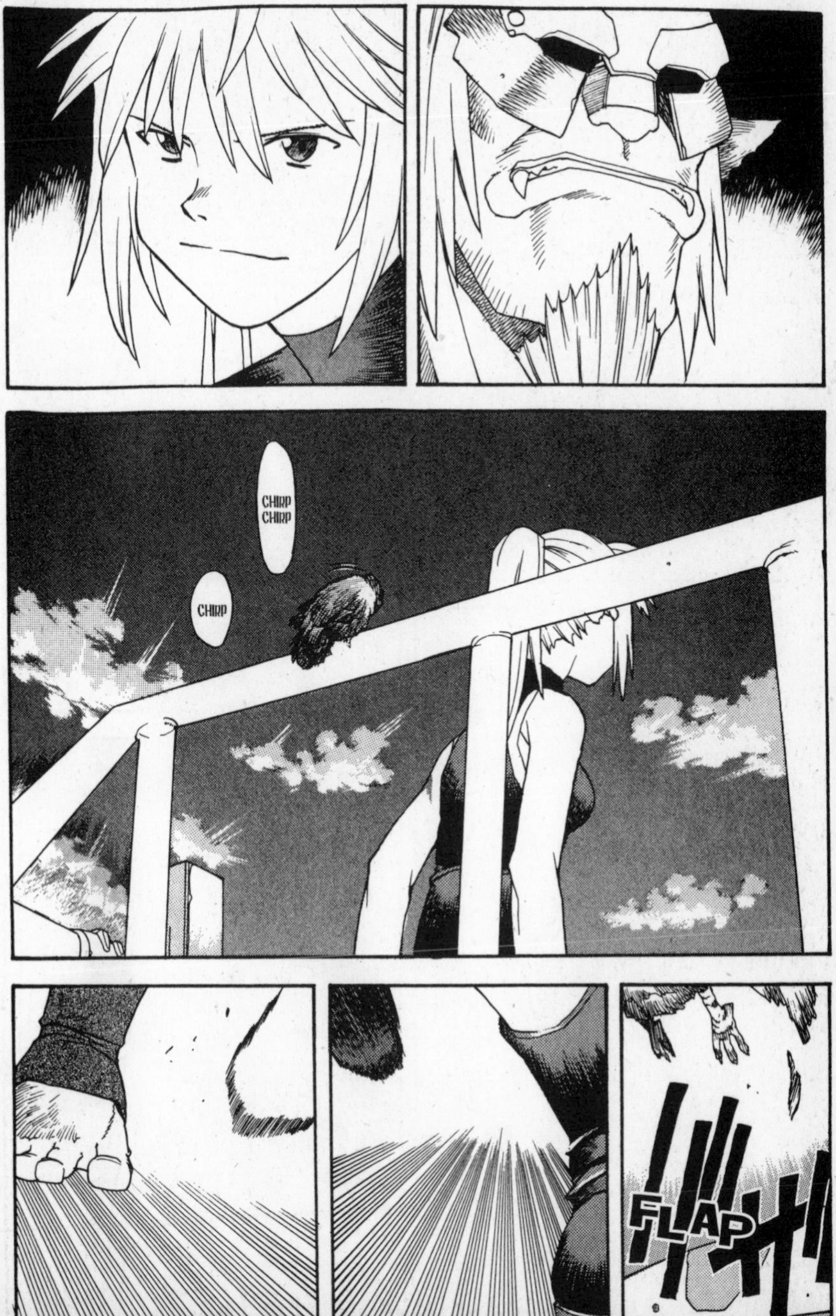
CHIRP
CHIRP
CHIRP
FLAP

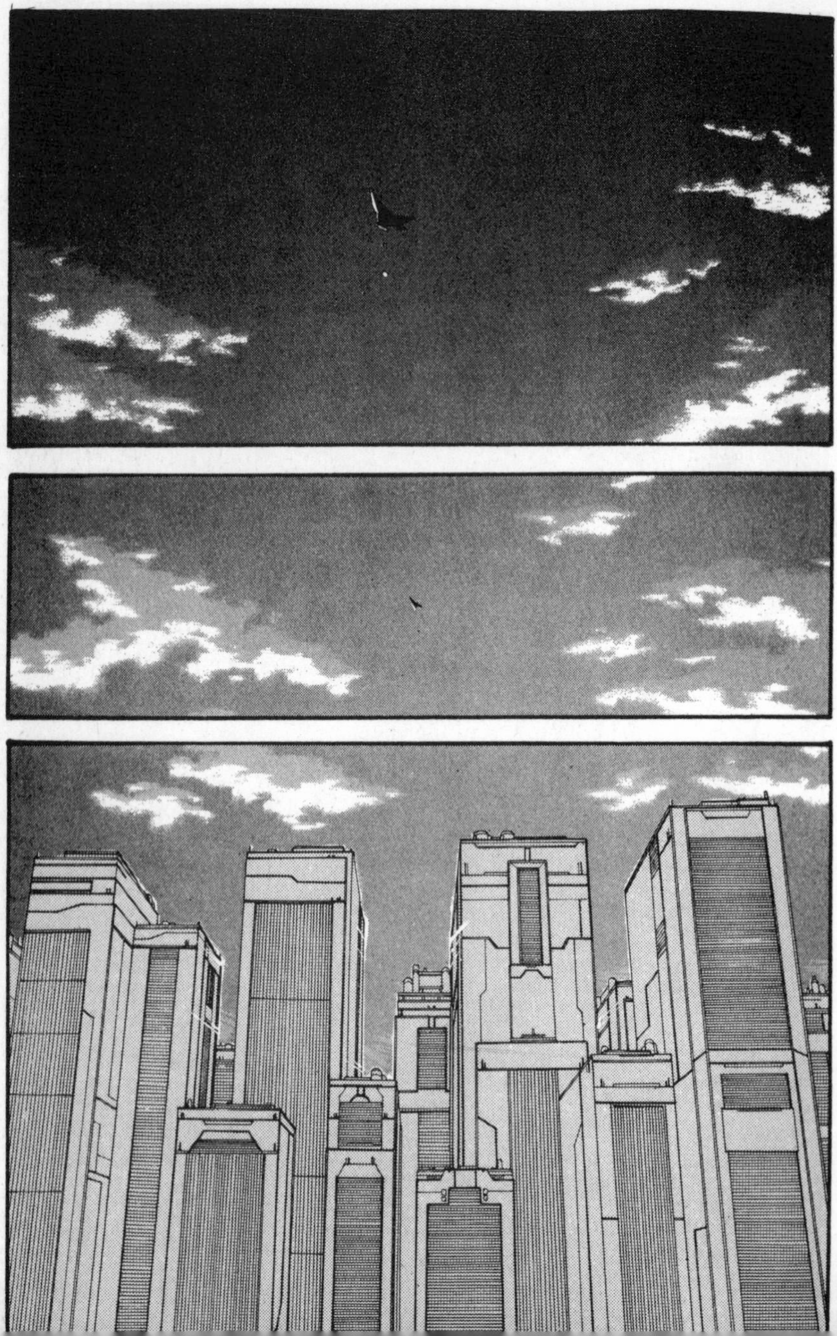

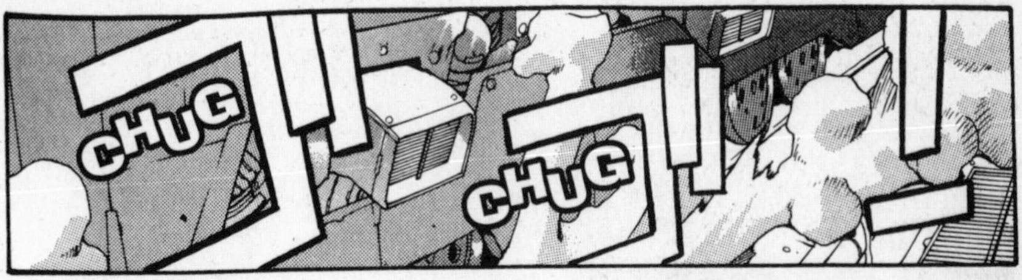
CHUG
CHUG
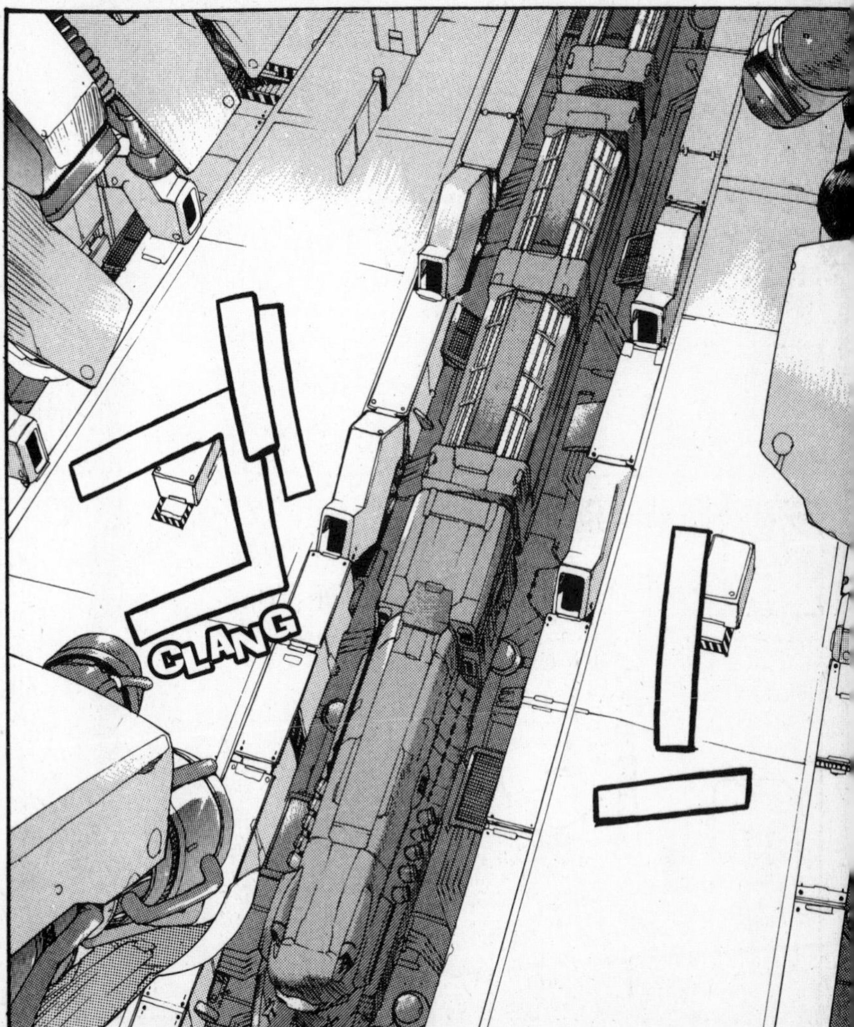
CLANG

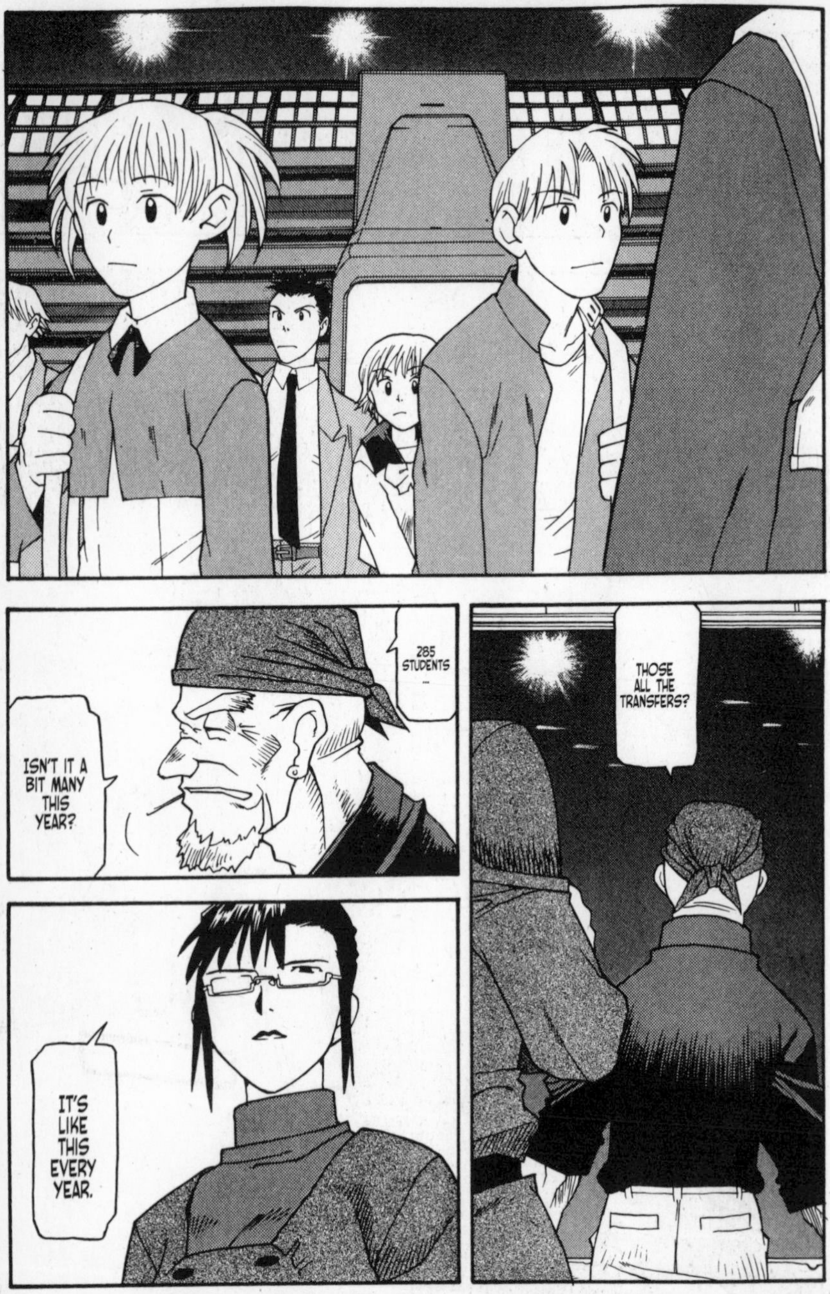
THOSE ALL THE TRANSFERS?
285 STUDENTS ...
ISN'T IT A BIT MANY THIS YEAR?
IT'S LIKE THIS EVERY YEAR.

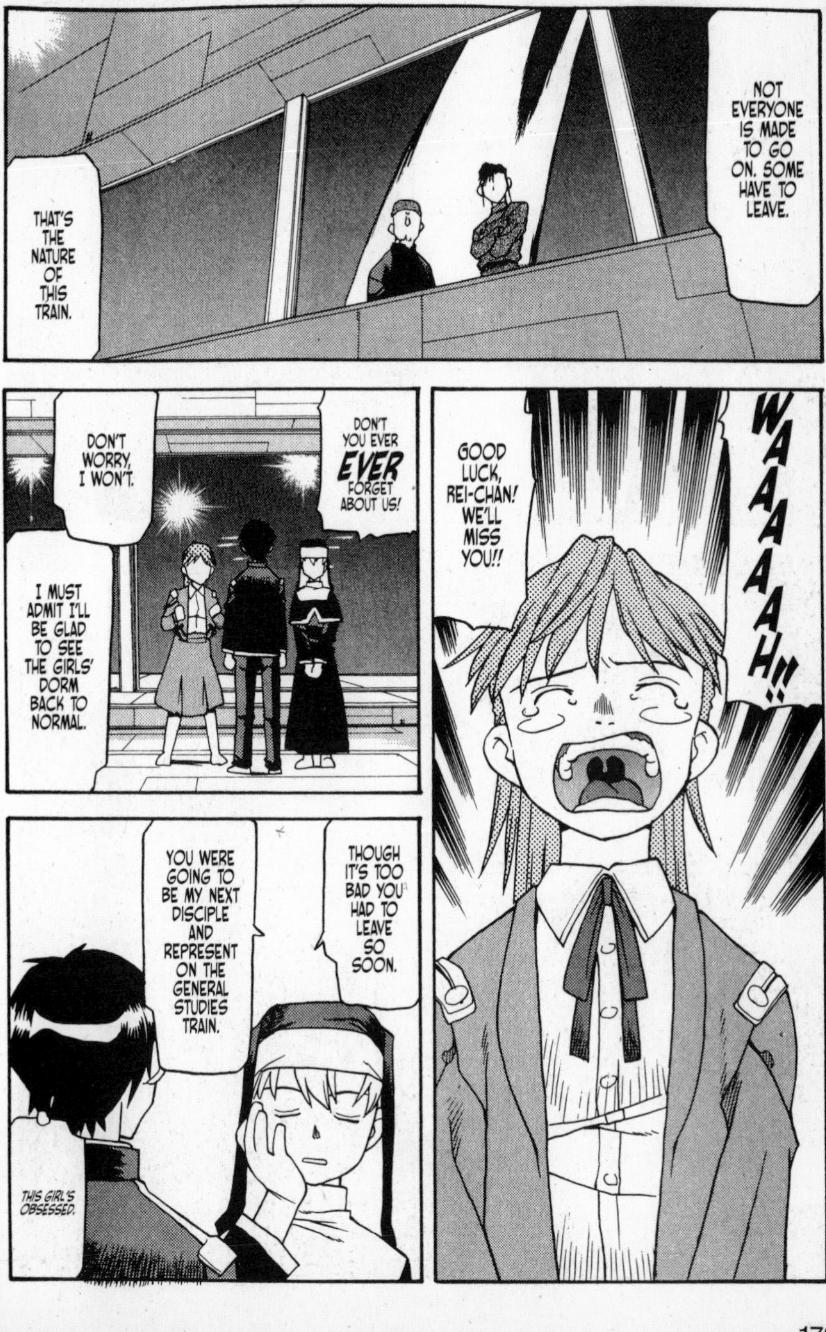
NOT EVERYONE IS MADE TO GO ON. SOME HAVE TO LEAVE.
THAT'S THE NATURE OF THIS TRAIN.
WAAAAAH!!
GOOD LUCK, REI-CHAN! WE'LL MISS YOU!!
DON'T YOU EVER EVER FORGET ABOUT US!
DON'T WORRY, I WON'T.
I MUST ADMIT I'LL BE GLAD TO SEE THE GIRLS' DORM BACK TO NORMAL.
THOUGH IT'S TOO BAD YOU HAD TO LEAVE SO SOON.
YOU WERE GOING TO BE MY NEXT DISCIPLE AND REPRESENT ON THE GENERAL STUDIES TRAIN.
THIS GIRL'S OBSESSED.

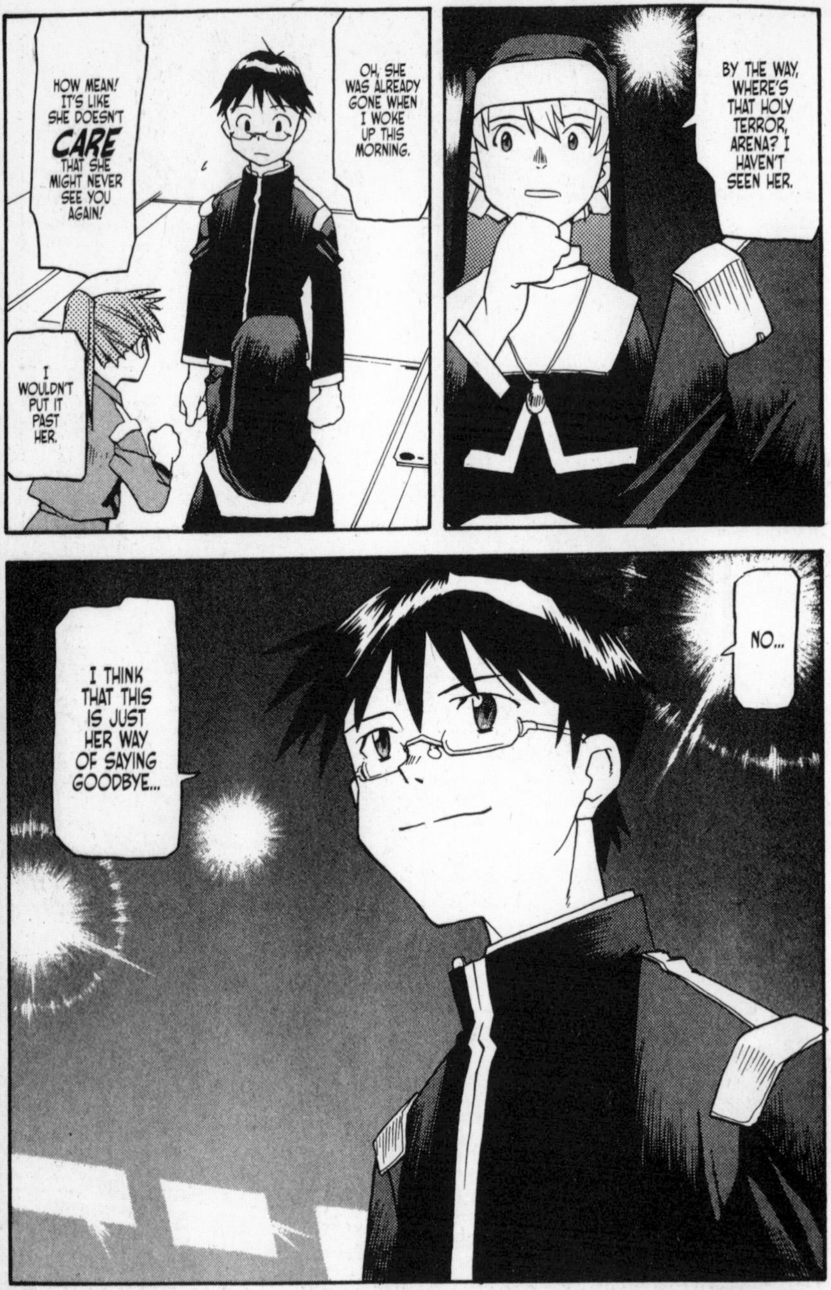
BY THE WAY, WHERE'S THAT HOLY TERROR, ARENA? I HAVEN'T SEEN HER.
OH, SHE WAS ALREADY GONE WHEN I WOKE UP THIS MORNING.
HOW MEAN! IT'S LIKE SHE DOESN'T CARE THAT SHE MIGHT NEVER SEE YOU AGAIN!
I WOULDN'T PUT IT PAST HER.
NO...
I THINK THAT THIS IS JUST HER WAY OF SAYING GOODBYE...

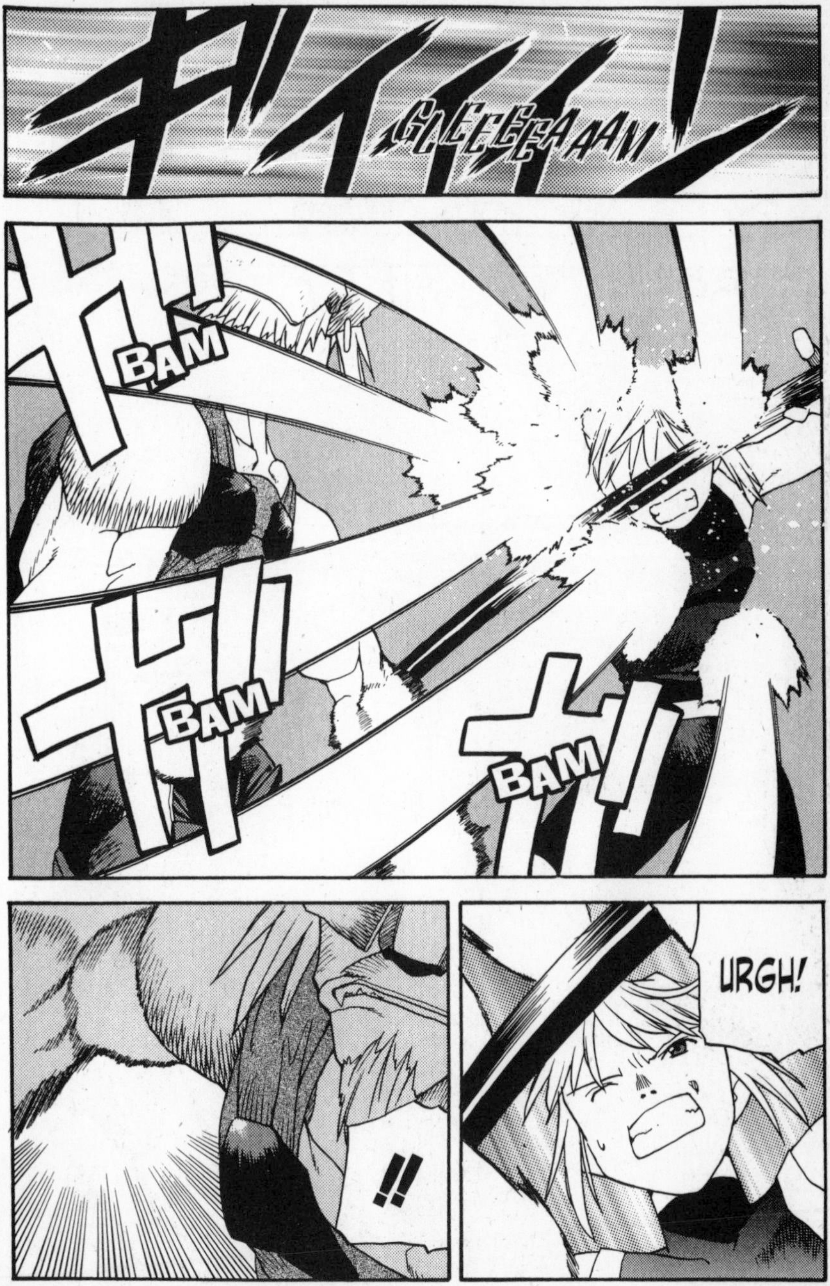
GLEEEEAAAM
BAM
BAM
BAM
URGH!
!!

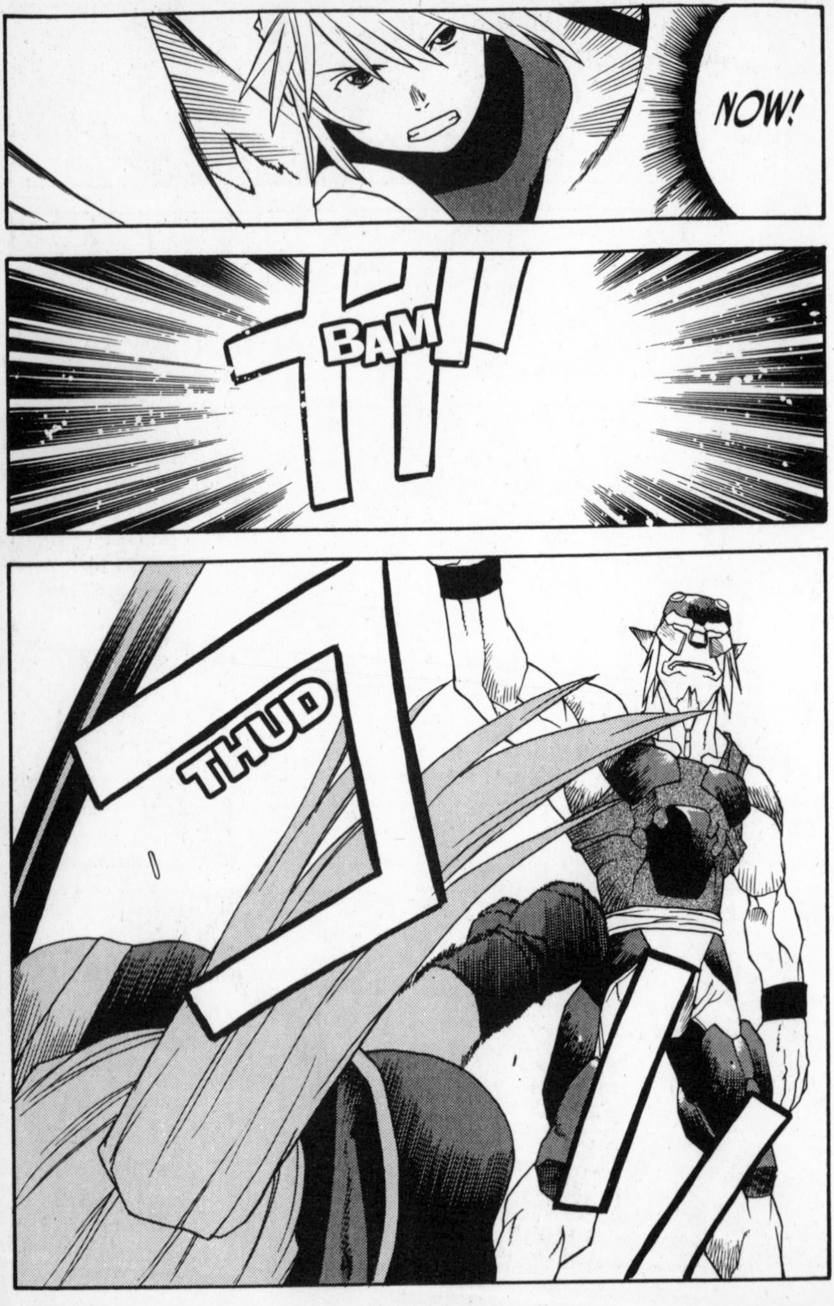
NOW!
BAM
THUD

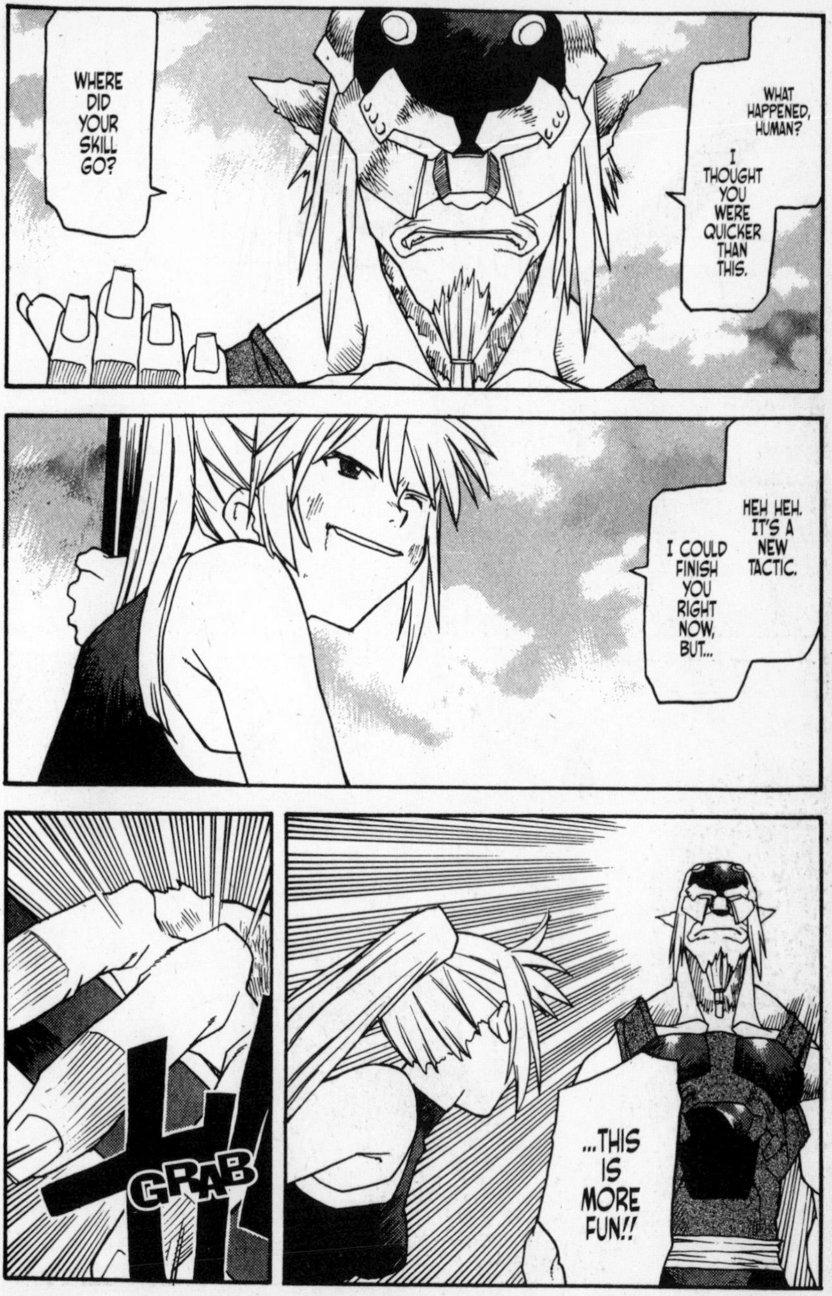
WHAT HAPPENED, HUMAN?
I THOUGHT YOU WERE QUICKER THAN THIS.
WHERE DID YOUR SKILL GO?
HEH HEH. IT'S A NEW TACTIC.
I COULD FINISH YOU RIGHT NOW, BUT...
...THIS IS MORE FUN!!
GRAB

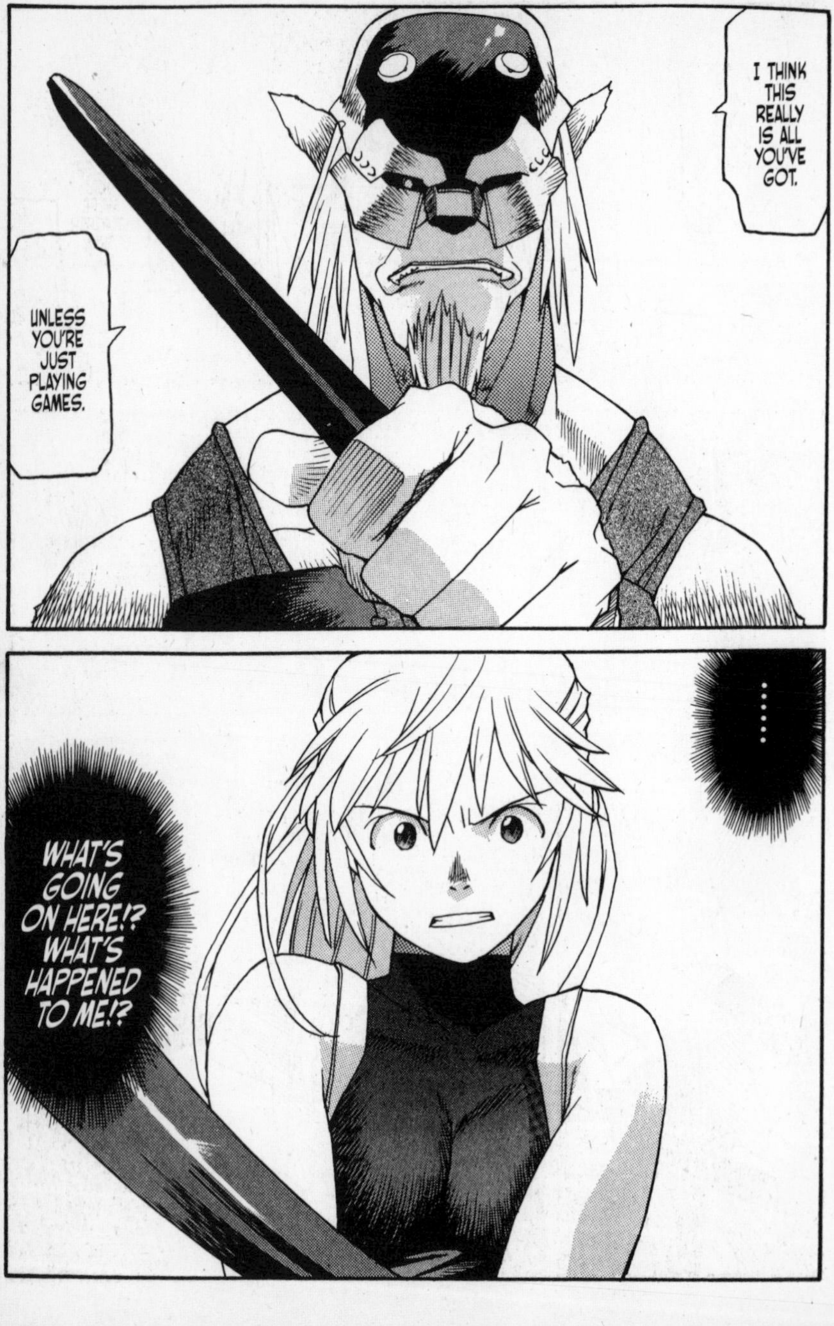
I THINK THIS REALLY IS ALL YOU'VE GOT.
UNLESS YOU'RE JUST PLAYING GAMES.
......
WHAT'S GOING ON HERE!? WHAT'S HAPPENED TO ME!?

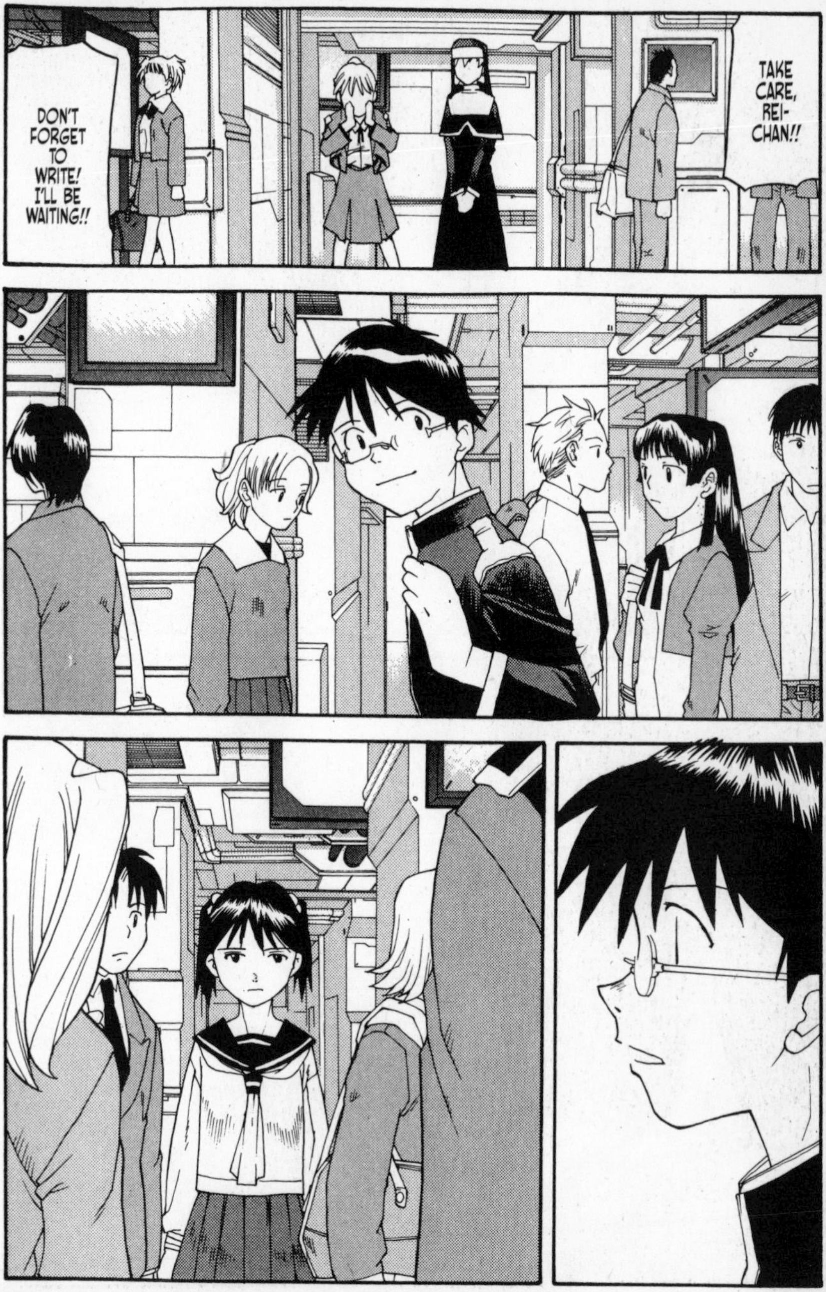
TAKE CARE, REI-CHAN!!
DON'T FORGET TO WRITE! I'LL BE WAITING!!

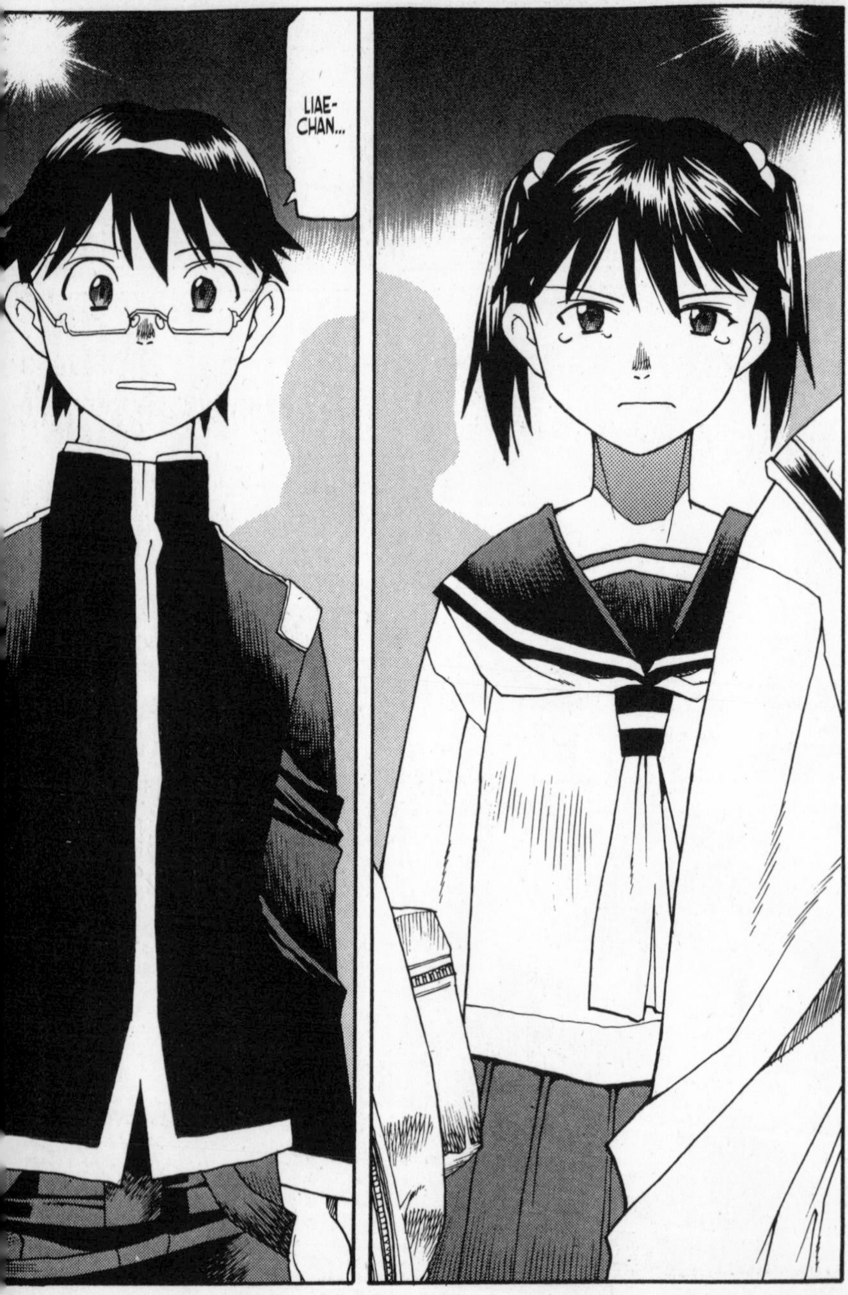
LIAE-CHAN...

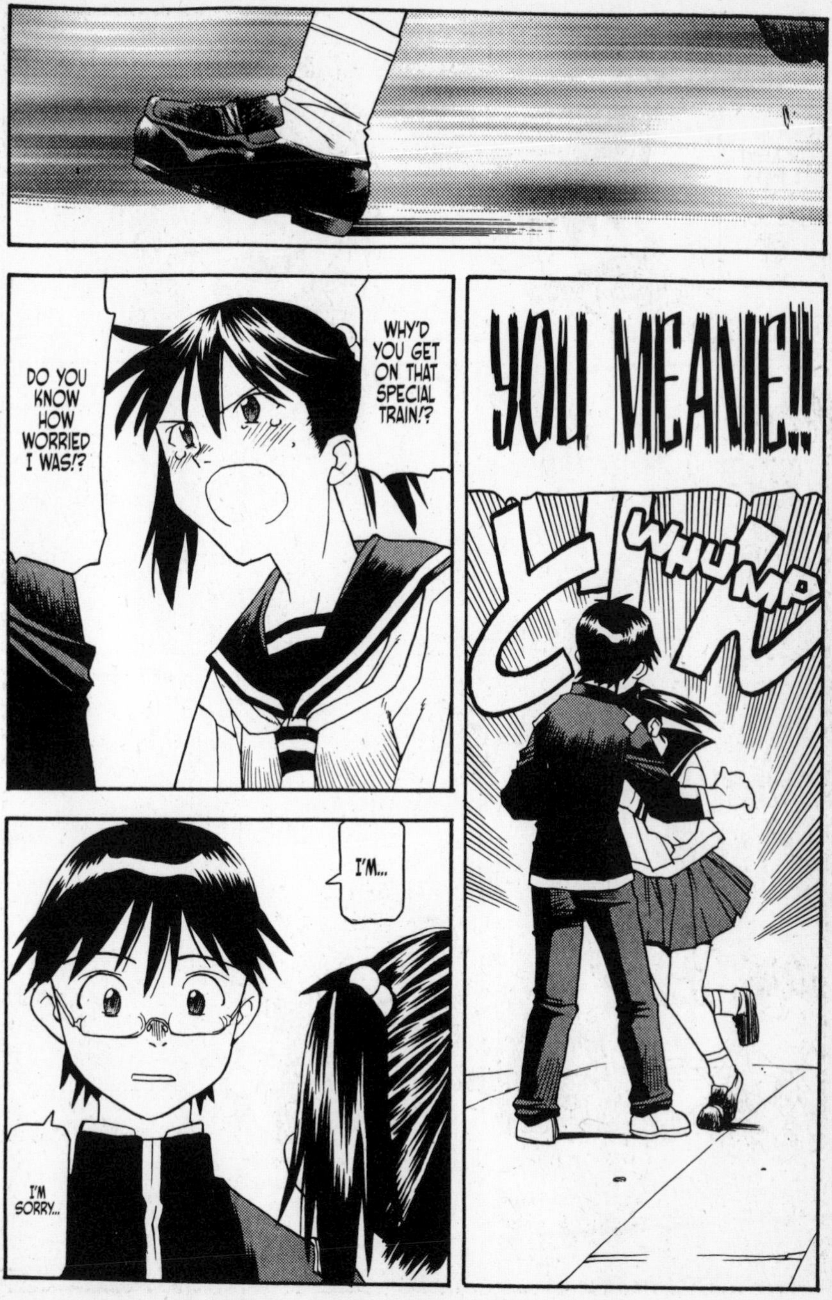
YOU MEANIE!!
WHUMP
WHY'D YOU GET ON THAT SPECIAL TRAIN!?
DO YOU KNOW HOW WORRIED I WAS!?
I'M...
I'M SORRY...

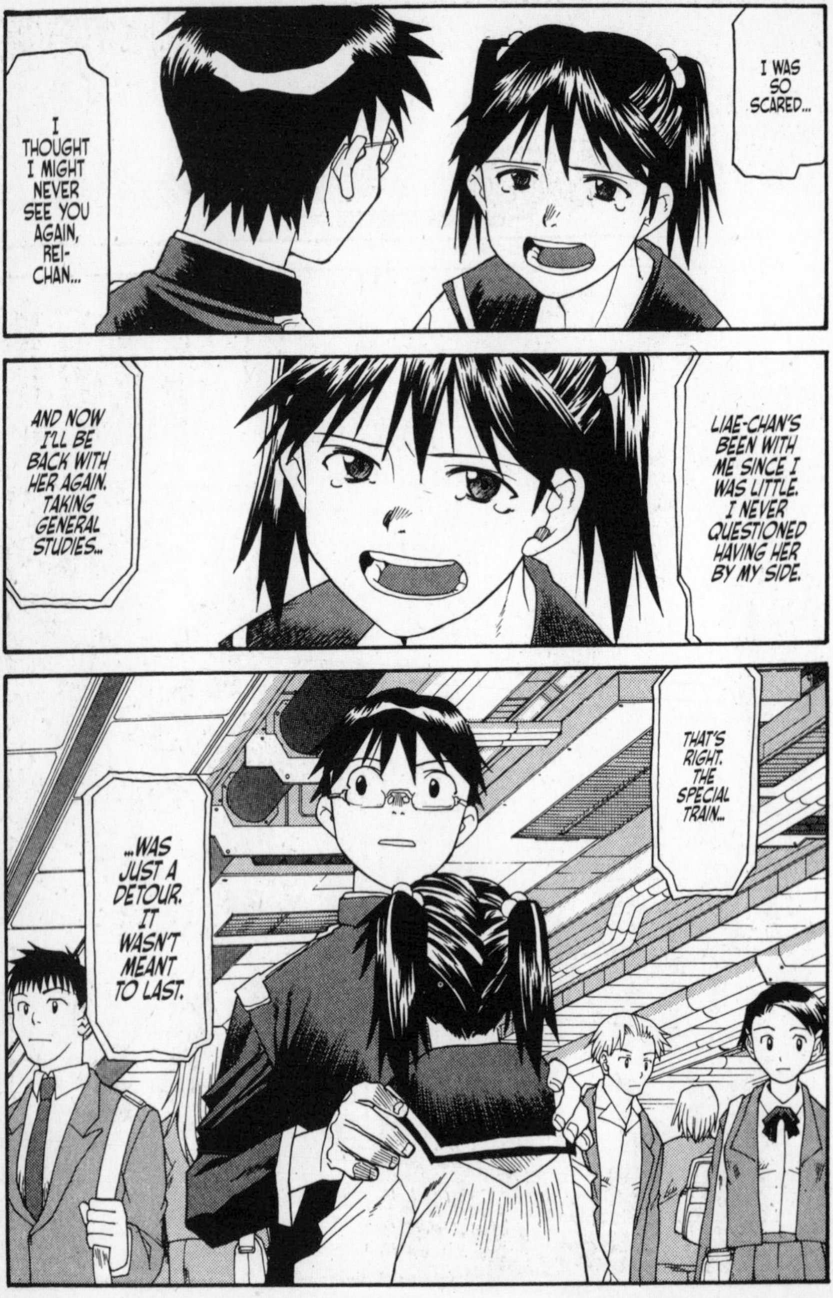
I WAS SO SCARED...
I THOUGHT I MIGHT NEVER SEE YOU AGAIN, REI-CHAN...
LIAE-CHAN'S BEEN WITH ME SINCE I WAS LITTLE. I NEVER QUESTIONED HAVING HER BY MY SIDE.
AND NOW I'LL BE BACK WITH HER AGAIN. TAKING GENERAL STUDIES...
THAT'S RIGHT. THE SPECIAL TRAIN...
...WAS JUST A DETOUR. IT WASN'T MEANT TO LAST.

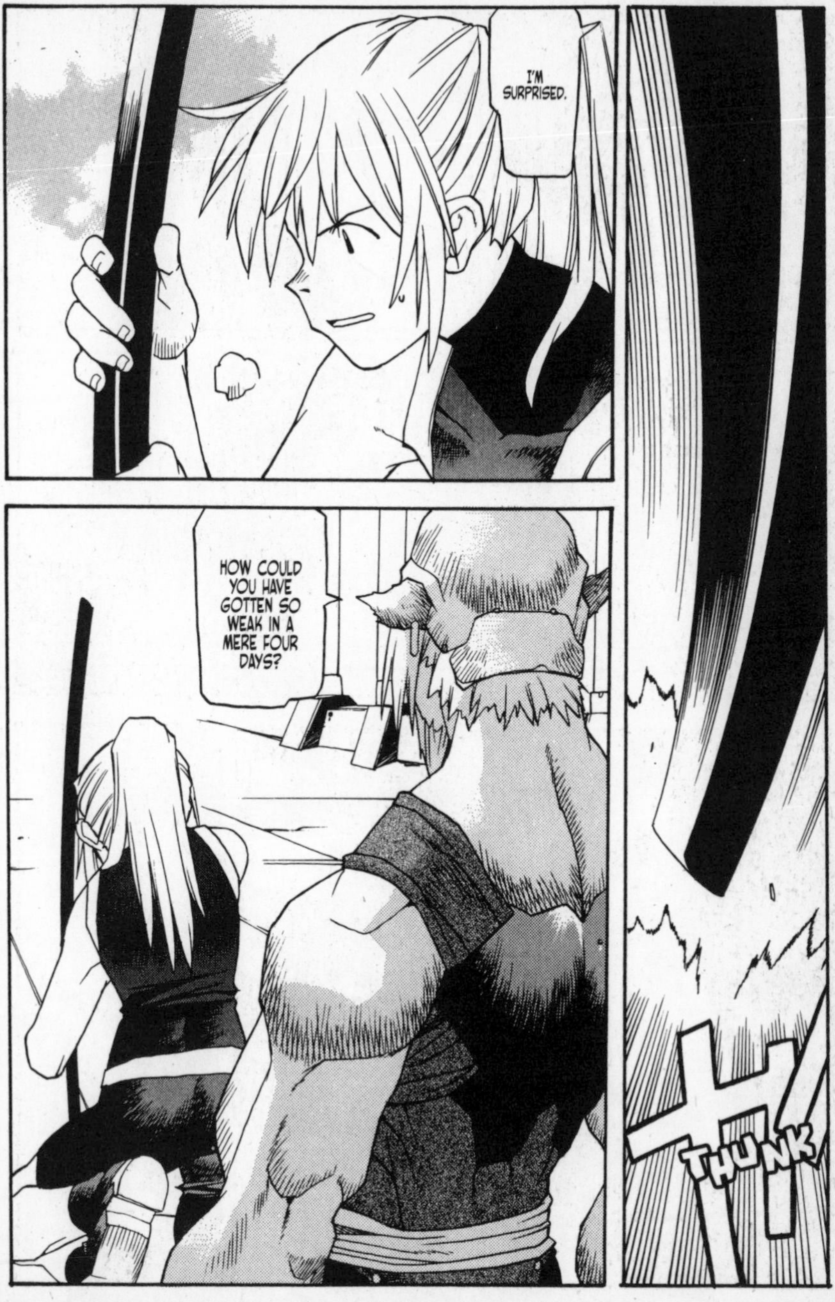
I'M SURPRISED.
HOW COULD YOU HAVE GOTTEN SO WEAK IN A MERE FOUR DAYS?
THUNK

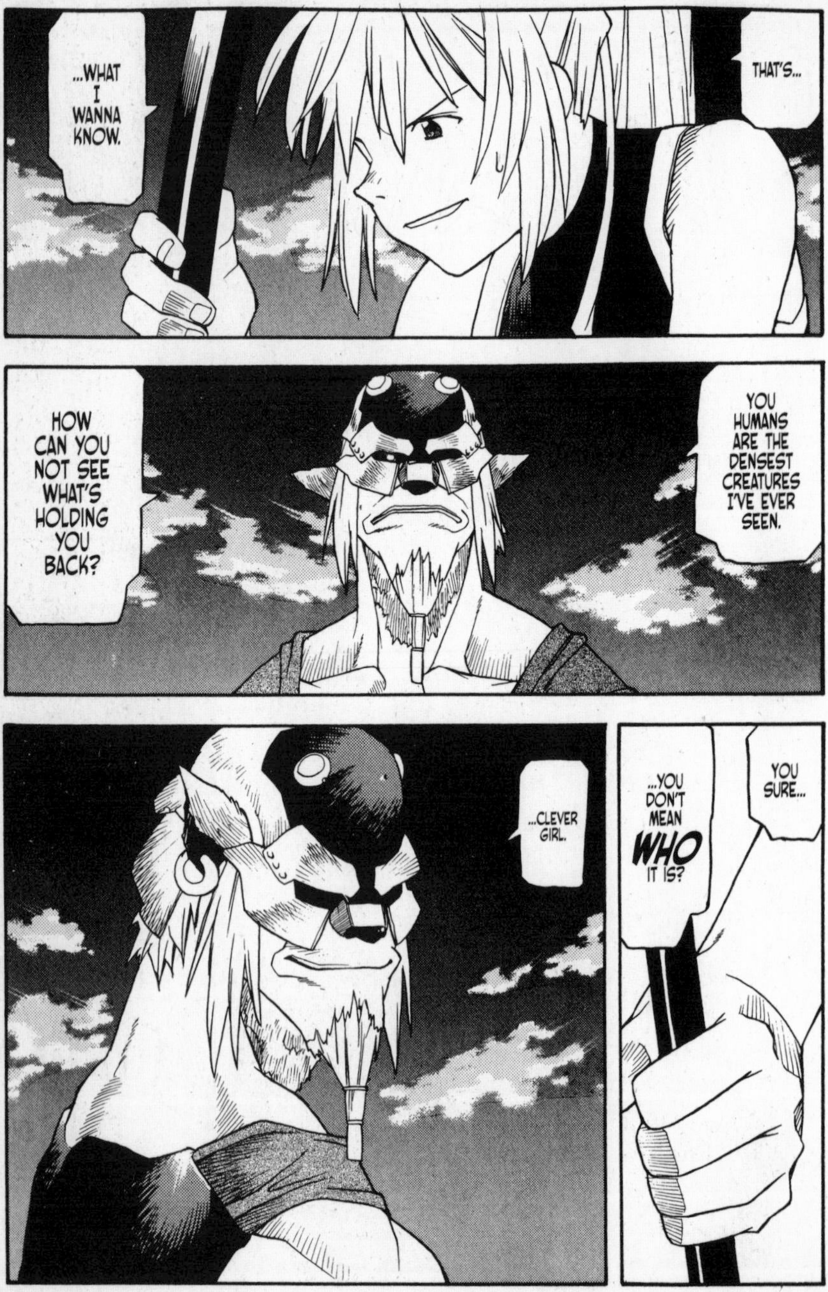
THAT'S...
...WHAT I WANNA KNOW.
YOU HUMANS ARE THE DENSEST CREATURES I'VE EVER SEEN.
HOW CAN YOU NOT SEE WHAT'S HOLDING YOU BACK?
YOU SURE...
...YOU DON'T MEAN WHO IT IS?
...CLEVER GIRL.

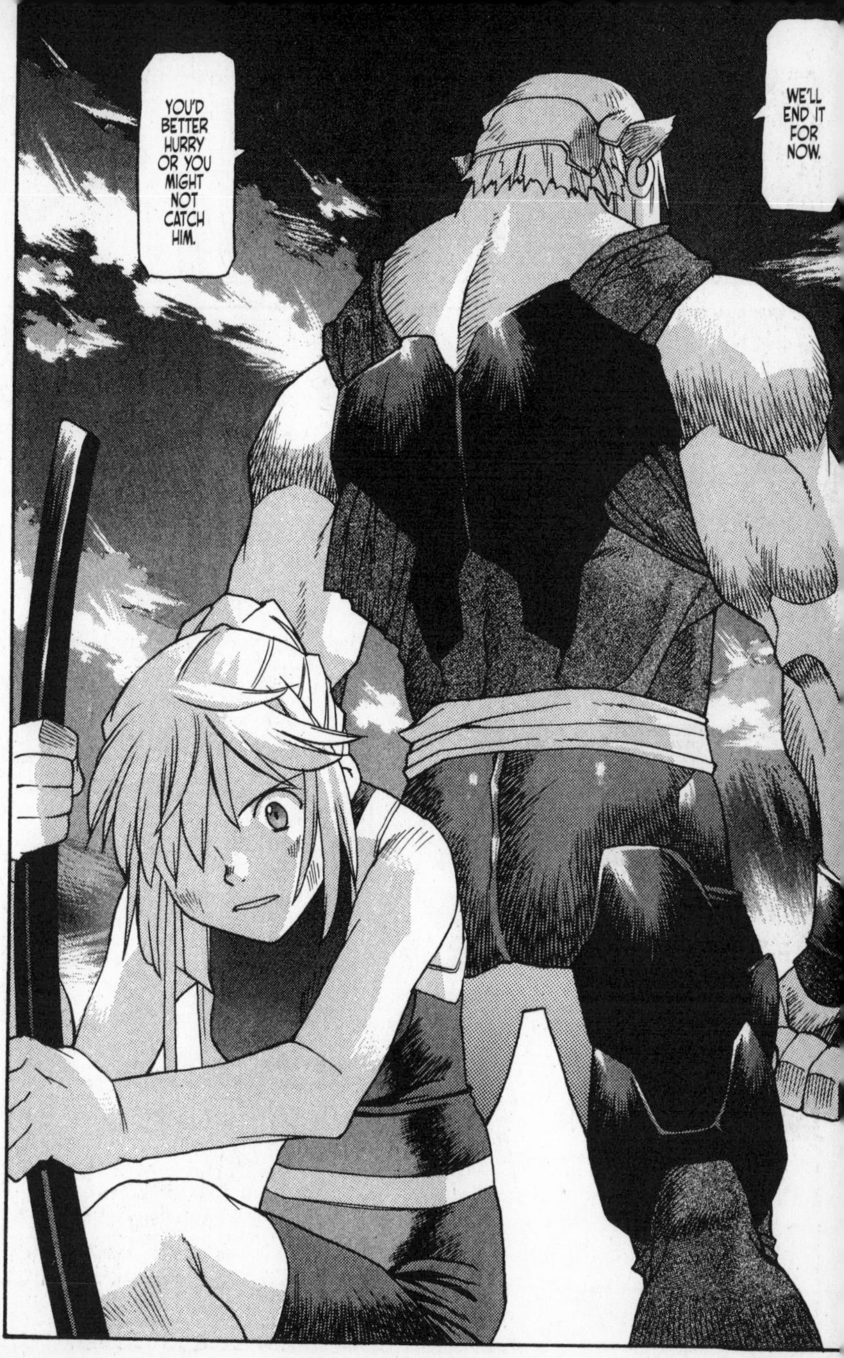
WE'LL END IT FOR NOW.
YOU'D BETTER HURRY OR YOU MIGHT NOT CATCH HIM.

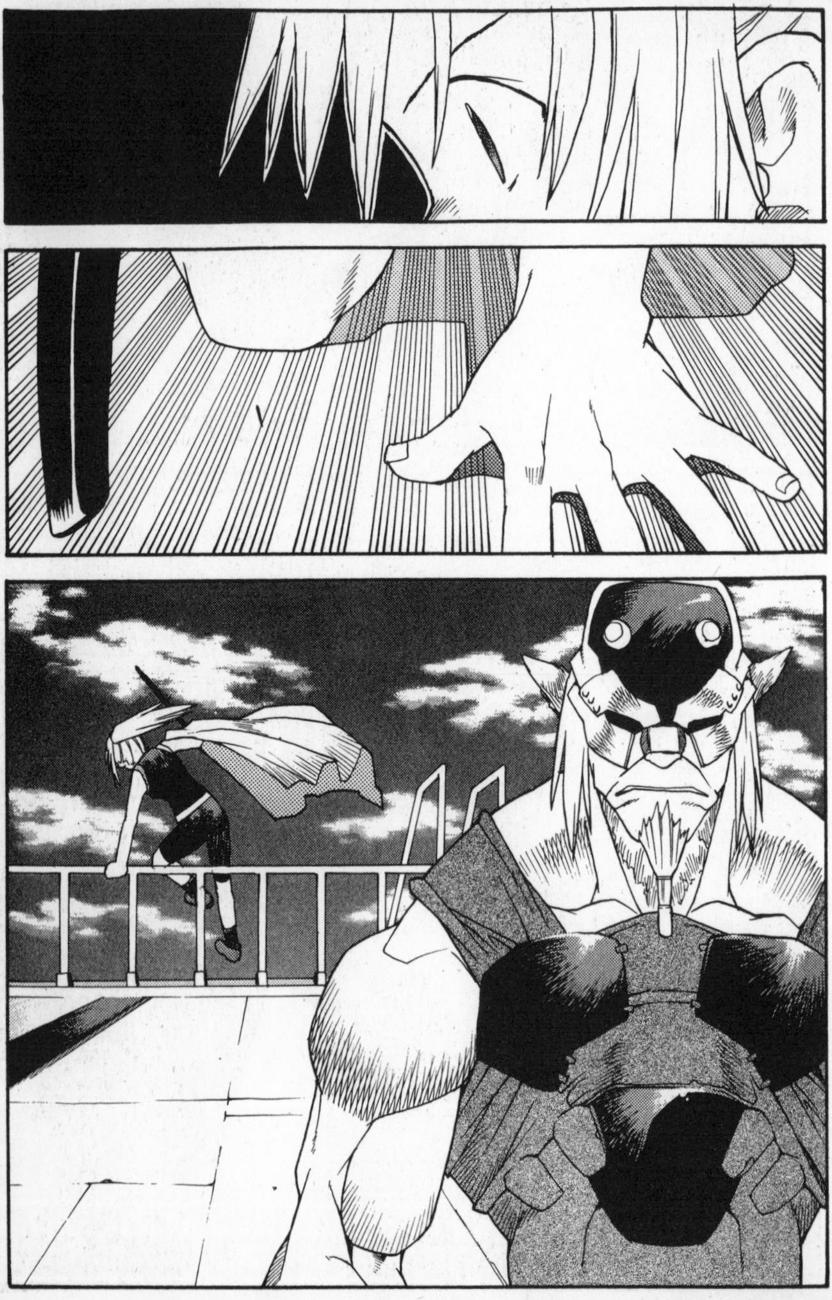

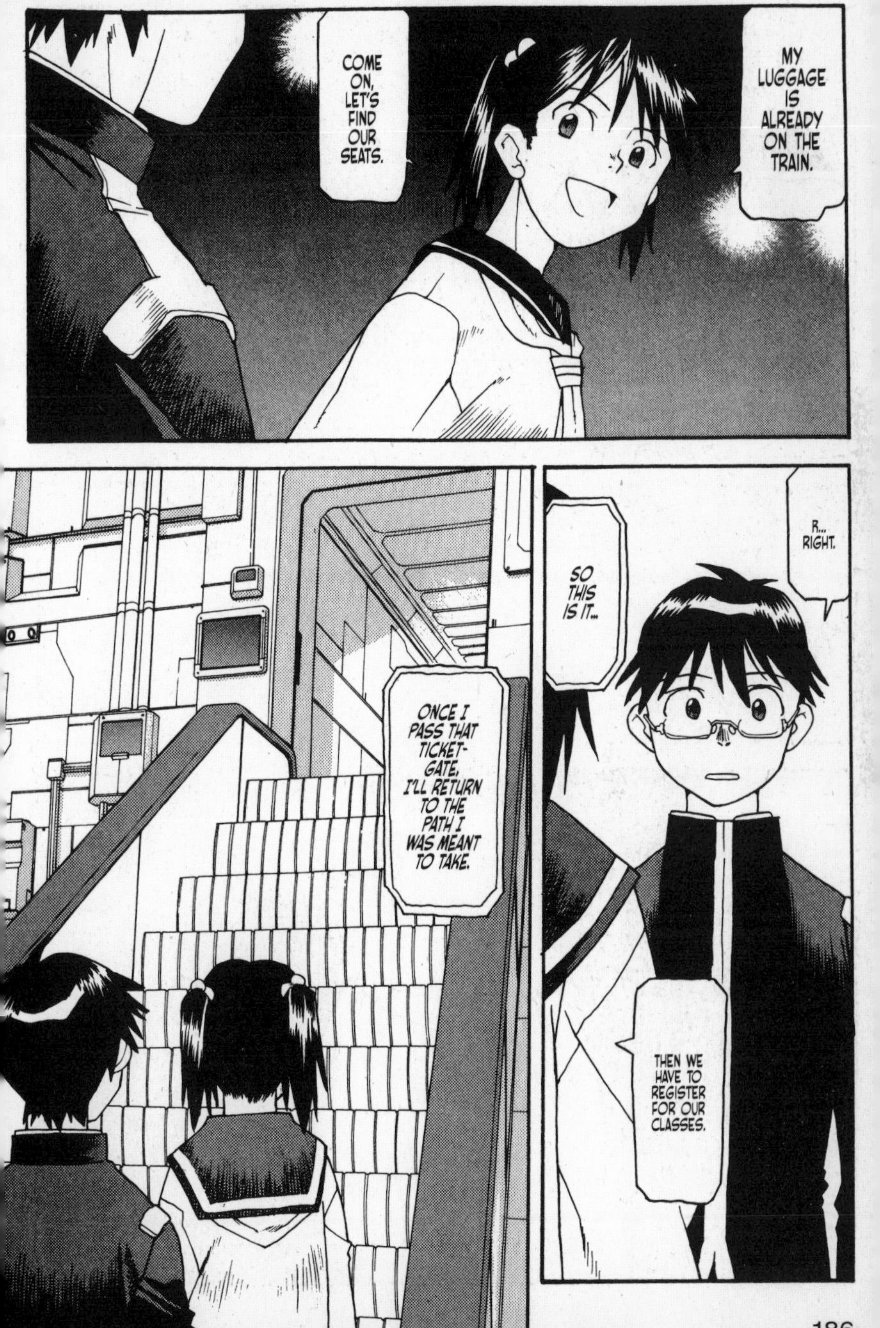
MY LUGGAGE IS ALREADY ON THE TRAIN.
COME ON, LET'S FIND OUR SEATS.
R... RIGHT.
SO THIS IS IT...
THEN WE HAVE TO REGISTER FOR OUR CLASSES.
ONCE I PASS THAT TICKET-GATE, I'LL RETURN TO THE PATH I WAS MEANT TO TAKE.

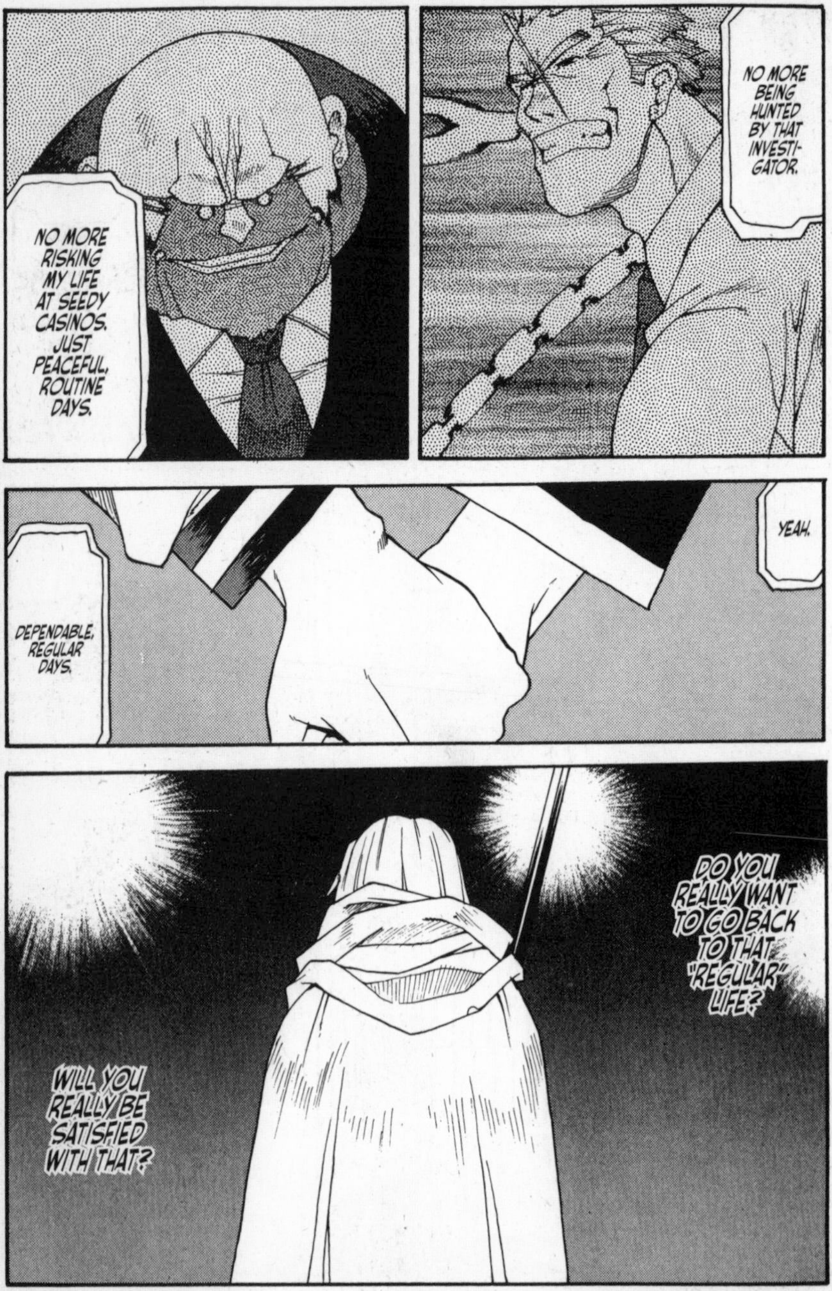
NO MORE BEING HUNTED BY THAT INVESTI-GATOR.
NO MORE RISKING MY LIFE AT SEEDY CASINOS. JUST PEACEFUL, ROUTINE DAYS.
YEAH.
DEPENDABLE, REGULAR DAYS.
DO YOU REALLY WANT TO GO BACK TO THAT "REGULAR" LIFE?
WILL YOU REALLY BE SATISFIED WITH THAT?

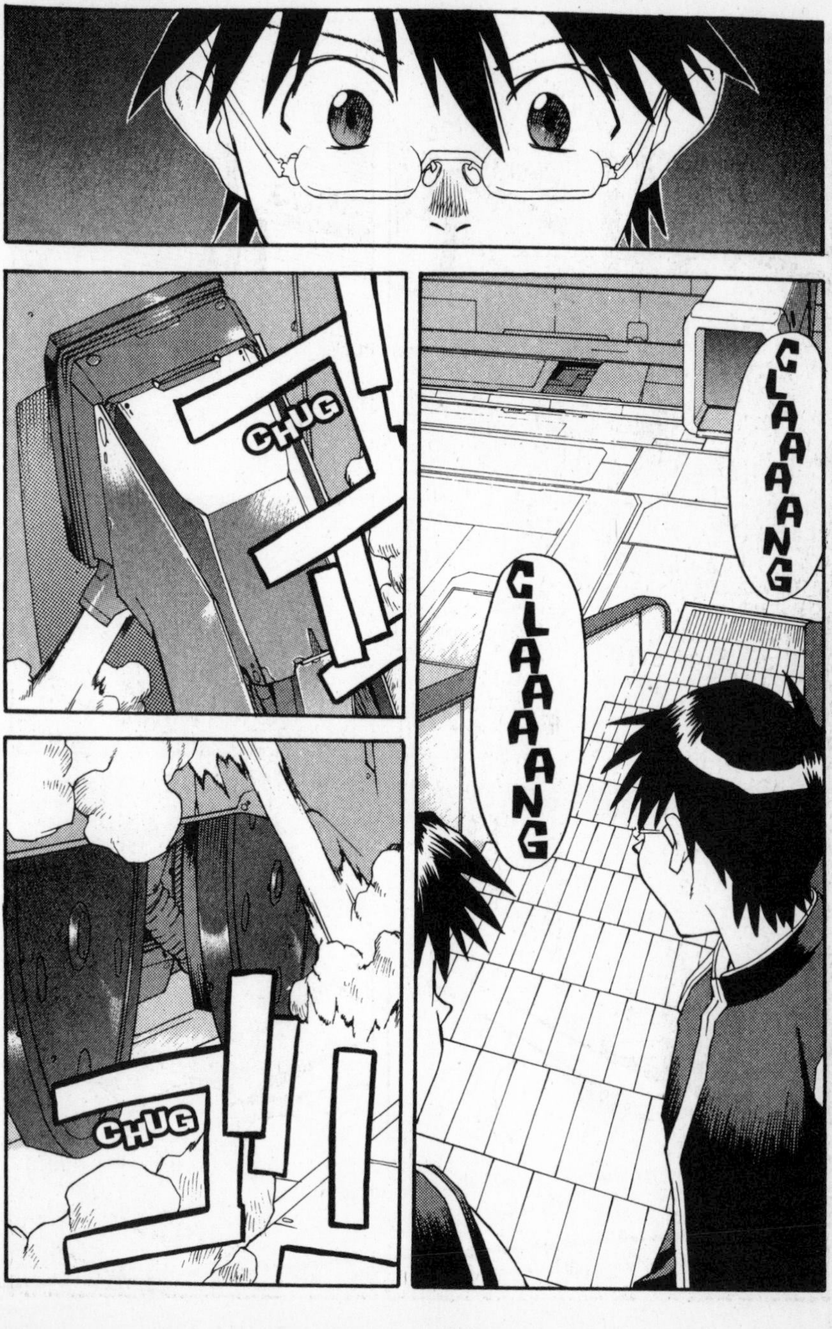
GLAAAANG
GLAAAANG
CHUG
CHUG

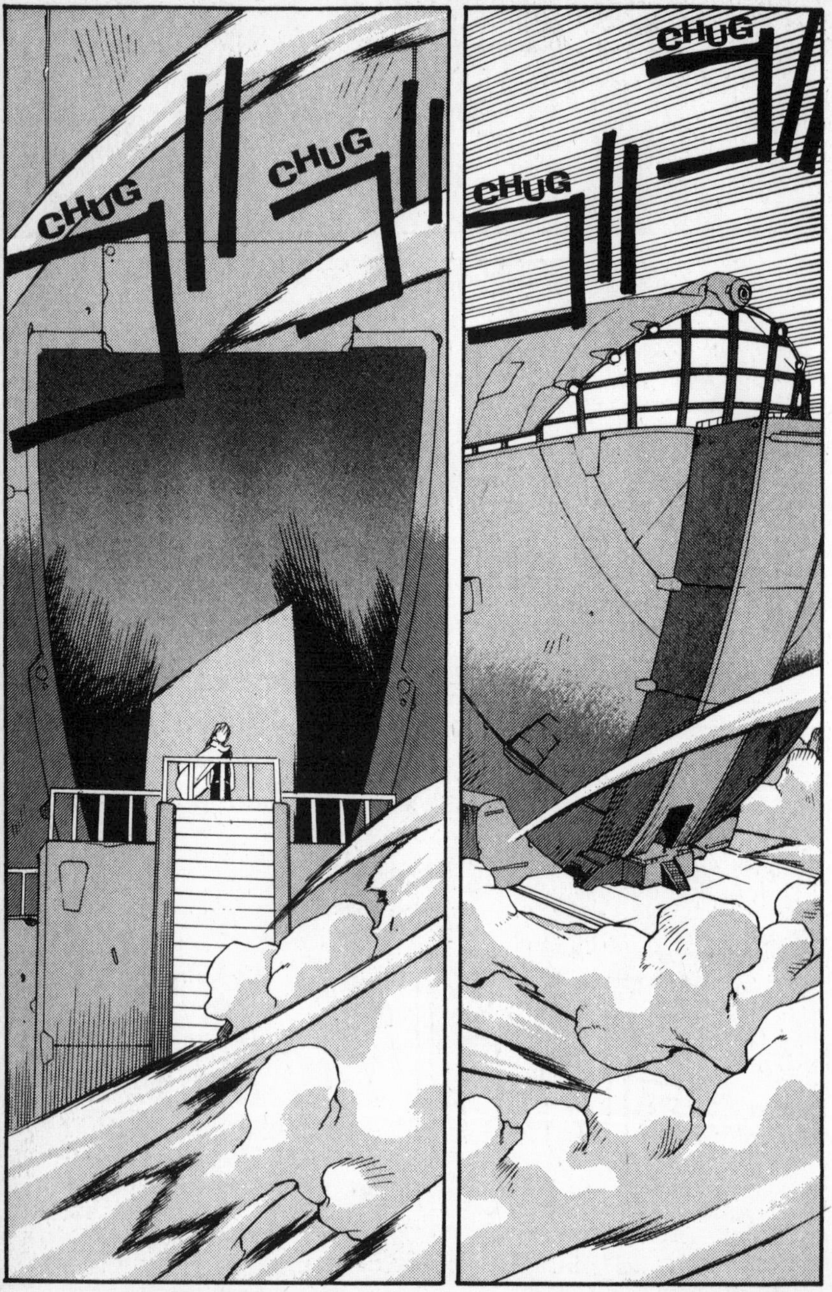
CHUG
CHUG
CHUG
CHUG

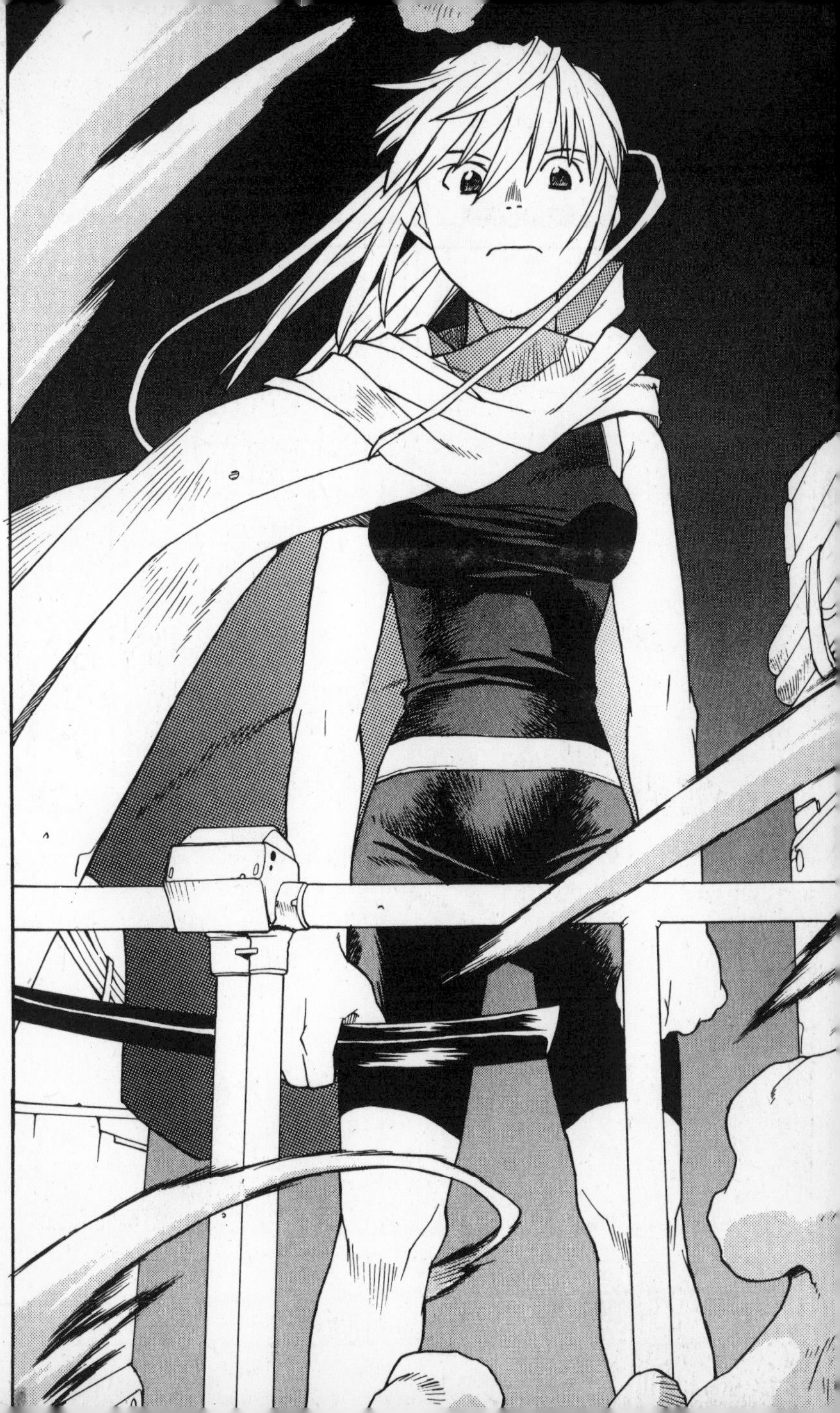

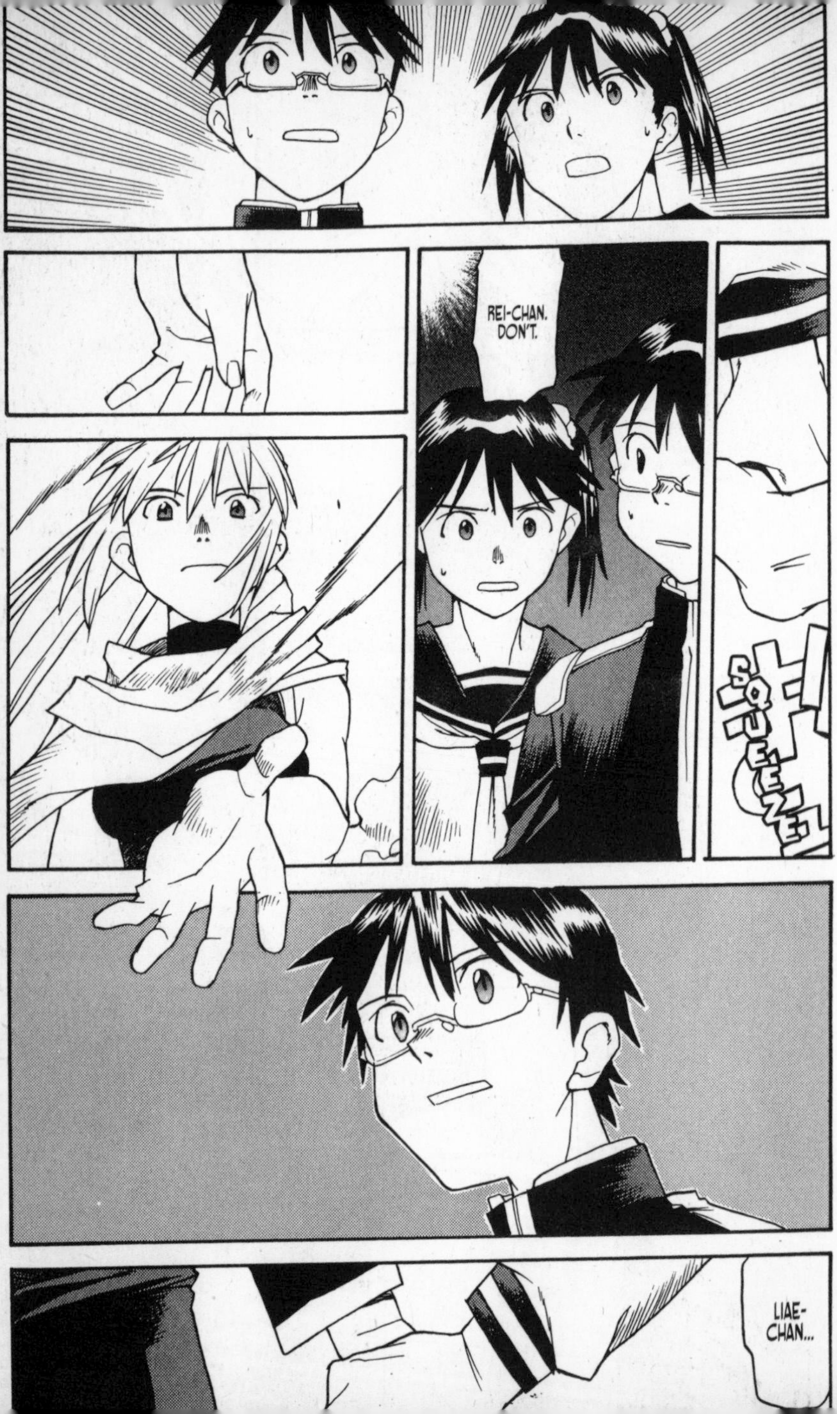
SQUEEZE!
REI-CHAN. DON'T.
LIAE-CHAN...

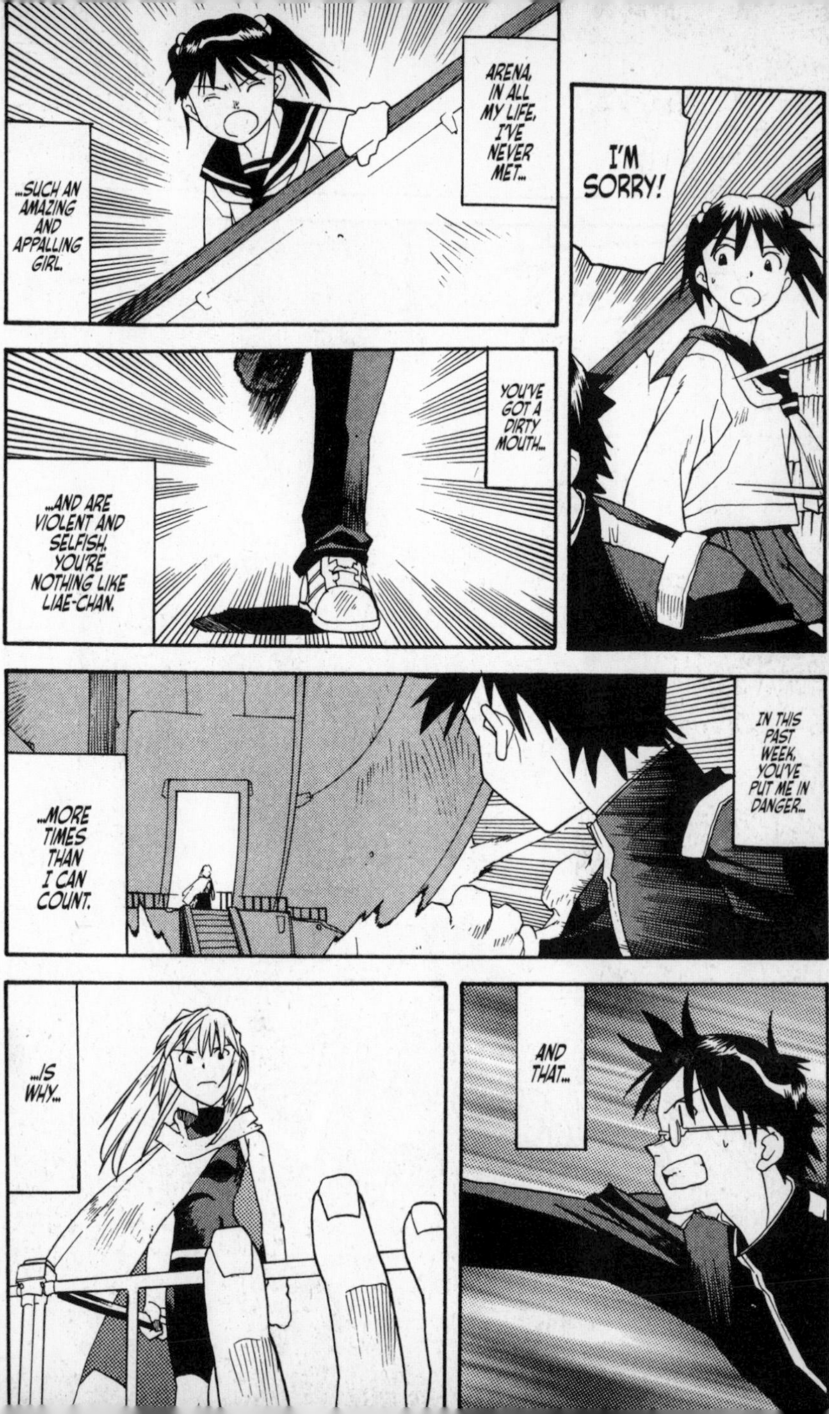

I'M SORRY!
ARENA, IN ALL MY LIFE, I'VE NEVER MET...
...SUCH AN AMAZING AND APPALLING GIRL.
YOU'VE GOT A DIRTY MOUTH...
...AND ARE VIOLENT AND SELFISH. YOU'RE NOTHING LIKE LIAE-CHAN.
IN THIS PAST WEEK, YOU'VE PUT ME IN DANGER...
...MORE TIMES THAN I CAN COUNT.
AND THAT...
...IS WHY...

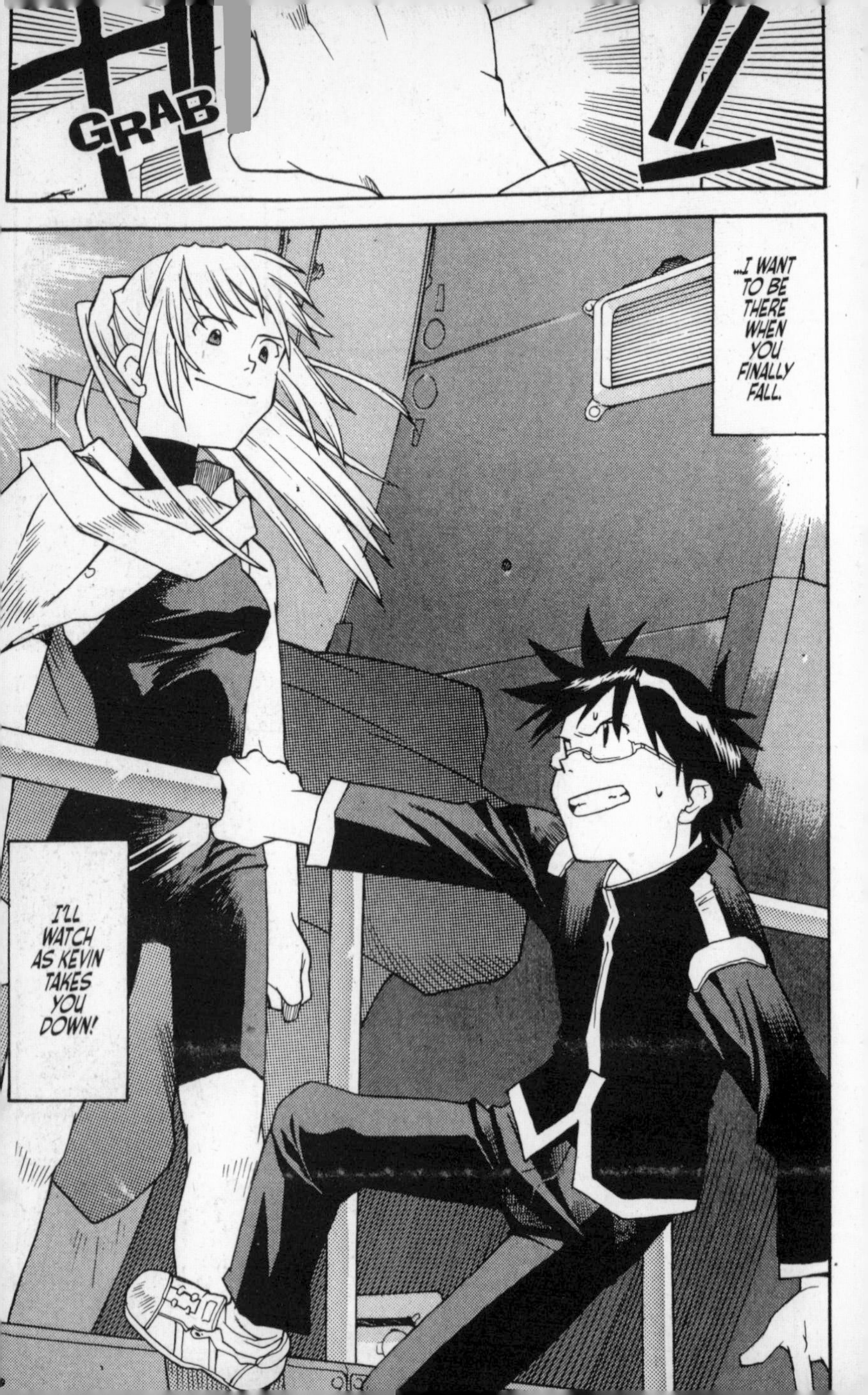
GRAB
...I WANT TO BE THERE WHEN YOU FINALLY FALL.
I'LL WATCH AS KEVIN TAKES YOU DOWN!

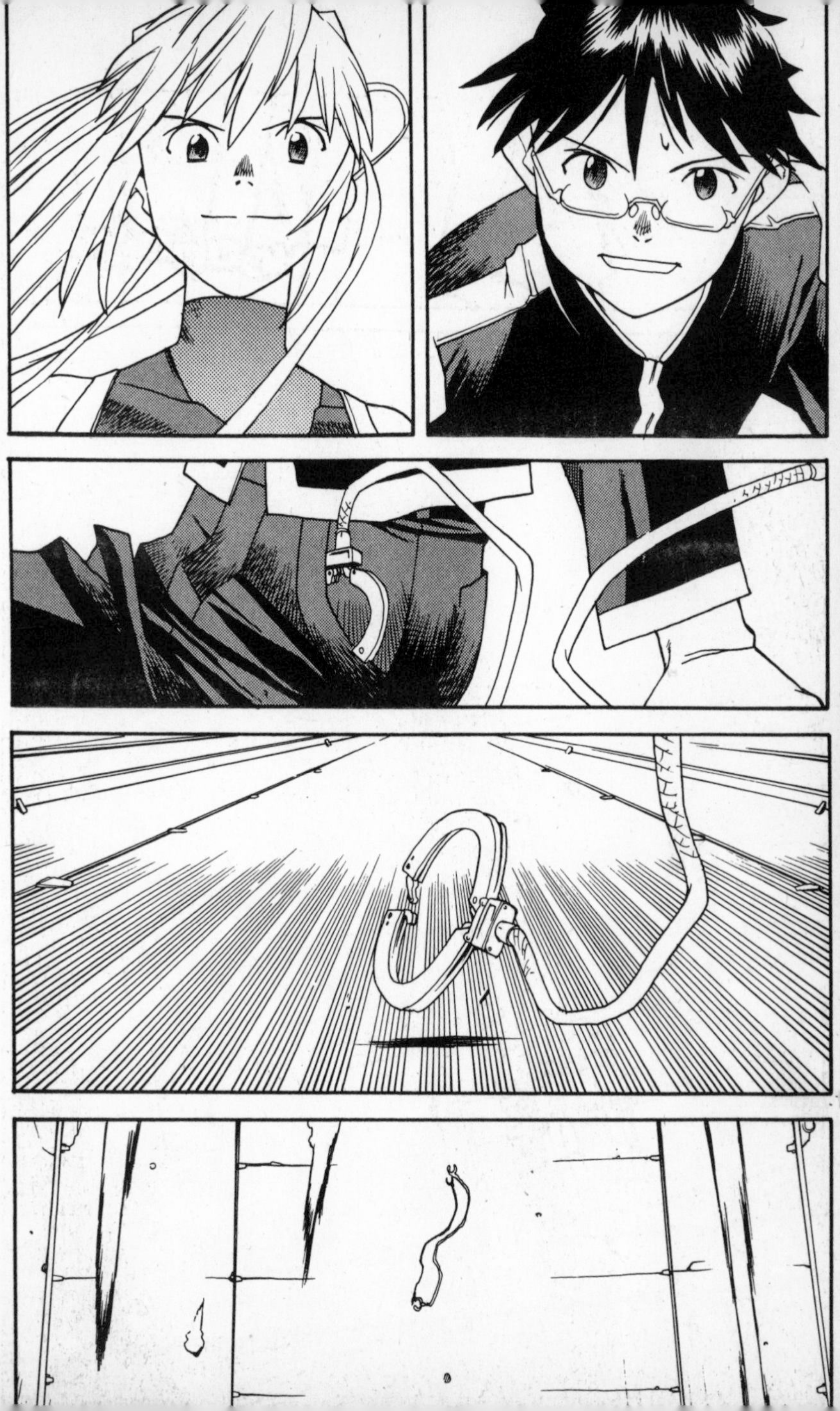

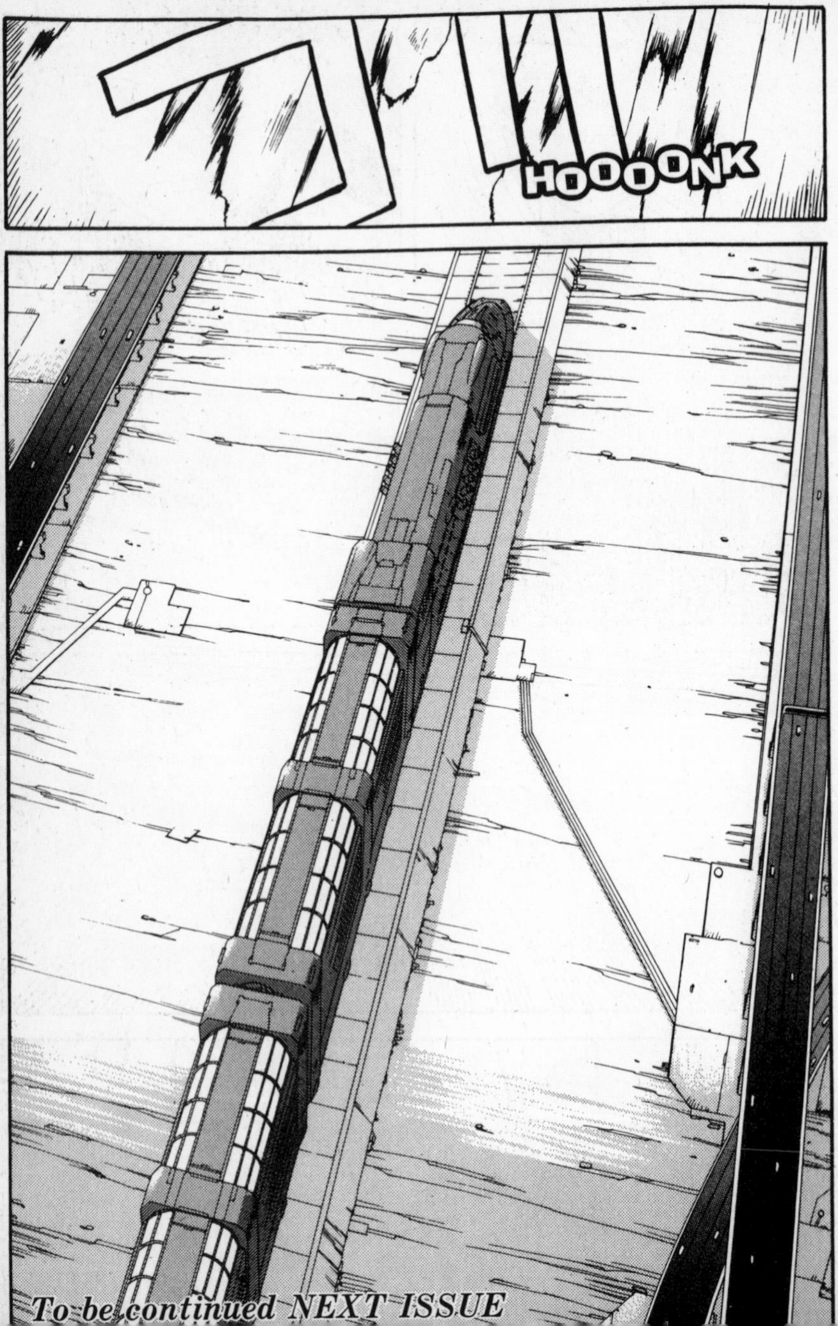
HOOOONK
To be continued NEXT ISSUE

TRAIN + TRAIN PROT WRITERS NOTE

FILE NO. 003

KONG SEEVAL

Lupin had Zenigata. Dr. Richard Kimble had Marshal Sam Gerard. I think the character who won't give up his pursuit always adds spice to the story. That's just what Kong is in this story as he tracks down the runaway, Arena. I had him in mind for a long time and even came up with his background: he's a military man who was discharged from the army after having respect issues with his superior advisor and so went into investigating (a pretty common pattern, I'm sure). His current case with Arena is more about the challenge than the reward, since it is really forcing him to try everything he's got. She's given him a good outlet for his willpower and passion, so his "trip" across Deloca is a little different from that of Reiichi and company. As for the chains on his arms, I got those from the bad guy in Jackie Chan's "Drunken Boxing 2." I think they're really bad-ass.

illustration by TOMOMASA TAKUMA. Text by HIDEYUKI K

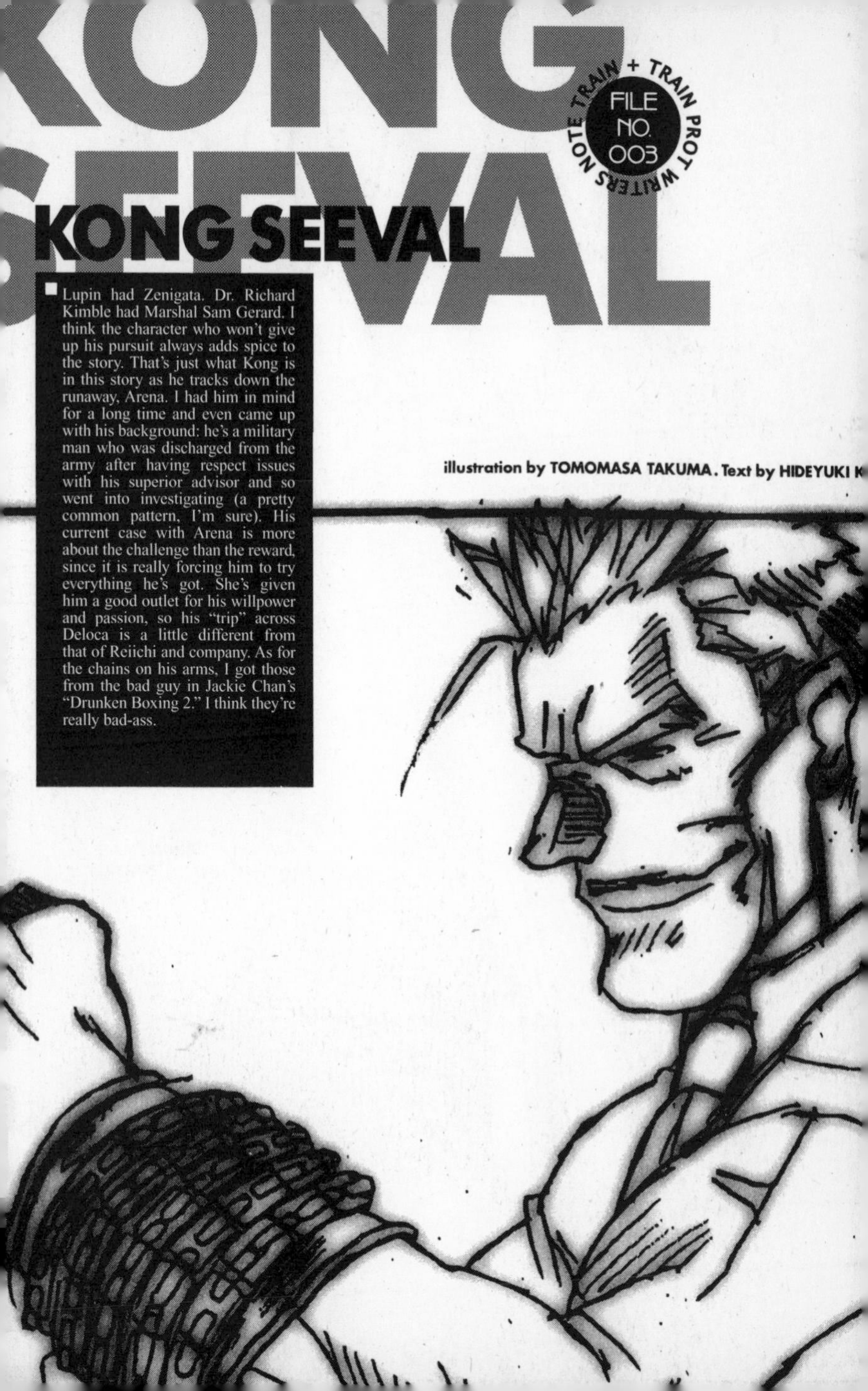

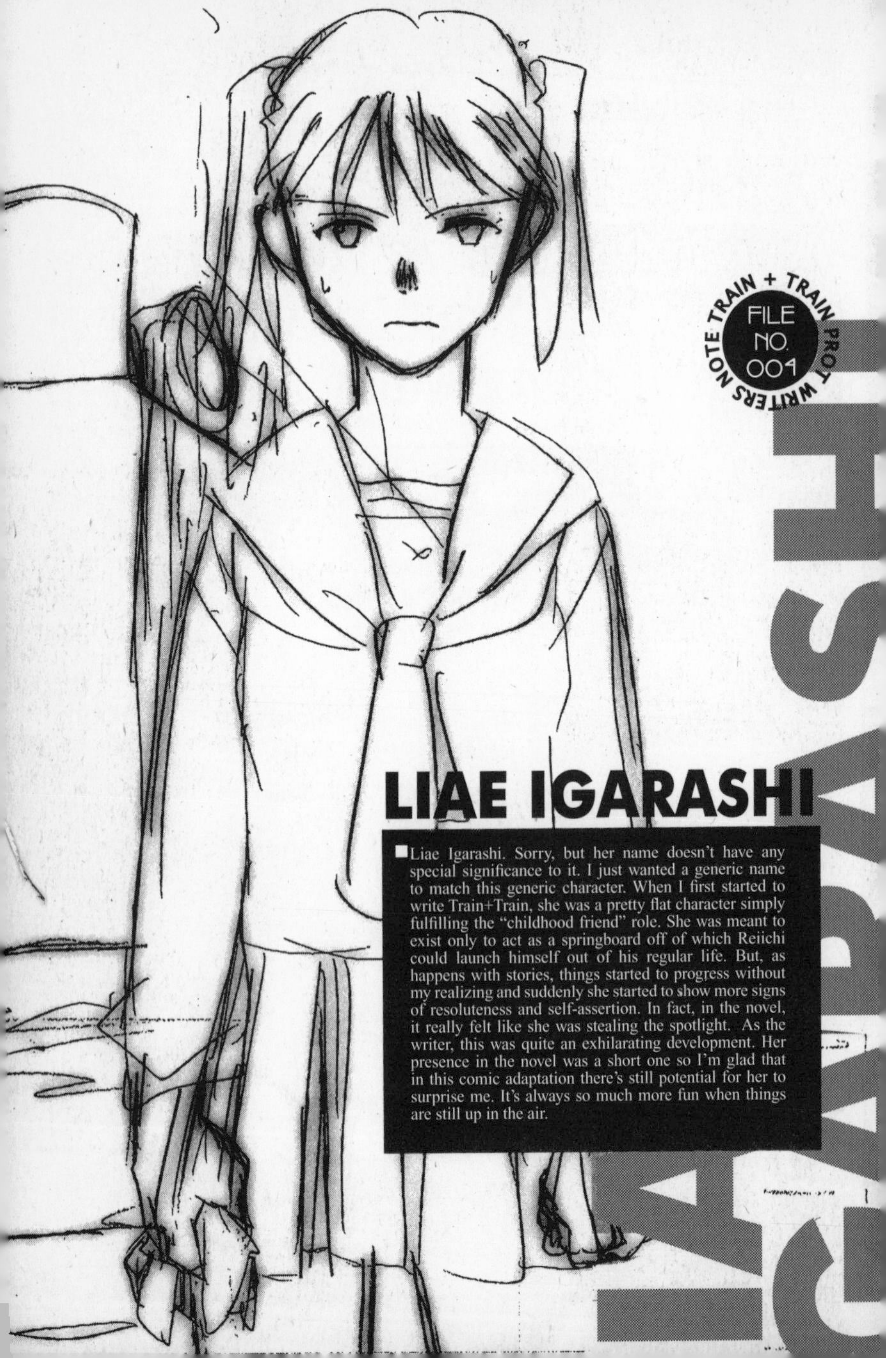

TRAIN + TRAIN PROT WRITERS NOTE
FILE NO. 004

LIAE IGARASHI

■Liae Igarashi. Sorry, but her name doesn't have any special significance to it. I just wanted a generic name to match this generic character. When I first started to write Train+Train, she was a pretty flat character simply fulfilling the "childhood friend" role. She was meant to exist only to act as a springboard off of which Reiichi could launch himself out of his regular life. But, as happens with stories, things started to progress without my realizing and suddenly she started to show more signs of resoluteness and self-assertion. In fact, in the novel, it really felt like she was stealing the spotlight. As the writer, this was quite an exhilarating development. Her presence in the novel was a short one so I'm glad that in this comic adaptation there's still potential for her to surprise me. It's always so much more fun when things are still up in the air.

IGARASHI

In volume 3 of TRAIN + TRAIN

Trapped in an icy cave, students of the Special Train must fight the forces of nature — *and each other!*

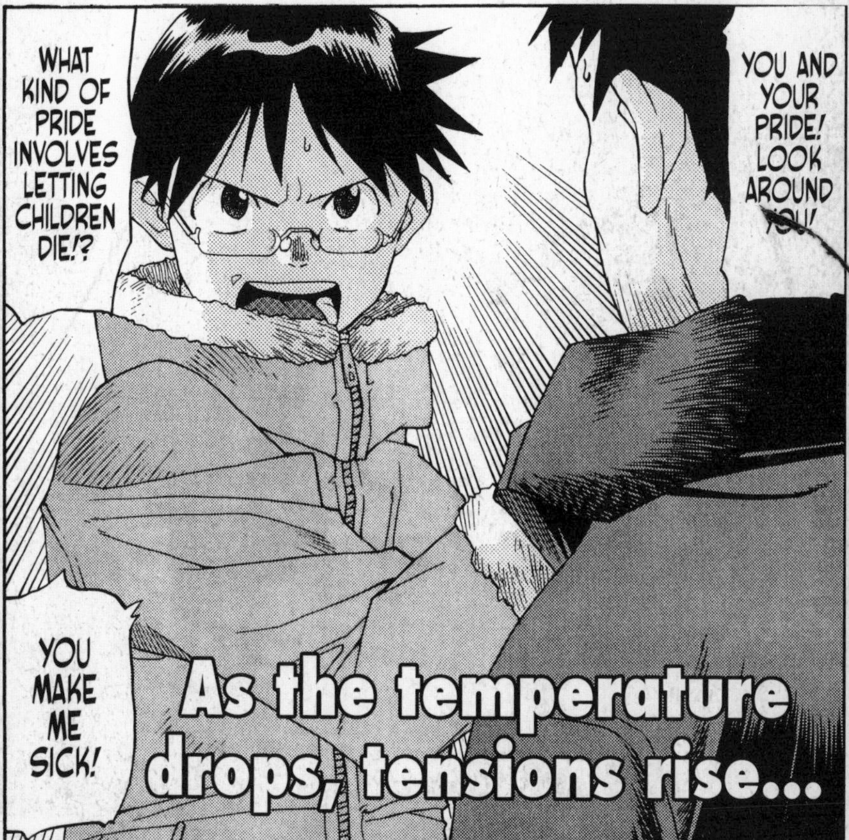
YOU AND YOUR PRIDE! LOOK AROUND YOU!
WHAT KIND OF PRIDE INVOLVES LETTING CHILDREN DIE!?
YOU MAKE ME SICK!

As the temperature drops, tensions rise...

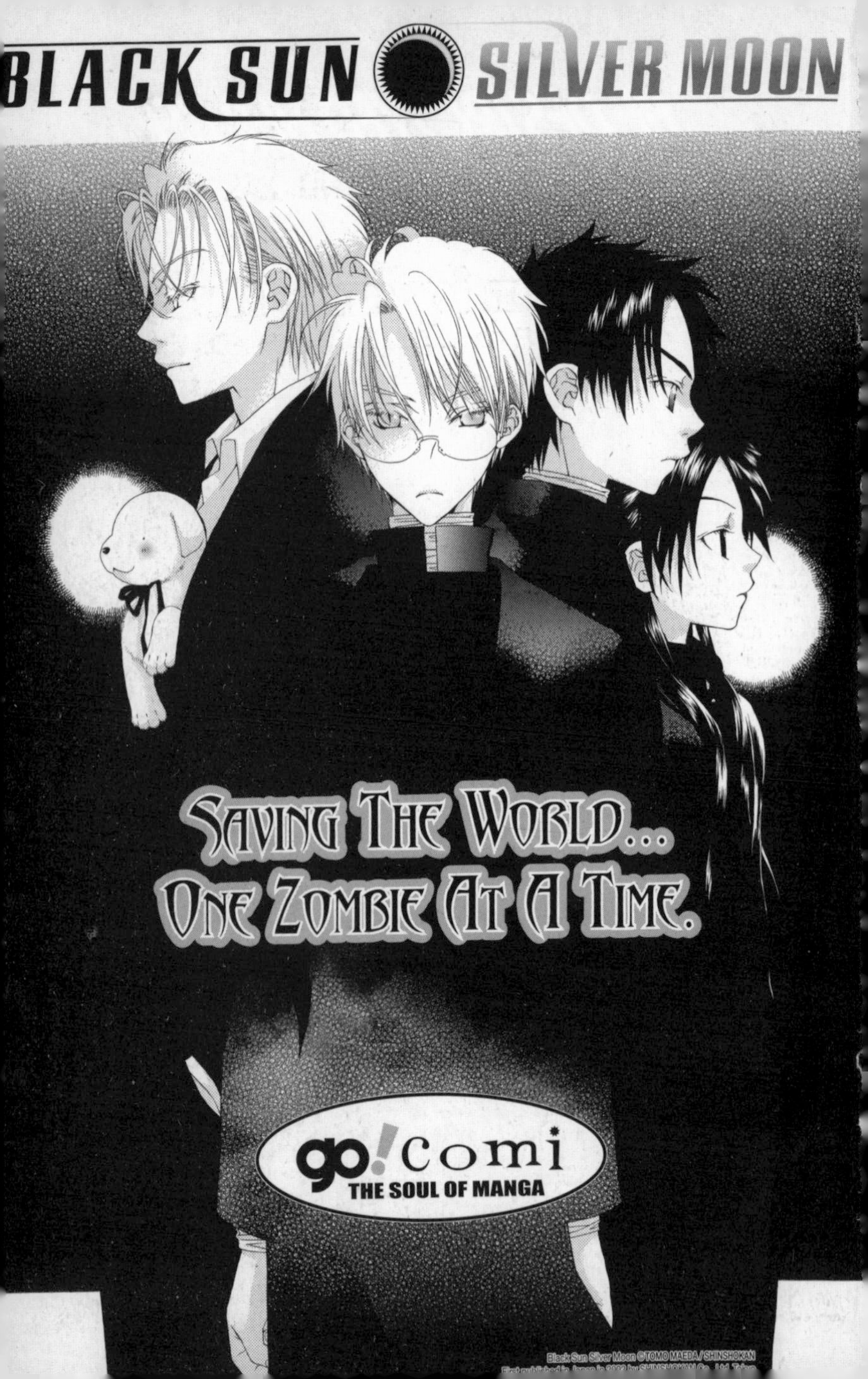
BLACK SUN SILVER MOON
SAVING THE WORLD...
ONE ZOMBIE AT A TIME.
go! comi
THE SOUL OF MANGA
Black Sun Silver Moon ©TOMO MAEDA / SHINSHOKAN

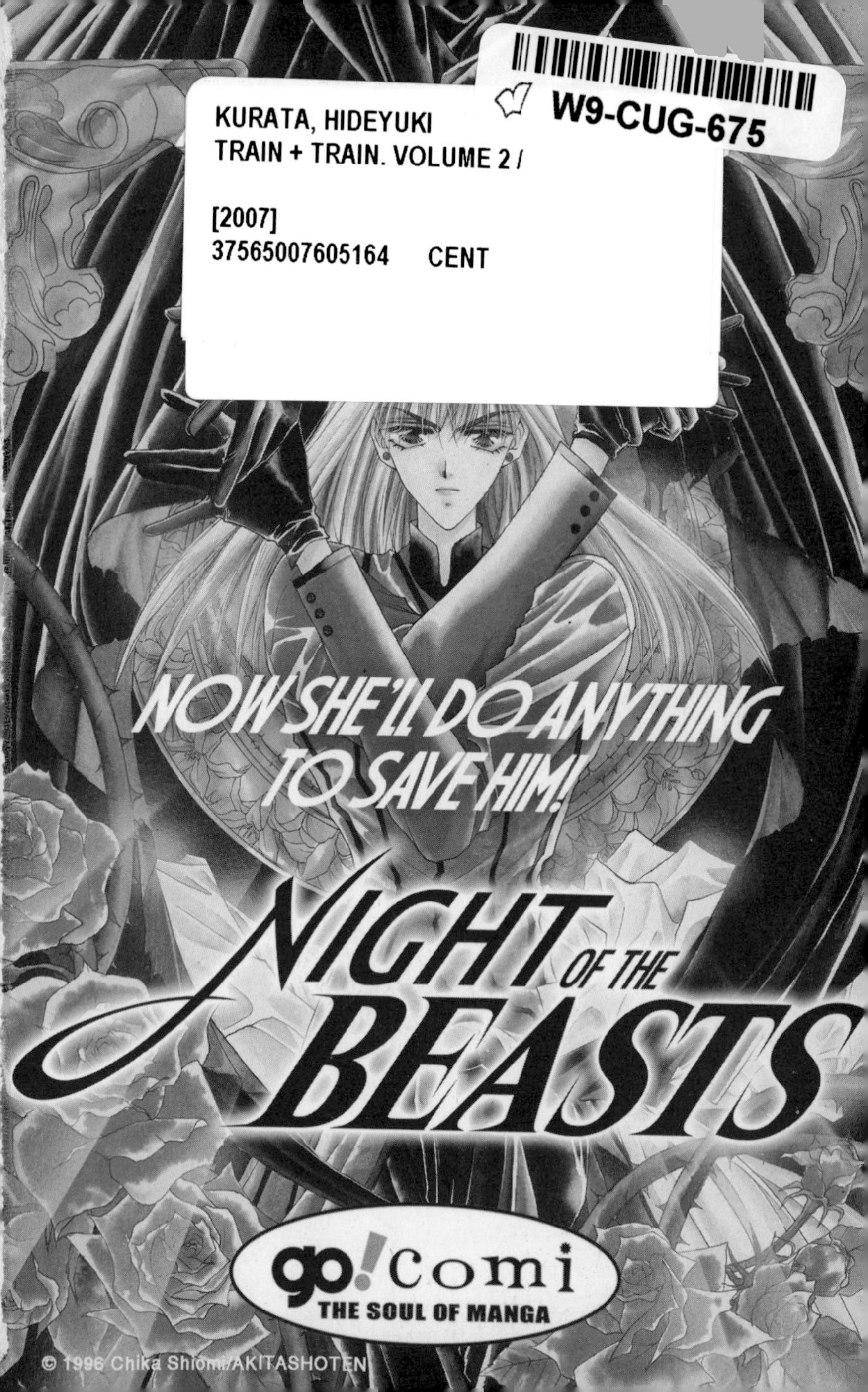
NOW SHE'LL DO ANYTHING TO SAVE HIM!
NIGHT OF THE BEASTS
go!comi
THE SOUL OF MANGA